The Problems of Disadvantaged Youth

**A National Bureau
of Economic Research
Conference Report**

The Problems of Disadvantaged Youth
An Economic Perspective

Edited by **Jonathan Gruber**

The University of Chicago Press

Chicago and London

JONATHAN GRUBER is professor of economics at the Massachusetts
Institute of Technology and Director of the Health Care Program at
the NBER, where he is a research associate and formerly directed the
Program on Children.

The University of Chicago Press, Chicago 60637
The University of Chicago Press, Ltd., London
© 2009 by the National Bureau of Economic Research
All rights reserved. Published 2009
Printed in the United States of America

18 17 16 15 14 13 12 11 10 09   1 2 3 4 5
ISBN-13: 978-0-226-30945-3 (cloth)
ISBN-10: 0-226-30945-2 (cloth)

Library of Congress Cataloging-in-Publication Data

The problems of disadvantaged youth : an economic perspective /
    edited by Jonathan Gruber.
        p. cm. — (A National Bureau of Economic Research conference
    report)
    Includes bibliographical references and index.
    ISBN-13: 978-0-226-30945-3 (alk. paper)
    ISBN-10: 0-226-30945-2 (alk. paper)
    1. Poor youth—United States—Social conditions. 2. Poor youth—
Education—United States. 3. Poor youth—Health and hygiene—
United States. I. Gruber, Jonathan. II. Series: National Bureau of
Economic Research conference report.
HV1431.P75 2009
362.7086'920973—dc22

                                                              2009003454

Relation of the Directors to the
Work and Publications of the
National Bureau of Economic Research

1. The object of the NBER is to ascertain and present to the economics profession, and to the public more generally, important economic facts and their interpretation in a scientific manner without policy recommendations. The Board of Directors is charged with the responsibility of ensuring that the work of the NBER is carried on in strict conformity with this object.

2. The President shall establish an internal review process to ensure that book manuscripts proposed for publication DO NOT contain policy recommendations. This shall apply both to the proceedings of conferences and to manuscripts by a single author or by one or more co-authors but shall not apply to authors of comments at NBER conferences who are not NBER affiliates.

3. No book manuscript reporting research shall be published by the NBER until the President has sent to each member of the Board a notice that a manuscript is recommended for publication and that in the President's opinion it is suitable for publication in accordance with the above principles of the NBER. Such notification will include a table of contents and an abstract or summary of the manuscript's content, a list of contributors if applicable, and a response form for use by Directors who desire a copy of the manuscript for review. Each manuscript shall contain a summary drawing attention to the nature and treatment of the problem studied and the main conclusions reached.

4. No volume shall be published until forty-five days have elapsed from the above notification of intention to publish it. During this period a copy shall be sent to any Director requesting it, and if any Director objects to publication on the grounds that the manuscript contains policy recommendations, the objection will be presented to the author(s) or editor(s). In case of dispute, all members of the Board shall be notified, and the President shall appoint an ad hoc committee of the Board to decide the matter; thirty days additional shall be granted for this purpose.

5. The President shall present annually to the Board a report describing the internal manuscript review process, any objections made by Directors before publication or by anyone after publication, any disputes about such matters, and how they were handled.

6. Publications of the NBER issued for informational purposes concerning the work of the Bureau, or issued to inform the public of the activities at the Bureau, including but not limited to the NBER Digest and Reporter, shall be consistent with the object stated in paragraph 1. They shall contain a specific disclaimer noting that they have not passed through the review procedures required in this resolution. The Executive Committee of the Board is charged with the review of all such publications from time to time.

7. NBER working papers and manuscripts distributed on the Bureau's web site are not deemed to be publications for the purpose of this resolution, but they shall be consistent with the object stated in paragraph 1. Working papers shall contain a specific disclaimer noting that they have not passed through the review procedures required in this resolution. The NBER's web site shall contain a similar disclaimer. The President shall establish an internal review process to ensure that the working papers and the web site do not contain policy recommendations, and shall report annually to the Board on this process and any concerns raised in connection with it.

8. Unless otherwise determined by the Board or exempted by the terms of paragraphs 6 and 7, a copy of this resolution shall be printed in each NBER publication as described in paragraph 2 above.

Contents

Acknowledgments

This project is part of the National Bureau of Economic Research's Program on Children, which seeks to bring economists together to study the range of issues related to child well-being. I am grateful to Martin Feldstein, former President of the NBER, for the suggestions and encouragement that provided the impetus for this project.

This project was supported by generous funding from the Annie E. Casey Foundation. I am grateful to Brian Lyght at the Casey Foundation for his assistance through the project. While I thank the Foundation for their support, I also acknowledge that the findings and conclusions presented in this report are those of the authors alone, and do not necessarily reflect the opinions of the Foundation.

The papers in this volume were presented at a conference at Amelia Island Plantation in April 2007. The NBER conference staff, and in particular Brett Maranjian, worked tirelessly to make this a terrific experience for everyone involved. Helena Fitz-Patrick was her usual expert self in guiding us through the review process and turning these papers into a final volume.

Introduction
What Have We Learned About the Problems of and Prospects for Disadvantaged Youth?

Jonathan Gruber

One of the most important public policy problems facing the United States today is the life prospects of disadvantaged youths. Youths from low income households, minority youths, and youths from broken families face a series of barriers to success that may have negative implications both today and in the future. Enumerating the problems facing disadvantaged youth in the United States is easy: poor educational opportunities, poor health care, high-crime environments, family dysfunction, and so on. What is much harder is to carefully document those problems across a broad spectrum of contexts. Moreover, it is difficult to assess the extent to which interventions can alleviate these causal impacts of disadvantage on current and long run youth outcomes.

The purpose of this volume is to take on these two challenges from an economics perspective. The volume brings together nine of the leading teams of empirical economics researchers in the country to address these questions from a number of different perspectives. The result is an innovative and comprehensive look at the issues facing youth in the United States in general, and disadvantaged youth in particular.

In this introduction, I provide an overview of the results provided in these studies. I review their findings and the important lessons drawn from each, as well as the lessons in aggregate for both the research and policy communities.

Jonathan Gruber is the associate head of the economics department and professor of economics at the Massachusetts Institute of Technology and a research associate of the National Bureau of Economic Research.

Summary of papers prepared for conference on the Economics of Disadvantaged Youth. I am grateful to the authors for writing such excellent papers and to the Annie E. Casey Foundation for research support.

The studies themselves fall into three different areas, so the book (and my discussion) groups them accordingly.

Before summarizing the work in the book, it is important to lay the groundwork for the chapters that follow. This set of chapters is *not* designed to be a comprehensive cataloging of all of the problems facing disadvantaged youth, but rather just a sampling of the economics approach to some of them. There is much more work to be done on other problems not addressed in this book, such as substance use and abuse, housing, and work training programs. My hope is that this introduction will introduce readers to tools that they can bring to bear on those questions as well.

Also, there is no one comprehensive definition of "disadvantaged" used in these chapters. There are a whole host of measures that can be used to measure disadvantage, and rather than impose a given measure on any one study, I urged the authors to cast a wide net and consider a variety of measures. The result is enough overlap across chapters that the interested reader can easily compare several studies along a given dimension of disadvantage (e.g., race or income deprivation).

Section I: Education

Clearly, a critical influence on the outcomes of disadvantaged youth is their educational opportunities. Numerous studies have shown that disadvantaged youth who obtain less education, or who are educated in lower quality schools, have worse life outcomes. But the difficulty with interpreting this finding is that those same disadvantaged youth who obtain low-quality education may have worse life outcomes for many reasons: maybe it is the youth with the most troubled home life, for example, who attend the worst schools. If it is the home life, and not the schools, that matters for youth outcomes, then we may be inappropriately focusing our policy attention on the educational arena. This project contains three separate studies that try to disentangle the causal effect of educational quality and quantity on disadvantaged youth.

The first is the study by David Figlio and Jeffrey Roth, "The Behavioral Consequences of Pre-Kindergarten Participation for Disadvantaged Youth." One of the most exciting public policy debates in the United States is over the role of the government in providing pre-kindergarten education for all children. Many other developed countries start state-funded education (and day care) much earlier than kindergarten. But evidence on the efficacy of early child interventions is mixed. On the one hand, a number of studies find that intensive pre-kindergarten interventions (such as the Perry Preschool and Abecedarian projects) and Head Start programs improve school readiness in the short run and generate less need for governmental services in the long run. On the other hand, the influential National Institute of Child Health and Development Study of Early Child Care and Youth Development find that children placed in day care at young ages display elevated levels of aggression and disobedience in elementary school. These mixed findings make it difficult to draw firm policy conclusions on the advisability of government support of expanded pre-kindergarten.

The Figlio and Roth chapter provides important new evidence on this debate by bringing to bear a unique new data set that links student birth records to pre-kindergarten participation for every child born in Florida in or after 1994 who subsequently attended public school in Florida. They also address an important issue that has plagued this literature: how to separate the impact of preschool programs from other factors that are correlated with preschool attendance. They do so by comparing siblings within the same family; they show that those who had access to a pre-kindergarten program through their locally-zoned elementary school when they were four years old were much more likely to attend pre-kindergarten than were their siblings who did not have access to a local program. The results here are striking: having a locally-zoned pre-K program raises the odds of attending pre-K, relative to a sibling without.

Using this innovative strategy, Figlio and Roth investigate the impact of pre-K attendance on behavioral problems and find that attending a pre-K program significantly reduces behavioral problems in elementary school. Interestingly, this impact is particularly large when the child lives in a very disadvantaged area, suggesting the value of public pre-K to such areas. In more advantaged areas, there was little effect of public pre-K.

The second chapter of the volume presents a study of the impacts of school choice by Julie Berry Cullen and Brian A. Jacob, entitled "Is Gaining Access to Selective Elementary Schools Gaining Ground? Evidence from Randomized Lotteries." As their chapter highlights, poor children attend much worse schools than their higher income counterparts. For example, in 2004 high-poverty districts received nearly $1,000 less per pupil in state and local revenues than low-poverty districts within the same state, and only 65 percent of teachers in high-poverty districts in California met the new federal guidelines for highly qualified teachers in 2004 to 2005, compared to 81 percent in low-poverty districts in the state. Perhaps as a result, the school outcomes of disadvantaged children are much worse than their more advantaged peers. For example, in the Chicago sample that the authors analyze, test scores for whites are more than 10 percent higher than for minorities, and test scores for those eligible for free student meals (a measure of low income) are 10 percent lower than those who are not eligible.

While there have been a number of initiatives to improve the educational opportunities available to low-income children, one of the most popular has been allowing students to opt out of their underperforming local school and choose another public school. But this initiative has proceeded largely in an evidence vacuum; as the authors point out, there is little to suggest that changing the school environment will improve the outcomes of these disadvantaged children.

Cullen and Jacob address this problem by using their own innovative data set, administrative records on over 50,000 children attending public elementary school in the Chicago Public School District (CPS). Under this system's "open enrollment" policy, students can apply to attend magnet schools and other public schools throughout the CPS, rather than their own local school. The other major innovation of their chapter is a clever means of addressing a common problem in this literature: it is the higher achieving students who will apply to attend more academically successful schools, biasing the results to suggest that better school quality leads to better outcomes. They address this shortcoming in a convincing manner, by noting that the most academically advanced schools in the CPS are oversubscribed, so that they allocate slots by randomized lottery. As a result, the authors can assess the causal impact of attending these schools by comparing those who apply and win the lottery, versus others who apply and are (randomly) denied entry to the school.

Their findings are striking. As expected, winning the lottery is closely associated with attending a higher quality school, as measured either by the average achievement level of peers in the school or by "value-added" indicators of the school's contribution to student learning. Yet there is no evidence that actually attending this better school has any positive impact on student outcomes over the subsequent five years! Students randomly assigned to higher achieving schools are themselves no likely to score higher on subsequent tests.

Most importantly from the perspective of this volume, they also find that there is no evidence that attending a higher achieving school matters for particular disadvantaged subgroups. The large differences in test scores that we see across groups do not in any way dissipate as the disadvantaged groups attend more selective schools. Perhaps this finding should not be surprising given that Cullen and Jacob find that two-thirds of the gap in achievement across groups is present *within* schools, and only one-third occurs across schools. The educational problems of the disadvantaged will not disappear simply by giving them access to better schools.

The third chapter in this series is Philip Oreopolous' study of laws restricting the ability of students to drop out of high school, "Would More Compulsory Schooling Help Disadvantaged Youth? Evidence from Recent Changes to School-Leaving Laws." Another source of educational difference by groups is the rate at which they drop out of high school. For example, students in low-income families are six times more likely to drop out than those in high income families. One policy intervention that can help to remediate this difference is compulsory schooling laws, which mandate that children stay in school until some minimum school-leaving age. Such laws were on the books for most of the twentieth century, but usually imposed school attendance only until ages of fourteen or fifteen. In the past few decades, however, states have revised these laws to require attendance to higher ages, in some states until age eighteen. If binding, these laws can reduce rates of dropping out, and thereby reduce the gap in attainment between advantaged and disadvantaged students.

Oreopolous' chapter provides a careful analysis of the impact of the recent increases in compulsory schooling ages. He first documents clearly that these laws have increased educational attainment. Moreover, even laws that raised the compulsory age to some point below graduation age still lowered dropout rates and promoted graduation, presumably by increasing interest in school and the willingness to "close out" high school once most of it was compulsory. He even finds that stricter compulsory schooling laws increase college attendance, presumably because high school graduates are in a better position to do the work required by college attendance.

In the second part of his chapter, Oreopolous asks whether the increased education mandated by these laws actually shows benefits for outcomes early in the working career. He finds clear evidence that it does: more education due to compulsory education laws leads to lower rates of unemployment and higher levels of family income.

A particularly important finding in this study is that the major effects of the compulsory schooling laws show up for Hispanic youth only. Thus, these laws appear to work to close the gap in educational attainment and labor market outcomes between Hispanics and whites, but not between blacks and whites. This suggest that compulsory schooling laws may be effective at reducing educational disparities along some dimensions but not others.

Section II: Health and Healthy Behaviors

Another dimension along which disadvantaged youth suffer relative to their advantaged counterparts is health status. These gaps arise from several sources: differences in inherited health status (genetic transmission); differences in treatment of illness; differences in environments that impact health status; and differences in risk-taking behaviors that determine health outcomes (such as smoking and drinking). Three of the chapters in this volume address important aspects of this set of issues.

The first is "Mental Health in Childhood and Human Capital," by Janet Currie and Mark Stabile. There has been increasing attention devoted to child mental health problems, with recent studies showing that one in five children in the United States suffers from mental or behavioral disorders. Currie and Stabile show that there are substantial gaps by socioeconomic status in these measures as well, with disadvantaged children in the United States and Canada exhibiting a 10 to 20 percent larger incidence of behavioral problems than more advantaged children.

Currie and Stabile's chapter is focused on documenting the long-term effects of children's mental health problems, an area that has attracted little attention from economists. They do so by examining the relationship between several common mental health conditions and future outcomes using large samples of children from the Canadian National Longitudinal Survey of Children and Youth (NLSCY), and the American National Longitudinal Survey of Youth (NLSY). They assess the impact of having conditions such as anxiety, depression, and Attention Deficit Hyperactivity Disorder (ADHD) as a child on later life outcomes such as young adult delinquency, grade repetition, and test scores. Once again, they face a difficult problem in this empirical analysis: children with mental health problems typically also face other barriers to success, and it is important for the purposes of the study to disentangle the role of mental health problems from the role played by these other factors. The authors address this concern by using sibling comparisons, comparing the long run outcomes of children who have these childhood mental health problems to the outcomes of their siblings without the problem.

Currie and Stabile find strong evidence that childhood ADHD is negatively associated with later life outcomes in both the United States and Canada, with more modest effects for other childhood mental health problems. They find, however, that there is relatively little consistent "buffering" effect of parental advantage on the impacts of childhood mental health problems on later outcomes. That is, the translation of poor child mental health to poor outcomes later in life is fairly consistent across groups of advantaged and disadvantaged children. As they note, this stands in contrast to work showing that the impact of physical health on later life outcomes is determined strongly by childhood advantage.

The next chapter in this section is Patricia M. Anderson, Kristin F. Butcher, and Diane Whitmore Schanzenbach's study of the determinants of childhood obesity, "Childhood Disadvantage and Obesity: Is Nature Trumping Nurture?" Childhood obesity is one of the leading public health concerns in the United States. The rate of child obesity tripled from 5 percent in the early 1970s to 15 percent thirty years later. Rates of obesity are even higher among disadvantaged youth. As the authors document, obesity rates were 17 percent among children in the lowest income quartile, as opposed to 11 percent in the highest quartile, and obesity rates are much higher for blacks and Hispanics than for whites.

One central question to raise about the high and differential obesity rate is the extent to which it is driven by parental influences. This chapter addresses that question head-on by examining the child-parent correlation in a measure of obesity, body mass index (BMI). In particular, the authors evaluate how this correlation has changed over time and whether the correlation operates differentially for disadvantaged groups. They undertake this study using the most comprehensive documentation of obesity in the United

States over time, the National Health and Nutrition Examination Survey (NHANES). The NHANES collects detailed data on weight and height for both parents and children, and has done so over four waves spanning from 1971 through 2004.

Anderson, Butcher, and Schanzenbach begin by showing that not only are disadvantaged children heavier than advantaged children, but that differential has been growing over time. For example, prior to 1980, families below the poverty line were no heavier than families above; by the end of the sample, they were 2.4 percent heavier than families at three times the poverty line. They then explore the elasticity of a child's BMI with respect to their mother's. They find that this elasticity grew from 0.14 (a 10 percent increase in mother's BMI led to a 1.4 percent increase in child BMI) in the first two waves to roughly 0.2 in the last two waves, a 50 percent increase. Using these elasticity estimates, the results imply that growth in parental BMI can explain about a third of growth in childhood obesity. They use data from another study, comparing biological to adopted children, to confirm that this intergenerational correlation occurs mostly as a result of biology and not shared environment.

They then explore the extent to which this elasticity differs for disadvantaged, relative to advantaged, groups. Surprisingly, despite the faster growth in obesity for the disadvantaged, there is no higher elasticity (nor faster growth in the elasticity). This finding suggests an important role for factors outside the household in combating the growth in obesity among both the advantaged and disadvantaged.

The final chapter in this section is the study of teen pregnancy by Melissa S. Kearney and Phillip B. Levine, "Socioeconomic Disadvantage and Early Childbearing." The United States has a rate of teen births well above other developed nations, with 5 percent of teens giving birth each year; in the United States roughly one-fifth of all women will give birth before the age of twenty. There is tremendous concern over the long run consequences for both the mother and the child of teen pregnancy, and therefore a major interest in understanding the causes of teen pregnancy. Kearney and Levine's chapter carefully investigates the role of socioeconomic disadvantage in driving teen pregnancy.

They begin by using the Panel Study of Income Dynamics (PSID) to document the strong correlation between various measures of disadvantage and teen child-bearing. But, as with the other studies in this volume, they are concerned that it is not the individual disadvantage per se that is driving these decisions; rather, girls who are born into a family characterized by socioeconomic disadvantage may also grow up in communities with social or cultural norms that lead to early childbearing. To address this concern, they turn to a cohort approach. Under this approach, they use data from the Vital Statistics to measure teenage birth rates across cohorts and states over a long period of time. They first find that the analysis at the cohort level shows a much stronger correlation between socioeconomic disadvantage (such as having a mother with low education or an unmarried mother) and child-bearing than does the analysis at the individual level. This suggests the presence of peer effects, whereby the consequences of disadvantage to some in an area can spill over to the behavior of others in that same area.

They then try to assess the shorter run impacts of a change in socioeconomic disadvantage on teen childbearing by comparing changes in cohort rates of disadvantage to changes in cohort rates of teen childbearing within states over time. They find that there is still a strong association, although weaker than when just comparing steady states: for each 10 percent increase in disadvantage there is at most a 2.5 percent rise in teen pregnancy, and the magnitude is much less for a number of disadvantage measures. This suggests that other social or cultural factors besides economic disadvantage are playing an important role in driving increases in teen pregnancy.

Section III: Contextual Influences

The final section of the book examines the role of contextual influences on the outcomes of disadvantaged children: the unemployment of their parents, the religiosity of the household, and the rate of crime in the neighborhood.

Marianne Page, Ann Huff Stevens, and Jason Lindo start this section by showing the impact of parental job dislocation on youth outcomes in "Parental Income Shocks and Outcomes of Disadvantaged Youth in the United States." Their chapter strikes at the fundamental question in government policy to help disadvantaged youth: will transferring income to disadvantaged families improve the outcomes of their children? This is obviously a very difficult question to answer since children in families with the highest incomes will have better long run outcomes for many reasons, of which income is only one. What is required to answer this question convincingly is a determinant of family income that is independent of the underlying correlation between the talents of parent and child.

Page, Stevens, and Lindo find such a determinant in job displacements. Specifically, they use data from the PSID to examine families who are similar over time, but where one family experiences a job displacement to an earner and the other family does not. They focus in particular on those who are displaced due to a plant closing, which is clearly independent of decisions made by the earner (and therefore independent of other determinants of the outcomes of their children). Such displacements have been shown in previous work, and are shown again here, to lead to sizeable family income losses.

Their main finding is surprising: those children who suffered income loss in childhood due to the job loss of a parent do not, on average, appear to have worse outcomes as adults. This finding casts significant doubt on the central role for the typical family of income levels in determining long run child outcomes. At the same time, they find that job loss-related income reductions do impact the long run outcomes of children from disadvantaged households. For example, among children who grew up in households with income below 1.5 times the poverty line, they are 36 percent less likely to have completed high school if a parent was displaced from their job (relative to comparable families without displacement), and 16 percent less likely to attend college. Thus, disadvantage at childhood makes children more susceptible to long run negative influences from lower household income.

The next chapter in this section is a study of the "buffering" effect of religious and social institutions by Rajeev Dehejia, Thomas DeLeire, Erzo F. P. Luttmer, and Josh Mitchell, "The Role of Religious and Social Organizations in the Lives of Disadvantaged Youth." As noted earlier, there is a substantial body of evidence that shows growing up in a disadvantaged household has negative consequences for later life outcomes—on average. Yet there is considerable variation in these later life outcomes, with some individuals escaping the grip of youth disadvantage. A key question is what factors might be associated with the ability to move out of disadvantage later in life. This chapter asks whether one such factor might be the role of religious or social organizations in the lives of disadvantaged youths.

The authors use the National Survey of Families and Households (NSFH), a panel data set that collects data on the religious and social participation of parents in 1987 to 1988, and follows up the outcomes of their children in 2001 to 2003. In this way, the authors can model these later child outcomes as a function of whether the family was disadvantaged roughly fifteen years earlier, and how that disadvantage interacts with the religious and social participation of the family at that time. The authors use a wide variety of measures of disadvantage, ranging from income to child characteristics, and an equally wide variety of measures of ultimate outcomes, ranging from education and income to subjective well-being. Given the large number of combinations of disadvantage and outcome that they examine (a total of 168), they are careful to ask whether the pattern of findings overall is consistent with a buffering role or not.

The findings are fairly conclusive: parental participation in religious organizations when the child is young does buffer the child against the negative consequences of disadvantage. For example, having a mother with no more than a high school education as a youth reduces the odds that a child attends college by 23 percentage points from a base of 65 percentage points, a decline of about one-third. Yet this effect is larger (31 percentage points) if the youth's family was an infrequent religious participant during childhood, and it is much smaller (16 percent) if the youth's family was a frequent religious participant. So the authors say that religious participation provided a "buffering" effect of roughly 50 percent. They do not find a similar buffering role for other social organizations.

The final chapter in this section is the study of the impact of neighborhood criminality on child outcomes by Anna Aizer, "Neighborhood Violence and Urban Youth." Her chapter opens with a striking fact: three-quarters of American children report having been exposed to neighborhood violence, and exposure to violence is closely associated with poor outcomes for children. Her ambitious chapter aims to explore this exposure in more detail and understand its consequences. She does so using a novel data set, the Los Angeles Family and Neighborhood Study (LA FANS), a survey of children and their families residing in sixty-five neighborhoods in Los Angeles. These data have information on the youth's individual exposure to violence, as well as information on test scores as a measure of youth outcomes. In addition, she creates an innovative measure of neighborhood violence: hospitalizations for assaults for individuals from that neighborhood.

Aizer finds that, in fact, there is no consistent evidence that exposure to violence, either at the individual or neighborhood level, is associated with reduced child outcomes once family disadvantage is controlled for. That is, the negative correlation one finds between exposure to violence and poor outcomes may not be due to the violence per se but to the other socioeconomic disadvantages present for those exposed to violence. Her results are not sufficiently statistically precise to say that violence does not matter, but she certainly raises the bar for those who would claim that exposure to violence, as opposed to other disadvantages, drives poor child outcomes.

Conclusion: How Does Disadvantage Matter?

This is a terrific set of papers, and together they cast new light on a series of important issues surrounding disadvantaged youth. It is hard to summarize clearly such a wide array of varying findings. But there are some general lessons that can be drawn from this body of work.

Lesson 1: Disadvantage Matters

The first lesson is the least surprising: childhood disadvantage has serious negative consequences for child outcomes—both in the short and long term. The studies in this volume document important differentials in a wide variety of outcomes between advantaged and disadvantaged children. In particular, relative to their more advantaged counterparts, children who have low family incomes, low parental education, or are from racial and ethnic minorities are susceptible to the following:

- More behavioral problems in school
- Lower school test scores
- More likely to drop out of high school
- More likely to be obese
- More likely to be teen mothers

- More likely to suffer from mental illness
- More exposed to violent crime

While not surprising, a number of these studies have brought to bear innovative approaches that allow the authors to separate the role of child disadvantage from other factors (such as genetics); that is, to move from a correlation between disadvantage and poor outcomes to a causal framework.

Lesson 2: Differential Impacts of Public Policy
and Other Outside Factors Are Mixed

Probably the most interesting question addressed by most of the chapters in this volume is whether public policies and other outside factors have a differential impact on children in disadvantaged households. The evidence here is surprisingly mixed. In a number of cases, this is shown to be the case:

- Figlio and Roth find that public pre-K has a strong effect on reducing behavioral problems in students who attend schools in disadvantaged areas, but not in students who attend schools in advantaged areas.
- Oreopolous finds that raising the minimum school-leaving age has a positive effect on later life outcomes for Hispanics, but not other groups.
- Page, Stevens, and Lindo find that income shocks to parents arising from job loss have effects on later life outcomes for poor but not for nonpoor children.
- Dehija, DeLeire, Luttmer, and Mitchell find that participation in religious organizations buffer the effects of disadvantage on later life outcomes.

Yet in a number of other cases, this turns out not to be the case:

- Cullen and Jacob find no evidence that moving to a higher "quality" public school has any impact on outcomes for either advantaged or disadvantaged youths.
- Anderson, Butcher, and Schanzenbach find no evidence that there is a higher translation of parental obesity to child obesity in disadvantaged relative to advantaged households.
- Currie and Stabile find no evidence that disadvantaged children see a particularly high translation of childhood mental illness to adult outcomes.

This disparity across the chapters is striking and suggests that context is very important in understanding the impact of protections against disadvantage. In some settings, such as pre-K schooling, high school dropping out, income shocks, or religious participation, there is a particularly strong "buffering" role to be played by interventions. In other settings, such as school choice or the translation of childhood mental illness to adult outcome, there is not. This is an important distinction because if there is a possible "buffering" role, then later interventions can help offset the implications of youth disadvantage; but if there is not, then policy must intervene to end the source of the disadvantage itself if it is to improve child outcomes. Clearly a next step for this research agenda is understanding why this set of buffering responses is so mixed. In particular, can we refine our understanding of the contexts where interventions do and do not offset the impact of family disadvantage?

I

Education

The Behavioral Consequences of Pre-Kindergarten Participation for Disadvantaged Youth

David Figlio and Jeffrey Roth

1.1 Introduction

Expanding access to pre-kindergarten for disadvantaged children has been widely advocated and hotly debated in recent years, and numerous state and local jurisdictions have introduced policies to offer pre-kindergarten to these populations. While the efficacy of Head Start and pre-kindergarten programs has been studied extensively, the focus of this line of research has been nearly exclusively on school readiness and student cognitive performance, with mixed evidence to date. The most compelling of these studies exploit cross-sibling comparisons (Currie and Thomas 2000; Garces, Thomas, and Currie 2002) and regression-discontinuity designs that take advantage of variation in Head Start funding rates (Ludwig and Miller 2007). These studies find general evidence that Head Start participation has long-term benefits in terms of schooling outcomes.

But from the inception of federal support to extend educational opportunity to three- and four-year-old low-income children, there has been a consistent dual emphasis on cognitive and social development. To the plan-

David Figlio is the Orrington Lunt Professor of Education and Social Policy, and a Faculty fellow of the Institute for Policy Research, Northwestern University, and a research associate of the National Bureau of Economic Research. Jeffrey Roth is an associate professor of pediatrics in the College of Medicine at the University of Florida.

This research was funded by the Annie E. Casey Foundation, the U.S. Department of Education, and the National Science Foundation. We thank them for their support but acknowledge that the findings and conclusions presented in this report are those of the authors alone, and do not necessarily reflect the opinions of the research funders. The authors are grateful to the Florida Departments of Education and Health for the individual-level data used in this analysis. They appreciate the helpful comments of Liz Cascio, Jens Ludwig, Jon Gruber, and participants at the NBER preconference and conference on the economics of disadvantaged youth as well as those at the 2006 APPAM conference. We are responsible for any remaining errors.

ners of Head Start in 1964, preparing disadvantaged youth to succeed in school required a "whole child" approach, one in which not only academic knowledge but also behavioral competence would be emphasized (Zigler and Styfco 2004). In addition to Head Start, the federal government also began to aid state efforts to provide local community-sponsored preschools through the mechanism of the Child Care and Development Block Grant program. This flow-through program subsidized child care programs whose quality standards were allowed to vary a great deal more than Head Start's. To supporters of Head Start, these state-subsidized early childhood programs "do not pretend to have anything to do with school readiness. They are essentially custodial programs whose only purpose is to enable poor parents to enter the work force" (Zigler and Styfco 2004, 53).

This issue—that preschool separates parents from children during crucial years of their development as a result of either an elective or required return to the workforce—remains at the heart of the debate over its potentially zero-sum benefit/harm ratio. Disadvantaged children may receive sufficient academic stimulation to compensate for missing or insufficient parental instruction, yet this cognitive benefit may be offset by two negatives: (a) low income children congregate in poor quality child care settings where unfamiliarity with appropriate social interaction is mutually reinforced; and (b) initiation into socially acceptable norms of behavior is conducted not consistently by family members but intermittently by a stranger. The preferred alternative outcome of preschool for disadvantaged youth is that it teaches school acculturation behavior in ways that improve student academic and behavioral outcomes once at school.

This chapter represents an attempt to systematically study the effects of pre-kindergarten participation on student behavior. We utilize a unique longitudinal data set that links student birth records to pre-kindergarten participation for every child born in Florida in or after 1994 who subsequently attended public school in Florida. Because pre-kindergarten participation is endogenous, we employ a novel identification strategy to estimate the effects of pre-kindergarten participation by comparing siblings within the same family. Families' access to pre-kindergarten can change over time as schools add or drop programs. We demonstrate that, within a family, the sibling with less costly access to public pre-kindergarten—measured by the fact that his or her locally-zoned elementary school offers a pre-kindergarten program when he or she is four years old—is considerably more likely to attend than the equally-eligible sibling who would have attended pre-kindergarten at a school other than his or her zoned elementary school, and use this differential access within a family as an instrument to predict public pre-kindergarten attendance. Using these differences in access within a family, we find that public pre-kindergarten participation apparently reduces behavioral problems in elementary school, especially when the child grows up in a particularly disadvantaged neighborhood.

1.2 Background

Research suggesting the possibly negative impact of preschool participation on children's subsequent elementary school behavior is embedded in the larger debate about the psychological consequences of children of any income level being separated from their parents in the first years of life. In the early 1980s educational psychologists began employing attachment theory (Bowlby 1973; Ainsworth et al. 1978) in their study of increasing numbers of infants and toddlers being placed in public or private child care as a result of mothers rapidly returning to the workforce. Attachment theory posited that for humans to become trusting and caring individuals they must, as infants, bond with their mothers in the first year of life. The theory predicted that disruption of this attachment process (primarily to a nurturant female) would result in a child who is unable to develop self control or form stable relationships. Jay Belsky was one of the first educational psychologists to claim to have found evidence confirming this prediction. Starting in the mid 1980s, Belsky issued a series of warnings (1986, 1988, 1990) that "early and extensive nonmaternal care carried risks in terms of increasing the probability of insecure infant-parent attachment relationships and promoting aggression and noncompliance during the toddler, preschool, and early primary school years" (Belsky 2002, 167). The research that Belsky cited was criticized on the grounds that it did not take into account the quality of the child care setting or the background characteristics of the children.

The decade of the 1990s saw a two-prong response to anxiety among both poor and nonpoor families that leaving their infants and toddlers in a group child care setting might promote adverse behavioral outcomes such as noncompliance and aggression. In the legislative arena, the National School Readiness Task Force issued a report in 1991 affirming that school readiness involved not only academic knowledge but also social competence. In 1994, Congress set school readiness to be first among the nation's eight education goals. By the year 2000, all children would have access to high-quality, developmentally appropriate preschool programs and would arrive at school able to "to maintain the mental alertness necessary" to learn (Public Law 103–227).

In the research arena, the National Institute of Child Health and Human Development (NICHD) commissioned a multicenter study of early child care and youth development. Since 1993, the NICHD Early Child Care Research Network has produced over sixty publications, many of which reach conflicting conclusions about the relationship between early child care and socioemotional development. Since the early 1990s, a great deal of research has been conducted on short- and long-run effects of children's early preschool experiences. Given that early childhood education represents a nexus of psychological theory, employment exigency, and cultural transmission, it is not surprising that findings in this body of research using nationally representative samples are decidedly mixed:

- The National Institute of Child Health and Human Development (NICHD) Study of Early Child Care and Youth Development (1998a) found no difference in problem behavior during the first three years among children reared exclusively at home and those who spent more than thirty hours per week in nonparental care.
- The NICHD Study of Early Child Care and Youth Development (1998b) found that mothering was a stronger and more consistent predictor of child outcomes than child care. There was little evidence that early, extensive, and continuous care was related to problematic child behavior. Child care quality was the most consistent predictor of child functioning.
- The NICHD Study of Early Child Care and Youth Development (2001) found that when quality and quantity of child care were controlled, the association between family factors and children's social-emotional development remained significant, thereby affirming that parents continue to have a meaningful effect on children's behavior despite considerable child care experience in the earliest years.
- The NICHD Study of Early Child Care and Youth Development (2003) found that children spending longer hours or more months in center care each year exhibit elevated levels of aggression and less effective impulse control.
- The national evaluation of Early Head Start (Love et al. 2005) found that children randomly assigned to the program (compared to a control group that could access any community service except Early Head Start) showed fewer problem behaviors and lower levels of aggressive behavior at twenty-four and thirty-six months. No evidence was found that more time in child care was associated with higher rates of aggressive behavior.
- First year findings from the *Head Start Impact Study* (U.S. Department of Health and Human Services 2005) reported effect sizes of -0.13 for total behavior problems and -0.16 for hyperactivity as reported by parents whose children were randomly assigned to Head Start. Control groups could enroll in available community non-Head Start services.
- A study of subsidized child care in Quebec found evidence of negative effects on a wide spectrum of child behavioral outcomes: hyperactivity-inattention, general anxiety, separation anxiety, and physical aggressiveness/opposition (Baker, Gruber, and Milligan 2005).
- Summarizing effect sizes, the NICHD Study of Early Child Care and Youth Development (2006) concluded that more child care hours predicted more behavior problems and conflict, according to care providers.

- Using Early Childhood Longitudinal Study data, Loeb et al. (2007) found that center-based care had a negative effect on sociobehavioral measures (with the exception of English proficient Hispanic children). Across the family income distribution, the younger the start age, the larger the negative effect. Intensity effects (more hours per day lead to more kindergarten teacher-report behavioral effects—measures of self control, interpersonal skills, and externalizing behavior) are moderated by family income and race.
- Also using Early Childhood Longitudinal Study, Magnuson, Ruhm, and Waldfogel (2007) found that participation in pre-kindergarten was associated with higher levels of behavior problems noted in the spring of first grade. This adverse relationship was somewhat attenuated for public school-located pre-kindergarten, particularly for students who continued to kindergarten in the same public school where they attended pre-kindergarten.

Parallel to the legislative and research activity at the national level, the decade of the 1990s saw states acting to extend pre-kindergarten into their K-20 educational framework. In Florida as in other states, this downward extension of public schooling to include three- and four-year-olds was partly to accommodate provisions of the Individuals with Disabilities Education Act (Public Law 99-457). Since disproportionate numbers of incoming low-income children were classified early in elementary school with special education exceptionalities such as speech and language impairment or emotional handicap, it was considered a worthwhile investment to provide these services in the context of a pre-kindergarten early intervention program (PKEI).

In funding the program, the Florida Legislature stipulated that priority be given to economically disadvantaged 3- and 4-year-old children whose family's income—up to 135 percent of the federal poverty level—made them free lunch eligible. Additional targets were children of migrant workers, children who had been abused, in foster care, prenatally exposed to drugs, and three- and four-year-olds not economically eligible who could participate with a fee adjusted for family income. Minimum operational parameters were set at six hours per day, five days per week during the school year with an option of extending services to ten hours per day year round. Public school PKEI teachers had to be certified in early childhood education; however, school districts could also choose to subcontract with community-based nonprofits such as Head Start or child care agencies to provide services to three- and four-year olds. Staff qualifications at nonpublic school providers were not as rigorous: a twelve-credit Child Development Associate credential (plus 120 hours of fieldwork) was acceptable to be a lead teacher. In either setting, the student-staff ratio was set at 10:1.

Throughout the 1990s, annual funding for PKEI hovered just under $100 million with enrollment averaging between 25,000 to 35,000 children per year. By the time our data collection period ended (2003), the program had been transferred out of the Department of Education to the quasi public-quasi private Partnership for School Readiness housed directly inside the Governor's Office. It has since been transferred to the Agency for Work-force Innovation, lending partial support to Zigler and Styfco's contention that the mission of many state-supported preschool programs is primarily to serve as day care for mothers on welfare who are required to enter the workforce.[1]

So far we have been focusing on the potentially negative behavioral consequences of preschool participation. To look at the glass half-full, considerable evidence has been accumulated that "emotional development and academic learning are far more closely intertwined in the early years. . . . Across a range of studies, the emotional, social, and behavioral competence of young children (such as higher levels of self-control and lower levels of acting out) predict their academic performance in first grade, over and above their cognitive skills and family backgrounds" (Raver and Knitzer 2002, 3). The collocation of academic knowledge and self regulation in the brain is the basis for both conceptual and empirical support in favor of preschool education. To life span economists such as James Heckman, estimated rates of return to investment in preschool programs far exceed their opportunity costs. These returns to investment would be due in part because younger persons have a longer horizon over which to recoup the fruits of their investments. In Heckman's human capital model (2000), noncognitive skills and informal learning play important roles in lifetime earnings (see also Heckman 2006; Heckman and Rubinstein 2001; Heckman, Stixrud, and Urzua 2006). Most long-run studies that find support for investment in high quality early childhood programs (e.g., High/Scope Perry Preschool, Carolina Abecedarian Project, Chicago Child-Parent Centers) do not make the economic case that disadvantaged program participants caught up to earning levels of more advantaged age peers but rather that society saved money through lower rates of antisocial, cost-positive behavior such as juvenile arrest, welfare dependency, and adult incarceration (Schweinhart et al. 2005; Reynolds et al. 2002). Indeed, Belfield et al. (2006) argue that the long-term effects on crime account for a very large share of the dollar-value benefits of the Perry Preschool treatment. On the other hand, Duncan et al. (2007), utilizing data from six longitudinal data sets in the United States, Canada, and the United Kingdom, found very limited evidence that self-regulation skills at kindergarten had lasting import for long-term academic and behavioral success.

In the opening years of the present accountability-driven decade, early

---

1. Cascio (2006) shows that mothers entered the workforce as a result of increased availability of state subsidized kindergarten.

childhood programs were not spared the press to quantify effects of participation. Head Start adopted a Child Outcomes Framework, and commissioned an impact study as did Early Head Start, both involving random assignment. Some state pre-kindergarten programs were evaluated on the basis of their graduates' performance in elementary school. It has become commonplace to find multilevel and growth curve models being used to investigate the relationship between treatment and proficiency. Calls for "analytical strategies aimed at explaining interindividual differences in intraindividual change" proliferate (Granger and Kivlighan 2003; Kaplan 2002). Adding to the need to be able to demonstrate value added results, the lingering controversy over possible detrimental behavioral effects of early nonmaternal, collective care has galvanized efforts to better measure and treat mental illness in children (Currie and Stabile, this volume).

In the forty years since the United States launched a nationwide program to extend equal opportunity to disadvantaged three- and four-year-olds, the mandate to provide instruction in both the cognitive and socioemotional domains has become subject to increased specificity. In Head Start's performance appraisal goals for 2007, "identifying behavioral problems in preschool children" is listed as a specific performance measure (U.S. Department of Health and Human Services/Administration for Children and Families/Office of Head Start 2007). A history of difficulty in adhering to the behavioral norms expected by schools is frequently used to explain students' poor academic performance (sometimes culminating in their exclusion from the testing pool). Thus, the burden on public pre-kindergarten programs to initiate students into socially acceptable forms of interaction has never been higher. Our study examines whether children who attended public school pre-kindergarten in Florida acquired a better grasp of socially acceptable behavior than their four-year-old peers who attended either a nonpublic preschool or no preschool at all.

This analysis makes several key advances over the existing literature. First, this is the first large-scale study to utilize administrative data on pre-kindergarten participation. This has the advantage of size: we observe the entire population of income-eligible students in the state of Florida born in or after 1989. Using administrative data also eliminates the potential for recall bias in measuring program participation; any student who participated in a public Head Start or school-based pre-kindergarten program in the state of Florida is observed in our data. Also, because we have matched child birth records, school-based pre-kindergarten participation records, and subsequent school behavior records for the entire state of Florida, we can rely on administratively-observed background factors and behavioral problems. (We measure behavioral problems by whether the child is referred for disciplinary action by their teachers.) Furthermore, our matching of birth vital records with school records allows us to compare within families, a strategy shared by Garces, Thomas, and Currie (2002).

Second, the use of population-based data allow us to stratify the estimated effects of pre-kindergarten participation in a number of different ways. With tens of thousands of income-eligible families with multiple children, we can estimate with confidence the differential effects of pre-kindergarten participation within families along a variety of dimensions, including birth conditions, maternal age, and education.

Third, and most importantly, this analysis introduces a novel identification strategy. In addition to within-family comparisons, we exploit the fact that local policy conditions outside of the control of specific families generate different effective prices of attending public pre-kindergarten for different siblings. Whereas all students who meet certain family income or health criteria are eligible for public pre-kindergarten participation, not all students have the same ease of access. For around 60 percent of income-eligible Florida students, the student's local zoned elementary school does not offer a public pre-kindergarten program. These students must in turn attend a pre-kindergarten site farther from their home, and perhaps without public transportation.

We argue that the presence of a pre-kindergarten program in the zoned elementary school should promote public pre-kindergarten participation for several reasons. One major reason is informational: parents are more likely to be aware of pre-kindergarten options when they have a child who attends a school that offers such a program, or when their neighbors have children who attend such a school. But transportation costs may also be a factor, even in cases when transportation to preschool is provided. This may be true for several reasons. Parents may not wish for their young children to be bused long distances, especially if they are alone. And it may be easier for parents to send their young children on a bus if they are accompanied by an older sibling or older neighbor whom the child knows; these are more likely to be the case if the pre-kindergarten is attached to the local zoned school. (In fact, the informational and neighbor-transportation factors are probably the strongest reasons for this increased likelihood of attending public pre-kindergarten when the locally zoned school offers the program, as first children attend pre-kindergarten at nearly the same rate as their younger siblings.) For all of these reasons, we suspect that it is the public school zone, rather than travel time and mileage, that matters most in determining whether children attend public pre-kindergarten programs.

We demonstrate that income-eligible students are highly responsive to the presence of a pre-kindergarten program at their zoned elementary school. Families with a pre-kindergarten program at their zoned elementary school are more than 60 percent more likely to send their children to a public pre-kindergarten program than are families without a pre-kindergarten program at their zoned school. And this pattern holds up within families as well: around 40 percent of families live in elementary school zones with a public pre-kindergarten program when one sibling is four but not when another sibling is four. This situation occurs either because the family changes residence, the zoning lines are redrawn, a school with a pre-kindergarten program dropped it, or because a school without a pre-kindergarten program added it. Regardless, within the same family, the sibling whose zoned elementary school has a pre-kindergarten program is 60 percent more likely to attend than the sibling without such a program at the zoned school. This probability holds when we exclude families who move, and look only at families with different access to public pre-kindergarten because of exogenous changes in local school policy. In this chapter we demonstrate that when one exploits within-family differences in access to pre-kindergarten, a positive estimated effect of pre-kindergarten on behavioral outcomes emerges.

1.3   Disadvantage and Behavior

How and why disadvantage correlates with behavior problems in school has been investigated by every social science discipline over the last fifty years in what now may seem like a quixotic quest for greater equality of opportunity. Two premises underlie myriad theoretical and empirical investigations of this relationship: first, students who misbehave are not learning; and second, the preponderance of students who misbehave are disadvantaged. Disruptive conduct is therefore problematic in both the short and long run: proximally, it obstructs acquisition of social and academic skills, and distally, it postpones mastery of situationally appropriate behavior and course content needed to exit disadvantaged circumstances.

The ongoing investigation of the association between disadvantage and misbehavior in school settings assess a multitude of levels, and, within levels, a multitude of factors that contribute to academic performance. Economists analyze noncognitive returns from investing in early intervention and familial resources (Heckman and Masterov 2007; Ram and Hou 2003); sociologists examine neighborhood effects and family structure (Duncan, Brookes-Gunn, and Klebanov 1994; Hao and Matsueda 2006); psychologists explore accumulated exposure to acute and chronic stressors such as perinatal complications, reduced access to healthcare, harsh and inconsistent parenting (McLoyd 1998; Barbarin et al. 2006); educators consider childcare quality, teacher expectations, and classification schemes entailed by high stakes testing (Berliner 2006; Bradley and Corwin 2002; NICHD 2005). While there have been efforts to organize these multiple levels and factors into overarching nested frameworks (see e.g., Aber, Jones, and Raver 2007), two issues remain unresolved: (a) the etiology of misbehavior (family-mediated or community-influenced); and (b) the circularity between disadvantage, behavior problems, and academic development. Since poor children arrive at school less ready to learn, they are more likely to exhibit frustration and diminished self-esteem, thereby increasing the probability of their becoming disruptive, noncompliant, overactive, and inattentive, which in turn exacerbates existing learning difficulties (Arnold and Doctoroff 2003).

A critique leveled at material deprivation models is that exogenous factors such as intelligence may be the cause of both family poverty and children's behavior and learning problems, and that such models erroneously ascribe patterns of association to income rather than to omitted variables (Mayer 1997). Contemporary interdisciplinary research uses mixed models to decompose the simultaneous deleterious effects of economic disadvantage on socioemotional competence and cognitive skills. However, the efficacy of public pre-kindergarten programs to mitigate the negative effects of material disadvantage has not been unambiguously demonstrated in these multilevel models.

A fundamental first step in any study of the relationship between disadvantage and behavior is to measure the degree to which disadvantaged students, measured along a number of dimensions, tend to misbehave at greater rates in school. Table 1.1 presents some basic facts about the rates of disciplinary problems in the first three years of school (typically, kinder-

Table 1.1   **Rates of disciplinary problems, by measure of student disadvantage**

	Year in school		
	First (kindergarten)	Second	Third
Individual measures of disadvantage			
Teenage mothers	0.043	0.065	0.084
Not teenage mother	0.033	0.049	0.070
Mother has less than high school degree	0.040	0.060	0.084
Mother has high school degree or greater	0.032	0.046	0.063
Mother is black	0.043	0.065	0.092
Mother is white	0.035	0.044	0.051
Parents were unmarried at time of birth	0.040	0.060	0.085
Parents were married at time of birth	0.027	0.038	0.048
Child had inadequate prenatal care	0.044	0.061	0.090
Child had adequate prenatal care	0.035	0.053	0.073
Neighborhood measures of disadvantage			
Above-median rate of free lunch eligibility	0.034	0.056	0.084
Below-median rate of free lunch eligibility	0.039	0.050	0.060
Above-median percent nongraduate mothers	0.035	0.059	0.086
Below-median percent nongraduate mothers	0.037	0.048	0.063

Notes: Disciplinary problems are defined as having been referred to the principal's office for disciplinary reasons at least once during the year. To be included in the analysis, students must be in families with at least two children who were born after 1989 and enrolled in school before 2002, and where all children in the family are recorded as being eligible to receive free lunch (i.e., self-reported income less than 130 percent of the poverty line) in every observed period in school. Families are defined as two or more children who share the same birth mother. Analysis sample: 59,418 children in 29,087 families.

garten through second grade, though we measure the year the child is in school rather than the grade) in the income-eligible population. We compare children who are considered to be disadvantaged along some individual dimension (having a teenage mother; having a mother with less than a high school diploma; having a black mother; having unmarried parents; or having inadequate prenatal care[2]) or neighborhood dimension (living in a neighborhood with above-median rates of free lunch eligibility or non-high school-graduate mothers) to those not considered to be disadvantaged along that same dimension. In table 1.1 and throughout the analysis, we restrict our attention to students who are income-eligible for pre-kindergarten programs at the time of potential enrollment in pre-kindergarten. We do not actually measure income eligibility with certainty; to be income-eligible; a family must have income below 100 percent of the poverty line. However, we only observe free lunch eligibility—less than 130 percent of the federal poverty level. We therefore restrict our analysis to the set of families where all students are consistently observed being eligible for free lunch in every potential time period—about 60 percent of the students who are free lunch eligible at any given time. We expect this more restrictive measure of income eligibility to nearly approximate the true eligible population. Our analysis sample consists of 59,418 children in 29,087 families where all students in the family are consistently observed to be free lunch eligible.

We find consistent evidence that relatively disadvantaged low-income children misbehave at a greater rate than do relatively advantaged low-income children, and that this absolute gap increases over time. For instance, in the first year of school, 4 percent of children born to low-income mothers with less than a high school degree have had serious disciplinary problems, as compared with 3.2 percent of children with low-income high school graduate mothers. By the third year of school, the rate differential between the two groups increases from 0.8 percentage points to 2.3 percentage points.

Our study question of interest is whether pre-kindergarten participants misbehave at greater rates than do eligible nonparticipants. Note that we cannot directly observe private pre-kindergarten (or community-based Head Start) participation, and therefore are comparing public pre-kindergarten attendees with all other income-eligible students. Table 1.2 compares the rates of disciplinary problems in school for income-eligible children who participated in pre-kindergarten programs to those of income-eligible nonparticipating children.

One observes in table 1.2 that students who attended public pre-kindergarten have slightly higher rates of disciplinary problems than students who did not attend public pre-kindergarten in their early years of school. One further observes that the same patterns hold up within fami-

---

2. We measure inadequate prenatal care according to the Kotelchuck index that relates the number of prenatal visits to gestational age of the child.

Table 1.2   Rates of disciplinary problems, by pre-kindergarten participation

	Year in school		
	First (kindergarten)	Second	Third
Nonparticipants	0.036	0.050	0.073
Pre-kindergarten participants	0.037	0.058	0.075
Within-family comparisons			
Nonparticipants	0.035	0.052	0.075
Pre-kindergarten participants	0.035	0.054	0.077

Notes: Disciplinary problems are defined as having been referred to the principal's office for disciplinary reasons at least once during the year. To be included in the analysis, students must be in families with at least two children who were born after 1989 and enrolled in school before 2002, and where all children in the family are recorded as being eligible to receive free lunch (i.e., self-reported income less than 130 percent of the poverty line) in every observed period in school. Families are defined as two or more children who share the same birth mother. Analysis sample: 59,418 children in 29,087 families.

lies. The finding in the raw data that public pre-kindergarten attendees are slightly more likely than nonattendees to have later discipline problems in the early grades could indicate that public pre-kindergarten is either ineffective in terms of engendering positive behavior or perhaps promotes noncompliant, acting-out behavior. But it could also indicate that students, even within a family, are negatively selected into public pre-kindergarten programs: the siblings most in need of socialization may be the ones that families choose to send to pre-kindergarten, while those who are reasonably well-socialized might not be sent. It could also be the case that families are transitioning in a manner that is unobservable to the researchers. The potential presence of endogeneity bias indicates the necessity of conducting instrumental variables regression.

1.4   Evidence of Instrument Relevance

As mentioned earlier, our instrumental variable is the presence of a public pre-kindergarten program in the public elementary school for which the student would be zoned at the time that he or she is four years old. Table 1.3 demonstrates that, in cross section, income-eligible children are much more likely to attend public pre-kindergarten when they have more direct access to it. Even though all students in our data set are eligible for public pre-kindergarten, typically with free transportation, the presence of a public pre-kindergarten program housed locally, in the same elementary school where older siblings and neighbors already attend, appears to have a powerful effect on public pre-kindergarten take-up. Comparing zip codes without community-based Head Start options, nearly 55 percent of income-eligible students attend public pre-kindergarten when the local zoned school offers

Table 1.3   **Attributes of families with different local pre-kindergarten options**

	Families whose local zoned school *offers* a pre-kindergarten program and whose zip code . . .		Families whose local zoned school *does not offer* a pre-kindergarten program and whose zip code . . .	
	has a community-based Head Start program	*does not have a* community-based Head Start program	*has a* community-based Head Start program	*does not have a* community-based Head Start program
Probability of eligible student attending public pre-kindergarten	0.534	0.547	0.221	0.260
Percent "eligible" in school zone	0.293	0.183	0.256	0.167
Percent black in school zone	0.441	0.250	0.324	0.179
Percent Hispanic in school zone	0.180	0.198	0.154	0.149
Percent mothers in school zone without high school degree	0.377	0.285	0.302	0.216
Percent married parents in school zone	0.494	0.641	0.569	0.690
Percent *eligible* black in school zone	0.635	0.488	0.563	0.433
Percent *eligible* mothers in school zone without high school degree	0.534	0.513	0.469	0.460
Percent *eligible* married parents in school zone	0.297	0.381	0.336	0.390

pre-kindergarten, while only 26 percent attend public pre-kindergarten when this is not the case. Note also that while the presence of a community-based Head Start program in the zip code area slightly reduces the likelihood that a child will attend a public pre-kindergarten program (53 percent when the zoned school offers pre-kindergarten, and 22 percent when it does not), it is clear that the overwhelming determinant of public pre-kindergarten entry is not the community-based Head Start option, but available public pre-kindergarten access.

Table 1.3 also makes clear that a cross-sectional analysis of participation, using geographic location as an instrument, is not appropriate. This table provides basic descriptive information, culled from the full set of students whose birth records and school records are matched in Florida, on the family attributes of students across geographic locations with differing levels of access to public pre-kindergarten and community-based Head Start programs. Comparing across the columns, one observes that the school zones where public pre-kindergarten is locally offered tend to be poorer (in terms of a higher percentage "eligible" for publicly-funded pre-kindergarten[3]), with larger fractions black and Hispanic, more mothers who are not high school graduates, and fewer married parents than are the school zones where public pre-kindergarten is not locally offered. Community-based Head Start programs tend to operate in zip code areas that are poorer still, with even higher eligibility rates, more black families (though not Hispanic families), and lower rates of parental marriage and maternal high school graduation. The same patterns hold whether one looks at the attributes of the entire population of families in the school zone or whether one looks only at the attributes of income-eligible families in the school zone.

Clearly, families residing in these different types of geographical locations differ in many measured and unmeasured aspects that are independent of whether they attend public pre-kindergarten, and in fact, it makes sense that public pre-kindergarten programs (and community-based Head Start programs) would tend to locate in communities where the need for these programs is greatest. For numerous reasons, cross-sectional analysis of pre-kindergarten participation will be subject to omitted variables bias. A natural way to take into account these family-specific omitted variables is to control for family fixed effects.

An immediate problem with family fixed effects is that there are many potential reasons why one sibling might participate in pre-kindergarten while another income-eligible sibling might not. For a family fixed effects strategy to be valid, it must be the case that siblings vary according to some

3. We put the word "eligible" in quotation marks because we do not observe eligibility per se. We estimate eligibility based on the student's family's history with free lunch eligibility in the school. We are likely understating the true rate of eligibility in Florida, but this understatement does not seem important for this comparison or for the empirical analysis that follows.

Table 1.4   **Between-family differences in pre-kindergarten attendance probabilities, by availability at zoned school**

Family type	Number of families	Probability of attending pre-kindergarten
No siblings' local zoned school at age four offers pre-kindergarten	11,458	0.346
Some, but not all, siblings' local zoned school at age four offers pre-kindergarten	12,107	0.425
All siblings' local zoned school at age four offers pre-kindergarten	5,522	0.562

exogenous factor that induces one sibling to participate in the program but not the other. We contend that siblings' public pre-kindergarten take-up varies within a family based on differences in local access to pre-kindergarten; fortunately, over 40 percent of all income-eligible families with multiple children experience a change in program offerings from one sibling to the next. Table 1.4 shows that many students without a public pre-kindergarten program immediately available still go to pre-kindergarten, but the probability of attending increases dramatically if the zoned school has a program.[4] Among families where the zoned school offered a pre-kindergarten program to all siblings observed in the data, 56 percent of income-eligible students attended public pre-kindergarten. On the other hand, among families for whom the zoned elementary school never offered pre-kindergarten, just 35 percent of income-eligible students attended pre-kindergarten. Table 1.5 shows again that families in the three groups presented in table 1.4 are very different, further underscoring the importance of conducting within-family comparisons.

Table 1.6 presents within-family information on public pre-kindergarten take up, by access levels. For the 12,107 "mixed" families, the sibling with the easier access to public pre-kindergarten attended these programs 52 percent of the time, while the sibling without such access attended these programs 33 percent of the time. These same differences are apparent when we compare within families of different types, stratified by maternal education, maternal age, and race. This evidence indicates that our instrumental variables strategy has a very strong and consistent (across subgroups) first stage.

---

4. Note that the public pre-kindergarten attendance rate is somewhat higher in the first row of table 1.4 than in the last two columns of table 1.3. This is due to differences in sample between the two tables. In table 1.3, all families, including those with just one child observed, are included, while in table 1.4, only families with two or more children observed are included. In addition, these sibling comparisons tend to be for more disadvantaged families (or families who are more consistently disadvantaged) than the potentially eligible population as a whole.

Table 1.5   **Differences in family attributes, by differences in availability at zoned school**

Family attributes	No siblings zoned for a school offering pre-kindergarten at age four	Some, but not all, siblings zoned for a school offering pre-kindergarten at age four	All siblings zoned for a school offering pre-kindergarten at age four
Teen mother	0.274	0.259	0.231
Mother with less than high school education	0.470	0.514	0.501
Black mother	0.544	0.658	0.671
Mother unmarried	0.649	0.714	0.685
Inadequate prenatal care for child	0.083	0.108	0.137

Note: The attributes reported above are those in place when the youngest observed child in the family was born.

Table 1.6   **Within-family differences in pre-kindergarten attendance probabilities, by availability at zoned school**

Family type	Sibling(s) whose local zoned school at age four offers pre-kindergarten	Sibling(s) whose local zoned school at age four does not offer pre-kindergarten
All eligible families	0.523	0.327
Mother teenaged at birth	0.537	0.345
Mother has less than high school education	0.515	0.320
Mother is black	0.562	0.355
Mother is nonblack	0.445	0.270

1.5   Regression Estimates

Table 1.7 presents regression analysis of the estimated effects of attending public pre-kindergarten on the probability of being disciplined. Each cell in the table represents a different regression specification; the columns reflect different years in school. (Typically a student in "year 2" would be in first grade, but we chose to treat kindergarten repeaters and "natural" first graders the same way.) The regression results presented in table 1.7 include controls for school fixed effects, as well as for student race, sex, free/reduced price lunch status (though in practice, all students will show up as free lunch eligible), maternal age at birth, maternal education at birth, maternal marital status, Medicaid status at birth, adequacy of prenatal care, complications of labor and delivery, birth order, and indicators for whether the student's birth weight is less than 1,000 g, 1,000–1,500 g, 1,500–2,500 g, or > 2,500 g (extremely low, very low, moderately low, or normal birth weight). The

Table 1.7   **Estimated effects of attending pre-kindergarten on probability of being disciplined**

Specification	Year 1 (kindergarten)	Year 2	Year 3
School fixed effects	−0.000	0.003	−0.004
	(0.002)	(0.002)	(0.003)
School and family fixed effects	0.000	0.001	0.003
	(0.002)	(0.002)	(0.003)
School and family fixed effects with instrumental variable	−0.025	−0.032	−0.003
	(0.009)	(0.011)	(0.015)
School and family fixed effects with instrumental variable—	−0.020	−0.043	−0.009
families with children all zoned for the same school	(0.012)	(0.015)	(0.018)
Male students	−0.041	−0.060	−0.022
	(0.011)	(0.015)	(0.021)
Female students	−0.003	0.009	0.001
	(0.007)	(0.010)	(0.016)
School fixed effects with instrumental variable	−0.018	−0.028	−0.002
	(0.006)	(0.010)	(0.015)

Notes: Standard errors adjusted for clustering at the school level are in parentheses beneath point estimates. Each cell represents a different regression specification. Regressions also include controls for race, sex, free/reduced price lunch status, maternal age at birth, maternal marital status, maternal education levels, Medicaid status at birth, prenatal care complications of labor and delivery, indicators for birth weight < 1,000 g, 1,000–1,500 g, 1,500–2,500 g, > 2,500 g, birth order and school fixed effects. The instrumental variable is an indicator for whether pre-kindergarten programs are offered at the student's zoned elementary school at age four. Disciplinary problems are defined as having been referred to the principal's office for disobeying school rules at least once during the year. To be included in the analysis, students must be in families with at least two children who were born after 1989 and enrolled in school before 2002, and where all children in the family are recorded as being eligible to receive free lunch (i.e., self-reported income less than 130 percent of the poverty line) in every observed period in school. Families are defined as two or more children who share the same birth mother. Analysis sample: 59,418 children in 29,087 families. Analysis sample for last row in table: 31,149 children in 15,248 families.

school fixed effect controls are important because schools may vary systematically in how they dispense and report discipline. As can be seen in the first row of table 1.7, one observes no apparent cross-sectional relationship between public pre-kindergarten participation and disciplinary problems in the first three years of school. The second row of the table presents the same analysis but with family fixed effects. The (non-)results remain robust; while there exist some sign changes between years, the magnitudes of the point estimates are trivial.

The third row of table 1.7 presents the instrumental variables regression results. As can be seen, there exists a negative and sizeable estimated effect of pre-kindergarten participation and behavioral problems in the first two years of school, and the estimated effect is no longer statistically significant in the third year of school. This evidence suggests that students who participated in public pre-kindergarten programs are less likely to be referred for disciplinary problems later than are nonparticipants. This result is at odds with much of the existing cross-sectional literature that demonstrates a positive relationship between pre-kindergarten participation and subsequent misbehavior.

However, there is reason to be skeptical of this finding. Our sample of within-family access changers consists of families who moved, families who did not move but who were rezoned from one school to another, where one school offers a pre-kindergarten program and the other does not, and families who did not move and were not rezoned, but the zoned school changed its pre-kindergarten offerings between siblings. The second source of variation—rezonings—is arguably the most exogenous source of variation, but fewer than 1 percent of these families changed access status as a consequence of rezoning. However, 45 percent of families did not move and were not rezoned, but had their access status change when their zoned elementary school either added or dropped its pre-kindergarten program. These students provide more plausible variation, and the fourth row of table 1.7 restricts the analysis to this set of students. We observe similar findings when we exclude students who changed access status because they changed residences, suggesting that endogenous location choice is not driving our within-family estimates. The fifth and sixth rows of table 1.7 stratify these findings by student sex: unsurprisingly, the results are concentrated exclusively in the male students, who are by far more likely to commit disciplinary infractions in the elementary grades.

While we believe that the within-family identification strategy is more credible than an identification strategy that exploits school changes in public pre-kindergarten offerings over time, because of the nonrandomness inherent in schools' and school districts' decisions to initiate or disband school-based pre-kindergarten programs, we are sensitive to the potential that cross-sibling spillovers may still undermine our within-family identification strategy. We suspect that the reasons that families are more likely to send their children to public pre-kindergarten programs when their local zoned elementary school offers such a program include both transportation and informational factors. In both of these cases, it may be the case that older siblings attending a public school could contribute to a younger sibling attending a public pre-kindergarten program at that same school. The potential presence of strong cross-sibling spillovers could undermine the credibility of this instrumental variable strategy. It turns out, however, that the comparisons in table 1.7 appear to be nearly independent of birth order. For instance, 51 percent of eligible first siblings attend pre-kindergarten when offered at their locally zoned elementary school, as compared with 53 percent of subsequent siblings. Therefore, the non-sibling-related factors associated with public pre-kindergarten participation at locally zoned elementary schools appear to be the dominant reasons for children's attendance.

That said, the potential presence of sibling spillovers driving our results remains. Therefore, in the last row of table 1.7 we repeat the same basic empirical strategy without the family fixed effects—in essence, exploiting cross-time changes in locally zoned schools' pre-kindergarten program offerings. When we do this analysis, the results are slightly smaller but broadly consistent with those found using family fixed effects, suggesting that the findings are not being driven by our decision to compare sibling pairs. In the remainder of this chapter, we will therefore continue to utilize our preferred within-family identification strategy using instrumental variables.

It is important to note that while a within-family instrumental variables strategy appears to be appropriate, a straight sibling comparison identification strategy is not. We find that models that control for family fixed effects yield results that are nearly identical to those that exclude family fixed effects—suggesting that within-family selection into pre-kindergarten programs apparently takes place. That our results differ substantially depending on whether or not one instruments for local access to pre-kindergarten programs indicates that researchers should exercise considerable caution when making cross-sibling comparisons.

Are these results evidence of a short-term benefit only of public pre-kindergarten participation? It may be the case that the absence of behavioral problems in the first two years of schooling puts a child on a different trajectory. Table 1.8 shows that students who had behavioral problems in kindergarten were much more likely to be classified as emotionally disabled or severely emotionally disturbed later on. Table 1.9 also presents instrumental variables regression analysis to show that public pre-kindergarten participation reduces the likelihood that a student, all else equal, will be classified as emotionally disabled in year two or year three of school. In fact, we observe this reduction even when we control also for a student's actual observed behavior. This finding suggests that public pre-kindergarten participation not only appears to reduce the degree of problem behavior, relative to the alternative of private preschool or no preschool for disadvantaged youth, but it also seems to further reduce the likelihood of later classification into special education classes for students with serious social-emotional handicaps—above and beyond the degree of behavioral problems observed.

Table 1.8   **Relationship between disciplinary problems and subsequent classification of emotional disability**

	Year 1 (kindergarten)	Year 2	Year 3
Probability of being classified as emotionally disabled or severely emotionally disturbed			
Students who were referred in kindergarten	0.016	0.025	0.026
Students not referred in kindergarten	0.001	0.001	0.002
Probability of being classified with any disability			
Students who were referred in kindergarten	0.049	0.064	0.056
Students not referred in kindergarten	0.025	0.028	0.031

Table 1.9   Estimated effects of attending pre-kindergarten on probability of being classified as emotionally disabled or severely emotionally disturbed: Instrumental variables regression with family fixed effects

Specification	Year 1 (kindergarten)	Year 2	Year 3
Probability of being classified as emotionally disabled or severely emotionally disturbed	−0.003 (0.001)	−0.020 (0.003)	−0.011 (0.004)
Probability of being classified, conditional on actual observed behavior	−0.002 (0.001)	−0.019 (0.003)	−0.013 (0.005)

Notes: Standard errors adjusted for clustering at the school level are in parentheses beneath point estimates. Each cell represents a different regression specification. Regressions also include controls for race, sex, free/reduced price lunch status, maternal age at birth, maternal marital status, maternal education levels, Medicaid status at birth, prenatal care complications of labor and delivery, indicators for birth weight < 1,000 g, 1,000–1,500 g, 1,500–2,500 g, > 2,500 g, birth order, and school and family fixed effects. The instrumental variable is an indicator for whether pre-kindergarten programs are offered at the student's zoned elementary school at age four. Disciplinary problems are defined as having been referred to the principal's office for disobeying school rules at least once during the year. To be included in the analysis, students must be in families with at least two children who were born after 1989 and enrolled in school before 2002, and where all children in the family are recorded as being eligible to receive free lunch (i.e., self-reported income less than 130 percent of the poverty line) in every observed period in school. Families are defined as two or more children who share the same birth mother. Analysis sample: 59,418 children in 29,087 families.

1.5.1   Falsification Exercise

Especially given the fact that the estimated effects of public pre-kindergarten are considerably different depending on whether or not we instrument for pre-kindergarten participation, one might be concerned that our instrumental variables findings are being driven by the identification strategy employed. We therefore propose a falsification exercise, in which we utilize an indicator for low birth weight (i.e., less than 2,500 g at birth) as our replacement dependent variable. Pre-kindergarten participation cannot influence low birth weight, but an unmeasured third variable (e.g., exposure to an environmental toxin) could be associated with birth weight, pre-kindergarten participation, and behavioral outcomes. Medical research indicates that low birth weight infants have a higher incidence of behavioral problems (Johnson 2007), so this association could be seen as a strong falsification test in the event of a finding of zero effect. Therefore, in table 1.10 we conduct this falsification test. Because birth weight is a covariate in our regular regression models, we estimate this model without any covariates except for school and family fixed effects. In order to make our comparisons consistent, we also repeat our instrumental variables regression with discipline as a dependent variable to make certain that differential treatment of covariates is not responsible for the differences in results. We conduct these

Table 1.10   **Falsification exercise: Instrumental variables evidence on low birth weight**

	Discipline in year 1 (kindergarten)	Discipline in year 2	Discipline in year 3	Low birth weight
School and family fixed effects with instrumental variable	−0.033 (0.009)	−0.026 (0.011)	−0.002 (0.014)	0.005 (0.012)
School and family fixed effects with instrumental variable—*families with children all zoned for the same school*	−0.020 (0.012)	−0.048 (0.016)	−0.028 (0.018)	0.007 (0.018)

Notes: Standard errors adjusted for clustering at the school level are in parentheses beneath point estimates. Each cell represents a different regression specification. To be included in the analysis, students must be in families with at least two children who were born after 1989 and enrolled in school before 2002, and where all children in the family are recorded as being eligible to receive free lunch (i.e., self-reported income less than 130 percent of the poverty line) in every observed period in school. Families are defined as two or more children who share the same birth mother. Analysis sample: 59,418 children in 29,087 families. Analysis sample for last row in table: 31,149 children in 15,248 families.

tests both for the full sample of families and for the set of families where all observed children were zoned for the same school.

We observe that the results are quite similar with regard to discipline as a dependent variable, regardless of whether or not we include the covariates in the model. There remains the general pattern of a negative relationship between pre-kindergarten participation and discipline in the first two years of school, with less evidence of a relationship in the third year. In the falsification exercise, however, there is no evidence of a relationship between low birth weight and pre-kindergarten participation in our instrumental variables models, providing further support for our instrumental variables identification strategy. Indeed, given the positive correlation between low birth weight and behavioral problems, the positive insignificant coefficient in the low birth weight specification is reassuring.

1.5.2   Differential Effects by Degree of Disadvantage

Earlier in this chapter, we show that income-eligible students who are considered disadvantaged under different dimensions tend to misbehave at greater rates than do income-eligible students who are considered to be relatively advantaged. We next investigate whether we observe differential estimated effects of pre-kindergarten participation for students of different degrees of advantage. Table 1.11 presents estimated effects of pre-kindergarten participation for different groups of income-eligible students, over the first two years of school, along the same measures of individual disadvantage presented in table 1.1.

As can be seen in table 1.11, there does not appear to be a consistent differential relationship between measures of disadvantage and the esti-

Table 1.11   **Estimated effects of attending pre-kindergarten on probability of being disciplined, by different measures of disadvantage: Instrumental variables estimates**

Student/family attribute	Year 1 (kindergarten)	Year 2
Student has teenage mother	−0.025	−0.040
	(0.025)	(0.030)
Student does not have teenage mother	−0.027	−0.034
	(0.009)	(0.012)
Mother has less than high school degree	−0.043	−0.043
	(0.015)	(0.019)
Mother has high school degree or greater	−0.014	−0.028
	(0.010)	(0.013)
Mother is black	−0.028	−0.042
	(0.011)	(0.015)
Mother is white	−0.059	−0.018
	(0.030)	(0.031)
Parents were unmarried at time of birth	−0.026	−0.032
	(0.012)	(0.015)
Parents were married at time of birth	−0.029	−0.040
	(0.013)	(0.017)
Child had inadequate prenatal care	0.003	−0.068
	(0.039)	(0.043)
Child had adequate prenatal care	−0.029	−0.032
	(0.010)	(0.012)

Notes: Standard errors adjusted for clustering at the school level are in parentheses beneath point estimates. Each cell represents a different regression specification. Regressions also include controls for race, sex, free/reduced price lunch status, maternal age at birth, maternal marital status, maternal education levels, Medicaid status at birth, prenatal care complications of labor and delivery, indicators for birth weight $< 1,000$ g, $1,000–1,500$ g, $1,500–2,500$ g, $> 2,500$ g, birth order, and school fixed effects. The instrumental variable is an indicator for whether pre-kindergarten programs are offered at the student's zoned elementary school at age four. Disciplinary problems are defined as having been referred to the principal's office for disobeying school rules at least once during the year. To be included in the analysis, students must be in families with at least two children who were born after 1989 and enrolled in school before 2002, and where all children in the family are recorded as being eligible to receive free lunch (i.e., self-reported income less than 130 percent of the poverty line) in every observed period in school. Families are defined as two or more children who share the same birth mother. Neighborhoods are designed by public school zones.

mated effects of pre-kindergarten participation. Children born to teenage mothers apparently experience the same effects of pre-kindergarten participation as those born to nonteenage mothers. The relative estimated effects of pre-kindergarten participation are unstable from year to year with regard to race or adequacy of prenatal care. Only with regard to maternal education levels does a relatively clear pattern emerge, suggesting that children of less educated mothers apparently exhibit fewer disciplinary referrals associated with pre-kindergarten participation. This finding, however, should be inter-

Table 1.12   Estimated effects of attending pre-kindergarten on probability of
being disciplined, by percentage eligible in the neighborhood, conditional
on community-based Head Start availability: Instrumental
variables estimates

Families residing in zip codes with community-based Head Start availability	Year 1 (kindergarten)	Year 2	Year 3
10th percentile of percentage eligible	0.025	−0.004	0.021
	(0.034)	(0.043)	(0.053)
90th percentile of percentage eligible	−0.085	−0.118	−0.056
	(0.021)	(0.026)	(0.031)
p-value of difference	0.00	0.00	0.00

Notes: Standard errors adjusted for clustering at the school level are in parentheses beneath point estimates. Each cell represents a different regression specification. Regressions also include controls for race, sex, free/reduced price lunch status, maternal age at birth, maternal marital status, maternal education levels, Medicaid status at birth, prenatal care complications of labor and delivery, indicators for birth weight < 1,000 g, 1,000–1,500 g, 1,500–2,500 g, > 2,500 g, birth order, and school fixed effects. The instrumental variable is an indicator for whether pre-kindergarten programs are offered at the student's zoned elementary school at age four. Disciplinary problems are defined as having been referred to the principal's office for disobeying school rules at least once during the year. To be included in the analysis, students must be in families with at least two children who were born after 1989 and enrolled in school before 2002, and where all children in the family are recorded as being eligible to receive free lunch (i.e., self-reported income less than 130 percent of the poverty line) in every observed period in school. Families are defined as two or more children who share the same birth mother. Neighborhoods are designed by public school zones.

preted with caution given the relative instability of the other comparisons presented in table 1.11.

While students with different individual-level measures of disadvantage might not experience differential estimated effects of pre-kindergarten participation, it may be the case that differences are present when families are stratified on the basis of neighborhood measures of disadvantage. In an attempt to gauge the degree to which these neighborhood differences might be at work, we repeat the same analysis but compare the estimated effects of public pre-kindergarten participation for students in relatively advantaged neighborhoods to those for students in relatively disadvantaged neighborhoods. We define neighborhood advantage in two different ways—one based on the percentage of children in the neighborhood who are eligible for public pre-kindergarten and one based on the percentage of children in the neighborhood whose mothers are not high school graduates. These results, reported in the table 1.12, indicate that the estimated effects of public pre-kindergarten are very highly related to measures of neighborhood disadvantage. Neighborhoods with fewer disadvantaged families tend to have small (or opposite-signed) estimated effects of public pre-kindergarten programs, while neighborhoods with more disadvantaged families tend to have large, significant estimated effects of public pre-kindergarten

Table 1.13   **Estimated differential effects of attending pre-kindergarten on probability of being disciplined: Instrumental variables regression with school and family fixed effects**

Family/student attribute	Year 1 (kindergarten)			Year 2		
	Below-median rate of free-lunch eligibility	Above-median rate of free-lunch eligibility	p-value of difference	Below-median rate of free-lunch eligibility	Above-median rate of free-lunch eligibility	p-value of difference
Teenage mother	−0.007	−0.044	0.17	0.007	−0.089	0.04
	(0.035)	(0.024)		(0.043)	(0.030)	
Mother's education less than high school	−0.034	−0.047	0.49	0.015	−0.096	0.00
	(0.021)	(0.016)		(0.026)	(0.020)	
Low birth weight	−0.015	−0.025	0.80	0.056	−0.035	0.16
	(0.045)	(0.026)		(0.069)	(0.032)	
Black mother	−0.004	−0.046	0.08	0.018	−0.087	0.00
	(0.018)	(0.011)		(0.025)	(0.015)	

Notes: Standard errors adjusted for clustering at the school level are in parentheses beneath point estimates. Each cell represents a different regression specification. Regressions also include controls for race, sex, free/reduced price lunch status, maternal age at birth, maternal marital status, maternal education levels, Medicaid status at birth, prenatal care complications of labor and delivery, indicators for birth weight < 1,000 g, 1,000–1,500 g, 1,500–2,500 g, > 2,500 g, birth order, and school and family fixed effects. The instrumental variable is an indicator for whether pre-kindergarten programs are offered at the student's local elementary school. Disciplinary problems are defined as having been referred to the principal's office for disobeying school rules at least once during the year. To be included in the analysis, students must be in families with at least two children who were born after 1989 and enrolled in school before 2002, and where all children in the family are recorded as being eligible to receive free lunch (i.e., self-reported income less than 130 percent of the poverty line) in every observed period in school. Families are defined as two or more children who share the same birth mother. Analysis sample: 59,418 children in 29,087 families.

programs.[5] These results suggest that public pre-kindergarten programs are most helpful in the most disadvantaged neighborhoods.

We next consider the two-way interaction between individual measures of disadvantage and neighborhood measures of disadvantage. Table 1.13 stratifies the estimated effects of public pre-kindergarten based on a series of family attributes—mother's age, education level, and race and child's birth weight—and further by measured neighborhood disadvantage, proxied using the rate of free-lunch eligibility in the neighborhood. We observe relative consistency across the various strata by year 2 along a series of dimensions: we find that public pre-kindergarten is associated with increased estimated rates of behavioral problems in relatively advantaged neighborhoods and decreased estimated rates of behavioral problems in relatively disadvantaged communities. The differences between these two rates tend to be statistically significant in year 2. While the results are rather noisy,

5. We have also stratified these neighborhoods by fraction eligible for pre-kindergarten participation and found very similar results.

Table 1.14   Estimated effects of attending pre-kindergarten on probability of being suspended or repeating a grade by year 3, by differing degrees of community disadvantage: Instrumental variables estimates

	Probability of being suspended by year 3	Probability of repeating a grade by year 3
Relatively advantaged neighborhoods: below-median rate of free lunch eligibility	0.055 (0.034)	0.031 (0.042)
Relatively disadvantaged neighborhoods: above-median rate of free lunch eligibility	−0.052 (0.019)	−0.036 (0.027)
p-value of difference	0.00	0.06

Notes: Standard errors adjusted for clustering at the school level are in parentheses beneath point estimates. Each cell represents a different regression specification. Regressions also include controls for race, sex, free/reduced price lunch status, maternal age at birth, maternal marital status, maternal education levels, Medicaid status at birth, prenatal care complications of labor and delivery, indicators for birth weight < 1,000 g, 1,000–1,500 g, 1,500–2,500 g, > 2,500 g, birth order, and school fixed effects. The instrumental variable is an indicator for whether pre-kindergarten programs are offered at the student's zoned elementary school at age four. To be included in the analysis, students must be in families with at least two children who were born after 1989 and enrolled in school before 2002, and where all children in the family are recorded as being eligible to receive free lunch (i.e., self-reported income less than 130 percent of the poverty line) in every observed period in school, and where all included students are observed through year 3 of school. Families are defined as two or more children who share the same birth mother.

nonetheless the general pattern of findings remains consistent with those already presented: the estimated beneficial effects of public pre-kindergarten programs are present in the relatively disadvantaged communities and not in the relatively advantaged communities.

1.5.3   Other Outcomes

We next turn to other outcomes besides basic discipline and emotionally disturbed classification. Specifically, in table 1.14 we consider the likelihood that a student will, by the end of his or her third year, either have been suspended out of school or repeated a grade.[6] These arguably represent more serious behavioral outcomes than referral to the principal's office for a rule infraction.

As can be seen in table 1.14, patterns similar to disciplinary problems emerge with regard to suspension and grade repetition: students participating in public pre-kindergarten programs are estimated to be significantly more likely to be suspended than are nonparticipants in relatively advantaged communities, and are significantly less likely to be suspended than are nonparticipants in relatively disadvantaged neighborhoods. The difference between the two is statistically significantly different from zero as well. The

---

6. We present outcomes at the end of year 3 because grade repetition and suspension are low-probability events, particularly in the first year or two of school.

patterns of signs are the same for grade repetition, but neither point estimate is statistically significant; the difference between the two, however, is statistically significant at the 7 percent level. These results, while suggestive, provide further evidence that there exist substantial differences in results between relatively advantaged versus relatively disadvantaged communities, most likely suggesting that the potential socializing benefits of public pre-kindergarten programs are strongest in the disadvantaged communities where socialization to institutional norms faces numerous obstacles.

1.7 Conclusion

We utilize a unique matched administrative data set and a novel identification strategy to study the effects of public pre-kindergarten participation on student behavioral outcomes. The analysis indicates that public pre-kindergarten leads to reduced student disciplinary problems and reduced rates of being classified emotionally disabled or severely emotionally disturbed. That said, we observe that the estimated benefit of public pre-kindergarten participation apparently depends crucially on the level of advantage of the neighborhood in which the student resides. We find that the favorable estimated effects of public pre-kindergarten programs are concentrated in the least advantaged communities.

In relatively advantaged neighborhoods, on the other hand, we do not find evidence that public pre-kindergarten programs have appreciable behavioral benefits. This may be due to differences in community institutions, neighborhood effects, or private pre-kindergarten alternatives in these more advantaged neighborhoods, or it may be that the families eligible for public pre-kindergarten who live in more advantaged neighborhoods tend to be more advantaged themselves than do their income-eligible counterparts in less advantaged neighborhoods. We will continue to investigate these differences in our future work.

References

Aber, J. L., S. M. Jones, and C. C. Raver. 2007. Poverty and child development: New perspectives on a defining issue. In *Child development and social policy: Knowledge for action,* ed. J. L. Aber, S. J. Bishop-Josef, S. M. Jones, K. T. McLearn, and D. A. Phillips, 149–66. Washington, D.C.: American Psychological Association.

Ainsworth, M. D. S., M. C. Blehar, E. Waters, and S. Wall. 1978. *Patterns of attachment: A psychological study of the strange situation.* Hillsdale, NJ: Erlbaum.

Arnold, D. H., and G. L. Doctoroff. 2003. The early education of socioeconomically disadvantaged children. *Annual Review of Psychology* 54 (January): 517–45.

Baker, M., J. Gruber, and K. Milligan. 2005. Universal childcare, maternal labor supply, and family well-being. NBER Working Paper no. 11832. Cambridge, MA: National Bureau of Economic Research, December.

Barbarin, O., D. Bryant, T. McCandies, M. Burchinal, D. Early, R. Clifford, R. Pianta, and C. Howes. 2006. Children enrolled in public pre-K: The relation of family life, neighborhood quality, and socioeconomic resources to early competence. *American Journal of Orthopsychiatry* 76 (2): 265–76.

Belfield, C., M. Nores, S. Barnett, and L. Schweinhart. 2006. The High/Scope Perry preschool program: Cost-benefit analysis using data from the age-40 followup. *Journal of Human Resources* 41 (1): 162–90.

Belsky, J. 1986. Infant day care: A cause for concern? *Zero to Three* 6:1–9.

———. 1988. The "effects" of infant day care reconsidered. *Early Childhood Research Quarterly* 3:235–72.

———. 1990. Developmental risks associated with infant day care: Attachment insecurity, noncompliance, and aggression? In *Psychosocial issues in day care,* ed. S. Chehrazi, 37–68. Washington, D.C.: American Psychiatric Press.

———. 2002. Quantity counts: Amount of child care and children's socioemotional development. *Developmental and Behavioral Pediatrics* 23 (3): 167–70.

Berliner, D.C. 2006. Our impoverished view of educational research. *Teachers College Record* 108 (6): 949–95.

Bowlby, J. 1973. *Attachment and loss.* New York: Basic Books.

Bradley, R. H., and R. F. Corwyn. 2002. Socioeconomic status and child development. *Annual Review of Psychology* 53 (February): 371–99.

Cascio, E. 2006. Do large investments in early education pay off? Long-term effects of introducing kindergartens into public schools. Dartmouth College, Working Paper.

Currie, J., and D. Thomas. 2000. School quality and the longer-term effects of Head Start. *Journal of Human Resources* 35 (4): 755–74.

Duncan, G. J., J. Brooks-Gunn, and P. K. Klebanov. 1994. Economic deprivation and early childhood development. *Child Development* 62 (2): 296–318.

Duncan, G. J., A. Claessens, A. C. Huston, L. S. Pagani, M. Engel, C. J. Dowsett, H. Sexton, et al. 2007. School readiness and later achievement. *Developmental Psychology* 43 (6): 1428–46.

Garces, E., D. Thomas, and J. Currie. 2002. Longer term effects of Head Start. *American Economic Review* 92 (4): 999–1012.

Granger, D., and K. Kivlighan. 2003. Integrating biological, behavioral, and social levels of analysis in early child development: Progress, problems, and prospects. *Child Development* 74 (4): 1058–63.

Hao, L., and R. L. Matsueda. 2006. Family dynamics through childhood: A sibling model of behavior problems. *Social Science Research* 35 (2): 500–24.

Heckman, J. 2000. Policies to foster human capital. *Research in Economics* 54 (1): 3–56.

———. 2006. Skill formation and the economics of investing in disadvantaged children. *Science* 312 (5782): 1900–02.

Heckman, J. J., and D. V. Masterov. 2007. The productivity argument for investing in young children. *Review of Agricultural Economics* 29 (3): 446–93.

Heckman, J. J., and Y. Rubinstein. 2001. The importance of noncognitive skills: Lessons from the GED testing program. *American Economic Review* 91 (2): 145–49.

Heckman, J. J., J. Stixrud, and S. Urzua. 2006. The effects of cognitive and noncognitive abilities on labor market outcomes and social behavior. *Journal of Labor Economics* 24 (3): 411–82.

Johnson, S. 2007. Cognitive and behavioural outcomes following very preterm birth. *Seminars in Fetal and Neonatal Medicine* 12 (5): 363–73.

Kaplan, D. 2002. Methodological advances in the analysis of individual growth with relevance to education policy. *Peabody Journal of Education* 77 (1): 189–215.

Loeb, S., M. Bridges, D. Bassok, B. Fuller, and R. Rumberger. 2007. How much is too much? The influence of preschool centers on children's social and cognitive development. *Economics of Education Review* 26 (1): 52–66.

Love, J., E. E. Kisker, C. Ross, J. Constantine, K. Boller, R. Chazan-Cohen, C. Brady-Smith, et al. 2005. The effectiveness of Early Head Start for 3-year-old children and their parents: Lessons for policy and programs. *Developmental Psychology* 41 (6): 885–901.

Ludwig, J., and D. Miller. 2007. Does Head Start improve children's life chances? Evidence from a regression-discontinuity approach. *Quarterly Journal of Economics* 122 (1): 158–208.

Magnuson, K. A., C. Ruhm, and J. Waldfogel. 2007. Does prekindergarten improve school preparation and performance? *Economics of Education Review* 26 (1): 33–51.

Mayer, S. E. 1997. *What money can't buy: Family income and children's life chances.* Cambridge, MA: Harvard University Press.

McLoyd, V. C. 1998. Socioeconomic disadvantage and child development. *American Psychologist* 53 (2): 185–204.

National Institute of Child Health and Human Development (NICHD) Early Child Care Network. 1998a. Early child care and self-control, compliance, and problem behavior at twenty-four and thirty-six months. *Child Development* 69 (4): 1145–70.

———. 1998b. Relations between family predictors and child outcomes: Are they weaker for children in child care? *Developmental Psychology* 34 (5): 1119–28.

———. 2001. Nonmaternal care and family factors in early development: An overview of the NICHD study of early child care. *Journal of Applied Developmental Psychology* 22 (4): 457–92.

———. 2003. Does amount of time in child care predict socioemotional adjustment during the transition to kindergarten? *Child Development* 74 (4): 976–1005.

NICHD Early Child Care Research Network. 2005. Duration and developmental timing of poverty and children's cognitive and social development from birth through third grade. *Child Development* 76 (4): 795–810.

———. 2006. Child-care effect sizes for the NICHD Study of Early Child Care and Youth Development. *American Psychologist* 61 (2): 99–116.

Ram, B., and F. Hou. 2003. Changes in family structure and child outcomes: Roles of economic and familial resources. *Policy Studies Journal* 31 (3): 309–30.

Raver, C. C., and J. Knitzer. 2002. Ready to enter: What research tells policymakers about strategies to promote social and emotional school readiness among three- and four-year-old children. Discussion Paper, National Center for Children in Poverty, Columbia University, Mailman School of Public Health.

Reynolds, A. J., J. A. Temple, D. L. Robertson, and E. A. Mann. 2002. Age 21 cost-benefit analysis of the Title I Chicago Child-Parent Centers. *Educational Evaluation and Policy Analysis* 24 (4): 267–303.

Schweinhart, L. J., J. Montie, Z. Xiang, W. S. Barnett, C. R. Belfield, and M. Nores. 2005. *Lifetime effects: The High/Scope Perry preschool study through age 40.* Ypsilanti, MI: High/Scope Press.

U.S. Department of Health and Human Services, Administration for Children and Families. 2005. *Head Start Impact Study: First year findings.* Washington, D.C.: Office of Planning, Research and Evaluation.

U.S. Department of Health and Human Services. 2007. Head Start Reauthorization: Public Law 110-134.

Zigler, E., and S. Styfco. 2004. *The Head Start debates.* Baltimore, MD: P. H. Brookes.

Is Gaining Access to Selective Elementary Schools Gaining Ground?
Evidence from Randomized Lotteries

Julie Berry Cullen and Brian A. Jacob

2.1 Introduction

In 2004, roughly 13 million children in the United States were living below the poverty line. While social programs enacted since the Great Society have done a great deal to mitigate the immediate effects of poverty, education has become increasingly important in escaping poverty. The returns to education, and to skill, have increased dramatically over the past forty years. Where it was once possible to earn a productive living with only the most rudimentary of academic skills, it is increasingly difficult to find a job that offers a living wage with anything less than a college degree (Murnane and Levy 1996).

At the same time, poor children attend schools that appear worse on a number of dimensions. In 2004, high-poverty districts received nearly $1,000 less per pupil in state and local revenues than low-poverty districts within the same state (Education Trust 2006). According to a recent analysis by *Educa-*

Julie Berry Cullen is an associate professor of economics at the University of California, San Diego, and a research associate of the National Bureau of Economic Research. Brian A. Jacob is the Walter Annenberg Professor of Education Policy and professor of economics at the Gerald R. Ford School of Public Policy, University of Michigan, and a research associate of the National Bureau of Economic Research.

This research was funded by the Annie E. Casey Foundation. We thank them for their support but acknowledge that the findings and conclusions presented in this report are those of the authors alone, and do not necessarily reflect the opinions of the Foundation.

We are grateful to John Easton, Joseph Hahn, Dan Bugler, Jack Harnedy, Amy Nowell, Andrea Ross, Frank Spoto, and John Quane for assistance in collecting the data. We would like to thank Jacob Vigdor and participants in the conference and preconference meetings for useful comments and suggestions. Addresses: Julie Cullen, Department of Economics, University of California, San Diego, 9500 Gilman Dr., La Jolla, CA 92093-0508, jbcullen@ucsd.edu; Brian Jacob, Gerald R. Ford School of Public Policy, University of Michigan, 735 South State Street, Ann Arbor, MI 48109, bajacob@umich.edu.

tion Week, only 65 percent of teachers in high-poverty districts in California met the new federal guidelines for highly qualified teachers in 2005, compared to 81 percent in low-poverty districts in the state (Keller 2005). In New York, 81 percent of teachers in high-poverty districts were highly qualified, compared to almost 100 percent in low-poverty areas.[1]

These facts have spurred many initiatives to improve school quality for disadvantaged children. For example, over the past three decades a number of states have passed school finance reforms to reduce disparities in revenues and to guarantee a minimum adequate level of spending for districts with difficult-to-educate student populations. The federal government also targets aid to schools with high poverty rates through the Title I program. Complementary policies have been introduced to ensure that available resources are used effectively, such as state charter school laws that allow alternative schools to compete with the traditional public schools and the federal No Child Left Behind school accountability legislation that requires states to adopt universal testing and minimum performance standards.

While it certainly seems plausible that attending a better school should improve student achievement, the existing evidence is far from clear. For example, many studies have shown that schools (and districts) with higher per pupil expenditures do not necessarily have higher achievement scores than schools (and districts) with less spending (Hanushek 1997). Similarly, recent evidence suggests that certified teachers are not substantially better at raising student performance than uncertified teachers (Boyd et al. 2005; Kane, Rockoff, and Staiger 2006). More generally, evidence from a recent housing mobility experiment suggests that poor children whose families are given the opportunity to move to a lower poverty neighborhood do not show improvement on a variety of academic measures, even after living in their new neighborhood for up to seven years (Kling, Liebman, and Katz 2007).

In addition, technical shortcomings of many of the studies in this literature make them difficult to interpret. The key difficulty is that families and students choose schools often at the same time they choose where to live. This means that characteristics of the chosen school may signal something about the child, such as level of motivation or degree of family support, rather than serving solely as an independent measure of the quantity and quality of inputs applied to the student. Resources will appear effective if otherwise able students tend to attend high resource schools, while they will appear ineffective if more resources are applied to less able students, as is the case with many state and federal compensatory education programs.

Hence, the importance of school quality is an open question. This is not simply an academic issue. As a society, we are faced with a number of impor-

---

1. See Clotfelter et al. (2007) for evidence on similar disparities across high and low poverty schools in North Carolina.

tant tradeoffs between competing goods—a cleaner environment, better health care, international aid, and so forth. Of course, one can argue that we are a wealthy country and can afford to have higher quality education for poor children as well as these other important goods. However, there is then the question of what is the most effective way to achieve a better education for disadvantaged children. Given the multiple disadvantages faced by poor families and the multiplicity of support services, along with the uncertainty regarding the impact of school quality on student outcomes, simply attending a better school may not be the most effective intervention.

In this chapter, we first review the existing evidence more completely and then provide new evidence on whether expanded access to sought-after schools can improve achievement. The setting we study is the "open enrollment" system in the Chicago Public Schools (CPS). Elementary students in Chicago can apply to gain access to public magnet schools and programs outside of their neighborhood school, but within the same school district. We use lottery data to avoid the critical issue of nonrandom selection of students into schools. All but a handful of academically advanced elementary schools use lotteries to allocate spots when oversubscribed, and we analyze nearly 450 lotteries for kindergarten and first grade slots at thirty-two popular schools in 2000 and 2001. Since those who randomly win and lose any given lottery will on average have the same characteristics, we can obtain unbiased estimates of the impact of gaining access to one of these schools through a straightforward comparison of subsequent mean outcomes across the two groups, as long as there is not selective attrition.

Comparing lottery winners and losers, we find that lottery winners attend higher quality schools as measured by both the average achievement level of peers in the school as well as by value-added indicators of the school's contribution to student learning. Yet tracking students for up to five years following the application, we do not find that winning a lottery systematically confers any evident academic benefits. This suggests that the strong cross-sectional relationship that we observe between test score performance and school quality for the typical CPS elementary student is largely spurious, and highlights the importance of using a research design that compares likes to likes.

In the discussion section following, we explore several possible explanations for our findings, including the possibility that the typical student may be choosing schools for nonacademic reasons (e.g., safety, proximity) and/or may experience benefits along dimensions we are unable to measure. Regardless of the explanation, the lack of a robust relationship between access to sought-after schools and achievement undermines the practical relevance of relying solely on enhanced school choice or higher inputs to remedy existing achievement gaps. Moreover, our cross-sectional results support this pessimistic view, demonstrating that much of the achievement gaps observed system-wide across race/ethnicity and income subgroups persist across students *within* schools.

The remainder of this chapter is structured as follows. Section 2.2 reviews the most relevant prior literature. Section 2.3 describes our data and empirical strategy. Section 2.4 presents our results, and section 2.5 discusses the implications of our findings for the construction of policies to benefit disadvantaged children.

2.2   Literature Review

This section begins by defining school quality and describing the potential channels through which school quality may influence student outcomes. We then provide a broad overview of the existing evidence on the strength and nature of the link between school quality and student outcomes. Rather than attempt to provide an exhaustive summary of findings, we emphasize the strengths and weaknesses of the variety of methods used.

2.2.1   Conceptual Framework

School quality is a complex and multidimensional concept. There are many ways that one might define school quality and, thus, many ways in which school quality might influence student outcomes. One of the most straightforward definitions of school quality involves the financial and other "tangible" resources available to students and teachers, including things such as adequate textbooks, new computers, clean and spacious classrooms, small class sizes, and highly qualified teachers. The theoretical mechanisms through which these factors could influence student performance are straightforward, even if there continue to be fierce debates about the actual empirical relationship between such resources and outcomes.

Another common measure of school quality involves the students themselves. Schools with higher performing and/or more motivated peers are often considered higher quality due to the influence that one's peers and their families have on one's own outcomes. Peers are thought to influence individual outcomes in a number of ways, from providing good role models (e.g., friends that think studying is "cool") to changing the expectations of the teacher and thus the pace and content of classroom curriculum (e.g., to the extent that the teacher focuses attention on the median or modal student in the class, higher-achieving peers may translate into a more rigorous curriculum).

There is a third aspect of school quality—the quality of the match between the school and an individual student—that is not as frequently discussed in the traditional literature. The focus on "match quality" recognizes that students have different learning styles and/or needs, and that what might be beneficial for one student might be benign or detrimental to another student. Indeed, this is one of the premises underlying many current school-choice programs, including charters and public school choice programs like the one analyzed in this chapter.

Given the multitude of channels through which various aspects of school quality could influence student outcomes, is it plausible to imagine that there might *not* be a relationship between school quality and student performance? While there is no way to be certain, several factors suggest that this relationship might not be particularly strong. First, there is considerable evidence on the primitive importance of the family, both in terms of genes and environment. Second, there are undoubtedly important interactions between home and school, some of which might serve to mitigate the importance of school quality. If, for example, parents view their financial or other support as, at least in part, a substitute for formal schooling, then we might expect parents to become more involved when their child is faced with an incompetent teacher or under-resourced school (e.g., they may seek out an after-school program or help the child more with their schoolwork at home). This type of behavior, while completely natural, will serve to undermine the relationship between school quality and student achievement. Third, unlike previous generations in this country and current generations in many developing countries, the vast majority of children in the United States today have what one might consider the bare essentials of an education. If school quality is most important at the very low and very high levels of quality, it may be that we simply cannot detect any important relationship in current U.S. data.

2.2.2   Existing Evidence

Researchers have long sought to examine how school quality influences child outcomes. This research falls into two broad categories. Perhaps the most common approach to this problem has been to measure the impact of observable school inputs such as spending per pupil, student-teacher ratios, and teacher credentials on student outcomes. Studies that analyze the impact of policies that dramatically reallocated resources, such as desegregation and school finance equalization, find a modest convergence in educational outcomes across previously advantaged and disadvantaged students (e.g., Card and Krueger 1996; Card and Payne 2002). But, the literature to date has yielded mixed results regarding the ability of policymakers to influence educational outcomes through less radical adjustments to the set of inputs to the educational process. See Hanushek (1997) for an overview of this literature, and Hanushek et al. (2005), Rockoff (2004), and Aaronson, Barrow, and Sander (2007) for recent evidence on the impact of observable teacher characteristics on value-added. There is a related and vast literature that seeks to estimate the impact of peer characteristics on individual educational outcomes, also with mixed results (Hoxby 2000; Zimmerman 2003; Graham 2004; Lefgren 2004).

The analysis in this chapter is most closely related to the second strand of school quality research that has focused on private schools and other "choice" schools. Studies in this strand have sought to compare the performance of students in public versus private schools, or traditional public schools versus magnet or charter schools, as a way to say something about the benefits of attending a "choice" school which, by its nature, is presumably "better" along some important dimension. Unfortunately, estimating a causal relationship between access to sought-after schools and student outcomes has proven difficult. In the United States, observational studies of private schools (Coleman, Hoffer, and Kilgore 1982; Bryk, Lee, and Holland 1993) and magnet schools (Blank 1983; Gamoran 1996) find that students who attend these schools experience better educational outcomes. But these studies suffer from a potentially important source of bias driven by the fact that children who attend private or "nontraditional" public schools may differ from their peers in ways that are difficult to capture in a statistical analysis, but may nonetheless be quite important in determining life outcomes.

The difficulty in drawing conclusions from comparing outcomes for students served in different schooling settings is clearly evident in the public debate over charter schools. The American Federation of Teachers (Nelson, Rosenberg, and Van Meter 2004) produced a study comparing the achievement of students in traditional and charter schools using national NAEP test score data, finding results unfavorable to charter schools. The study has been strongly criticized for controlling for so few of the differences in characteristics in the student populations, particularly given that many charter schools are explicitly designed to serve at-risk students. A concurrent Hoxby (2004) study compares charter and public school student performance in neighboring schools with similar racial compositions, and comes to a starkly different conclusion. However, the findings of this study have also been challenged because of the relative crudeness of the school matching procedure (Carnoy et al. 2005).

Researchers have attempted to address these selection concerns in several ways. One method is to use longitudinal student level data, so that the same student can be tracked in different settings. If a student's prior test score serves as a summary statistic for that student's potential, then any changes from the baseline as compared to similarly able students can be attributed to the schooling choice. More recently, researchers have recognized that students differ not only in their current level of achievement, but also in their learning trajectory. Even more problematic for school choice studies, students may choose to switch schools in response to unexpectedly good or bad outcomes. Although some studies rely exclusively on past outcome histories to control for student heterogeneity, most incorporate these data along with other strategies.

One alternative method, instrumental variables, attempts to identify differences in access to and take-up of school choice options that are arguably as good as randomly distributed across students with differing propensities to achieve and learn. A number of researchers have attempted to use this strategy to ascertain the causal impact of attending a Catholic school. In an early influential paper, for example, Evans and Schwab (1995) use affiliation with the Catholic church as an instrument for attending a Catholic school. The idea here is that students who are affiliated with the Catholic church are more likely than other students to attend Catholic schools, so that one can infer the effectiveness of Catholic schooling by comparing the educational outcomes of Catholic children with those of other children (regardless of whether the student in particular attends Catholic school). Of course, the key assumption underlying this strategy is that Catholic children do not differ from other children in any way that (a) researchers cannot control for in their model and (b) will influence educational outcomes through channels other than attending a Catholic school. To support this assumption, Evans and Schwab (1995) document that Catholics are very close to the national average on a variety of socioeconomic indicators. However, as others have noted, Catholics may well differ from others in less easily measurable ways that could still have an important impact on schooling outcomes (Neal 1997; Altonji, Elder, and Taber 2005).

One straightforward example pointed out by Neal (1997) is that students who attend Catholic schools might be more likely to self-report that they are affiliated with the Catholic church, regardless of their families' religious affiliations, which would introduce a mechanical correlation that could bias the results. Instead, Neal (1997) uses a student's proximity to Catholic schools as an instrument for attending this type of school. Insofar as students who live near Catholic schools are more likely to attend them, this is a plausible instrument. The assumption of this approach, however, is that a family's residential location—specifically whether it is close to a Catholic school or not—is not associated with any unmeasured family characteristics that might influence a student's outcomes independent of the type of school the student attends. This assumption would be violated not only if neighborhoods with Catholic schools tend to be somewhat wealthier, for example, than other neighborhoods, but also if such neighborhoods are different in less tangible ways, such as having a greater sense of community (or what is often referred to in the sociology literature as social capital). Given the difficulty of finding a valid instrument, it is perhaps not surprising that these studies have found mixed effects, with some showing benefits (Evans and Schwab 1995) and others showing little or no effect (Sander 1996; Neal 1997).

More recently, there have been a series of studies that exploit randomized lotteries. The Milwaukee voucher program, offering vouchers to a limited number of low-income students to attend one of three private nonsectarian schools in the district, is the most prominent of these. Although in theory randomization provides an ideal context for evaluating the benefits of expanding students' choice sets, in the Milwaukee case less than half of the unsuccessful applicants returned to the public schools and those who did return were from less educated, lower income families (Witte 1997). As described in greater detail following, this type of selective attrition can seriously bias any statistical analysis of student outcomes. It is therefore not surprising that analyses of the Milwaukee program obtain sharply conflicting estimates of the impact on achievement depending upon the assumptions made to deal with the attrition of lottery losers from the sample (Witte, Sterr, and Thorn 1995; Greene, Peterson, and Du 1997; Witte 1997; Rouse 1998).

Evidence from other small-scale school choice experiments in the United States is similarly mixed. For example, Peterson, Myers, and Howell (1998) and Howell and Peterson (2002) find that the opportunity to attend a private school modestly increases student achievement for low-achieving African-American students in New York City, Dayton, and Washington, D.C. A reanalysis of the New York City experiment by Krueger and Zhu (2003), however, suggests that even claims of modest benefits may be overstated.

Our own prior work examining the impact of attending magnet high schools in Chicago (Cullen, Jacob, and Levitt 2006) is part of the growing set of studies relying on explicit randomization. A comparison between lottery winners and losers reveals that students who win attend better high schools along a number of dimensions, including higher peer achievement and attainment levels. Nonetheless, we find little evidence that winning a lottery provides any systematic benefit across a wide variety of traditional academic measures. Lottery winners do, however, experience improvements on a subset of nontraditional outcome measures, such as self-reported disciplinary incidents and arrest rates.

Recent work examining public school choice in the Charlotte-Mecklenburg School District (CMSD) highlights the importance of accounting for heterogeneity in treatment effects. Hastings, Kane, and Staiger (2006) measure the impact of attending one's "first choice" school by comparing outcomes of lottery winners and losers. And, like Cullen, Jacob, and Levitt (2006), they find that winning the lottery (and, thus, attending a desired school) has, on average, no impact on a student's academic performance, but does seem to moderate at least some nonacademic outcomes.

The primary innovation of the analysis is that the authors use information from parental rankings of up to three most-preferred schools on school choice application forms to infer the weight that each family places on academics. For example, parents that passed up nearby schools and chose a high-achieving school farther from their house were assumed to place a high value on academics. When the authors incorporate this information into their analysis, they find that those students whose parents place a high weight on academics experience significant test score gains from attending their first-choice school, while those whose parents place little value on academics actually experience test score declines from attending their desired school. Moreover, the gains do not seem to be driven by differences in the likelihood that winners end up attending a school with higher test scores, but rather appear to be attributable to improvements in idiosyncratic match quality. If in fact true, the policy implications are unclear, since the schools that deliver achievement gains for the subset of highly motivated parents and students do not seem to confer gains more generally.[2]

In this chapter, we further explore the impact of attending a choice school, considering elementary school students in Chicago Public Schools. An important limitation of our high school study is that the results may not generalize to younger students. It may be that high school is too late for students to benefit from improvements in their schooling environment, so that the option to attend a magnet school may have a stronger impact on students at younger ages (Heckman 2007; Heckman and Masterov 2007). We also attempt—within the constraints of the available data—to test for the presence of heterogeneous effects by preference for academics following the lead of Hastings, Kane, and Staiger (2006).

2.3   Data and Empirical Strategy

This section describes the data and methodology for our analysis of elementary school students in Chicago. We start by describing the school system and its choice program, and then explain how we use the lottery data to estimate the academic return to attending a better school.

2.3.1   Background on the Chicago Public Schools

Over 400,000 students are enrolled in the Chicago Public Schools (CPS) in grades K through 12. As in most urban districts, students in the system are disproportionately minority (more than two-thirds) and poverty rates are well above those for the nation as a whole. Given the high rates of disadvantage and poor overall performance relative to national norms, our analysis provides evidence on the net benefits of providing choice to students with otherwise limited opportunities.

The Chicago Public Schools has one of the most extensive school choice programs available.[3] At the elementary school level, each student is guaranteed admission to an assigned neighborhood school, but can also apply to any of at least 200 CPS magnet schools or regular schools with magnet

2. While the study is carefully done, there are still reasons to question the validity of the findings. It seems likely that whether high-preference students ultimately enroll in a CMSD school will be more sensitive to whether they win or not, so that the degree of attrition could be directly related to measured preferences and potentially generate the observed pattern of findings. Below, we show evidence that differential attrition does vary systematically across similar sample splits in the Chicago setting.

3. School choice was first instituted in Chicago in response to a 1980 desegregation consent decree with the federal government. The goal of the consent decree was to create schools that roughly matched the racial composition of the school system. Since that time, the size and scope of school choice has expanded dramatically.

programs. Indeed, more than a third of all elementary students in CPS in 2000 and 2001 elected to attend a school other than the school assigned.

In order to attend a school other than the assigned school, a student must submit an application in the spring of the preceding year.[4] A student must reside within the school district, but does not need to be currently enrolled in CPS in order to submit an application. Moreover, the application process is extremely easy. Parents simply fill out a one-page form listing basic information such as their name and address, and the grade the student will be entering. They can either mail the form into the district office, or drop it off at their home school. There is no limit on the number of schools to which a student can apply. In most cases, if the number of applicants exceeds the number of available positions, randomized lotteries are used to determine the allocation of spots. For a limited number of selective programs admission is based on criteria such as test scores, and lotteries are not used.

For programs using lotteries, there are explicit rules governing the way in which the lotteries are conducted. Because of desegregation goals and variation in the number of available slots at different grade levels, lotteries are typically conducted separately for each gender-race-grade combination. Also, a particular school may house multiple magnet programs, each of which conducts separate lotteries. As a consequence, one school can potentially have a large number of lotteries each year.[5]

2.3.2 The Data

Working with CPS, we obtained access to detailed administrative data that provide us information on student enrollment and achievement for all students over a number of years. Moreover, unique CPS student identification numbers allow us to track students over time as they change schools or if they leave and then reenter the school system.

For the purpose of this study, we obtained data on school choice applications submitted in spring 2000 and 2001 for enrollment in the following fall. The application data include the name, race, gender, date of birth, home address, and grade of each applicant, as well as the program the student is applying to, whether that application was part of a lottery and, if so, whether the application was selected or not. In our prior work, we examined students applying to high school (Cullen, Jacob, and Levitt 2006). Here, we focus on students applying to kindergarten and first grade, which are the principal entry grades for elementary school. The subset of the applicants attend-

---

4. Transportation is provided to students gaining access to elementary magnet schools (but not to magnet school programs housed in neighborhood schools) if they live more than 1.5 miles but less than six miles from the school.

5. There is a further layer of complexity with regard to lotteries, namely that schools also reserve a share of available seats and conduct special lotteries for siblings of current students ("sibling lotteries") and for students who live nearby ("proximity lotteries"). Because such lotteries are rarely oversubscribed, they do not provide useful variation for our empirical work.

ing public school at the time of the application (32 percent) report their unique CPS identification number directly on the application, and this can be directly used to link students to the administrative records.[6] For the other applicants, we utilize a probabilistic matching technique to link applicants to subsequent administrative records using name, date of birth, gender, and race/ethnicity.[7]

The full sample of applications for kindergarten and first grade openings includes 51,775 applications to 207 choice elementary schools. Only ten of these schools are academically advanced schools that have selective test-based admissions policies. While nearly one in every five applications is to these schools, less than one percent of elementary school students and six percent of applicants are served by these schools. All other schools assign slots by randomized lotteries if oversubscribed.

Given our research design—which involves comparing students who won a lottery with their peers who lost the same lottery—our analysis is necessarily limited to the set of lotteries where there were at least some winners and losers. Among applications to lottery schools, 50.2 percent were to lotteries with both winners and losers, 42.0 percent were to lotteries with no winners and 7.8 percent were to lotteries with no losers. A lottery will not have any winners if the campus is unable to accept applications to a specific grade due to overcrowding. Since we cannot estimate any treatment effects, we exclude applications to both types of degenerate lotteries from our analysis.

Two factors drive differences in the availability of slots for applicants across lottery schools and, hence, determine whether a campus is included in our analysis or not. First, much of the variation in capacity is geographic, with space constraints pervasive in the booming neighborhoods in the Northwest, Southwest, and South regions of the city (Neighborhood Capital Budget Group 1999). Second, the availability of *any* slots for applicants at the entry grade levels is only an issue for neighborhood schools that house magnet programs, since these schools have to first accommodate students living in the attendance zone. The overcrowded choice schools are neighborhood schools concentrated in the congested regions that otherwise appear similar on observable dimensions (e.g., average achievement level) to the campuses included in our analysis, while the schools that hold uncontested lotteries are substantially lower-performing.

After excluding another 10.8 percent of applications to nondegenerate lotteries at schools with fewer than 100 lottery participants across the two cohorts, we are left with 15,403 applications from 7,469 students to thirty-two schools. The great majority of the applications (79.1 percent) are for

6. The fraction applying from inside CPS is, not surprisingly, lower for pre-kindergarten applicants to kindergarten slots (24.7 percent). For applicants to first grade slots, the fraction is 42.9 percent.

7. The matching process works extremely well. We verify that we correctly identify nearly 95 percent of students with an existing CPS ID at the time of application.

kindergarten slots. Most of the schools (twenty-two) are magnet schools that accept students from throughout the district and organize the curriculum around a specific theme (e.g., math/science, humanities, fine arts, or world language). No students are assigned to these schools by default. The remaining schools also serve neighborhood students, but enrollment is dominated by students from outside the neighborhood drawn to magnet programs housed at the schools. Overall, these lotteries are quite competitive, with the typical application having a 13.3 percent chance of being selected. Because a student can apply to multiple lotteries, roughly one out of every four students in the sample wins at least one lottery.

We examine student outcomes through the spring of 2005, when those applying to kindergarten from our 2000 cohort will have progressed to fourth grade, and those applying to first grade will have progressed to fifth grade. Applicants from the 2001 cohort can be tracked for only four, rather than five, years subsequent to the application. We are able to track students as long as, and only if, they are enrolled in CPS. Among our outcome measures for applicants who attend CPS schools are indicators for whether the student is currently receiving special education services and whether the student has been retained (i.e., is repeating a grade).

The academic outcomes that we focus on most are achievement test scores. Students in CPS take the Iowa Test of Basic Skills (ITBS), which is a nationally-normed multiple-choice exam that measures student proficiency in reading comprehension and a variety of basic math skills. The tests are mandatory and universally administered to CPS elementary students, starting in third grade. In our sample, more than 99 percent of students enrolled in these grades have valid test score data, including students who receive special education or bilingual education services. Schools have discretion over whether to administer the tests to first and second grade students (none do to kindergarteners), so that some elementary schools assess students using the ITBS exams while others use alternative assessments for which results are not automatically reported to the district. We observe ITBS scores for 79.8 percent of enrolled first grade students, and for 87.1 percent of second grade students. The choice to administer ITBS at these grade levels appears to be idiosyncratic, since the schools that choose to do so do not differ in systematic ways from the schools that do not.[8]

The reading and math tests are designed so that a student's scores across grades can be mapped to a rate of learning. The scale is set so that a score of 185 represents achievement of the typical student in the nation in third grade, and a score of 200 is the same for fourth grade. Typical national achievement gains steadily decline from 15 points for fourth graders to 11 points for eighth graders, reflecting the idea that younger students learn

---

8. This is also supported by the findings in table 1.6 that enrolled lottery winners are no more or less likely to have valid ITBS scores than enrolled lottery losers.

more than older ones. The major advantage of using these standard scores is that a one unit change represents the same amount of learning regardless of the location on the scale, which facilitates comparisons across students in different grades and at different points in time.

2.3.3   Empirical Strategy

In theory, lottery-induced randomization provides a simple solution to the problem of endogenous sorting of students. Because lottery outcomes are randomly assigned, winners and losers of a particular lottery will be identical on average, in terms of unobservable as well as observable characteristics. Consequently, a simple difference of observed mean outcomes between students who win and lose the lottery provides a consistent estimate of the impact of winning the lottery.

In the presence of J independently conducted lotteries, we could in principle generate J different estimates δ_j that capture the marginal impact of being allowed admission to the school represented by lottery j:

(1) $\delta_j = E(Y_i \mid Win_{ij} = 1; Apply_{ij} = 1) - E(Y_i \mid Win_{ij} = 0; Apply_{ij} = 1)$,

where Y is some outcome measure for student i, Win_{ij} is a binary variable indicating whether the student won lottery j, and $Apply_{ij}$ is a binary variable equal to one if the student applied to the lottery and zero otherwise. Then, δ_j indicates whether winners are systematically higher or lower on the outcome Y than losers in the same lottery. Note that it is also legitimate to estimate separate treatment effects for subgroups of students, as long as the sample is split according to characteristics that are predetermined at the time of application.

While δ_j is clearly an unbiased estimate of the impact of winning this lottery, it is important to consider its interpretation. The parameter measures the impact of winning *conditional* on deciding to apply, which means that any findings may not generalize to nonapplicants. Also, because not all winners choose to attend the lottery school, δ_j measures the impact of having the *option* to attend the lottery school, or the intention-to-treat (ITT) effect. One can also infer the treatment effect for actually attending the lottery school, called the treatment-on-the-treated (TOT) effect, by scaling the ITT effect by the increased likelihood of attending the school for winners. For example, if winners are 50 percentage points more likely to attend, then the impact of actually attending would be twice as large as the observed mean difference in outcomes between winners and losers.

In practice, the standard errors for particular lotteries and subgroups within lotteries in our data are too large to make such school-specific estimates informative. Therefore, we instead pool information across the lotteries:

(2) $Y_i = \delta(Win\_Lottery_{ia}) + \Gamma(Lottery_a) + e_{ia}$,

where the subscripts i and a index students and applications, respectively. Variable $Win\_Lottery_{ia}$ is a binary variable that indicates whether application a for student i was a lottery winner, $Lottery_a$ is a vector of fixed effects indicating the lottery to which the observation refers, and e is a stochastic error term. In this specification, the δ coefficient is simply a weighted average of the δ_j's for the various lotteries.[9]

The unit of analysis in this model is a student-application. Students will appear more than once in the data if they applied for multiple lotteries. Moreover, a student who won one lottery but lost another lottery will serve as a member of the "treatment group" in the first case, and a member of the "control group" in the second case.[10] While this setup may seem odd, it builds on the logic of estimating separate lottery effects and does indeed produce consistent parameter estimates. For the intuition, recall that winners and losers in each lottery will be balanced along all observed *and* unobserved dimensions due to the randomization. While a certain fraction of winners in any given lottery may have applied to and won other lotteries, the same is true for losers in that lottery. Our estimates capture the impact of winning a lottery *conditional* on the set of other lotteries to which an individual applied to and may have won. What multiple applications do influence is the magnitude of the treatment effect (e.g., the change in the quality of the school attended) associated with winning any given lottery.

In addition to pooling applications across lotteries, we pool student outcome information across the years 2001 to 2005 to further increase precision. Rather than estimating equation (2) separately by year, we form a panel where the unit of observation becomes the application by year since the application. We then estimate ordinary least-squares regressions of the form:[11]

$$(3) \qquad Y_{it} = \delta(Win\_Lottery_{ia}) + \Gamma(Lottery_a) + \mathbf{X}_i\boldsymbol{\beta} + \Pi(g_{it}) + e_{ita}.$$

The specifications include separate indicators for each cohort, initial application grade, and current year combination (g_{it}), to absorb mean differences across students who applied in different years and to different grades and are observed in a different number of years since application. We also include a set of student demographic and home census tract characteristics, as well as variables measuring the number and types of applications submitted by

---

9. The weight for lottery j is equal to $N_j P_j(1 - P_j)/[\Sigma_j N_j P_j(1 - P_j)]$, where N_j is the number of students entered in lottery j and P_j is the proportion of students entered in lottery j who win the lottery. Holding the likelihood of winning constant, weights are proportional to the number of students in the lottery. The closer a lottery is to having half the applicants win, the more weight it receives.

10. On average, students in our analysis sample participate in two lotteries, and the typical winner has about a one in five chance of winning another lottery (as does the typical loser).

11. For the binary dependent variables, we confirmed that the reported coefficients estimated from linear probability models are always quite similar to the mean marginal effects estimated from comparable Probit specifications.

the student, that are all predetermined at the time of application ($\mathbf{X}_i$). These covariates increase precision by absorbing residual variation. Since the lottery balances students along these dimensions, the results will not be sensitive to this conditioning unless there is selective attrition from the sample, under which circumstances these controls will then help to mitigate any bias. In order to account for correlation in outcomes for the same student across applications and years, we report robust standard errors that allow for clustering at the student level. This clustering ensures that we do not overstate the precision of our inferences by recognizing that observations from the same student do not provide as much independent information as observations from different students.[12]

2.4   Results

In this section, we present the main results of our analysis. We begin by providing some basic statistics on the differences in student performance and school quality between more and less advantaged students in the Chicago Public Schools. We then explore the relationship between school quality and student outcomes in CPS using a common but naïve approach—namely, simple regression analysis that does not account for student self-selection into magnet schools. Third, we turn to our lottery sample in order to better isolate the causal impact of attending a sought-after school. Before presenting our main findings, we show a set of results aimed at exploring the scope for differential attrition. In presenting the main results of our analysis, we pay careful attention to understanding the magnitude of the effects, the statistical power of the estimates, and the distinction between ITT and TOT estimates.

2.4.1   A Preliminary Look at Differences in Student Outcomes and School Quality in Chicago

Table 2.1 presents some descriptive statistics to highlight the differences in school quality and academic performance between more and less advantaged children in CPS. It is worth noting that the differences revealed in these figures are likely an understatement of the actual differences since the most advantaged families in the Chicago metropolitan area do not attend CPS, with one in every five elementary students opting instead for private schools. The table compares students along three dimensions of socioeconomic status: race/ethnicity, individual poverty status, and neighborhood poverty status. The statistics are based on the sample of all third grade students enrolled in CPS in 2004 and 2005. These are the same years that the majority of our applicants, those applying for kindergarten slots, are enrolled in

---

12. Where appropriate, we tested sensitivity to allowing for clustering at the level of the school attended instead and found quite similar levels of precision.

Table 2.1   Summary statistics for all CPS third grade students

	Student race/ethnicity			Student poverty status		Tract poverty level	
	White (1)	Black (2)	Hispanic (3)	Ineligible for free/reduced-price lunch (4)	Eligible for free/reduced-price lunch (5)	Poverty rate ≤ 25% (6)	Poverty rate > 25% (7)
Share of 3rd grade enrollment	0.074	0.510	0.390	0.116	0.884	0.562	0.438
Student achievement							
In special education in 3rd grade	0.176	0.120	0.109	0.136	0.116	0.124	0.112
Took the ITBS reading/math exams	0.975	0.980	0.968	0.974	0.975	0.974	0.976
3rd grade reading standard score	194.3	174.8	176.8	193.4	175.4	180.7	173.4
3rd grade math standard score	194.1	176.8	182.3	193.2	179.1	183.9	176.7
Elementary school characteristics							
Mean peer composite 3rd grade score	190.2	177.3	179.8	188.9	178.3	182.1	176.4
Mean value-added 3rd–4th grades	0.741	−0.004	0.098	0.960	0.009	0.330	−0.151
Academically advanced school	0.062	0.010	0.016	0.081	0.009	0.026	0.007
Magnet school	0.103	0.058	0.054	0.142	0.051	0.064	0.059
School included in our analysis	0.127	0.055	0.045	0.159	0.046	0.071	0.045
Number of observations	4,603	31,630	24,196	7,225	54,831	34,846	27,210

Notes: The statistics are based on the sample of all third grade students enrolled in CPS in 2004 and 2005, the same years that most kindergarten applicants from our two application cohorts attended third grade. Each column presents means for the subsample indicated by the column heading. A value of 185 for the reading or math standard score indicates that the student is performing at the national average, and a difference of fifteen points represents a year's worth of learning for the typical third grade student. The mean peer composite third grade score is the average combined reading and math standard score for third grade students at the school. Mean value-added is the average "gain" on reading and math exams between third and fourth grades, controlling for prior scores and demographic characteristics. This is calculated by extracting the mean residual by campus from student-level regressions of fourth grade reading and math standard scores (separately) on flexible controls for third grade reading and math scores, and student demographic and neighborhood characteristics. A positive number indicates that the typical student at the school is progressing more quickly than similar students at other schools. Academically advanced schools include classical schools and regional gifted centers that have test-based admissions policies. Magnet schools organize their curricula around a specific theme (e.g., math/science, fine arts, world language, or humanities) and accept students from throughout the city via computerized lottery.

third grade. Each column presents means for the subsample indicated by the column heading.

The top panel documents dramatic differences in performance between advantaged and disadvantaged students. The average standard reading and math scores of white third grade students in CPS are both 194, which are substantially above the overall national averages of 185. However, black and hispanic children in Chicago score roughly twenty points lower than white children, implying a deficit of more than one year of learning. Similar differences are apparent when low-income students who are eligible for free or reduced-price lunch[13] and/or live in high poverty neighborhoods are compared with their more advantaged peers.

The bottom panel reveals equally striking differences in school quality.[14] White children are nearly six times more likely to attend academically advanced schools and nearly twice as likely to attend magnet schools relative to black and hispanic children. Similarly, students who are not eligible for free or reduced-price lunch attend schools where mean third grade test scores are roughly ten points—or two-thirds of a year's worth of learning—higher than eligible students.[15] Of course, this may simply reflect the fact that more advantaged students have higher initial ability levels than disadvantaged students. In order to explore the contribution of the school itself, we calculated a crude value-added measure for each school equal to the average deviation of students' fourth grade reading and math standard scores from expected, given students' prior scores and demographic characteristics.[16] While still not perfect, this measure should come a great deal closer to capturing school quality than simply the level of achievement. Yet the differences in school value-added across demographic groups are, if anything, even more strik-

13. Eligibility for the federally assisted meal programs operated in schools is a useful indicator of household income. Students are eligible for free (reduced-price) lunch if income is below 130 (185) percent of the relevant federal poverty threshold given the household size. The fraction eligible for meal assistance is a measure of student disadvantage commonly factored into federal and state funding allocation rules.

14. Natural dimensions of school quality that we do not consider include financial resources and teacher quality. In CPS, funding is allocated largely by formula whereby schools with larger populations of poor, special education, and language minority students receive compensatory funding, making it difficult to interpret higher levels of expenditures as a signal of quality. Some information on teacher characteristics by school is available, but we were unable to find a measure that both varied across schools and had an unambiguous association with the quality of instruction.

15. This score is the average composite reading and math standard score for third grade students in the 2000 and 2001 cohorts at the school. This is the group of students attending when our sample was in the process of applying.

16. Specifically, using all fourth graders in 2000 and 2001, we separately regressed reading and math standard scores on demographic variables (race/ethnicity, gender, age, and free/reduced-price lunch eligibility) and twenty indicators each for location of third grade reading and of third grade math scores by 5 percentile point ranges of the third grade test score distribution. The control variables explain approximately 60 and 70 percent of the variation in fourth grade reading and math scores, respectively. We then predict the residuals, and average these residuals across students by campus.

ing than the differences in achievement levels. Black and hispanic children in CPS, for example, attend schools with value-added scores close to zero whereas white children attend schools with value-added scores of roughly 0.7, indicating that students at these schools improve nearly one point each year relative to similar CPS students at less effective schools.

The statistics presented in table 2.1 paint a portrait of a school system with highly unequal outcomes across demographic groups, and provide some evidence that children from more advantaged backgrounds attend higher quality schools. This does not prove that the differences in school quality are responsible for the differences in student outcomes, however. Indeed, this type of correlation is exactly what one would expect if children from more advantaged families have a greater inclination and/or ability to find a good school for their children and also provide the type of home support that fosters high academic achievement.

Table 2.2 explores the correlation between school quality and student achievement more closely. Using the same sample (i.e., all third grade students enrolled in CPS in 2004 and 2005), we estimate a series of regressions where the dependent variable is the average of the student's third grade reading and math standard scores. Each column presents the results from a separate regression, with the difference being the specific set of controls included. In all cases, the control set includes student demographic and neighborhood characteristics as detailed in the notes to the table. Our goal is to see to what extent it appears that different levels of school quality can help to explain outcome inequities across student groups, under the assumption that students who choose to attend better schools would otherwise have similar outcomes to other students. These results provide a benchmark for comparison to our later results.

The specification in column (1) shows the relationship between student achievement and student race and poverty status with no school-level controls. We see that black and hispanic children score seven to eight points lower than otherwise similar white children, and students eligible for free or reduced-price lunch score roughly nine points lower than otherwise similar ineligible students. These differences are large relative to the scale of the scores, as every fifteen points represents the amount of learning a typical student can expect in a year.

In column (2), we control for both the school mean achievement level as well as the school value-added measure, both of which are calculated for earlier cohorts of students in the school so that they are not "mechanically" related to the performance of students in our analysis sample. We see a significant positive relationship between both school quality measures and student outcomes. For example, the coefficient of 0.58 on mean achievement level indicates that students who attend schools where prior students scored ten points higher score, on average, 5.8 points higher themselves. Perhaps more interestingly, the coefficients on student race and poverty status drop

Table 2.2   Correlation between academic achievement and school quality

	Dependent variable: 3rd grade composite standard score							
	Sample: All 3rd graders in 2004 and 2005					Sample: Analysis 3rd graders		
Independent variable	(1)	(2)	(3)	(4)	(5)	(6)	(7)	(8)
	Student characteristic							
Black	−8.3**	−6.3**	−7.0**	−6.6**	−7.1**	−12.6**	−12.4**	−13.2**
	(0.6)	(0.6)	(0.4)	(0.6)	(0.4)	(2.0)	(1.9)	(1.5)
Hispanic	−6.5**	−4.9**	−5.3**	−4.9**	−5.2**	−11.8**	−11.0**	−11.3**
	(0.5)	(0.5)	(0.3)	(0.5)	(0.3)	(1.7)	(1.7)	(1.4)
Eligible for free/reduced-price lunch	−9.4**	−6.3**	−5.8**	−5.8**	−5.5**	−9.9**	−5.0**	−4.5**
	(0.6)	(0.3)	(0.3)	(0.3)	(0.3)	(1.3)	(0.9)	(0.9)
Applied to at least one lottery school	—	—	—	2.9**	2.8**	—	—	—
				(0.4)	(0.4)			
Applied to at least one academically advanced school	—	—	—	6.7**	5.6**	—	—	—
				(0.7)	(0.5)			
	School characteristic							
Mean peer composite 3rd grade score	—	0.583**	—	0.520**	—	—	0.557**	—
		(0.026)		(0.025)			(0.057)	
Mean value-added 3rd–4th grades	—	0.241**	—	0.209**	—	—	0.124	—
		(0.057)		(0.053)			(0.153)	
Includes school fixed effects	N	N	Y	N	Y	N	N	Y

Notes: The sample in the left panel is all third grade students enrolled in CPS in 2004 and 2005 with nonmissing ITBS tests scores. The sample in the right panel is the subset of these students that participated in contested lotteries for kindergarten slots in 2001 and 2002, and so comprise part of our lottery analysis sample. The dependent variable is the mean of the student's third grade reading and math standard scores. Coefficient estimates are shown for the control variables indicated in the rows, with standard errors that are robust to unspecified correlation across students within the same elementary schools in parentheses. What differs across the columns is whether and which controls for school quality and student applications are included. In addition to the variables shown, all specifications include an indicator for 2005, student demographic characteristics (Asian, Native American, gender, age), and home tract characteristics (population, fraction black, fraction Hispanic, median income, poverty rate, fraction female-headed households, fraction of adults highest degree high school, fraction of adults completed at least some college, fraction homeowners, unemployment rate, share of students grades K–8 attending private school, 1994 crime index). The school characteristics are described in the notes to table 2.1.

**Significant at the 5 percent level.

*Significant at the 10 percent level.

noticeably when these school quality measures are included. Even conditional on these measures of the quality of the school attended, however, poor and minority children substantially underperform their peers, scoring five to six points lower.

These two variables may well miss many important aspects of school quality, however. For this reason, the specification in column (3) adds separate indicators for each school to the control set, so that the estimates shown here come from a comparison of students within the same schools. While there may still be some within-school differences in school quality across race or poverty status (e.g., special enrichment programs for higher-achieving students in the school, or ability tracking that places more advantaged students with better teachers), this approach will account for any difficult-to-measure school-level quality factors, such as the ability of the principal or the level of parent/community involvement. We continue to find that poor and minority children score five to seven points lower than their peers in the *same* school. This comparison provides a useful bound on the potential impact of school quality. These results tell us that even if we attribute as great a role as possible to schools by ignoring that able students are likely to choose better schools, completely equalizing school quality would reduce the achievement gap by less than one-fifth to one-third.

Why are the estimates of the impact of school quality likely to be overstated in these regressions? The primary concern is that it does not account for unobservable factors such as student motivation or family support that might be correlated with school quality and student performance. While it appears that better schools lead to better outcomes, it may simply be that better students attend these schools, and would perform well regardless—and vice versa for worse students. The specifications in columns (4) and (5) introduce proxies for motivation and ability to test how these moderate the results. Our proxies come from our application data. We know which of these students expressed an interest in attending a choice school for kindergarten. The results show that students who applied to any lottery-based or academically advanced (i.e., test-based) magnet school do in fact score between three and seven points higher than other students. Notably, adding these two indicators reduces the point estimate for the effect of mean school peer achievement by more than 10 percent. Column (5), which includes school fixed effects, shows that applicants are outperforming students attending the same schools. Clearly, students who seek out better schools are not like other students.

Table 2.3 directly compares our sample of lottery participants and the general CPS population. Column (1) begins by displaying the summary statistics for the full sample of participants in our nondegenerate lottery sample. Columns (2) and (3) focus on students enrolled in pre-kindergarten at the time of the applications, comparing lottery participants (column [2]) with students who were not observed submitting any applications to choice

Table 2.3　　　　　**Summary statistics for lottery applicants**

| Background characteristic | All lottery participants (1) | Students enrolled in CPS in PK at time of application | | |
		Lottery participants (2)	Nonapplicants (3)	Difference (2) – (3)
Student characteristics				
Applying to kindergarten	0.720	1	—	—
Applying to 1st grade	0.280	0	—	—
White	0.156	0.122	0.076	0.047**
Black	0.620	0.526	0.475	0.051**
Hispanic	0.161	0.239	0.416	−0.177**
Asian	0.058	0.107	0.032	0.075**
Male	0.492	0.508	0.520	−0.012
Age on Sept. 1 of school year following application	5.77	5.53	5.57	−0.05**
Eligible for free/reduced-price lunch[a]	n.a.	0.412	0.799	−0.387**
Living with a biological parent[a]	n.a.	0.876	0.813	0.063**
Enrolled in CPS at the time of application	0.303	1	1	—
Received special education in PK[a]	n.a.	0.073	0.108	−0.035**
Received bilingual education in PK[a]	n.a.	0.260	0.314	−0.054**
Tract poverty rate	0.208	0.212	0.261	−0.049**
Tract fraction completed at least some college	0.492	0.465	0.363	0.102**
Predicted 3rd grade composite score	192.0	192.1	180.7	11.4**
Default kindergarten school characteristics				
Fraction eligible for free/reduced-price lunch	0.860	0.869	0.902	−0.033**
Fraction black	0.591	0.507	0.493	0.014
Fraction hispanic	0.270	0.327	0.400	−0.073**
Mean peer composite 3rd grade score	179.2	179.5	178.6	0.9**
Mean value-added 3rd–4th grades	0.157	0.155	−0.237	0.392**

Notes: The unit of observation is the student. There are 7,469 students participating in at least one of the lotteries included in our analysis. Mean characteristics for these lottery participants are shown in column (1). Column (2) restricts the sample to the 1,309 lottery participants enrolled in CPS in pre-kindergarten at the time of the application. There are 31,050 students enrolled in pre-kindergarten in CPS in spring 2000 and spring 2001 that we do not observe submitting an application to a choice school. Mean characteristics for these students are shown in column (3). n.a. = not available.

[a]These variables are only available for students enrolled in CPS at the time of application.

**Significant at the 5 percent level.

*Significant at the 10 percent level.

schools (column [3]). The first point to note is that lottery participants tend to be relatively more advantaged than other CPS students on a variety of dimensions. Participants are disproportionately white and asian relative to the broader CPS population, and they live in neighborhoods with lower poverty rates. As a way to quantify the implications of these differences for achievement, we predicted third grade scores for these students as a function of student and neighborhood background characteristics.[17] Given the differences in these, lottery participants would be predicted to score more than eleven points higher on average on future reading and math exams than nonapplicants.

The bottom panel of table 2.3 demonstrates that lottery participants and nonapplicants have access to neighborhood schools of somewhat unequal quality. The neighborhood elementary schools for lottery participants have lower proportions of students who receive free or reduced-price lunch, and higher achievement levels and value-added. Since lottery participants are generally applying to higher-ranking schools than their neighborhood schools, differential take-up of school choice will tend to lead to larger differences in the characteristics of the schools actually attended than those that are observed for the default school.

Given these differences, it is reasonable to ask whether the relationship between student demographics, school quality, and student performance operate differently within our sample of lottery participants relative to the general CPS population. It is possible, for example, that lottery participants come from supportive family environments that mitigate the importance of school quality for these students. To explore this possibility, columns (6) to (8) of table 2.2 reproduce our cross-sectional regressions of student performance on student characteristics and school quality for our analysis sample. The results in column (6) indicate that race and poverty gaps are even larger among our lottery sample. The estimated effect of school quality in column (7) suggests that peer ability continues to be correlated with individual performance in the analysis sample.[18]

In summary, it appears that lottery participants differ from other CPS students in many important and readily observable ways, such as race and poverty status. Moreover, the results in columns (4) to (5) of table 2.2 indicate that lottery participants differ along other unobservable dimensions that exert an additional influence on their academic performance. It is precisely for this reason that lottery-induced randomization is likely to be important

17. Specifically, we regressed third grade reading and math standard scores (separately) on the background characteristics that are available for all applicants and enrolled students: race/ethnicity, gender, and the set of home tract variables detailed in the notes to table 2.2. We then averaged the two predicted values for each student.

18. Mean value-added is no longer statistically significantly related to own achievement, though the point estimate is still sizeable. The loss of precision is attributable to a correlation between the two school quality measures that is twice as strong in the analysis sample.

for drawing conclusions about the causal impact of school quality on the students in our sample. We now turn to this task.

2.4.2   Using Lotteries to Estimate the Causal Impact of School Quality on Student Outcomes

The Lottery Schools

Students in our analysis sample applied to at least one of thirty-two schools that admitted students through a competitive lottery. Table 2.4 illustrates that these schools vary widely in terms of quality. In column (1), for example, we see that the average third grade test scores in these schools ranged from 206 in LaSalle Language Academy to 176 in Ericson Scholastic Academy. This thirty-point difference is equivalent to two entire years worth of learning. In other words, the average third grade student in LaSalle is roughly two years ahead of the average student at Ericson. In the majority of the lottery schools, however, students scored above the national average (i.e., 185 points), a considerable feat considering the high levels of poverty in CPS and that none of these schools accept students on the basis of academic ability. Column (2) shows that students at most of these schools are learning at a faster rate than otherwise similar students in CPS, since the value-added measures are generally positive. Finally, columns (3) and (4) report measures reflecting the popularity of the schools. Column (3) shows the fraction of applicants who were rejected, which captures the competitiveness of the lottery. Column (4) shows the fraction of lottery winners who actually choose to enroll in the school when given the opportunity.

There is substantial variation across schools along all of these dimensions. Schools with high mean achievement tend to be popular with students, as measured by either the competitiveness of the lotteries or the take-up rates of lottery winners (the correlation between columns [1] and [3] is .56 and between columns [1] and [4] is .64). Notably, the schools that we identify as high value-added are somewhat less popular schools (the correlations between our value-added measure and the acceptance and take-up rates are both .45). In terms of the number of lottery participants, the high-achieving schools are overrepresented.

Empirical Concern 1: Valid Randomization

The key to our research design rests on the assumption that admission to our sample of schools was determined randomly. The CPS officials indicate that the lotteries used to determine admission were conducted using a computer algorithm that generated random numbers. However, given the importance of this issue, we confirm that the randomization indeed occurred. If the lotteries were conducted properly, then one would predict that the winners and losers of a given lottery will be, on average, perfectly balanced on all predetermined characteristics. We test this by estimating

Table 2.4   Chicago public elementary schools represented in the analysis

School name	Mean peer composite 3rd grade score (1)	Mean value-added 3rd–4th grades (2)	Fraction of applicants rejected (3)	Fraction of accepted applicants enrolling (4)	Number of participants in analysis lotteries (5)	Average size of 3rd grade class (6)
LaSalle Language Academy[m]	206.0[a]	3.09	0.93	0.57[a]	1,372	65
Hawthorne Scholastic Academy[m]	202.7[a]	2.29	0.91	0.65[a]	674	63
Jackson Language Academy[m]	199.9[a]	4.77[a]	0.92	0.59[a]	714	62
Thorp Scholastic Academy[m]	198.5[a]	2.79	0.85	0.46	444	85
Stone Scholastic Academy[m]	197.9[a]	−1.30	0.89	0.47	718	61
Sheridan Math/Science Academy[m]	196.9[a]	−0.06	0.82	0.71[a]	423	58
Franklin Fine Arts Center[m]	194.7[a]	8.28[a]	0.96[a]	0.62[a]	511	42
Ray Elementary School	193.6[a]	5.46[a]	0.89	0.51[a]	223	91
Beasley Academic Magnet[m]	192.5	4.31[a]	0.83	0.38	696	156
Newberry Math/Science Academy[m]	192.5	4.36[a]	0.94[a]	0.41	1,045	65
Gunsaulus Scholastic Academy[m]	192.2	2.02	0.77	0.66[a]	216	72
Blaine Elementary School	190.8	4.69[a]	0.56	0.13	337	45
Owen Scholastic Academy[m]	190.4	5.19[a]	0.91	0.54[a]	188	28
Galileo Scholastic Academy[m]	190.1	2.09	0.98[a]	0.17	120	68
Black Magnet School[m]	189.6	4.06[a]	0.95[a]	0.46	1,369	55
Vanderpoel Magnet School[m]	189.2	3.33	0.95[a]	0.48	798	29
Pershing Magnet School[m]	188.1	1.63	0.95[a]	0.35	248	31
Burnside Scholastic Academy[m]	186.9	2.19	0.87	0.46	601	84
Disney Magnet School[m]	186.7	−0.07	0.90	0.35	1,970	178

	(1)	(2)			(6)
Hamilton Elementary School	186.0	−5.47	0.44	0.05	233	58
Turner-Drew Language Academy[m]	186.0	3.53	0.94[a]	0.38	271	29
Mayer Elementary School	184.7	1.84	0.73	0.10	372	83
Sayre Language Academy[m]	183.6	3.11	0.84	0.36	503	59
Budlong Elementary School	183.0	−1.08	0.93[b]	0.11	114	103
Agassiz Elementary School	182.9	2.88	0.53	0.11	115	64
Alcott Elementary School	181.8	0.98	0.55	0.17	133	47
Audubon Elementary School	181.6	−1.14	0.64	0.14	159	51
De Diego Community Academy	181.6	−0.71	0.39	0.38	146	137
Sabin Magnet School[m]	181.4	−2.72	0.83	0.32	160	61
Nettelhorst Elementary School	179.6	−2.46	0.50	0.04	155	69
Jensen Scholastic Academy[m]	179.0	−2.27	0.76	0.42	131	73
Ericson Scholastic Academy[m]	176.2	2.29	0.44	0.39	244	98
CPS Elementary School Average	180.1	0.34	n.a.	n.a.	n.a.	86.8

Notes: The summary statistics in columns (1) and (2) are based on all students enrolled in these elementary schools in spring 2000 and spring 2001, at the time of application for our two cohorts. Column (1) reports the mean composite reading and math standard scores for third graders at the school, where a value of 185 indicates that students are performing at the national average. Value-added in column (2) is calculated as described in table 2.1. The statistics reported in columns (3) and (4) are averages across all 2000 and 2001 applications, regardless of whether an individual application is involved in a nondegenerate lottery or not. Column (5) refers to applications to the nondegenerate lotteries included in the empirical analysis. Column (6) shows average third grade enrollment across 2000 and 2001 at the campus. The bottom row shows mean values across all 456 regular elementary schools in the CPS in fiscal years 2000 and 2001. Magnet schools, denoted by [m], accept students from throughout the district. No students are assigned to these schools by default. The other schools are neighborhood schools that also operate magnet cluster programs that enroll students from outside the attendance area.

n.a. = not available.

[a]The elementary school is in the top quartile of analysis schools on this measure.

the cross-sectional equation (2) for a series of student demographic and neighborhood variables that are predetermined at the time of the lottery, as well as variables capturing the number and types of applications submitted by the student. In results not presented here (but available from the authors upon request), we find that the number of statistically significant differences between winners and losers are no more than would be expected by chance if the lotteries were, in fact, truly random. Hence, we conclude that the lotteries were conducted properly.

Empirical Concern 2: Selective Attrition

Even if the lotteries are valid randomizations, however, the fact that not all applicants end up enrolling in CPS may bias our findings since we only observe subsequent student outcomes for CPS students. Of course, if the students who choose to remain in CPS are identical to their peers who choose to leave CPS, then the attrition of some students from our sample will not influence the results of our analysis. On the other hand, if this attrition is nonrandom, then it could bias our findings. For example, imagine that high-achieving students' decisions about whether to remain in a city public school are more sensitive to whether they win the lottery at a choice school or not. That is, they are more likely to stay if they win, and to leave if they lose. In this case, the sample of winners we observe in subsequent years will contain a disproportionate share of these "good" students relative to the sample of lottery losers—even if the full sample of winners and losers were identical at the time of the lottery. This type of attrition would lead us to overstate the benefits of winning a lottery and attending a higher quality school. Conversely, if students who leave CPS when they lose the lottery tend to be the lower-achieving students (which might be the case if families are more concerned about prospects for an "at-risk" child in a traditional public school), then our results would tend to understate any benefits of attending a higher quality school.

We provide evidence on the degree of overall attrition and test for whether it is selective in table 2.5. The first row shows results from estimating equation (3) with an indicator for enrollment in CPS as the dependent variable, for the overall sample and for various student subgroups. We do not condition on observable characteristics for these diagnostic analyses—the only variables included as controls are the set of lottery indicators. Recall that we pool observations across multiple years, so that this outcome indicates whether a student is enrolled in CPS in each year following the lottery. As a baseline, it is useful to consider the fraction of lottery losers subsequently enrolled in CPS. The fraction .527 in square brackets in the first column indicates that the typical lottery loser is enrolled in 52.7 percent of post-lottery years. The fact that relatively few students end up enrolling reflects the selective nature of the sample. The students who applied for choice schools indicated a willingness to look beyond their neighborhood school.

Table 2.5 The impact of winning a lottery on enrollment and attrition

Dependent variable	All students (1)	Student race/ethnicity			Student poverty status[a]		Tract poverty level	
		White (2)	Black (3)	Hispanic (4)	Ineligible for free/reduced-price lunch (5)	Eligible for free/reduced-price lunch (6)	Poverty rate ≤ 25% (7)	Poverty rate > 25% (8)
Currently enrolled in CPS	0.050** (0.012) [0.527]	0.053* (0.028) [0.420]	0.045** (0.018) [0.534]	0.078** (0.025) [0.609]	n.a.		0.066** (0.015) [0.516]	0.026 (0.024) [0.559]
Conditional on current enrollment								
Predicted 3rd grade composite score	-0.15 (0.23) {10.75}	0.29 (0.51) {6.38}	-0.18 (0.32) {7.49}	-0.51 (0.44) {7.29}	-0.00 (0.32) {11.53}	-0.50* (0.30) {8.38}	-0.28 (0.27) {10.68}	0.21 (0.35) {7.71}
Number of observations	70,114	13,063	41,115	11,625	n.a.	n.a.	51,218	18,896
Number of observations conditional on enrollment	37,569	5,620	22,241	7,283	18,541	18,795	26,836	10,733

Notes: Each cell reports the coefficient on an indicator for being selected from separate ordinary least squares regressions of the dependent variables indicated by the row headings. The control set also includes a full set of lottery fixed effects. Eicker-White robust standard errors are shown in parentheses, clustered by student. Either the mean [ ] or the standard deviation { } of the dependent variable among lottery losers is shown beneath the standard error. The results shown in the first column are based on the full sample of applications involved in nondegenerate lotteries. The remaining columns are based on various subsamples. n.a. = not available.

[a]Eligibility for free/reduced-price lunch is only defined for students enrolled in CPS.

**Significant at the 5 percent level.

*Significant at the 10 percent level.

The estimated coefficients on the indicator for being selected in the lottery for that application reveals that, while many students in our sample choose to attend school outside of CPS, the difference in enrollment between winners and losers is modest. For example, the coefficient of .050 in column (1) indicates that students who win a lottery are five percentage points more likely to be enrolled in CPS in subsequent years than their counterparts in the same lottery who are not selected. Given the baseline enrollment rate of 52.7 percent, we infer that selection in the lottery increases the likelihood of enrolling by roughly 9 percent.

While the extent of differential attrition is modest, if the students who left CPS because they did not win a lottery were substantially different from their counterparts who won a lottery and therefore remained, we would be concerned about the validity of our estimates. Row 2 explores this concern by examining the subsample of winners and losers enrolled in CPS. Rather than examine a series of background characteristics separately, we use a summary measure—namely, the student's predicted third grade achievement score (reading and math combined). We predict this on the basis of a linear regression that includes a host of student and neighborhood characteristics at the time of application, as well as indicators for the number of applications and acceptances to test-based schools observed for the student.

If the lottery losers who left were systematically different than their winning counterparts who remained, we would expect there to be a significant relationship between selection in the lottery and student characteristics among enrolled students. However, as we see in row 2, there is no such relationship across the subsamples we examine, other than for low-income students, where winners appear to be slightly negatively selected. Moreover, the estimates are small in magnitude and precisely estimated across the board. For example, the estimate of –0.15 in column (1) is tiny relative to the standard deviation of the predicted third grade score measure (10.75) shown in brackets. This provides some evidence that the differential attrition we observe overall and across demographic groups will not skew our baseline estimates.[19] However, we reconsider the issue of selective attrition when we examine whether the effect of winning a lottery varies according to the induced change in school quality or the family's revealed preference for academics, since any differences between winners and losers could be exaggerated in these types of sample splits.

2.4.3   Baseline Estimates of the Effect of Winning a Lottery on Student Outcomes

Having established that lottery applicants differ in important observable and unobservable ways from nonapplicants, the choice-school lotteries were

19. Of course, it is still possible that winners who were induced to remain in CPS are different in unobservable ways (e.g., they have more or less supportive families), which could lead to a bias in our findings.

indeed random, and selective attrition is unlikely to be a substantial concern in our analysis, we now proceed to our main results, shown in table 2.6. Each column refers to a different student subgroup and each row reports the results for a different outcome variable. Though we present results for various student subgroups, we focus our discussion on the overall results where the precision of our estimates is greatest. In each case, our estimates are based on ordinary least squares regressions of the type shown in equation (3), pooling across years since the application. Robust standard errors clustered by student are shown in parentheses, and the mean of the outcome variable for lottery losers is shown in square brackets.

We first present results that characterize the nature of the treatment for winners. How does winning affect their schooling? The top row of table 2.6 shows the likelihood of attending the lottery school, conditional on enrolling in CPS. If all winners chose to attend the lottery school to which they applied and the losers were precluded from attending, we would expect to find a point estimate of 1, indicating that winning the lottery shifts the likelihood of attending the lottery school from 0 to 100 percent. That is not what we see. In our case, 8.2 percent of lottery losers end up enrolling in the school, likely moving off the waitlist. The estimate of 0.312 indicates that students who won the lottery were 31.2 percentage points more likely to attend that school, implying that winners take up the option to attend approximately 39 percent of the time. So, while the attendance rate is nearly five times higher among winners than losers, less than half of the students who win a lottery end up attending the school. This is not surprising since about one in five of the winners in any given lottery included in our analysis had successful applications to at least one other lottery-based school, and many also applied to the academically advanced programs with selective admissions. However, it is due to this slippage that any differences in mean outcomes between winners and losers have to be scaled up in order to be interpreted as impacts of attending the lottery school.

Rows 2 and 3 characterize the change in exposure to school quality that is induced by winning a lottery. For example, the estimates in row 2 for the overall sample indicate that students who won a lottery attend schools where students from prior cohorts scored roughly 2.3 points higher than at schools attended by lottery losers. Given a standard deviation of 12.1 points among the control group, this translates into a 20 percent increase in this measure of school quality. The results in row 3 indicate that winning a lottery also increases the quality of the school a child attends as measured in terms of value-added, and to a similar degree.

However, it is again important to realize that these estimates only reflect the effect of winning the lottery, not the effect of actually attending the lottery school. For example, in order to obtain an estimate of the effect of attending the lottery school for which the student gained admission on mean peer achievement, it is necessary to divide 2.3 by the estimate of the fraction of years spent at the lottery school shown in row 1. Doing so, one

Table 2.6   The impact of winning a lottery on student outcomes

Dependent variable	All students (1)	Student race/ethnicity			Student poverty status		Tract poverty level	
		White (2)	Black (3)	Hispanic (4)	Ineligible for free/reduced-price lunch (5)	Eligible for free/reduced-price lunch (6)	Poverty rate ≤ 25% (7)	Poverty rate > 25% (8)
Attending school for which lottery applies	0.312** (0.015) [0.082]	0.210** (0.029) [0.105]	0.377** (0.021) [0.073]	0.275** (0.030) [0.083]	0.278** (0.019) [0.084]	0.367** (0.023) [0.080]	0.299** (0.017) [0.082]	0.381** (0.030) [0.081]
Characteristics of school attended								
Mean peer composite 3rd grade score (in 2000/2001)	2.34** (0.28) {12.1}	1.90** (0.65) {10.8}	2.67** (0.41) {11.7}	2.23** (0.53) {10.9}	1.50** (0.39) {12.7}	3.02** (0.40) {10.4}	2.04** (0.32) {12.2}	3.42** (0.54) {10.8}
Mean value-added 3rd–4th grades (in 2000/2001)	0.45** (0.08) {3.19}	0.41** (0.20) {3.05}	0.51** (0.12) {3.23}	0.53** (0.16) {3.12}	0.24** (0.11) {3.18}	0.64** (0.13) {3.12}	0.45** (0.10) {3.22}	0.57** (0.17) {3.09}
Student outcomes								
Retained in grade	-0.002 (0.002) [0.019]	0.005 (0.004) [0.007]	-0.002 (0.004) [0.023]	-0.006 (0.005) [0.018]	0.001 (0.003) [0.012]	-0.004 (0.004) [0.025]	-0.004 (0.003) [0.016]	0.005 (0.006) [0.025]

In special education	-0.003	0.000	0.010	-0.035*	-0.022*	0.019	0.000	0.008
	(0.009)	(0.020)	(0.012)	(0.019)	(0.012)	(0.013)	(0.010)	(0.019)
	[0.084]	[0.092]	[0.085]	[0.092]	[0.095]	[0.073]	[0.084]	[0.083]
Missing ITBS test scores	-0.007	-0.010	-0.000	-0.008	-0.006	-0.010	-0.002	-0.010
	(0.005)	(0.013)	(0.006)	(0.014)	(0.008)	(0.007)	(0.006)	(0.011)
	[0.265]	[0.306]	[0.220]	[0.357]	[0.279]	[0.254]	[0.270]	[0.253]
Composite (mean) reading and math standard score	0.17	0.02	-0.37	0.86	-0.18	-0.87	0.25	-0.99
	(0.53)	(1.23)	(0.75)	(1.07)	(0.74)	(0.78)	(0.64)	(1.05)
	{19.6}	{18.8}	{18.1}	{18.8}	{19.9}	{18.1}	{19.7}	{18.2}
Number of observations	37,569	5,620	22,241	7,283	18,541	18,795	26,836	10,733

Notes: Each cell reports the coefficient on an indicator for being selected from separate ordinary least squares regressions of the dependent variables indicated by the row headings. The control set includes a full set of lottery fixed effects as well as student demographic characteristics, home census tract characteristics, and student application patterns. Eicker-White robust standard errors are shown in parentheses, clustered by student. Either the mean [] or the standard deviation {} of the dependent variable among lottery losers is shown beneath the standard error. The results shown in column (1) are based on the full sample of applications involved in nondegenerate lotteries from students currently enrolled in CPS. The remaining columns are based on various subsamples.

**Significant at the 5 percent level.

*Significant at the 10 percent level.

finds that students who actually attend the lottery school after winning a lottery experience peers who score roughly 7 points higher in reading and math (2.3/.312 ≈ 7.4 points, or more than 60 percent of the control group standard deviation) than they would have had they lost the lottery. This suggests that attending a sought-after school can substantially change a student's educational experience.

Now that we have established that winners are attending what appear to be better schools, the bottom panel of table 2.6 evaluates whether this leads to better academic outcomes.[20] The outcome measures include an indicator for whether the student is repeating a grade (defined starting after the first year following the application), an indicator for whether the student currently receives special education services, an indicator for whether ITBS test scores from the spring administration are available for the student, and the student's composite (reading and math) test score. Recall that we are estimating these results on a panel that includes either four or five years of outcome data for each student.

Focusing on the results for the full sample of students shown in column (1), we find little evidence that winning the lottery had any impact on student achievement. Despite the fact that winners, on average, attend schools with higher achievement levels and value-added measures, test scores of these students are virtually identical to their peers who lost the lottery. There is no indication that these students were any more or less likely to receive special education services, to be retained in grade, or to take the standardized exams.

While the average student does not appear to benefit from winning a lottery, it is possible that the opportunity to attend a more desirable school has a greater impact for disadvantaged students. To explore this possibility, columns (2) through (8) of table 2.6 present results separately for various subgroups. Looking at the subgroup analyses in columns (2) through (8), we see no evidence that winning a lottery had a discernible positive impact on test scores for any subgroup.

While these results suggest that attending a higher quality school does not improve academic achievement for young children, it is worth exploring the magnitude and precision of our estimates more carefully. To begin, recall that the estimates presented in table 2.6 reflect the average difference between lottery winners and losers regardless of the school they end up attending. This ITT estimate captures the effect of the *opportunity* to attend the school, where the treatment refers to attendance at the school. As shown previously, in order to understand the effect of attending a lottery school, one needs to divide the outcome estimates by the figures shown in row 1. Doing so for

---

20. However, even without changes in observable school quality, winners should presumably benefit from better match quality. They have gained a schooling option they expressed an interest in having.

the test score result, one gets 0.17/0.31 ≈ 0.55. We can calculate an approximate 95 percent confidence interval (ignoring the variability in the estimated attendance response) of attending the lottery school as 0.55 ± (0.53/0.31) × 1.96. = 0.55 ± 3.35. This means that attending a sought-after lottery school leads to a change in test performance of –2.8 to +3.9 points. Given the standard deviation of test scores in our control group is 19.6, we can rule out average increases in achievement from attending a lottery school (for all sample years following the application) of more than 20 percent of a standard deviation. Hence, we can rule out modest or large impacts, but cannot discount the possibility that attending a choice school has a small positive (or negative) impact on achievement.

It is also useful to compare these estimates to our earlier cross-sectional estimates of the impact of mean peer achievement on own achievement. The point estimate of 0.52 in column (4) of table 2.2 indicates that a one point increase in mean peer achievement is associated with a half a point increase in the student's own third grade test score. The estimates in row 2 of table 2.6 show that the typical winner attends a school with mean peer achievement 2.34 points higher than the typical lottery loser. Together, these imply that lottery winners should score 1.2 points (2.34 × 0.52, with an approximate 95 percent confidence interval of ±0.11) higher themselves. This is the upper bound of the ITT effect implied by our test score estimate of 0.17 (0.53) in table 2.6. Hence, if one believes that there are no other channels through which attending a choice school would improve one's achievement, we cannot quite rule out the OLS estimates. However, to the extent that there are any other significant pathways through which choice impacts student outcomes (including the demonstrated independent effect of measured value-added), then we can infer the naïve OLS estimates are inflated.

2.4.4   Interaction Effects of Winning a Lottery on Student Outcomes

Though we can rule out sizeable academic benefits from winning the lottery on average, it is possible that the impact varies depending on the nature of the treatment and the reasons for choosing the application schools. We present results from specifications that allow for differential impacts along these lines in table 2.7.

The first row of table 2.7 explores whether our estimates vary by the number of years since the application. Recall that our sample includes information on student outcomes for up to five years following application. To the extent that the effects of attending a high quality school are cumulative, we would expect the benefit of attending a choice school to increase with time. To explore this possibility, we estimate the specification shown in equation (3), but include an interaction between being selected in the lottery and years since application (with the first year normalized to zero). Note that the main effect (years since application) is subsumed by other variables in our control

Table 2.7   Impact of winning a lottery—interactions

Interaction variable	Enrolled in CPS		Predicted 3rd grade combined score (conditional on enrolling)		Mean peer composite 3rd grade score at campus attended (in 2000/2001)		Student's composite reading and math standard score	
	Selected (1a)	Interaction (1b)	Selected (2a)	Interaction (2b)	Selected (3a)	Interaction (3b)	Selected (4a)	Interaction (4b)
Treatment exposure								
Years since application	0.069**	−0.011**	−0.22	−0.03	2.98**	−0.33**	0.18	−0.01
	(0.013)	(0.003)	(0.28)	(0.06)	(0.36)	(0.10)	(0.61)	(0.24)
Intensity of treatment								
Potential gain in mean peer composite 3rd grade score [μ = 4.4 σ = 10.0]	0.037**	0.003**	−0.32	0.01	1.73**	0.12**	0.06	0.00
	(0.013)	(0.001)	(0.21)	(0.03)	(0.29)	(0.04)	(0.58)	(0.06)
Preference for school quality								
Mean residual [μ = −0.4, σ = 6.0]	0.057**	0.004**	−0.35	−0.05	2.32**	0.05	0.14	−0.02
	(0.013)	(0.002)	(0.24)	(0.04)	(0.33)	(0.05)	(0.56)	(0.09)

Notes: The cells report results from separate ordinary least squares regressions of the independent variables indicated by the column headings. The control set includes a full set of lottery fixed effects as well as student demographic characteristics, home census tract characteristics, and student application patterns (when the dependent variable is other than student's predicted third grade score). The estimated coefficients on the indicator for being selected and the interaction between this indicator and the variable indicated by the row heading are reported in paired columns. Eicker-White robust standard errors are shown in parentheses, clustered by student. The results are based on the full sample of applications involved in nondegenerate lotteries.

**Significant at the 5 percent level.

*Significant at the 10 percent level.

set (i.e., the indicators for each cohort, initial application grade, and current year combination).

The table shows results for four different outcomes. In order to examine whether attrition changed across years since the application, columns (1a) and (1b) show the main effect for being selected and the interaction with years since application for a model where the outcome measure is an indicator for whether the student was enrolled in CPS. The coefficient of -0.011 on the interaction between winning a lottery and the number of years since the application indicates that the *difference* in enrollment rates between lottery winners and losers *shrinks* over time. In the initial year after the application, lottery winners are estimated to be 6.9 percentage points more likely to be enrolled. Five years following the application, winners are only 2.5 percentage points $(6.9 - 4 \times 1.1)$ more likely to be enrolled in CPS. This convergence between winners and losers is driven both by further exit from CPS of some lottery winners as well as later entry by lottery losers.

In order to examine whether selective attrition changed across years since the application, columns (2a) and (2b) show the main effect and interaction term for a model where the outcome measure is the student's predicted third grade test score. There is no evidence that selective attrition differed as time elapsed.

The results in columns (3a) and (3b) focus on the mean peer achievement in the school(s) that the student actually attends, which provides an indication of the "treatment" effect of winning a lottery. The coefficient estimate of -0.33 on the interaction term indicates that the "benefit" of winning a lottery, in terms of the quality of school attended, diminishes somewhat over time. This may be due to the fact that students who lost the lottery continue to seek opportunities to attend better schools, and so slowly "catch-up" with their peers who were initially lucky enough to win the lottery.

Columns (4a) and (4b) show the results for student achievement. Here we see no indication that the benefit from winning the lottery changed over time. The fact that achievement effects do not increase with longer "exposure" to the "treatment" (i.e., a longer period of time in the choice school) could be taken as further evidence that the link between schools and test scores is weak. On the other hand, the fact that the quality differential diminishes over time might serve to mitigate the greater length of exposure. In either case, these results speak to the potential importance of compensating behavior on the part of families.

To get more directly at any heterogeneity according to intensity of the treatment, row 2 presents a similar specification where the interaction term is the potential gain in mean peer achievement (and we add the main effect to the specification as well). This measure varies by student and application, and is defined as the difference between the peer achievement in the application school and the level of peer achievement the student is likely to experience if he or she does not win the lottery to the application school.[21] Not surprisingly, winners are increasingly more likely than losers to enroll as the potential gain increases, though it continues to appear that remaining winners and losers are not systematically different from one another. The change in school quality experienced by winners, by definition, increases with the potential gain, as documented in columns (3a) and (3b). Yet, we see no interaction between potential gains and achievement effects in columns (4a) and (4b). In other words, the effect of winning a lottery is no different for those students who sought out high-achieving schools compared with otherwise comparable students who applied to schools with lower test scores. So, the apparent lack of benefits for the overall sample cannot simply be explained by gains for some and losses for others due to differences in what winning confers in terms of changes in the schooling environment.

As a final test, we consider the possibility that the overall null effect masks test score gains from the choices made by students expressly interested in academics, and test score losses for those more willing to trade-off distance or other school features against academic quality. This test is motivated by the finding of Hastings, Kane, and Staiger (2006) that, among non-white students, those students whose parents exhibit the strongest preferences for academic quality benefit from the opportunity to attend a more-preferred choice school, while those seeking same-race settings are harmed (in terms of test score outcomes). Moreover, the apparent test score gains and losses appear to come from idiosyncratic match quality, rather than aspects of quality that are enjoyed by all students at a school.

Note that the potential gains interaction described will, to a large extent, capture parent preferences for academic quality since the measure incorporates the family's choice of application schools. However, this measure varies by application as well as student, and also incorporates information on the student's likely default option. To the extent that families who care strongly about academics make sure their children attend a high-achieving school regardless of the lottery outcome (e.g., through application to test-based schools), the potential gain measure may understate the family's preference for academics. For these reasons, we create a more direct measure of parent preference for academics.

While the structure of the school choice program in Chicago does not allow us to calculate the same type of preference measure, we are able to create a similar indicator to explore this possibility in our sample. We estimate a regression of the following form:

$$(4) \qquad Q_{ia} = \mathbf{X}_i\boldsymbol{\beta} + \boldsymbol{\Gamma}(\mathbf{Z}_i) + e_{ia},$$

where Q_{ia} is the average combined (reading and math) test score in the school that student i applied to in application a, $\mathbf{X}_i$ is a vector of student demo-

---

21. The expected quality of a student's alternative options is inferred from the mean experienced by lottery losers from the same neighborhood (there are seventy-seven community areas) who are predicted to be in the same quintile of third grade achievement.

graphics and home tract characteristics, Z_i is a vector of community area fixed effects, and e is a stochastic error term. We then average the residuals across applications for each student and use this as a measure of the family's preference for academics. The intuition behind our measure is that the parents who apply to schools with the highest achievement levels—conditional on their observable demographics and the neighborhood in which they live, which captures the distance to various schooling options—place the greatest weight on academics. Note that it is likely that *all* of the families in our analysis sample place more weight on academics than the average CPS family since they have taken the step of applying for a choice school rather than simply attending their default neighborhood school, and we observe average improvements in observable school quality for winners (as do Hastings, Kane, and Staiger 2006). However, there remains significant variation in revealed preferences among students in our lottery sample, and our measure has a standard deviation of six points.

The results in row 3 of table 2.7 are based on a specification that adds an interaction between this academic preference measure and winning the lottery (as well as the main effect for the academic preference measure). In columns (1a) and (1b), we see that there is a systematic relationship between preference for school quality and attrition. Specifically, the coefficient of 0.004 on the interaction term in column (1b) indicates that students whose parents express a greater preference for academic quality are *more* likely to leave CPS if they lose the lottery. While the difference in enrollment rates between winners and losers increases with the parents' preference for academic quality, the results in columns (2a) and (2b) provide no evidence that the attrition is more selective (along observable dimensions) among high-preference parents. Of course, it is still possible that student attrition was selective along unobservable dimensions such as parental motivation or family support. The results in columns (3a) and (3b) show that the improvement in measured school quality induced by winning does not vary by preferences. This is somewhat surprising given that one would expect families with a stronger preference for academics to end up in higher-achieving schools if they win the lottery. On the other hand, this result is consistent with the findings in Hastings, Kane, and Staiger (2006), and likely reflects the fact that a family's preferences as measured by application behavior is strongly correlated with the student's next-best alternative. However, unlike the Hastings, Kane, and Staiger (2006) analysis of Charlotte-Mecklenburg, the achievement results in columns (4a) and (4b) reveal no test score gains from winning a lottery in the Chicago setting, even among high-preference families.

2.5   Conclusions and Implications

The original analysis conducted in this chapter suggests that schools are a blunt instrument for improving the achievement of disadvantaged students. First, for elementary school students in CPS, we demonstrate that the gap in achievement across advantaged and disadvantaged students is two-thirds as great within schools as across schools. The great inequities that we observed in school quality across these groups, then, cannot explain the bulk of the differences in outcomes. Further, this surely overstates the role for schools. Part of the convergence in outcomes within schools as compared to across schools is due to the fact that minority and poor students who attend the same schools are similar in family background and other characteristics that are difficult to measure. These students would have more similar outcomes regardless of their shared schooling experience.

We then use lotteries to examine whether elementary school students who gain access to desirable schools do better. The great advantage is that randomly selected winners and losers are by definition exchangeable. Although students in our sample often take advantage of winning a lottery by attending that school, and on average lottery winners attend schools that are better on observable dimensions than the schools attended by lottery losers, we observe no systematic improvement in student performance among winners relative to losers. This finding is surprising since students who win contested lotteries would be expected to fare better because of access to better resources, better peers, or a program that better suits their learning needs for idiosyncratic reasons. The fact that these students do not appear to benefit further undermines the likelihood that changes in broad aspects of school quality will radically change students' fates.

There are several explanations for the lack of average positive effects. One possibility is that attending a choice school is a substitute for parental involvement. In prior work, however, we find only weak support for this hypothesis (Cullen, Jacob, and Levitt 2006). Another explanation is that students winning lotteries may have to travel much greater distances to school, which might interfere with academic success. However, in results not shown here, we find that the travel costs experienced by lottery winners appear to be quite small, and thus unlikely to explain our results.

The coexistence of intense competition for entry and little academic benefit to students winning the lotteries could indicate that parents are not well-informed about the education production function, and mistake higher school outputs for higher school value-added. Alternatively, parents and children might apply to magnet schools for predominantly nonacademic reasons, in which case systematic academic gains would not be expected. Indeed, studies of school choice programs that attempt to ascertain parent preferences generally conclude that parents value factors such as convenience (i.e., distance from home to school) and the racial composition of the school at least as much as measures of academic quality (Glazerman 1998; Hastings, Kane, and Staiger 2005). In the Chicago setting, however, we are unable to find evidence that either winning a lottery that induces a large change in mean peer achievement or choosing with academic motivations in mind confers any greater benefits.

The type of school choice we analyze in this chapter is particularly relevant to the current federal accountability mandate insofar as our analysis focuses on public schools in a large, disadvantaged urban district. This form of choice is the most common form of choice available to students in urban areas (National Center for Education Statistics 1997), and it is likely to become even more prevalent under the recent federal education legislation of No Child Left Behind. School districts that accept Title I funds must allow students at lagging schools to attend other schools in the district, giving preference to low achieving and low income students. We cautiously conclude that access to "better" schools is likely to be less effective than more targeted interventions.

Appendix

Table 2A.1   **Data sources**

Data	Source	Construction
Academic Outcomes	CPS Board	Information on enrollment, special education placement, and retention is from administrative records provided by the Board. Special education status covers a variety of disabilities ranging from mild learning disabilities to severe physical handicaps. Standardized test scores are from separate administrative test files provided by the Board. Students are tested in grades 1–8 on the Iowa Test of Basic Skills (ITBS), which is a nationally-normed standardized achievement exam. The scores that we use are developmental standard scores, which are designed so that a unit change represents the same amount of learning at all points on the scale.
Student Demographics	CPS Board	Student demographic variables (race, gender, age) come directly from information reported on the applications. Eligibility for free or reduced-price lunch is only available for students who enroll in CPS, and is recorded each spring.
Neighborhood Characteristics	2000 Census, CPS Board, and CCSR	We mapped the home addresses reported on the application files to census tracts. Basic information on the student's census tract, such as median household income and percent below the poverty line, comes from the 2000 Census. The crime composite was provided by the Consortium on Chicago School Research (CCSR) and is an index created by factor analysis using official block group level crime statistics for 1994. The variable used in this analysis is a tract-level average, weighted by the total population in each block group.

References

Aaronson, D., L. Barrow, and W. Sander. 2007. Teachers and student achievement in the Chicago public high schools. *Journal of Labor Economics* 25 (1): 95–135.

Altonji, J. G., T. E. Elder, and C. R. Taber. 2005. An evaluation of instrumental variable strategies for estimating the effects of Catholic schooling. *Journal of Human Resources* 40 (4): 791–821.

Blank, R. K. 1983. Survey of magnet schools: Analyzing a model for quality integrated education. Washington, D.C.: ABT Associates for the Department of Education.

Boyd, D., P. Grossman, H. Lankford, S. Loeb, and J. Wyckoff. 2005. How changes in entry requirements alter the teacher workforce and affect student achievement. NBER Working Paper no. 11844. Cambridge, MA: National Bureau of Economic Research, December.

Bryk, A. S., V. A. Lee, and P. B. Holland. 1993. *Catholic schools and the common good.* Cambridge, MA: Harvard University Press.

Card, D., and A. B. Krueger. 1996. School resources and student outcomes: An overview of the literature and new evidence from North and South Carolina. *The Journal of Economic Perspectives* 10 (4): 31–40.

Card, D., and A. A. Payne. 2002. School finance reform, the distribution of school spending, and the distribution of student test scores. *Journal of Public Economics* 83 (1): 49–82.

Carnoy, M., R. Jacobsen, L. Mishel, and R. Rothstein. 2005. The charter school dust-up: Examining evidence on enrollment and achievement. Washington, D.C.: Economic Policy Institute.

Clotfelter, C. T., H. F. Ladd, J. L. Vigdor, and J. Wheeler. 2007. High poverty schools and the distribution of teachers and principals. *North Carolina Law Review* 85 (5): 1345–80.

Coleman, J. S., T. Hoffer, and S. Kilgore. 1982. *High school achievement: Public, Catholic and private schools compared.* New York: Basic Books.

Cullen, J. B., B. A. Jacob, and S. Levitt. 2006. The effect of school choice on participants: Evidence from randomized lotteries. *Econometrica* 74 (5): 1191–1230.

Education Trust. 2006. Funding gaps 2006. Washington, D.C.: The Education Trust.

Evans, W. N., and R. M. Schwab. 1995. Finishing high school and starting college: Do Catholic schools make a difference? *Quarterly Journal of Economics* 110 (4): 941–74.

Gamoran, A. 1996. Student achievement in public magnet, public comprehensive, and private city high schools. *Educational Evaluation and Policy Analysis* 18 (1): 1–18.

Glazerman, S. 1998. *Determinants and consequences of parental school choice.* PhD diss. University of Chicago, Harris School of Public Policy.

Graham, B. S. 2004. Identifying social interactions through excess variance contrasts. Harvard University. Unpublished Manuscript.

Greene, J. P., P. E. Peterson, and J. Du. 1997. *The effectiveness of school choice: The Milwaukee experiment.* Cambridge, MA: Program on Education Policy and Governance, Harvard University.

Hanushek, E. A. 1997. Assessing the effects of school resources on student performance: An update. *Educational Evaluation and Policy Analysis* 19 (2): 141–64.

Hanushek, E. A., J. Kain, D. M. O'Brien, and S. G. Rivkin. 2005. The market for teacher quality. NBER Working Paper no. 11154. Cambridge, MA: National Bureau of Economic Research, February.

Hastings, J. S., T. Kane, and D. Staiger. 2005. Parental preferences and school competition: Evidence from a public school choice program. NBER Working Paper no. 11805. Cambridge, MA: National Bureau of Economic Research, November.

———. 2006. Preferences and heterogeneous treatment effects in a public school choice lottery. NBER Working Paper no. 12145. Cambridge, MA: National Bureau of Economic Research, April.

Heckman, J. 2007. The economics, technology and neuroscience of human capability formation. *Proceedings of the National Academy of Sciences* 104 (33): 13250–5.

Heckman, J., and D. V. Masterov. 2007. The productivity argument for investing in young children. *Review of Agricultural Economics* 29 (3): 446–93.

Howell, W. G., and P. E. Peterson. 2002. The education gap: Vouchers and urban schools. Washington, D.C.: Brookings Institution.

Hoxby, C. M. 2000. Peer effects in the classroom: Learning from race and gender variation. NBER Working Paper no. 7867. Cambridge, MA: National Bureau of Economic Research, August.

———. 2004. Achievement in charter schools and regular public schools in the U.S.: Understanding the differences. Harvard University. Unpublished Manuscript.

Kane, T. J., J. E. Rockoff, and D. O. Staiger. 2006. What does certification tell us about teacher effectiveness? Evidence from New York City. NBER Working Paper no. 12155. Cambridge, MA: National Bureau of Economic Research, April.

Keller, B. 2005. Actual measures of "highly qualified" teachers just beginning to come to light across nation. *Education Week* 25 (15): S6.

Kling, J., J. Liebman, and L. Katz. 2007. Experimental analysis of neighborhood effects. *Econometrica* 75 (1): 83–119.

Krueger, A. B., and P. Zhu. 2003. Another look at the New York City school voucher experiment. NBER Working Paper no. 9418. Cambridge, MA: National Bureau of Economic Research, January.

Lefgren, L. 2004. Educational peer effects and the Chicago public schools. *Journal of Urban Economics* 56 (2): 169–91.

Murnane, R. J., and F. Levy. 1996. Teaching the new basic skills: Principles for educating children to thrive in a changing economy. New York: The Free Press.

National Center for Education Statistics (NCES). 1997. Public school choice programs, 1993–94: Availability and student participation. Washington, D.C.: National Center for Education Statistics, Department of Education.

Neighborhood Capital Budget Group (NCBG). 1999. Rebuilding our schools brick by brick. Chicago, IL: NCBG.

Neal, D. 1997. The effects of Catholic secondary schooling on educational attainment. *Journal of Labor Economics* 15 (January): 98–123.

Nelson, F. H., B. Rosenberg, N. Van Meter. 2004. Charter school achievement on the 2003 national assessment of education progress. Washington, D.C.: American Federation of Teachers.

Peterson, P. E., D. Myers, and W. G. Howell. 1998. An evaluation of the New York City school choice scholarship program: The first year. Cambridge, MA: Mathematica Policy Research and the Harvard Program on Education Policy and Governance.

Rockoff, J. E. 2004. The impact of individual teachers on student achievement: Evidence from panel data. *American Economic Review* 94 (2): 247–52.

Rouse, C. E. 1998. Private school vouchers and student achievement: An evaluation of the Milwaukee parental choice program. *Quarterly Journal of Economics* 113 (2): 553–602.

Sander, W. 1996. Catholic grade schools and academic achievement. *Journal of Human Resources* 31 (3): 540–48.

Witte, J. F. 1997. Achievement effects of the Milwaukee voucher program. New Orleans: American Economics Association Annual Meeting.

Witte, J. F., T. D. Sterr, and C. A. Thorn. 1995. Fifth-year report: Milwaukee parental choice program. Madison, WI: University of Wisconsin.

Zimmerman, D. 2003. Peer effects in academic outcomes: Evidence from a natural experiment. *The Review of Economics and Statistics* 85 (1): 9–23.

Would More Compulsory Schooling Help Disadvantaged Youth?
Evidence From Recent Changes to School-Leaving Laws

Philip Oreopoulos

3.1 Introduction

High school dropout rates have changed little over the last thirty years. In the early 1970s, 17 percent of U.S. youths aged eighteen to twenty-four and not in high school had not completed their degree. This figure (from the National Center for Education Statistics [NCES 2003]) fell slowly to 14 percent by 1990, and has since leveled off. Dropout rates are higher among blacks and substantially higher among hispanics. Noncompletion is also related to family income. During the twelve months ending in October 2001, high school students living in low-income families dropped out of school at six times the rate of their peers from high-income families (NCES 2005).

Policymakers and administrators often grapple with finding ways to reduce the number of dropouts. Some consider lowering class size, others consider making the curriculum easier, or targeting students at risk earlier. An additional possibility, also considered recently by several states, is to raise the minimum school leaving age. The compulsory school leaving age restricts the minimum length of time students must spend in school before having the legal option to leave. Laws that determine this age have been around for many decades, in some cases more than one hundred years, and have been updated periodically.

Some of the best evidence suggesting that high school dropouts gain, on average, from staying on comes from historical changes in compulsory

Philip Oreopoulos is an associate professor of economics at the University of Toronto and a faculty research fellow of the National Bureau of Economic Research.

This research was funded by the Annie E. Casey Foundation. I thank them for their support but acknowledge that the findings and conclusions presented in this report are those of the author alone, and do not necessarily reflect the opinions of the Foundation.

school laws. Previous studies have consistently shown that individuals compelled to stay in school also experience large gains to social-economic outcomes. For the United States, Angrist and Krueger (1991) and Acemoglu and Angrist (2001) estimated (using very different methodologies) that annual adult earnings are about 10 percent higher for students compelled to stay a year longer in school. For the United Kingdom, Harmon and Walker (1995) found about 14 percent higher earnings from school compulsion. And for Canada, I found similar gains using provincial law changes between 1915 and 1970 for would-be dropouts compelled to stay in school. Other studies have found that additional high school lowers the likelihood of committing crime (Lochner and Moretti 2004), of dying young (Lleras-Muney 2005), and lowers the chances of teen pregnancy (Black, Devereux, and Salvanes 2004).

These earlier reports, however, examine effects from raising the minimum school leaving age to fourteen, fifteen, or sixteen many decades ago, often before the 1950s. The circumstances behind dropout decisions back then were quite different than the circumstances behind dropout decisions today. The demand for skilled workers has increased, and the gains from additional education attainment may also have increased. On the other hand, more students today graduate from high school and obtain post-secondary education. Today's dropouts come from relatively poorer families. From the 2000 census, 73 percent of dropouts under twenty and living at home have parents with household income below the twenty-fifth percentile, compared to 55 percent of dropouts from the 1960 census. It is not clear whether compelling these individuals to remain in school beyond sixteen would generate the same effects found in earlier studies.

Many states have discussed raising the school leaving age to seventeen or eighteen, almost making high school completion compulsory. In fact, twenty-nine states have already increased the minimum school leaving age above sixteen, although often with exceptions.

This chapter uses these recent changes to the school leaving age to explore the potential for compulsory schooling to serve as an effective policy from improving current social-economic outcomes, especially for today's disadvantaged youths. The purpose is to present new evidence and discussion for considering whether to support such policies. Support for or against compulsory school laws often is presented without theoretical or empirical foundation. And past studies only indicate compulsory school laws appear to have been effective in generating adult gains for would-be dropouts many decades ago.

The first part of the chapter focuses on whether these recent changes and experiences had any impact on increasing school enrollment and attainment. Section 3.2 describes the recent law changes in the United States. In section 3.3, I estimate whether changes to the school leaving age above sixteen made some students drop out later, graduate, and even decide to enroll in college.

As the reader will see following, many of the law changes included exceptions, were poorly enforced, or had little punishment for noncompliance. The recent increases in the school leaving age had only a small, but still significant, impact on increasing school completion rates, as well as college attendance.

The second part of the chapter estimates the subsequent impact on earnings and on other labor market outcomes for the small fraction affected by these laws. I discuss in section 3.4 the methodology for estimating these effects. Section 3.5 presents the results. Notably, the results reveal very similar findings to the more historic studies. I estimate individuals compelled to stay in school beyond the age of sixteen experience significantly higher earnings and higher opportunities for employment in their early careers.

Finally, I conclude in section 3.6. Taken together with the consistent previous evidence, the overall results suggest raising the school leaving age above sixteen offers significant gains to earnings and employment outcomes, on average, to students that otherwise would have left sooner. One recommendation is that, if states are serious about lowering dropout rates through compulsory schooling, they need to better enforce these laws and promote their potential benefits to administrators, parents, and students. While allowing exceptions are probably necessary, greater initial enforcement may help establish an acceptance from youth to stay in school. Students may also find it easier to accept staying if schools also offer more curriculum choice (offering more trait-based training, for example), as some governments have already done. Ideally, compulsory school laws work through threat of enforcement rather than through actual enforcement.

3.2 Recent Changes to Compulsory Schooling Laws in the United States

Many states in the United States have a minimum school leaving age of seventeen or eighteen. The annual National Center for Education Statistics' (NCES') Education Digest lists these laws. Figure 3.1 shows the minimum school leaving age between 1970 and 2005 for states with a minimum school leaving age set above sixteen at least once during this period (and for the District of Columbia). Figure 3.2 shows the other states.[1] Several, like Rhode Island, Florida, and Nebraska, upgraded their compulsory school laws only in the last few years. Others like Oklahoma, Oregon, and Utah, however, have had a minimum leaving age set above sixteen for more than two decades. Figure 3.3 shows the estimated effects of minimum school leaving age above sixteen on school enrollment in the 2000 to 2003 Current Population Surveys (excluding June, July, and August). Figure 3.4 shows the estimated effects of

---

1. Hawaii and Alaska are left out of this chapter's analysis since their demographics and economies differ significantly from the other states. However, results are similar when including them in the regressions.

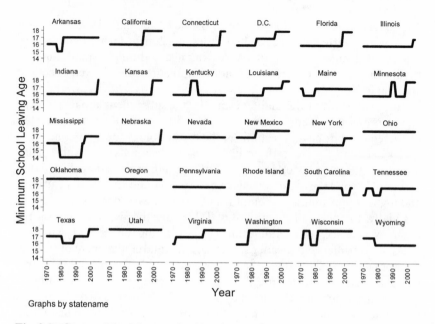

Graphs by statename

Fig. 3.1   States with minimum school leaving age greater than sixteen, at least once between 1970–2003

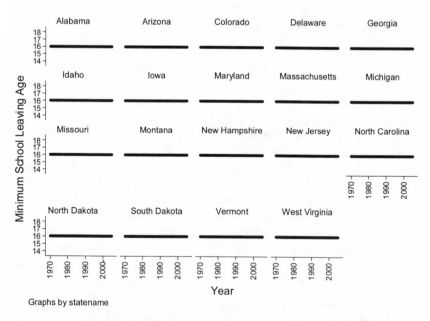

Graphs by statename

Fig. 3.2   States with minimum school leaving age sixteen or less, 1970–2003

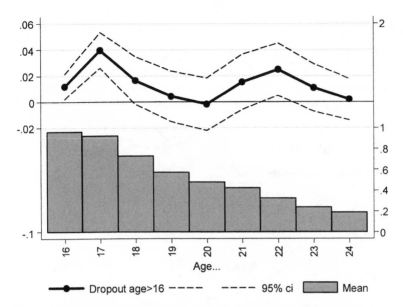

Fig. 3.3   Estimated effects of minimum school leaving age above sixteen on school enrollment 2000 to 2003 current population surveys, excluding June, July, and August

Note: Each black dot on top half of the figure represents a separate regression by age category. An indicator variable for whether in school was regressed on whether an individual faced a dropout age above sixteen in their state of residence when they were sixteen years old, plus nine region fixed effects. The estimated coefficients for the effects of facing a higher dropout age are reported here for each age group. The dotted lines outline the 95 percent confidence interval. The bars in the bottom half of the figure indicate the fraction of sample in each age group in school.

minimum school leaving age above sixteen on grade attainment in the 2000 to 2003 Current Population Surveys (twenty- to twenty-four-year-olds).

The strange pattern from a few states raising then lowering the leaving age hints that more is going on. A closer look at the legislation reveals that there is much more to compulsory school laws than a specific age range within which individuals must remain in school. There are exceptions if a student works, exemptions with parental consent, and various degrees of enforcement and repercussions for noncompliance. Table 3.1 lists some of these exceptions and exemptions for states with school leaving laws above sixteen in 2005. The information comes directly from the States' Statutes or Codes. The descriptions do not capture the full details of the law, but rather provide a sense of the intricacies behind compulsory schooling policy.

In several states, students can leave earlier than the set minimum school leaving age if they work instead. In other cases, students can leave with parental consent. Kansas allows dropping out before the recorded minimum age if, after a counseling session, both student and parent sign a disclaimer

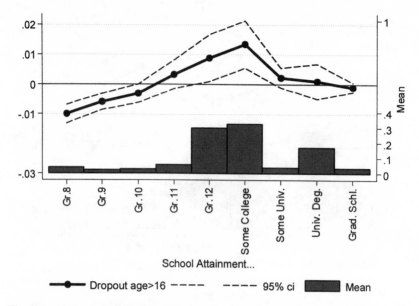

Fig. 3.4   Estimated effects of minimum school leaving age above sixteen on grade attainment 2000 to 2003 Current Population Surveys, twenty- to twenty-four-year-olds

Note: An indicator variable for the school attainment indicated along the x-axis was regressed on whether an individual twenty to twenty-four years old in the 2000 to 2003 CPS faced a dropout age above sixteen in their state of residence when they were sixteen, plus nine region fixed effects. The estimated coefficients for the effects of facing a higher dropout age are reported here for school attainment level. The dotted lines outline the 95 percent confidence interval. The bars in the bottom half of the figure indicate the fraction of sample in each education level.

acknowledging a list of academic skills the student may not yet have acquired and average earnings differences between dropouts and graduates.[2]

Some students disengage and drop out illegally because compulsory schooling policies are either not well enforced, or punishment for habitual

2. Interestingly, the Kansas State Department of Education (2005) suggests administrators use the following information in the counseling session:

Level of education completed	Lifetime earnings (US$)	Median weekly earnings in 2003 (US$)	Unemployment rate in 2003 (%)
Not a high school grad.	993,466	396	8.8
High school grad.	1,298,316	554	5.5
Some college	1,462,379	622	5.2
Associate degree	1,527,582	672	4.0
Bachelor's degree	2,173,417	900	3.3
Master's degree	2,312,426	1,064	2.9
Doctorate	2,907,904	1,307	1.7
Professional	3,013,000	1,349	2.1

Table 3.1   2005 compulsory school law legislation for states with minimum school leaving ages greater than 16

State	School leaving age	Punishment for habitual truancy	Major exemptions
Arkansas	17	Up to $500 (for parent)	16+ and in adult ed. 10 hrs a week
California	18	Community service (for student and/or parent); juvenile delinquent school (student); parent education, $1,000 fine	Work permit
Connecticut	18	Social and rehabilitation service (parent and/or child)	16+ and parent's consent or work permit
District of Columbia	18	Parent subject to community service, fine, or imprisonment	17+, part-time school if working
Illinois	17	Community service (for child), graduation incentives program, misdemeanor (parents and/or child)	Working
Indiana	18	Ineligible for driver's license, misdemeanor (parents and/or child)	16+ and student, parent, and principal agree to withdrawal
Kansas	18	Social and rehabilitation service (parent and/or child)	Parent consent and signing of disclaimer that child lacks skills and earnings will be lower
Louisiana	18	Up to $250, or 30 days imprisonment	17+ and parent consent
Maine	17	None mentioned	15+, parent consent, part-time school, and working
Minnesota	18	Misdemeanor (parents and/or child)	16+ and parental consent
Mississippi	17	Misdemeanor (parent), foster care (child)	None
Nebraska	18	Misdemeanor (parents and/or child)	16+ and parent consent or need to work
Nevada	17	Advisory board meeting, misdemeanor (parent), foster care (child)	Distant from school or need to work or 14+ and working

(*continued*)

Table 3.1   (continued)

State	School leaving age	Punishment for habitual truancy	Major exemptions
New Mexico	18	Ineligible for driver's license, social and rehabilitation service (child), misdemeanor (parent)	17+ and working
New York	17	Fine or imprisonment	16+ and working
Ohio	18	Misdemeanor (parents and/or child)	Work permit
Oklahoma	18	Misdemeanor (parents and/or child)	16+, principal and parent consent
Oregon	18	Notice to parent	16+, parent consent, and working
Pennsylvania	17	Misdemeanor (parents and/or child)	None
Rhode Island	18	Fine or imprisonment	16+ and parent consent
South Carolina	17	Fine or imprisonment	Need to work
Tennessee	17	Misdemeanor (parents and/or child), truancy school	None
Texas	18	Misdemeanor (parents and/or child), truancy school	None
Utah	18	Misdemeanor (parents and/or child), truancy school	16+ and working
Virginia	18	Misdemeanor (parents and/or child)	Parent consent
Washington	18	Misdemeanor (parents and/or child) social and rehabilitation service (parent and/or child)	16+ and working
Wisconsin	18	Fine or imprisonment	None

Table 3.2   School attainment by school leaving age faced at age 16, 2000–2005

	School leaving age faced at age 16		
	16	17	18
Fraction of sixteen-year-olds in school during school year	96.6	96.3	97.1
Fraction of seventeen-year-olds in school during school year	92.3	92.4	93.9
Fraction of eighteen-year-olds in school during school year	75.4	75.2	74.8
Fraction of twenty- to twenty-four-year-olds with high school degree or some post-secondary	88.9	87.2	89.6
Fraction of twenty- to twenty-four-year-olds with some post-secondary	54.7	52.6	55.4

Notes: Data are from the NBER's extracts of the Merged Outgoing Rotation Files of the Current Population Survey. The years included for this table are for 2000 to 2005. The "In School" variable is equal to one if individual is coded as being enrolled part-time or full-time in school the week of the survey.

truancy is not severe enough to deter them. Administrators may be reluctant to pursue court action, especially in cases where students are disruptive in class and do not appear interested in school. In virtually every state, the primary action when a student begins to disengage from school (through absenteeism) is to notify a parent or guardian and counsel him or her to encourage the child to attend. Some states require parents to pay fines or even face imprisonment for a child that regularly skips school. Children themselves can face termination of driving privileges (see Burke 2005), community service, or be forced to attend a juvenile detention facility. In practice, only a fraction of habitually truant students are disciplined by the state. In Tennessee, for example, most attendance officers believe that their caseload is too large and that they face difficulty contacting truant students' families (Palmisano and Potts 2004). Only general guidelines are provided by the state to determine habitual truancy, and schools have little financial incentive to improve attendance.

If the minimum school leaving age affects at least some would-be dropouts, we should expect to observe more sixteen- and seventeen-year-olds in school in states that have school leaving ages of seventeen or eighteen, respectively, compared to states with a leaving age of sixteen. In states that provide no exceptions to a leaving age of eighteen, we should observe virtually all sixteen- and seventeen-year-olds in school. To check this, table 3.2 presents the fraction of sixteen-, seventeen-, and eighteen-year-olds in school during the 2000 to 2005 school year, categorized by the minimum leaving age faced at age sixteen.[3]

3. These proportions are calculated from responses in the 2000 to 2005 outgoing rotation files of the Current Population Survey, excluding the months of June, July, and August and using population weights. I matched the state school leaving ages to the year in which an individual was sixteen in their current state of residence. The data appendix provides additional details.

Most sixteen-year-olds are in school regardless of the minimum school leaving age they face. The fraction of students in school at age sixteen is about the same across states with different school leaving ages. The fraction of seventeen-year-olds in school does not spike up for youths in states with a school leaving age of eighteen, as we might expect to see: 6.1 percent of seventeen-year-olds in states with a leaving age of eighteen have left, compared to 7.7 percent in states with a leaving age of sixteen. Table 3.2 also presents education attainment measures for twenty- to twenty-four-year-olds. There are no substantial differences in the dropout rate or attainment rate across states with different leaving ages. One reason for this may be states that tend to have more restrictive compulsory schooling laws also have more students that tend to drop out, and this limits our ability to observe the effects of these age limits. I address this in the next section. The finding that many students leave before the legally mandated age suggests the exceptions, exemptions, and lack of enforcement of these laws weakens their effectiveness in keeping youths in school.

3.3   The Effect of Raising the School Leaving Age on School Enrollment and Attainment

This section presents a more systematic analysis of the effects of recent U.S. changes in school leaving ages on school enrollment and attainment. The appendix provides details of the data. The analysis uses the monthly outgoing rotation files of the Current Population Survey (CPS) between 1979 and 2005 and the American Community Surveys (ACS) between 2000 and 2005. To focus on recent changes to compulsory schooling laws, the baseline sample is limited to those aged twenty to twenty-nine. Individuals are matched to the state school leaving age faced at age sixteen using state of residence (for the CPS sample) or state of birth (for the ACS sample).[4]

The main regression model to estimate the effects of raising the school leaving age above sixteen is the following:

$$(1) \qquad EDUC_{iscy} = \gamma(DROPAGE_{sc} > 16) + \delta_s + \delta_c + \delta_y + \delta_{iscy},$$

where $EDUC_{iscy}$ is a measure of education attainment measure for individual i, in state or from state s, born in year c, surveyed in year y. The variable $DROPAGE_{sc} > 16$ is equal to one if the individual faced a school leaving age above sixteen when he or she was sixteen years old in state s. The variable equals zero otherwise, and e_{iscy} is the error term. The regression includes fixed effects for state of residence (CPS) or birth (ACS), birth cohort, and survey year. These variables control for perennial differences in state education

---

4. I include immigrants that arrived before age seventeen in the ACS and all immigrants in the CPS, since most twenty- to twenty-nine-year-old immigrants faced compulsory schooling laws in the United States. The results are similar excluding them, and available on request.

attainment that do not vary over time, as well as national trends in education attainment that do vary over time. I also examine the results with linear birth cohort trends for each state.[5]

The variable of interest, γ, is the average effect of facing a school leaving age above sixteen on educational attainment. Table 3.3 shows estimates of γ under alternative specifications using the CPS sample of twenty- to twenty-nine-year-olds who were sixteen years old between 1970 and 2001. Table 3.4 shows the same estimates using the ACS sample of twenty- to twenty-nine-year-olds who were sixteen years old between 1987 and 2001. The appendix tables show similar results with alternative sample specifications.

The first column of table 3.3 replaces the state fixed effects in equation (1) with nine region fixed effects. The identification of the compulsory schooling effects in this case comes not just from changes in the school leaving laws, but also from state-to-state variation in the leaving age within a region. I estimate, on average, raising the school leaving age above sixteen increases an individual's years of schooling by 0.13 years. Replacing region with state fixed effects in column (5) controls for average differences in attainment across states over the entire period. This specification (equation [1]) does not significantly change the estimated effect. Finally, in column (6), I add state-specific linear cohort trends to examine the possibility the results are driven by state differences in overall education attainment trends. This cautious specification makes estimation of the compulsory schooling law effect more difficult, since some of the trends may absorb some of the effects. Under this specification, however, we still identify a similar effect—0.11 more years of schooling—from higher school leaving laws.

The second and third rows show the same results, but with high school completion and college enrollment as outcome variables. The results also indicate that raising the school leaving age above sixteen decreases the dropout rate and increases college or university entrance. From the main specification in column (5), raising the school leaving age above sixteen decreases the fraction of twenty- to twenty-four-year-olds with less education than a high school degree by 1.3 percentage points. Even though compulsory schooling laws do not mandate any college education, I also find raising the school leaving age above sixteen increases the fraction of youths with at least some college or university. One story consistent with this finding is that some individuals compelled to stay longer in high school become more interested in college education or view higher education as less daunting an obstacle

5. The data are first aggregated into cell means at the state, cohort, survey year, gender, and race level, and weighted by cell population size. The standard-errors reported cluster for state · cohort-specific heteroskedasticity using the Huber-White methodology. Standard errors from clustering only by state are larger, but the first stage and second stage estimates remain statistically significant at the 10 percent p-value criteria for most of the school attainment and labor market outcome variables.

Table 3.3 The effects of recent compulsory schooling laws on school attainment, ages 20–29, year at age 16 between 1970 to 2001, current population survey data

		Regression coefficient (standard error in parenthesis)					
	Mean	Dropout age faced at age 16			Dummy for faced dropout age > 16 at age 16		
Dependent variable	(standard deviation)						
Years of schooling	13.0	0.1239	0.128	0.1088	0.0645	0.0721	0.0655
	(2.4)	(0.0198)***	(0.0197)***	(0.0276)***	(0.0093)***	(0.0130)***	(0.0158)***
Never completed high school	0.134	−0.0129	−0.0165	−0.0181	−0.0148	−0.0064	−0.0108
	(0.340)	(0.0027)***	(0.0029)***	(0.0038)***	(0.0012)***	(0.0018)***	(0.0022)***
Some college	0.489	0.015	0.0093	0.0192	−0.0042	0.0066	0.0111
	(0.500)	(0.0035)***	(0.0033)***	(0.0047)***	(0.0019)**	(0.0022)***	(0.0027)***
Cell size observations		44,946	44,946	44,946	44,946	44,946	44,946
Region fixed effects		No	Yes	No	Yes	No	No
State fixed effects		Yes	No	Yes	No	Yes	Yes
Cohort fixed effects		Yes	Yes	No	Yes	Yes	No
Survey year fixed effects		Yes	Yes	Yes	Yes	Yes	Yes
Cohort · state linear trend		No	No	Yes	No	No	Yes

Notes: Data are from the NBER's extracts of the 1979–2005 Merged Outgoing Rotation Files of the Current Population Survey and collapsed into cell means by year of birth, state of residence, age, race, and gender (regressions are weighted by cell population size). All regressions include year of birth fixed effects, and region or state fixed effects where indicated. The sample includes twenty- to twenty-nine-year-olds who were aged sixteen between 1970 and 2001. Standard errors are clustered by state and year of birth.

***Significant at the 1 percent level.

**Significant at the 5 percent level.

*Significant at the 10 percent level.

Table 3.4 The effects of recent compulsory schooling laws on school attainment, ages 20–29, year at age 16 between 1987 to 2001, American Community Survey Data

Dependent variable	Mean (standard deviation)	Regression coefficient (standard error in parenthesis)					
		Dropout age faced at age 16			Dummy for faced dropout age > 16 at age 16		
Years of schooling	13.4	0.09	0.0878	0.0045	0.0548	0.0651	0.0234
	(2.4)	(0.0240)***	(0.0341)**	(0.0504)	(0.0105)***	(0.0142)***	(0.0215)
Never completed high school	0.123	−0.0117	−0.0124	0.0002	−0.0146	−0.0078	−0.0028
	(0.329)	(0.0038)***	(0.0043)***	(0.0042)	(0.0013)***	(0.0019)***	(0.0021)
Some college	0.576	0.0105	0.0014	−0.0031	0.0016	0.003	0.0027
	(0.494)	(0.0039)***	(0.0049)	(0.0067)	(0.0022)	(0.0021)	(0.0027)
Cell size observations		64,948	64,948	64,948	64,948	64,948	64,948
Region fixed effects		Yes	No	No	Yes	No	No
State fixed effects		No	Yes	Yes	No	Yes	Yes
Cohort fixed effects		Yes	Yes	No	Yes	No	No
Survey year fixed effects		Yes	Yes	Yes	Yes	Yes	Yes
Cohort · state linear trend		No	No	Yes	No	Yes	Yes

Notes: Data are from the 2000–2005 American Community Surveys and collapsed into cell means by year of birth, state of residence, age, race, and gender (regressions are weighted by cell population size). All regressions include year of birth fixed effects, and region or state fixed effects where indicated. The sample includes twenty- to twenty-nine-year-olds who were aged sixteen between 1987 and 2001. Standard errors are clustered by state and year of birth.

***Significant at the 1 percent level.

**Significant at the 5 percent level.

*Significant at the 10 percent level.

Table 3.5   Differences in compulsory schooling law effects on total years of schooling completed, by exceptions to law and time

	Data: Current Population Surveys			
	Differences by states with law exemptions and small punishments			
Dropout age above 16	0.1239	0.0841	0.1323	0.0841
	(0.0198)***	(0.0207)***	(0.0208)***	(0.0207)***
Can leave earlier with parental consent or work permit		0.0796 (0.0380)**		0.1037 (0.0403)**
Misdemeanor or no punishment			−0.126 (0.0499)**	−0.1785 (0.0570)***
Cell size observations	44,946	44,946	44,946	44,946
	Data: American Community Surveys			
	Differences by states with law exemptions and small punishments			
Dropout age above 16	0.0878	0.0455	0.0897	0.045
	(0.0341)**	(0.0664)	(0.0347)***	(0.0665)
Can leave earlier with parental consent or work permit		0.0565 (0.0787)		0.0602 (0.0793)
Misdemeanor or no punishment			−0.1021 (0.0664)	−0.1197 (0.0686)*
Cell size observations	64,948	64,948	64,948	64,948

Notes: Data are from the 1979–2005 Merged Outgoing Rotation Files of the Current Population Survey and the 2000–2005 American Community Surveys. Data are collapsed into cell means by year of birth, state of residence, age, race, and gender (regressions are weighted by cell population size). All regressions include year of birth and state fixed effects (state of residence for CPS and state of birth for ACS). The sample includes twenty- to twenty-nine-year-olds who were aged sixteen between 1970 and 2001 in the CPS and between 1987 and 2001 in the ACS. Standard errors are clustered by state and year of birth.
***Significant at the 1 percent level.
**Significant at the 5 percent level.
*Significant at the 10 percent level.

than when they were younger.[6] The analogous estimates in table 3.4 using the ACS data are similar, but less precise.

Table 3.5 explores whether the estimated effects from raising the minimum school leaving age are weaker for states that allow exemptions or small punishments. The results are mixed. Column (2) shows the estimated effects from raising the compulsory schooling age above sixteen for states that allow early exit with a working permit or parental consent, compared to states that do not allow early exit. The results indicate that states with exemptions are not associated with weaker school attainment effects from raising the

6. The other set of results in the first three columns use the actual school leaving age as the dependent variable (sixteen, seventeen, or eighteen) instead of the dummy variable indicating a school leaving age above sixteen for the main specification. The results are similar and imply greater school attainment effects for states that raised their school leaving age to eighteen instead of seventeen.

school leaving age. In fact, these show impact on school attainment from raising the age minimum. On the other hand, column (3) shows the estimated effects from raising the compulsory schooling age above sixteen for states that associate truancy with a misdemeanor charge or no punishment at all. The estimated effects are smaller and statistically insignificant from zero compared to other states. Taken together, the impact from weaker laws on raising the school leaving age is not clear cut.

What is notable about these findings is that the effects are small, given that the strict interpretation of the law implies virtually no teenager should be allowed to leave before age sixteen. The other notable finding is that the more restrictive compulsory schooling laws also appear to increase college attainment. This is not the case in earlier studies (e.g., Acemoglu and Angrist 2001). The option of college may seem more possible from the standpoint of a high school graduate compared to a high school dropout.

3.4   Methodology for Estimating the Effect of Raising the School Leaving Age on Subsequent Employment and Wages, among Those Affected by the Law Change

This section briefly describes the methodology for estimating the effects of compulsory schooling from raising the school leaving age above sixteen on unemployment, earnings, and other labor market outcomes.

Consider the same regression model in equation (1), but using unemployment status as the dependent variable:

$$(2) \quad UNEMP_{iscy} = \lambda(DROPAGE_{sc} > 16) + u_s + u_c + u_s + u_y + u_{iscy},$$

where $UNEMP_{iscy}$ is equal to one if individual i (now older), living in state s, born in year c, surveyed in year y is unemployed, zero otherwise. Equation (2) is known as the reduced form equation. The coefficient λ captures the average effect of raising the school leaving age above sixteen on the unemployment rate for *everyone* in the sample. Of course, not everyone is affected by the change in law. What we want to estimate instead is the impact from an increase in the dropout age for those that end up taking one more year of school. For example, suppose the increase in the dropout age makes 50 percent of the population take one more year of school ($\gamma = 0.50$). We can estimate the impact of raising the school leaving age on those 50 percent by dividing λ by 0.50. If an increase in the dropout age increases total number of school years by 0.50 and an increase in the dropout age decreases average unemployment by 0.02, then we can deduce the effect from taking one more year of compulsory schooling decreases average unemployment by 0.04 (0.02/0.50), or λ/γ.

Thus, to estimate the effect of one more year of compulsory schooling (from raising the school leaving age above sixteen), we simply rescale our estimate in (2) by the estimated increase in school years in (1). Another way of looking at this is to suppose raising the school leaving age caused everyone to take one more year of school. Then our estimate in (2) would give us exactly the effect of one more year of school on the likelihood of being unemployed ($\lambda/1$).

For this approach to work, changes in the school leaving age must be unrelated to changes in state demographic or institutional characteristics that also affect school attainment. Also, if raising the school leaving age does not affect an individual's education attainment (e.g., whether facing a dropout age of sixteen or eighteen, she intends to graduate), raising it also does not affect her unemployment rate. Another way to describe this instrumental variables method is in two stages. In the first stage, we estimate education attainment differences caused only from changes in the school leaving age (the first stage is equation [1]). In the second stage, we estimate:

$$(3) \qquad UNEMP_{iscy} = \beta EDUC\_HAT_{scy} + v_s + v_c + v_y + v_{iscy},$$

where $EDUC\_HAT_{SC}$ is an individual's predicted education based on the first stage. The coefficient β is the average effect from one year of education, caused from a change in the compulsory school leaving age. It is equivalent to λ/γ.

3.5   The Effect of Compulsory Schooling on Subsequent Employment and Wages

Tables 3.6 and 3.7 show estimates of the effects of a year of compulsory schooling on early career outcomes, using the instrumental variables methodology discussed in the last section. The top panels show the reduced form results of the average effects from facing a higher school leaving age on the labor market outcomes for the entire sample, whether affected by the laws or not. The bottom panels show the estimated average effects for just those affected by these laws (those compelled to stay in school). The sample in table 3.6 includes all twenty- to twenty-nine-year-olds in the CPS that were sixteen years old between 1970 and 2001. Table 3.7 uses a similar sample, but from the ACS.[7]

Column (1) shows the results using region fixed effects instead of state fixed effects. This specification lets us estimate the effects of compulsory schooling using cross-section variation in state laws, but requires the assumption that this within-region variation is not related to other factors that could explain education or labor market outcome differences. Table 3.6 indicates that an additional year of compulsory schooling, caused from increasing the

---

7. The first three columns use the dummy variable for whether an individual faced a school leaving above age sixteen as the instrument. The last three columns use the actual dropout age faced as the instrument.

Table 3.6 Reduced form and IV regressions of labor market outcomes and compulsory schooling, ages 20–29, year at age 16 between 1970 and 2001, Current Population Survey Data

Reduced form coefficient

Dependent variable	Mean: full sample (standard deviation)	Dropout age faced at age 16 (1)	Dropout age faced at age 16 (2)	Dropout age faced at age 16 (3)	Dummy for faced dropout age > 16 at age 16 (1)	Dummy for faced dropout age > 16 at age 16 (2)	Dummy for faced dropout age > 16 at age 16 (3)
Unemployed	0.066 (0.249)	−0.0028 (0.0010)***	−0.0045 (0.0012)***	−0.0069 (0.0013)***	−0.0014 (0.0005)***	−0.0018 (0.0007)**	−0.0038 (0.0008)***
Not working	0.199 (0.400)	−0.0159 (0.0020)***	−0.0063 (0.0023)***	−0.0032 (0.0030)	−0.0078 (0.0010)***	−0.0027 (0.0014)*	−0.0004 (0.0017)
Log weekly earnings for those working > 25 hrs/week	9.7 (0.583)	0.0093 (0.0052)*	0.0133 (0.0065)**	0.0235 (0.0060)***	0.0108 (0.0046)**	0.0039 (0.0039)	0.0128 (0.0034)***

Total years of schooling coefficient, instrumented by compulsory schooling law

Dependent variable	Mean: dropout sample (standard deviation)	Instrument: Dropout age faced at age 16 (1)	Instrument: Dropout age faced at age 16 (2)	Instrument: Dropout age faced at age 16 (3)	Instrument: Dropout age > 16 at age 16 (1)	Instrument: Dropout age > 16 at age 16 (2)	Instrument: Dropout age > 16 at age 16 (3)
Unemployed	0.117 (0.322)	−0.0222 (0.0083)***	−0.036 (0.0103)***	−0.0631 (0.0173)***	−0.0219 (0.0074)***	−0.0252 (0.0100)**	−0.0583 (0.0163)***
Not working	0.329 (0.470)	−0.1246 (0.0228)***	−0.0507 (0.0189)***	−0.0289 (0.0262)	−0.1217 (0.0215)***	−0.0372 (0.0198)*	−0.0057 (0.0256)
Log weekly earnings for those working > 25 hrs/week	9.4 (0.525)	0.0722 (0.0391)*	0.1077 (0.0551)*	0.2152 (0.0708)***	0.1114 (0.0427)***	0.0547 (0.0547)	0.1959 (0.0633)***
Cell size observations		44,946	44,946	44,946	44,946	44,946	44,946
Region fixed effects		Yes	No	No	Yes	No	No
State fixed effects		No	Yes	Yes	No	Yes	Yes
Cohort fixed effects		Yes	Yes	Yes	Yes	Yes	Yes
Survey year fixed effects		Yes	Yes	Yes	Yes	Yes	Yes
Cohort · state linear trend		No	Yes	Yes	No	Yes	Yes

Notes: The top panel shows reduced form results from regressing total years of schooling on the dropout age faced at age sixteen. Data are from the 1979–2005 Merged Outgoing Rotation Files of the Current Population Survey and collapsed into cell means by year of birth, state of residence, age, race, and gender (regressions are weighted by cell population size). All regressions include year of birth fixed effects, and region or state fixed effects where indicated. The sample includes twenty- to twenty-nine-year-olds who were aged sixteen between 1970 and 2001. Standard errors are clustered by state and year of birth.

***Significant at the 1 percent level.
**Significant at the 5 percent level.
*Significant at the 10 percent level.

Table 3.7 Reduced form and IV regressions of labor market outcomes and compulsory schooling, ages 20–29, year at age sixteen between 1987 and 2001, American community survey data

Dependent variable	Mean: full sample (standard deviation)	Reduced form coefficient					
		Dropout age faced at age 16			Dummy for faced dropout age > 16 at age 16		
Unemployed	0.094 (0.292)	-0.005 (0.0021)**	-0.0052 (0.0027)*	-0.0051 (0.0038)	-0.0064 (0.0008)***	-0.0015 (0.0015)	-0.0019 (0.0023)
Not working	0.265 (0.441)	-0.0068 (0.0034)**	-0.0102 (0.0048)**	0.0013 (0.0073)	-0.0088 (0.0014)***	0.0049 (0.0019)**	0.0003 (0.0036)
Log weekly earnings for those working > 25 hrs/week	9.892 (0.76)	0.0069 (0.0062)	-0.0072 (0.0122)	0.0159 (0.0282)	0.0016 (0.0029)	0.0053 (0.0044)	0.0005 (0.0132)
Log family income	10.541 (1.04)	0.0006 (0.0092)	0.0373 (0.0106)***	0.0029 (0.0148)	-0.0025 (0.0046)	0.0201 (0.0054)***	0.0068 (0.0085)
In low skilled job for those working > 25 hrs/week	0.284 (0.451)	-0.0056 (0.0025)**	-0.0145 (0.0049)***	0.0046 (0.0085)	-0.0004 (0.0014)	-0.0102 (0.0023)***	0.0017 (0.0042)
Below poverty line	0.153 (0.360)	-0.0029 (0.0025)	-0.0071 (0.0033)**	-0.0025 (0.0046)	-0.0045 (0.0011)***	-0.0037 (0.0015)**	-0.0014 (0.0019)
On welfare	0.020 (0.139)	-0.0013 (0.0009)	-0.0049 (0.0013)***	-0.002 (0.0016)	-0.0003 (0.0004)	-0.0023 (0.0007)***	-0.0017 (0.0008)**

Dependent variable	Mean: Dropout sample (standard deviation)	Total years of schooling coefficient, instrumented by compulsory schooling law					
		Instrument: Dropout age faced at age 16			Instrument: Dropout age > 16 at age 16		
Unemployed	0.218 (0.413)	-0.0522 (0.0194)***	-0.0541 (0.0267)**	-3.5366 (127.8186)	-0.1196 (0.0254)***	-0.0218 (0.0219)	-0.0809 (0.0883)
Not working	0.446 (0.497)	-0.0754 (0.0320)**	-0.1167 (0.0901)	0.0699 (0.0445)	-0.1601 (0.0351)***	-0.075 (0.0395)*	0.014 (0.1615)

Log weekly earnings for those working > 25 hrs/week	9.687	0.1205	−0.3066	−0.0269	0.0719	0.1573	0.0131
	(0.70)	(0.0932)	(0.8596)	(1.0599)	(0.1190)	(0.1074)	(1.6746)
Log family income	10.201	0.0063	0.4185	−0.0683	−0.0436	0.3069	0.2838
	(1.07)	(0.1015)	(0.1580)***	(1.2696)	(0.0846)	(0.0918)***	(0.5434)
In low skilled job for those working > 25 hrs/week	0.524	−0.0983	−0.6311	−0.1536	−0.0172	−0.3058	−0.2295
	(0.499)	(0.0393)**	(0.7139)	(0.1840)	(0.0592)	(0.0918)***	(0.5245)
Below poverty line	0.284	−0.0321	−0.0806	−0.048	−0.0799	−0.0563	−0.0572
	(0.451)	(0.0242)	(0.0321)**	(0.0344)***	(0.0193)***	(0.0218)***	(0.0758)
On welfare	0.054	−0.0142	−0.0554	0.0094	−0.0053	−0.0357	−0.072
	(0.226)	(0.0088)	(0.0204)***	(0.0146)	(0.0070)	(0.0111)***	(0.0817)
Cell size observations		64,948	64,948	64,948	64,948	64,948	64,948
Region fixed effects		Yes	No	No	Yes	No	No
State fixed effects		No	Yes	Yes	No	Yes	Yes
Cohort fixed effects		Yes	Yes	No	Yes	Yes	No
Survey year fixed effects		Yes	Yes	Yes	Yes	Yes	Yes
Cohort · state linear trend		No	No	Yes	No	No	Yes

Notes: The top panel shows reduced form results from regressing total years of schooling on the dropout age faced at age sixteen. Data are from the 2000–2005 American Community Surveys and collapsed into cell means by year of birth, state of residence, age, race, and gender (regressions are weighted by cell population size). All regressions include year of birth fixed effects, and region or state fixed effects where indicated. The sample includes twenty- to twenty-nine-year-olds who were aged sixteen between 1987 and 2001. Standard errors are clustered by state and year of birth.

***Significant at the 1 percent level.

**Significant at the 5 percent level.

*Significant at the 10 percent level.

school leaving age above sixteen, lowers the likelihood of unemployment by 2.2 percentage points.[8] The effect on the likelihood of working at all for this age group is large, but imprecisely estimated.

Column (2) shows the main results that include state fixed effects, so that identification of the effects of compulsory schooling comes only from changes in the minimum school leaving age. A year of compulsory schooling from these law changes decreases the probability of being unemployed by 3.6 percentage points and decreases the probability of not working by 5.1 percentage points. Since some individuals affected by the law changes may still be in school (at the post-secondary level), I measure the effect of compulsory schooling on weekly earnings only for those in the sample working at least twenty-five hours per week. The return to compulsory schooling on weekly earnings is 10.8 percent, an estimate not much different from earlier studies that use older birth cohorts.

Column (3) shows results from estimating the model that allows for underlying linear birth cohort trends for each state. This specification makes the assumption required for causal interpretation of the results more likely, but at the expense of possibly absorbing variation driven by the school leaving ages and making the estimates less precise. Nevertheless, with this model, the estimates for the effects of compulsory schooling on unemployment and not working are similar to those in column (2), and the effects on weekly earnings are greater. Columns (4) to (6) show similar estimates using the actual dropout age faced by individuals at age sixteen as the instrumental variable in equation (1).

The estimated effects using the ACS in table 3.7 are consistent with the CPS results. While the estimates are less precise, the results suggest significant reductions in the likelihood of ending up unemployed, below the poverty line, or on welfare from additional compulsory schooling. The ACS results also hint at higher income effects and a reduction in the likelihood of working in a low-skilled occupation.[9]

Finally, the baseline estimates for the effects of compulsory schooling on overall education attainment and labor market outcomes are shown in appendix tables 3A.1 and 3A.2 under alternative sample specifications. Table 3A.1 indicates increases in the minimum school leaving age had almost identical effects for males and females, but little influence on blacks. An explanation for these racial differences is not readily apparent. Table 3A.2 shows results for different age groups and over different periods. The results are not sensitive to including thirty- to thirty-nine-year-olds, who were affected by earlier law changes than twenty- to twenty-nine-year-olds. The estimated

---

8. Unemployment is defined as not working and looking for work.

9. Individuals are defined as working in low skilled occupations if they are categorized as operatives, service workers, or laborers in the ACS using the 1950 occupation classification (codes between 600 and 920). The ACS also defines individuals with poverty status as those in families with total incomes below the Census poverty line, adjusted for family size.

impact from raising the school leaving age above sixteen is also similar comparing cohorts affected between 1970 and 1985 and those affected between 1986 and 2001.

3.6 Conclusion

This chapter uses recent experiences with raising the school leaving age to seventeen and eighteen to assess whether such policies can increase school attainment and improve career outcomes. The results suggest that recent and more restrictive compulsory schooling laws reduced dropout rates, increased college enrollment, and improved several social economic indicators. Some caution is warranted because focusing on more recent law changes leads to less precision. But the consistent findings with the previous studies are suggestive that compulsory high school at later ages can benefit disadvantaged youth.

States that increased the school leaving age above sixteen saw average years of schooling for twenty- to twenty-nine-year-olds' increase by about 0.13 years, and high school dropout rates fall by about 1.4 percentage points. Raising the age limit also increased college attendance by about 1.5 percent, even though college is not compulsory. Perhaps this finding indicates that would-be dropouts reconsider post-secondary options after getting close to, or completing, a high school degree.

Among students affected by the more restrictive laws, I estimate that additional compulsory schooling significantly improved their early career outcomes by lowering the likelihood of being unemployed and increasing earnings, on average. These individuals were also less likely to fall below the poverty line and less likely to receive welfare.

Exceptions, leniency, and weak consequences for truancy substantially weakened the effectiveness of these laws in increasing school attainment. Exceptions may be desirable because some students would obviously not benefit from staying on. The results in this chapter do not capture whether those students for whom exceptions were made gain from being forced to stay. While allowing exceptions might be necessary, the results suggest that more resolve may be needed in cases where students begin to disengage from high school. Compulsory schooling laws could exist in the backdrop in an environment where students do not consider leaving school before the minimum possible age because virtually no one does. Greater initial enforcement may help establish an acceptance from youth to stay in school and limit the need to enforce such laws in the future. Students may also find it easier to accept staying if schools also offer more curriculum choice (offering more trait-based training, for example), as some governments have already done (for example, in the province of Ontario, Canada).

Finding large gains to individuals from compelling them to stay in school raises the question of why dropouts drop out in the first place. Why do young persons leave school early if staying on generates attractive gains, on average, to their careers? The possibility that students cannot afford to stay in high school seems unlikely. Many dropouts do not work. Among sixteen- and seventeen-year-olds recorded in the 2000 Census as not in school, only 55 percent are in the labor force, and 90 percent still live at home with parents.

Several alternative explanations for dropout behavior exist. First, dropouts may simply abhor school. Poor classroom performance and condescending attitudes from other students and teachers may make students want to leave as soon as possible, even at the expense of forgoing large returns (Lee and Burkam 2003). Removing reasons for school distaste, in this case, could go a long way in reducing dropout rates. Second, dropouts may be myopic. Myopic students that temporarily downplay or ignore future consequences of their decisions—as considered by Laibson (1997) and O'Donoghue and Rabin (1999)—may prefer dropping out to staying on but later prefer staying on to dropping out. A third alternative is that cultural or peer pressures might dominate adolescent decision making and lead to dropout behavior. Cultural norms that devalue schooling, a lack of emotional support, or low acceptance for higher education among peers may exacerbate students' distaste for school beyond the minimum (e.g., Akerlof and Kranton 2002; Coleman 1961). A final consideration is that students may simply mispredict, underestimating the real expected benefit from staying in school longer. Students' guesses about gains from schooling are often wildly off the mark from those estimated by social scientists (e.g., Dominitz, Fischoff, and Manski 2000). Teenagers from more disadvantaged family backgrounds are more likely to predict lower gains from additional schooling than those from more affluent families—not just for high school, but higher education as well. Perhaps the main reason why students from low-income households more often drop out or fail to continue on to college is not poverty per se, or debt aversion, but a systematic tendency among this group to overestimate the costs and underestimate the benefits of education.[10]

Raising the school leaving age may offer an effective and affordable means to increase education attainment among the least educated and improve their subsequent employment circumstances and earnings potential.

Data Appendix

The Current Population Survey (CPS) is a large, nationally representative data set and tracks school attainment and labor force outcomes monthly for over twenty-five years. It records an individual's state of residence, which

10. For a more detailed discussion about the implications of these results for explaining dropout behavior, see Oreopoulos (2007).

is used in this chapter to predict the minimum school leaving age faced at sixteen years of age. Since an individual may have moved before sixteen, this chapter also estimates effects using American Community Survey (ACS) data, which contain information on state of birth. The ACS data is smaller, but records several additional labor market outcome variables not included in the CPS.

The National Bureau of Economic Research's extracts of the CPS outgoing rotation files cover the period between 1979 and 2005. The CPS, administered by the U.S. Bureau of Labor Statistics, collects monthly household data about employment and labor markets for about 30,000 nationally representative individuals aged sixteen. It is the source of the used to calculate the unemployment rate in the United States. The extract contains variables related to employment, such as hours worked, earnings, industry, occupation, education, and unionization. The extracts also contain many background variables: age, sex, race, ethnicity, and geographic location.

Every household that enters the CPS is interviewed each month for four months, then ignored for eight months, then interviewed again for four more months. In a given month, there are about 120,000 individuals sampled, but only one-fourth of the sample exit the survey and are not interviewed the following month. Usual weekly hours/earning questions are asked only to households in their fourth and eighth interview. Data from these outgoing interviews are combined for every year between 1979 and 2005 to create the extract, for a total sample size over 8.6 million.[11] To examine recent compulsory school law changes, the base data set includes only sixteen- to twenty-nine-year-olds aged sixteen between 1970 and 2001. This restriction cuts the sample down to about 1.8 million.

Some of the variable definitions change from survey to survey and were adjusted to make year to year comparisons consistent. The years of schooling variable is the highest grade completed plus the number of years of college. This variable is recorded in every CPS survey from 1979 to 1992 (the gradeat variable), and is capped at 17. Following Acemoglu and Angrist (2001), I combine this variable with the education categorical variable from the 1992 survey onwards (grade 92) by assigning imputed years of schooling to each category for males and females using the imputation method in Park (1994). A high school dropout is defined as an individual with less than twelve years of schooling. An individual with some college education is defined as an individual with more than twelve years of schooling. An individual in school is defined as an individual reporting in the CPS being enrolled in high school or college in the previous week, excluding surveys

11. Individuals in these files are interviewed twice, so the combined data set contains two observations for almost all individuals one year apart. The analysis adjusts for heteroskedasticity from having the same individual in the data set twice by first aggregating the entire data set into cells by survey year, birth cohort, gender, and region, and uses Huber-White standard errors clustered at the cohort-region level.

taken in the months between June and August. This variable is only available from the CPS since 1984 and for individuals aged twenty-four or less.

I use the NBER extract's imputed weekly earnings (earnwke), which is actual weekly earnings among those who report it, and reported hourly earnings times hours worked per week for individuals who report earnings in hours. Definitions of unemployment (not working but looking for work) and not working come directly from the imputed labor force participation measures of the CPS (ftpt79, ftpt89, ftpt94).

The 2000 to 2005 American Community Surveys were extracted from the Integrated Public Use Microdata System-USA (IPUMS-USA) website (http://usa.ipums.org/usa/). The ACS is administered by the U.S. Census Bureau and replaces the long form in the decennial census. It is an ongoing, nationally representative survey that included approximately 400,000 persons in 2000, 1.1 million persons between 2001 and 2004, and 2.9 million persons in 2005. As with the more recent education attainment variable in the CPS, the ACS survey records highest grade or highest level of schooling completed. Years of schooling was computed using the highest grade completed for high school dropouts and imputed years of schooling using the method in Park (1994) for high school graduates. The combined ACS sample includes U.S.-born and immigrants that arrived into the country before age seventeen.

The minimum school leaving age data come from various years of the National Center for Education Statistic's (NCES's) Education Digest. Individuals in the CPS were matched according to the minimum school leaving age they would have faced at age sixteen and assuming an individual's high school state was the same as her current state of residence. The CPS does not record state of birth. Individuals in the ACS were matched according to their state of birth, or state of residence for immigrants.

Much of the main analysis in the chapter uses the data collapsed into cell means, aggregated by survey year, birth cohort, state of residence, gender, and race. All regressions and tabulations use either noninstitutional population weights (weight) or "working weights," which reflect the population of individuals working at least twenty-five hours a week.

Table 3A.1   **Compulsory schooling effects by sex and race**

Dependent variable	Full sample	Males	Females	Nonblacks	Blacks
Effect of facing dropout age > 16 on total years of schooling					
Total years of schooling	0.1239	0.1299	0.1201	0.1398	−0.0039
(CPS data)	(0.0198)***	(0.0234)***	(0.0228)***	(0.0227)***	(0.0240)
Cell size observations	44,946	22,281	22,665	25,479	19,467
Total years of schooling	0.0878	0.078	0.0925	0.0955	0.0007
(ACS data)	(0.0341)**	(0.0402)*	(0.0411)**	(0.0379)**	(0.0400)
Cell size observations	64,948	32,537	32,411	44,345	20,603
Estimated effect of year of schooling on labor market outcomes					
Unemployed	−0.036	−0.0337	−0.0392	−0.0301	0.4854
(CPS data)	(0.0103)***	(0.0140)**	(0.0127)***	(0.0094)***	(3.2884)
Not working	−0.0507	−0.0059	−0.0897	−0.0487	0.284
(CPS data)	(0.0189)***	(0.0189)	(0.0270)***	(0.0172)***	(2.5668)
Log weekly earnings for those	0.1077	0.1265	0.0819	0.0873	−4.2359
working > 25 hrs/week	(0.0551)*	(0.0586)**	(0.0583)	(0.0479)*	(25.1092)
(CPS data)					
Unemployed	−0.0541	−0.0469	−0.0625	−0.0184	−0.3473
(ACS data)	(0.0267)**	(0.0420)	(0.0442)	(0.0217)	(0.4950)
Not working	−0.1167	−0.087	−0.1305	−0.1542	−0.5364
(ACS data)	(0.0901)	(0.0782)	(0.1155)	(0.0994)	(34.0168)
Log weekly earnings for those	−0.3066	−0.304	−0.3509	−0.4663	5.1164
working > 25 hrs/week	(0.8596)	(0.9293)	(0.9054)	(1.2287)	(24.7673)
Log family income	0.4185	0.4528	0.4242	0.365	0.3175
(ACS data)	(0.1580)***	(0.2552)*	(0.1796)**	(0.1586)**	(1.0084)
In "low skilled job" for those	−0.6311	−1.0171	−0.3923	−0.7738	−4.4497
working > 25 hrs/week	(0.7139)	(1.8516)	(0.3705)	(1.0202)	(235.1214)
Below poverty line	−0.0806	−0.068	−0.1041	−0.0679	−2.2975
(ACS data)	(0.0321)**	(0.0490)	(0.0468)**	(0.0356)*	(121.9384)
On welfare	−0.0554	−0.0092	−0.1042	−0.0513	0.073
(ACS data)	(0.0204)***	(0.0104)	(0.0415)**	(0.0204)**	(0.230)

Notes: The top panel shows "First Stage" results from regressing total years of schooling on the dropout age faced at age sixteen. Data are from the 2000 to 2005 American Community Surveys and collapsed into cell means by year of birth, state of residence, age, race, and gender (regressions are weighted by cell population size). All regressions include year of birth fixed effects and state fixed effects. Standard errors are clustered by state and year of birth. The second panel shows instrumental variable estimates of labor market outcomes regressed on total years of schooling, with schooling instrumented by the dropout age faced at age sixteen.

***Significant at the 1 percent level.
**Significant at the 5 percent level.
*Significant at the 10 percent level.

Table 3A.2   Sensitivity analysis

Dependent variable						
	Effect of facing dropout age > 16 on total years of schooling					
Total years of schooling (CPS data)	0.1239 (0.0198)***	0.1221 (0.0202)***	0.1203 (0.0162)***	0.1157 (0.0205)***	0.1995 (0.0382)***	0.129051 (0.020)***
Cell size observations	44,946	23,309	75,239	25,084	21,578	44,946
Total years of schooling (ACS data)	0.0878 (0.0341)**	0.0906 (0.0359)**	0.0717 (0.0229)***	n.a.	n.a.	0.0863 (0.0337)**
Cell size observations	64,948	10,290	131,167	n.a.	n.a.	64,948
	Estimated effect of year of schooling on labor market outcomes					
Unemployed (CPS data)	−0.036 (0.0103)***	−0.0297 (0.0126)**	−0.026 (0.0063)***	−0.0944 (0.0191)***	−0.0183 (0.0110)*	−0.0345 (0.0101)***
Not working (CPS data)	−0.0507 (0.0189)***	−0.0236 (0.0185)	−0.0447 (0.0143)***	−0.0747 (0.0217)***	−0.0159 (0.0265)	−0.0522 (0.0189)***
Log weekly earnings for those working > 25 hrs/week (CPS data)	0.1077 (0.0551)*	0.0847 (0.0568)	0.1452 (0.0468)***	0.1659 (0.0640)***	0.1277 (0.0603)**	0.1121 (0.0550)**
Unemployed (ACS data)	−0.0541 (0.0267)**	−0.0701 (0.0333)**	−0.0219 (0.0264)	n.a.	n.a.	−0.0555 (0.0269)**
Not working (ACS data)	−0.1167	−0.0634	−0.1322	n.a.	n.a.	0.1151

	(0901)					
(ACS data)	(0.0901)	(0.0907)	n.a.	(0.0757)*	n.a.	(0.0897)
Log weekly earnings for those working > 25 hrs/week	−0.3066	−0.0225	n.a.	−27.3351	n.a.	−0.2876
	(0.8596)	(0.6498)		(1,567.6844)		(0.7670)
Log family income	0.4185	0.4552	n.a.	0.3521	n.a.	0.4097
(ACS data)	(0.1580)***	(0.1759)***		(0.1286)***		(0.1568)***
In "low skilled job" for those working > 25 hrs/week	−0.6311	−0.534	n.a.	8.6247	n.a.	−0.5497
	(0.7139)	(0.7187)		(130.0150)		(0.5595)
Below poverty line	−0.0806	−0.0981	n.a.	−0.0671	n.a.	−0.082
(ACS data)	(0.0321)**	(0.0382)**		(0.0280)**		(0.0324)**
On welfare	−0.0554	−0.0563	n.a.	−0.0493	n.a.	−0.0533
(ACS data)	(0.0204)***	(0.0217)***		(0.0160)***		(0.0200)***
Age	20–29	20–24	20–29	20–39	20–29	20–29
Years at age 16	1970–2000	1970–2000	1970–1985	1970–2000	1985–2000	1985–2000
Cluster group	State/Cohort	State/Cohort	State/Cohort	State/Cohort	State/Cohort	State/Cohort
Ignore transient law changes?	No	No	No	No	No	Yes

Notes: The top panel shows "First Stage" results form regressing total years of schooling on the dropout age faced at age sixteen. Data are from the 1979–2005 CPS and 2000–2005 ACS and collapsed into cell means by year of birth, state of residence, age, race, and gender (regressions are weighted by cell population size). All regressions include year of birth fixed effects and state fixed effects. The second panel shows instrumental variable estimates of labor market outcomes regressed on total years of schooling, with schooling instrumented by the dropout age faced at age sixteen. The bottom of the table indicates the variation of the sample and standard error cluster group used.

***Significant at the 1 percent level.
**Significant at the 5 percent level.
*Significant at the 10 percent level.

References

Acemoglu, D., and J. Angrist. 2001. How large are human capital externalities? Evidence from compulsory schooling laws. *NBER Macroannual*: 9–59.

Akerlof, G., and R. Kranton. 2002. Identity and schooling: Some lessons for the economics of education. *Journal of Economic Literature* 40 (4): 1167–1201.

Angrist, J. D., and A. Krueger. 1991. Does compulsory school attendance affect schooling and earnings? *Quarterly Journal of Economics* 106 (4): 979–1014.

Black, S. E., P. J. Devereux, and K. G. Salvanes. 2004. Fast times at Ridgemont High? The effect of compulsory schooling laws on teenage births. NBER Working Paper no. 10911. Cambridge, MA: National Bureau of Economic Research, November.

Burke, M. 2005. Sanctions on driving privileges. *StateNotes: Accountability/Sanctions*, Education Commission of the States, March.

Coleman, J. S. 1961. *The adolescent society.* New York: The Free Press.

Dominitz, J., B. Fischoff, and C. F. Manski. 2001. Who are youth at-risk? Expectations evidence in the NLSY-97. In *Social awakenings: Adolescents' behavior as adulthood approaches,* ed. R. T. Michael. New York: Russell Sage Publications.

Harmon, C., and I. Walker. 1995. Estimates of the economic return to schooling for the United Kingdom. *American Economic Review* 85 (5): 1278–86.

Kansas State Department of Education. 2005. Compulsory attendance requirements for a child 16 or 17 years of age. Memo to Superintendents, High School Principals, and Counselors, from Dal M. Dennis, Deputy Commissioner of Education, and Veryl D. Peter, Director, School Finance, March 2.

Laibson, D. 1997. Golden eggs and hyperbolic discounting. *Quarterly Journal of Economics* 112 (2): 443–77.

Lee, V. E., and D. T. Burkam. 2003. Dropping out of high school: The role of school organization and structure. *American Educational Research Journal* 40 (2): 353–93.

Lochner, L., and E. Moretti. 2004. The effect of education on crime: Evidence from prison inmates, arrests, and self-reports. *American Economic Review* 94 (1): 155–89.

National Center for Education Statistics. 2003. The condition of education. Available at: http://nces.ed.gov/.

O'Donoghue, T., and M. Rabin. 1999. Doing it now or later. *American Economic Review* 89 (1): 103–24.

Oreopoulos, P. 2007. Do dropouts drop out too soon? Wealth, health, and happiness from compulsory schooling. *Journal of Public Economics* 91 (11–12): 2213–29.

Palmisano, A., and K. Potts. 2004. Teaching to empty desks: The effects of truancy in Tennessee schools. Report from the Tennessee Office of Education Accountability, January.

Park, J. H. 1994. Estimation of sheepskin effects and returns to schooling using the old and new CPS measures of educational attainment. Working Paper 338, Princeton Industrial Relations Section, December.

II

Health and Healthy Behaviors

Mental Health in Childhood and Human Capital

Janet Currie and Mark Stabile

4.1 Introduction

The prevalence and importance of child mental health problems have been increasingly recognized in recent years. The Methodology for Epidemiology of Mental Disorders in Children and Adolescents (MECA) Study cited in the 1999 U.S. Surgeon General's Report on Mental Health states that approximately one in five children and adolescents in the United States exhibit some impairment from mental or behavioral disorders, 11 percent have significant functional impairments, and 5 percent suffer extreme functional impairment (Shaffer et al. 1996; U.S. Department of Health and Human Services [DHHS] 1999).[1] These are very large numbers of children.

It is surprising, then, that there is relatively little longitudinal research documenting the long-term effects of children's mental health problems, and virtually no research attempting to identify the types of mental health problems that are most deleterious to children's future prospects. Instead, most studies assume that childhood mental health problems will have negative

Janet Currie is the Sami Mnaymneh Professor of Economics at Columbia University, and a research associate of the National Bureau of Economic Research. Mark Stabile is an associate professor of business economics and public policy at the Rotman School of Management and the School of Public Policy and Governance, University of Toronto, and a faculty research fellow of the National Bureau of Economic Research.

The authors are grateful to the Social Science and Humanities Research Council of Canada for financial support. We thank Joshua Goodman and Yeefei Chia for excellent research assistance and Kelly Bedard, Jon Gruber, and Jane Waldfogel for helpful comments. This research was funded by the Annie E. Casey Foundation. We thank them for their support but acknowledge that the findings and conclusions presented in this report are those of the authors alone, and do not necessarily reflect the opinions of the Foundation.

1. Offord et al. (1987) report that in the Canadian province of Ontario, 18 percent of children have moderate to severe emotional or behavioral problems.

effects and work to document the prevalence of these conditions, examine the efficacy of specific interventions (usually in small and nonexperimental settings), or examine the factors that might be related to the development of mental health conditions.

Our work aims to fill this gap in the literature by examining the relationship between several common mental health conditions and future outcomes using large samples of children from the Canadian National Longitudinal Survey of Children and Youth (NLSCY), and the American National Longitudinal Survey of Youth (NLSY). The most common mental health disorders of childhood are anxiety and mood disorders such as depression, and what the Surgeon General's report refers to as "disruptive disorders." Attention Deficit Hyperactivity Disorder (ADHD) is the largest single diagnosis within the second category, followed by aggression or conduct disorders. Hence, we examine indicators for these three types of disorders (depression/anxiety, ADHD, and conduct disorders) in addition to a more general index of behavior problems.

Our work makes several contributions to the existing literature. First, we use "screener" questions that were asked of all children. It is problematic to rely on diagnosed cases, because mental illness may be either overdiagnosed (if, for example, parents seek to justify their child's poor outcomes, or schools have incentives to get low achieving children into special education, Cullen [2003]) or underdiagnosed (given stigma) relevant to its true prevalence. Screener questions focus on specific behaviors that are not linked to any specific mental condition in the questionnaires, and hence are less likely to yield biased responses.[2] While a high score on a screening questionnaire is not equivalent to a clinical diagnosis, in most cases the first step in diagnosing a mental illness would be to administer such a screener to the parents of the troubled child.

---

2. One of the difficulties in diagnosing mental health problems in children is that there are no "objective" criteria that a third party can observe, and often the children themselves cannot accurately report their symptoms. Therefore, mental health problems in children are typically diagnosed by independently asking a child's parents and teachers a series of questions about their behaviors. For example, for ADHD, a parent would be asked nine questions about inattention (including whether the child "often has trouble keeping attention on tasks or play activities" or "often does not seem to listen when spoken to directly"), and nine questions about hyperactivity/impulsivity (such as, "often fidgets with hands or feet or squirms in seat" and "often has trouble waiting one's turn"). For a diagnosis, the parent would have to answer yes to six or more questions in each category, and the practitioner would have to decide that the behavior was inappropriate for the child's developmental level. In addition, the behavior must have persisted for at least six months, started before the child was seven years old, and be causing them impairment in two or more settings. This diagnostic process raises the problem that parents whose children are having difficulties in school may be more likely to focus on their child's behavior and answer yes to screener questions. This would lead us to overstate the relationship between mental health problems and outcomes. To the extent that anxious parents apply the same level of scrutiny to both children, sibling fixed effects models may help to control for differences in parental reporting propensities.

Second, existing longitudinal studies that examine the effects of mental health conditions on child outcomes suggest that they are associated with significantly worse outcomes. But it is possible that poorer outcomes reflect other problems suffered by children with these conditions (or possibly even the effects of other problems that contributed to their poor mental health). For example, in the United States, the estimated prevalence of ADHD is almost twice as high in families with income less than $20,000 compared to families of higher income (Cuffe et al. 2003).[3] The Surgeon General's report concludes that the risk of developing a mental health disorder is higher for children who are prenatally exposed to drugs, alcohol or tobacco, low birth weight children, and those who suffer from abuse or exposure to traumatic events. All of these circumstances are more likely in poor families and may have independent effects on child outcomes. Hence, we use sibling comparisons in order to try to control for omitted factors that might be correlated with both poorer outcomes and mental health conditions.

Third, poor children with mental health conditions may also receive less effective treatment than other children, and thus be at "double jeopardy" for ill effects. Hence, we ask whether the effects of mental health conditions differ by family income, or by mother's education.

We find that behavior problems have a large negative effect on future educational outcomes. The most consistent effects across the two countries are found for ADHD. In models that include sibling fixed effects, anxiety/depression is found to increase grade repetition but has no effect on the other outcomes we examine (such as test scores), suggesting that depression acts through a mechanism other than decreasing cognitive performance. Conduct disorders are also found to have broadly negative effects in the United States, while in Canada they reduce the probability that sixteen- to nineteen-year-old youths are in school but do not have significant effects on other outcomes. We find little evidence that these effects are modified by family income or maternal education.

Our results are robust to controlling for other diagnosed learning disabilities or birth weight or excluding children with other diagnosed learning disabilities, and to different ways of handling treated children. We also find that the effects of mental health conditions on test scores are large relative to those of other chronic conditions of childhood (though both mental health conditions and chronic physical conditions increase the probability of grade repetition). Finally, when we control both for past and current mental health problems, we find that past mental health problems have significant negative

3. Other studies that find a relationship between income and ADHD prevalence include: Korenman, Miller, and Sjaastad (1995); McLeod and Shanahan (1993); Dooley et al. (1998); Dooley and Stewart (2003); Phipps and Curtis (2003); and Lipman, Offord, and Boyle (1994).

effects on test scores, suggesting that the effects of persistent mental health problems in children are cumulative.

4.2   Background

Three strands of the previous literature are relevant to our study. First, and perhaps most similar to our work, are studies that look at the longer term consequences of behavior problems in relatively large samples. Kessler et al. (1995) uses data from the U.S. National Comorbidity Study, which surveyed 8,098 respondents fifteen to fifty-four years old from 1990 to 1992 and assessed their current psychiatric health as well as collecting information about past diagnoses of mental problems. Using retrospective questions about onset, they find that those with early onset psychiatric problems were less likely to have graduated from high school or attended college.

Farmer (1993, 1995) uses data from the British National Child Development Survey (the NCDS), which follows the cohort of all British children born in a single week in March 1958, to examine the consequences of childhood "externalizing" behavioral problems on men's outcomes at age twenty-three. She finds that children who fell into the top decile of an aggregate behavior problems score at ages seven, eleven, or sixteen had lower educational attainment, earnings, and probabilities of employment at age twenty-three.[4] Gregg and Machin (1998) also use the NCDS data and find that behavioral problems at age seven are related to poorer educational attainment at age sixteen, which in turn is associated with poor labor market outcomes at ages twenty-three and thirty-three.

A similar study of a cohort of all New Zealand children born between 1971 and 1973 in Dunedin found that those with behavior problems at age seven to nine were more likely to be unemployed at age fifteen to twenty-one (Caspi et al. 1998). Miech et al. (1999) examine adolescents from this cohort who met diagnostic criteria for four types of disorders—anxiety, depression, hyperactivity, and conduct disorders when they were evaluated at age fifteen—and who were followed up to age twenty. They find that youths with hyperactivity and conduct disorders obtained significantly less schooling, while anxiety and depression had little effect on schooling levels.

More recently, McLeod and Kaiser (2004) use the NLSY data to show that children who had behavior problems at ages six to eight are less likely to graduate from high school or to attend college, even after conditioning on maternal characteristics. Like Miech et al. (1999) they find that in models that included both "internalizing" and "externalizing" behavior problems, only the latter were significant predictors of future outcomes. One limitation

---

4. Her regressions control for parent's aspirations for the child, the type of school attended, the ability group of the child, and whether they are in special education. Hence, her analysis attempts to measure the effects of externalizing behavior over and above its effects on these determinants of educational attainment.

of this study is that it focuses on a relatively small number of children who, given the design of the NLSY, were born primarily to young mothers.

Several studies focus on particular "externalizing" mental health conditions. Mannuzza and Klein (2000) review three studies of the long-term outcomes of children with ADHD. In one study, children diagnosed with ADHD were matched to controls from the same school who had never exhibited *any* behavior problems and had never failed a grade; in a second study, controls were recruited at the nine-year follow-up from nonpsychiatric patients in the same medical center who had never had behavior problems; and in a third study, ADHD children sampled from a range of San Francisco schools were compared to non-ADHD children from the same group of schools.

These comparisons consistently show that the ADHD children had worse outcomes in adolescence and young adulthood than control children. For example, they had completed less schooling and were more likely to have continuing mental health problems. However, by excluding children with any behavior problems from the control groups, the studies might overstate the effects of ADHD. Also, the studies do not address the possibility that the negative outcomes might be caused by other factors related to a diagnosis of ADHD, such as poverty, the presence of other learning disabilities, or the fact that many people diagnosed with ADHD end up in special education.[5]

Currie and Stabile (2006) address these problems by examining the effects of ADHD in sibling fixed effects models. This study builds on the previous one by considering a broader range of mental health problems that might be correlated with ADHD (and so might have contributed to the estimated effects of ADHD in our previous paper).

Perhaps the most widely known studies of the long-term effects of aggression or conduct disorders are associated with Richard Tremblay, who tracked a group of 1,037 boys from kindergarten to age fifteen in Montreal, Canada. He found that boys who were highly aggressive in kindergarten were much more likely to be persistently aggressive, and that this was most true of children of young or less educated mothers (cf. Nagin and Tremblay 1999). Campbell et al. (2006) use data from the NICHD Study of Early Child Care and Youth Development to track children from twenty-four months to twelve years of age, and find that children who persist in moderate or high levels of physical aggression past kindergarten have higher levels of externalizing problems as preteens.

A third strand of related research examines the importance of "noncognitive skills." For example, Blanden, Gregg, and Macmillan (2006) ask whether

---

5. These studies do not address the question of whether outcomes were better for ADHD children who were treated—in fact, there appears to be virtually no research examining the longer-term effects of treatment on achievement (Wigal et al. 1999).

rising returns to noncognitive skills can explain growing income inequality. In their analysis of the 1958 and 1970 British birth cohort data sets, they include characteristics such as "hyper" and "anxious" as well as measures such as "self esteem" and "extrovert" as measures of noncognitive skills and find that rising returns to positive mental characteristics do indeed account for some of the increase in inequality between the two cohorts. However, Heckman, Stixrud, and Urzua (2006) conceptualize noncognitive skills as innate traits (similar to native ability) and measure them using the Rotter Locus of Control Scale and the Rosenberg Self Esteem Scale. They conclude that such noncognitive skills are important determinants of academic and economic success. It seems clear that these measures of noncognitive skills are likely to capture some aspects of mental health as well as innate character traits. In this chapter, we focus on identifiable mental health problems and their long-term impacts.

Our work differs from previous work using longitudinal data sets by emphasizing sibling fixed-effects models to control for omitted variables bias, and by examining interactions between parental SES and the impact of mental health conditions. Fixed effects methods offer a powerful way to control for unobserved or imperfectly measured characteristics of households that might be associated with both a higher probability of mental health problems and with outcomes. We also investigate outcomes in a more recent cohort of children than many of the previous studies, and offer a comparison between the United States and Canada.

The comparison between the United States and Canada is interesting because one might expect the underlying propensity to have mental health conditions to be similar in the United States and Canada, although the reported incidence of diagnosed mental health conditions is lower in Canada and children are less likely to be treated for mental health conditions in Canada than in the United States.[6] Hence, it is of interest to see whether these conditions have similar effects on the prospects of children in the two countries. Moreover, the conditions we focus on are measured slightly differently in the two countries, so the comparison also offers a way to deter-

6. Currie and Stabile (2006) report that both the NLSY and the NLSCY have information about drug and psychiatric treatment for mental health conditions. In 1994, only 1.4 percent of the Canadian children reported drug treatment compared to 3.3 percent of the American children. The NLSCY asks specifically about Ritalin, tranquilizers, and nerve pills, whereas the NLSY asks a more general question about medications used to control activity levels or behavior. The Canadian children were also less likely to have seen a psychiatrist, resulting in overall treatment rates of 4.7 percent, compared to 9.6 percent for the American children. These differences in mean rates of treatment are surprising in view of differences in the insurance regimes in the two countries: in Canada, psychiatric treatment is covered under public health insurance, and all of the provinces have drug plans for low-income families. In the United States, many private insurance plans severely restrict the coverage of mental health treatment, and Medicaid (the public system of health insurance for low income children) offers only limited coverage of psychiatric treatment. The low treatment rates in Canada may reflect greater stigma attached to mental illness, less faith in the efficacy of treatment, or both.

mine whether the results are sensitive to slight differences in the screener questions used.

4.3   Data

We use data from the Canadian National Longitudinal Survey of Children and Youth (NLSCY) and from the American NLSY. The NLSCY is a national longitudinal data set that surveyed 22,831 children ages zero to eleven and their families beginning in 1994. Follow-up surveys were conducted biannually up to 2002. We restrict our sample to those children between the ages of four and eleven in 1994, since only parents of children in this age range completed the ADHD screener. This restriction yields 5,604 children. For analyses that use Canadian math test scores we have a smaller sample of approximately 2,293.[7] We use the NLSCY data to ask how mental health screener scores in 1994 affect outcomes in 2002.

The NLSY began in 1979 with a survey of approximately 6,000 young men and 6,000 young women between the ages of fourteen and twenty-one. These young people have been followed up every year up to the present. In 1986, the NLSY began assessing the children of the female NLSY respondents at two year intervals. Given the differences in the design of the two studies, and the large amounts of missing data in the NLSY, we use the NLSY data to see how the average hyperactivity score measured over the 1990 to 1994 period affects the average outcomes of children in the 1998 to 2004 waves.[8] This procedure yields a maximum sample of 3,758 children. We restrict the age range of the NLSY children to be greater than four and less than twelve years of age in 1994. This makes the Canadian and U.S. samples comparable, and it has the additional benefit of making the NLSY sample more representative. The mothers of the NLSY children represented a nationally representative cohort of fourteen- to twenty-one-year-old women in 1978. But since women of lower socioeconomic status tend to have children at younger ages, the NLSY sample of children is disadvantaged relative to a nationally representative cross section of children, and this problem is more pronounced when the oldest children (who were born to the youngest mothers, on average) are included.

The measurement of mental health conditions is key for our analysis. The diagnostic criterion for the mental health conditions we examine are laid out in the *Diagnostic and Statistical Manual of Mental Disorders, Fourth Edition*

7. In cycle 5 the response rate for the mathematics test was 81 percent. Currie and Stabile (2006) discuss an analysis of the nonresponses to the NLSCY math tests for previous cycles performed by Statistics Canada, which reports little difference between responders and nonresponders at that time. In the cycle 5 codebook, Statistics Canada notes that the response rate is lower in higher grades, and higher among students who performed well on previous cycle math tests.

8. We also tried using the average for 2000 to 2004, but found that this reduced the sample size by at least half.

(American Psychiatric Association 1994). In order to be diagnosed, a child must exhibit several symptoms over some period of time, and must suffer impairment from those symptoms. The measures available in our surveys, as in most surveys, are questions that are asked to parents about symptoms. These questions are subsets of the questions that appear in the DSM-IV for each disorder.

We do not have information about whether the symptoms are causing impairments, but given the way that mental health conditions are diagnosed, it is likely that children who are having problems in school are more likely to be judged to be "impaired" by their symptoms in the school setting than those who are not. Hence, whatever the underlying symptoms, there is likely to be a spurious relationship between schooling achievement and mental health problems, particularly those "externalizing" problems that are likely to be disruptive in a school setting. Given this problem, it is useful to focus on answers to screeners that are administered to all children rather than on diagnosed cases. The administration of parental questionnaires that are similar (though more detailed) than the screeners we use here is almost always the first step in the diagnosis of child mental health conditions.

In the NLSCY data, the parents of all children aged four through eleven in 1994 were asked a series of questions about the child's behavior (we list the questions in the data appendix, which is available online at http://www.nber .org/books/grub07-2/). The responses to these questions are categorized by disorder, and then added together to determine a hyperactivity score (eight questions), an emotional behavior score (eight questions), and an aggressive behavior score (six questions) for the child. We use these three measures separately, as well as creating a combined Behavior Problems Index (BPI) based on these three measures, plus an indirect aggression score, a prosocial behavior score, and a property offense score. This measure is meant to be similar to the overall Behavior Problems Index in the NLSY.[9]

The NLSY Behavior Problems Index is asked to parents of children four to fourteen. There are twenty-six questions asked to all children, and two questions asked only to children who have been to school. Five of the questions can be used to create a hyperactivity subscale, six can be used to form a conduct disorder subscale, and five can be used to form an anxiety/depression subscale. These scores are standardized by the child's age. We convert this standardized score to one that has the same range as the scores in the Canadian data. In addition to the specific subscales, we also estimate models

9. Children in the NLSCY are asked different questions related to the same mental health conditions, depending on their age. To avoid complications in combining scores across ages we focus on children four to eleven in 1994 who are all asked the identical set of questions. Questions also vary slightly across cycles and as a result we take scores for all children from the same cycle. Each score is measured on a scale of either 1 through 16 or 1 through 12 (depending on the number of underlying questions), and the combined behavioral problems index is then simply the added total of these scores reflecting the number of total symptoms the child exhibits across health conditions.

using the overall behavior problems index. More information about how these scores are computed in both samples is available in the data appendix (http://www.nber.org/chapters/c1105.pdf).

In the NLSY, parents were also asked whether their children had any conditions that limited their normal activities. If they answered in the affirmative, parents were asked to identify the limitation. This suite of questions was used to identify children who had been diagnosed with a "learning disability." In the Canadian NLSCY, we use a question on whether the child has been diagnosed with a learning disability that is asked in the series of questions on chronic conditions. Below, we examine the effects of mental health problems in a sample of children (excluding those with diagnosed learning disabilities) in an effort to isolate the effects of particular mental health conditions themselves. We also estimate models that include both behavior problems and other learning disabilities in order to assess the comparative magnitude of the effects. Using the Canadian data on chronic conditions, we also compare the effects of behavior problems to those of chronic physical conditions.

We focus on a set of outcomes that are intended to capture the child's human capital accumulation, broadly defined. These include: grade repetition, mathematics scores, reading scores, and special education. We also examine delinquency, which one might think of as a measure of "negative human capital," since children who are delinquent might be viewed as building capital in antisocial or criminal activities. Further details about the construction of these variables are available in the data appendix, but some general discussion is warranted here.

Grade repetition is an important outcome, in that it is predictive of eventual schooling attainment. Because whether or not someone has ever repeated a grade is a cumulative measure, we ask whether the child repeated a grade between 1994 (when hyperactivity is measured) and 2004. Mathematics and reading scores are two more immediate measures of schooling achievement. The NLSY assesses children using the Peabody Individual Achievement Tests (PIATs) for mathematics and reading recognition. These tests are administered in the home. In the NLSCY, mathematics tests were administered in schools to children in grades two through ten and are based on the Canadian Achievement Tests. The NLSCY began collecting a reading test score in its first three cycles but dropped this measure in subsequent cycles. Therefore, we are only able to include a math test score from the Canadian data for the 2002 cycle. We convert all of the test scores to Z-scores.

The special education variable is available only in the NLSY (and not the NLSCY) for the years used in this study. Special education is an important variable to consider, because special education children tend to lag behind their peers throughout their schooling and are more likely to drop out.

The measure of delinquency that we construct using NLSY data corresponds closely to that used by the U.S. Department of Justice (DIJ) for this age group. The DIJ definition includes illegal drug use or sales, "destroyed property," "stolen something worth more than $50," "committed assault," and whether they have ever been arrested (Puzzanchera 2000). The NLSCY measure is slightly broader in that it also includes questions about whether children have been questioned by police, or have run away from home. Questions about drug use and delinquency are answered by the child in both surveys. Because the questions pertaining to different age groups of children are somewhat different, we estimated models separately for ten- to fourteen-year-olds and fifteen and older children in the NLSY, and for children less than sixteen and sixteen to nineteen in the NLSCY. For simplicity we present delinquency results only for children sixteen to nineteen years old. Results for younger children were similar.

We use total *permanent* household income as our measure of income. This variable is constructed by taking the mean income for all available waves in the NLSCY, and for waves from 1990 to 2004 in the NLSY. We average income over all waves for two reasons. First, child outcomes are likely to be more strongly affected by permanent than by transitory income. Second, the impact of random measurement error in income will be attenuated by averaging.[10]

Means of all of our measures are shown for all children with nonmissing mental health scores in columns (1) and (4) of table 4.1. Columns (2) and (5) show means for the sample of children with siblings, who will be the focus in our fixed effects models. In the NLSY, all siblings in sampled households are interviewed, whereas in the NLSCY, one randomly chosen sibling of the target child is interviewed. Columns (3) and (6) show the number of siblings with a within-family difference in the variable in question, since these are the children who will identify the effects of hyperactivity in our models.

This table suggests that the sibling sample is quite similar to the "full" sample of children, and that there are sufficient numbers of siblings with differences in outcomes to pursue a fixed effects strategy for most of our outcomes. The table highlights similarities and differences between the U.S. and Canadian samples. The U.S. children are slightly older and born to somewhat younger mothers on average, as one would expect. They are also more likely to have mothers who are depressed or who have an activity limitation. All of these differences as well as differences in other observable variables in the two data sets are controlled for in our Ordinary Least Squares (OLS) models, and many of them will be absorbed by family fixed effects in the fixed effects models.

A comparison of the distributions of NLSCY and NLSY scores are shown in table 4.2. Across all measures, the children in the NLSCY sample are more

10. In cases where the household income is not reported, the NLSCY imputes it. We include a dummy variable for the imputation of household income in all of our analyses. We also reestimated all our analyses, omitting individuals for whom income had been imputed in order to be sure that there was nothing peculiar about the income imputation process. Our analyses are robust to these checks.

Table 4.1   Means table for sample of children with all behavioral scores nonmissing

	U.S.			Canada		
	Complete sample	Sibling sample	# of siblings with differences	Complete sample	Sibling sample	# of siblings with differences
U.S./Canada behavioral scores (1994)						
Total/Combined	6.837	6.833	2,340	3.862	3.845	2,260
Hyperactivity	5.150	5.023	2,300	4.648	4.404	2,040
Antisocial/Aggression	4.865	4.943	2,291	1.439	1.504	1,546
Depressed/Emotional disorder	4.529	4.553	2,316	2.562	2.419	1,820
Outcomes						
Young adult delinquency	0.462	0.459	888	0.368	0.359	152
Grade repetition	0.081	0.083	348	0.096	0.082	280
In school	0.833	0.835	322	0.818	0.863	106
Standardized math score	0.034	0.007	1,346	0.195	0.258	412
Standardized reading score	0.213	0.156	1,340			
Enrolled in special education	0.085	0.087	200			
Robustness covariates (1994)						
Child undergoing any treatment	0.093	0.094	337	0.045	0.042	176
Child has learning disability	0.025	0.026	122	0.025	0.026	116
Other covariates (1994)						
Age of child	8.114	8.129		7.310	7.273	
Male child	0.514	0.514		0.494	0.495	
Firstborn child	0.385	0.297		0.456	0.362	
Permanent income ($100,000)	0.522	0.523		0.651	0.686	
Mother has less than high school education	0.223	0.225		0.211	0.186	
Ln(Family size)	1.434	1.525		1.429	1.495	
Mother teen at child's birth	0.039	0.044		0.042	0.027	
Mother's age at child's birth	24.854	24.762		27.476	27.551	
Mother depressed or has activity limitation	0.232	0.223		0.156	0.146	
Mother is immigrant	0.080	0.085		0.074	0.075	
Two-parent household	0.830	0.847		0.878	0.912	
Number of children in sample	3,758	2,358		5,604	2,374	

Notes: We measure all behavioral scores, robustness covariates, and other covariates in 1994 for Canadian data and over the 1990–1994 interval for U.S. data. Outcomes are measured in 2002 for Canadian data and over the 1998–2004 interval for U.S. data (except for permanent income, which is averaged for both countries over all available years). For further details on the definitions and constructions of these variables, see the data appendix.

Table 4.2   Distribution of behavioral scores (% of children with each score)

Score	Total/Combined		Hyperactivity		Antisocial/Aggression		Depressed/Emotional disorder	
	U.S.	Canada	U.S.	Canada	U.S.	Canada	U.S.	Canada
0	0.93	1.00	11.63	10.30	8.30	43.18	17.03	24.52
1	2.34	8.12	6.17	11.71	13.84	22.84	4.34	18.72
2	3.19	14.10	7.13	11.22	8.14	12.92	7.53	15.95
3	5.06	24.18	9.90	10.76	7.45	7.74	7.00	11.92
4	8.46	21.32	10.40	9.92	12.59	4.93	18.65	8.74
5	11.12	13.95	6.95	8.64	8.99	3.48	9.50	6.28
6	15.43	7.48	13.60	9.08	7.82	2.44	7.69	5.30
7	15.22	4.84	7.08	7.73	11.07	1.09	11.20	3.23
8	11.26	2.57	11.15	6.51	5.96	0.59	5.30	2.57
9	10.24	0.00	4.60	4.39	4.39	0.32	4.15	1.20
10	6.17	1.34	4.28	3.14	4.66	0.20	3.62	0.64
11	4.63	0.50	3.17	2.11	2.63	0.15	1.57	0.29
12	2.90	0.36	1.92	1.28	1.57	0.12	1.57	0.37
13	1.17	0.16	1.30	1.23	1.68	0.00	0.48	0.18
14 to 16	1.86	0.09	0.72	1.98	0.91	0.00	0.37	0.10

Notes: Canadian children are assigned integer scores from 0 to 16. American children's scores have been scaled to fit in this range, then rounded to the nearest integer for purposes of this table. For further details, see the data appendix.

Table 4.3   Correlations between behavioral scores and learning disability in U.S. sample

	Total	Hyperactivity	Antisocial	Depressed	Learning disability
Total	1.00				
Hyperactivity	0.80	1.00			
Antisocial	0.78	0.57	1.00		
Depressed	0.77	0.52	0.49	1.00	
Learning disability	0.16	0.18	0.11	0.10	1.00

likely to have scores in the lowest part of the distribution. For the BPI, for example, approximately 30 percent of the Canadian sample has a score of 0 through 2, whereas approximately 11 percent of the U.S. sample falls in this range. While the ninetieth percentile of the hyperactivity distribution is similar across the two samples (nine out of sixteen for NLSCY and ten out of sixteen for the NLSY), the ninetieth percentile for the conduct/aggression scores and the depression/emotional scores are lower in Canada. This is also reflected in the BPI score distribution, which include these scores as component parts. Table 4.3 shows that while the measures are correlated with one another, there is unique information about the child in each measure. The correlations between hyperactivity, conduct disorder, and depression are all approximately 0.5. The correlations between the BPI, which includes these measures, and any one measure are considerably higher, between 0.7 and 0.8. It is interesting that correlations between the various types of behavior problems and other learning disabilities are rather low. The strongest correlation is between other learning disabilities and ADHD, at .18.

An important question is whether we expect the effect of mental health symptoms to be roughly linear, or whether scores above some threshold have much more deleterious effects? People often think about illness in terms of thresholds—only people with blood pressure above a set cutoff are diagnosed with high blood pressure, and only people whose insulin function is subject to a certain degree of impairment are diagnosed with diabetes. However, in both of these examples, recent research has shown that persons with readings below the relevant thresholds for diagnosis still suffer from negative effects. This could also be the case with mental health problems.

Figure 4.1 shows nonparametric Lowess plots of outcomes against our behavior scores for the United States and Canada. There are two striking things about these pictures. First, for grade repetition, math score, and delinquent behavior they are remarkably similar for the United States and Canada despite differences in samples, educational systems, variable definitions, and so on. Second, all of the outcomes except delinquency and remaining in school change approximately linearly with mental health scores. This observation suggests that even children with scores low enough that they would never be diagnosed with a problem may nevertheless suffer ill effects of certain behaviors. Hence, in what follows, we focus on the linear scores.

4.4 Methods

We begin by estimating OLS models of the relationship between our behavioral scores in 1994 and future outcomes, controlling for a wide range of other potentially confounding variables, including permanent income; maternal health status, education, and family structure (in 1994); child age (single year of age dummies), whether the child is firstborn, and sex. These models have the following form:

$$(1) \qquad outcome_i = \alpha + \beta \mathbf{MENTAL94}_i + \lambda \mathbf{X94}_i + \varepsilon_i,$$

where *outcome* is one of the outcomes described previously, **MENTAL94** is a vector of the three child mental health scores, and **X** is the vector of covariates previously described. If high scores on the screener are positively correlated with other factors that have a negative effect on child outcomes, then these estimates will overstate the true effect of poor mental health.

We next attempt to control for unobserved heterogeneity by estimating family fixed effects models:

$$(2) \qquad outcome_{if} = \alpha + \beta \mathbf{MENTAL94}_{if} + \lambda \mathbf{Z94}_{if} + \mu_f + \varepsilon_{if}.$$

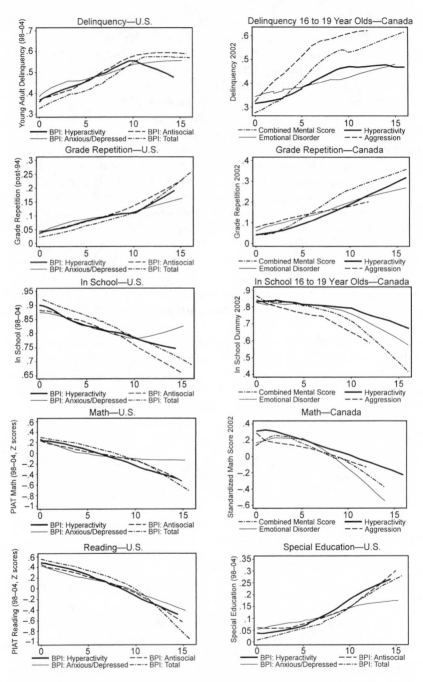

Fig. 4.1   The relationship between mental health measure and outcomes

In these models, the **Z** vector is similar to **X** but omits factors common to both siblings, and the f subscript indexes families. A comparison of (1) and (2) will indicate whether OLS estimates are driven by omitted variables at the family level. Evidently, there may be individual-level factors that are important and that will not be captured by family fixed effects.[11] However, it is impractical to estimate models with child fixed effects because externalizing mental health problems like ADHD and conduct disorder often manifest themselves before the child's seventh birthday and exhibit considerable stability over time.[12] Given the crudeness of our measures, changes in these scores over time for the same child could easily reflect measurement error, rather than true changes in mental health status.

If a high mental health problem score for one sibling has negative effects on the achievement of other siblings in the household, then the difference between the two siblings will provide an under-estimate of the effects of the deleterious effects of mental health problems. Estimates of (2) may also be biased downwards by random measurement error in the mental health scores. Measurement error is a potentially important problem in this and all of the past studies relying on parental reports of children's mental health disorders (cf. Offord et al. 1987; Garrett 1996; Glied et al. 1997).

One way to judge the importance of measurement error is to compare the OLS and fixed effects estimates. If we believe that mental health status is likely to be similar between siblings, then the measured within family variation may be more "noisy" than the between family variation. In this case we might expect increased attenuation bias in the fixed effects estimates. However, as we show following, where they are statistically significant, the OLS and fixed effects estimates are generally similar so that measurement error (or potential spillover effects, as noted previously) may not be such an important problem.

A third potential problem is that a small number of children in our samples are being treated for behavior problems, but it is difficult to tell exactly what they are being treated for using our data. To the extent that treatment is effective in altering behavior, children who are being treated will have lower

---

11. Because of the way that the NLSY sample was constructed, it is possible for children to have been measured some years apart. We have also reestimated the models shown in table 4.4, keeping only siblings who are within three years of age. This reduces our sample size by about two-thirds, but has remarkably little effect on the estimated coefficients. The coefficients corresponding to table 4.4 are: .017 (delinquency), .009 (grade repetition), −.004 (in school), −.027 (math), −.033 (reading), and .013 (special education). In the NLSCY all children, both between and within families, are measured at the same point in time and so there is no difference in family structure between siblings at the time the mental health questions are asked.

12. For a diagnosis of ADHD, symptoms have to have been manifest before the child was seven years old. While conduct disorder is often diagnosed later, Kim-Cohen et al. (2005) use the DSM-IV guidelines to assess conduct disorder in a large sample of four-and-a-half- to five-year-olds and find that those who had three or more symptoms at age five (about 6.6 percent of the sample) were significantly more likely than other children to also have conduct disorder at age seven.

behavior problem scores than they otherwise would have. But if treatment has no consistent impact on cognitive outcomes such as test scores (as the Surgeon General's report concludes, and see also Wigal et al. [1999]) then failing to account for treatment will bias our estimates. For example, if all ADHD children were treated, it might appear that even low ADHD scores were associated with significantly poorer outcomes, and our results would be biased upwards.

It would be extremely interesting to be able to conduct our own analysis of the impact of treatment on outcomes. However, the very small number of children who are treated (especially in Canada) and the endogenous nature of treatment decisions (along with the lack of plausible instruments for treatment) make this difficult. Instead, we take two alternative approaches to the problem of treated children. First, we simply exclude the treated children. If treatment were applied randomly to the population of children, then these estimates would provide an unbiased estimate of the effects of untreated mental health problems on outcomes. Second, in models that use the overall behavior problem index, we impute the ninetieth percentile BPI score to all of the treated children. This is equivalent to assuming that only children with high scores are treated. As we will show, neither alternative has much impact on our estimates, given the small numbers of children being treated.

Finally, we turn to an investigation of the extent to which the effects of mental health problems are mediated by income. The OLS models we estimate have the following form:

$$(3) \qquad outcome_i = \alpha + \beta(income)_i + \phi income_i \cdot \textbf{MENTAL94}_i$$
$$+ \chi \textbf{MENTAL94}_i + \lambda \textbf{X94}_i + \varepsilon_i,$$

where now income has been broken out of the **X** vector, and interacted with a mental health score. A positive coefficient on the interaction term (in the case of a positive outcome) would suggest that the negative effects of mental health problems were mitigated in high income children. In addition to including interactions with linear income, we also use interactions between the mental health scores and having a mother who is a high school dropout, and between the mental health scores and being in poverty.

4.5   Results

Table 4.4 presents our baseline OLS estimates of the effects of mental health problems on child outcomes in the United States and Canada along with the corresponding fixed effects (FE) estimates. We present both OLS and FE estimates for the combined BPI index, and for each of the three individual scores.

Table 4.4 indicates that children with higher hyperactivity scores have

Table 4.4   The effects of behavioral scores on various outcomes: OLS vs. fixed effects

	Young adult delinquency		Grade repetition		In school		Standardized math score		Standardized reading score	Special education
	U.S.	Canada	U.S.	Canada	U.S.	Canada	U.S.	Canada	U.S.	U.S.
1. OLS										
Total/Combined score	0.016***	0.023***	0.007***	0.019***	−0.005**	−0.007*	−0.028***	−0.019*	−0.045***	0.013***
	[4.88]	[4.13]	[3.97]	[7.86]	[1.97]	[1.78]	[4.69]	[1.66]	[6.68]	[5.95]
R^2	0.09	0.08	0.06	0.07	0.12	0.20	0.22	0.09	0.19	0.06
Number of observations	3,204	2,185	3,566	5,594	2,467	2,493	2,559	2,293	2,559	2,715
2. Fixed effects										
Total/Combined score	0.007	0.019	0.013***	0.016***	−0.005	−0.008	−0.047***	−0.078**	−0.047***	0.013***
	[0.88]	[0.96]	[3.15]	[3.47]	[0.69]	[0.64]	[3.59]	[2.07]	[3.22]	[2.76]
R^2	0.75	0.93	0.69	0.86	0.80	0.95	0.86	0.94	0.86	0.79
Number of observations	3,226	2,185	3,592	5,594	2,484	2,493	2,577	2,293	2,577	2,736
3. OLS										
Hyperactivity score	0.010***	0.010***	0.005***	0.013***	−0.004	−0.005**	−0.032***	−0.024***	−0.044***	0.012***
	[3.85]	[3.34]	[3.43]	[9.95]	[1.56]	[2.55]	[6.26]	[3.91]	[7.72]	[6.20]
R^2	0.08	0.08	0.06	0.08	0.11	0.20	0.23	0.09	0.20	0.06
Number of observations	3,204	2,278	3,566	5,822	2,468	2,599	2,558	2,380	2,558	2,716
4. Fixed effects										
Hyperactivity score	0.006	0.008	0.008***	0.010***	−0.009	−0.005	−0.041***	−0.073***	−0.038***	0.013***
	[1.08]	[0.79]	[2.67]	[4.69]	[1.60]	[0.88]	[4.51]	[4.11]	[3.69]	[3.93]
R^2	0.75	0.93	0.70	0.86	0.80	0.95	0.86	0.94	0.86	0.79
Number of observations	3,226	2,278	3,591	5,822	2,485	2,599	2,575	2,380	2,575	2,736

(continued)

Table 4.4 (continued)

	Young adult delinquency		Grade repetition		In school		Standardized math score		Standardized reading score	Special education
	U.S.	Canada	U.S.	Canada	U.S.	Canada	U.S.	Canada	U.S.	U.S.
5. OLS										
Antisocial/Aggression score	0.015***	0.024***	0.006***	0.008***	−0.005**	−0.014***	−0.018***	−0.021**	−0.031***	0.008***
	[5.52]	[3.90]	[4.03]	[3.38]	[2.09]	[3.21]	[3.43]	[1.96]	[5.38]	[4.46]
R^2	0.09	0.08	0.06	0.06	0.12	0.20	0.22	0.09	0.19	0.05
Number of observations	3,197	2,278	3,559	5,816	2,465	2,598	2,554	2,377	2,554	2,709
6. Fixed effects										
Antisocial/Aggression score	0.010*	0.034	0.008***	0.008	−0.007	−0.034*	−0.023**	−0.047	−0.026**	0.005
	[1.73]	[1.40]	[2.60]	[1.79]	[1.20]	[2.35]	[2.52]	[1.40]	[2.50]	[1.37]
R^2	0.75	0.93	0.70	0.86	0.80	0.95	0.86	0.94	0.86	0.78
Number of observations	3,220	2,278	3,586	5,816	2,482	2,598	2,573	2,377	2,573	2,731
7. OLS										
Depressed/Emotional disorder score	0.008***	0.007*	0.005***	0.009***	−0.004	0.000	−0.017***	0.001	−0.028***	0.007***
	[3.03]	[1.72]	[3.58]	[5.16]	[1.56]	[0.06]	[3.16]	[0.10]	[4.67]	[3.41]
R^2	0.08	0.07	0.06	0.06	0.12	0.20	0.22	0.09	0.19	0.05
Number of observations	3,207	2,281	3,571	5,831	2,469	2,603	2,562	2,386	2,562	2,719
8. Fixed effects										
Depressed/Emotional disorder score	−0.002	0.006	0.008***	0.006	0.002	−0.001	−0.014	0.039	−0.017	0.002
	[0.27]	[0.41]	[2.64]	[1.87]	[0.41]	[0.12]	[1.37]	[1.33]	[1.48]	[0.40]
R^2	0.75	0.93	0.70	0.86	0.80	0.95	0.86	0.94	0.86	0.78
Number of observations	3,230	2,281	3,598	5,831	2,486	2,603	2,581	2,386	2,581	2,741

9. OLS

Total/Combined score	0.004	0.016	−0.004	0.010**	−0.002	0.004	0.019	0.050**	0.020	0.009
	[0.38]	[1.31]	[0.79]	[2.12]	[0.28]	[0.50]	[1.03]	[2.23]	[0.95]	[1.47]
Hyperactivity score	0.002	0.004	0.003	0.010***	0.000	−0.006*	−0.038***	−0.040***	−0.044***	0.007**
	[0.52]	[0.92]	[1.08]	[5.25]	[0.04]	[1.92]	[4.32]	[4.43]	[4.34]	[2.38]
Antisocial/Aggression score	0.012**	0.014	0.006**	−0.008**	−0.003	−0.014**	−0.007	−0.029**	−0.016*	0.001
	[2.58]	[1.59]	[2.40]	[2.39]	[0.83]	[2.27]	[0.82]	[1.98]	[1.70]	[0.24]
Depressed/Emotional disorder score	−0.001	−0.007	0.004*	0.001	0.000	0.006	−0.006	0.008	−0.011	−0.004
	[0.31]	[1.39]	[1.65]	[0.35]	[0.02]	[1.55]	[0.65]	[0.66]	[1.06]	[1.31]
R^2	0.09	0.08	0.06	0.08	0.12	0.20	0.23	0.10	0.20	0.06
Number of observations	3,181	2,185	3,540	5,594	2,459	2,493	2,537	2,293	2,537	2,693

10. Fixed effects

Total/Combined score	−0.010	−0.063	−0.006	0.003	0.010	0.033	−0.012	0.051	−0.004	0.008
	[0.53]	[1.76]	[0.62]	[0.33]	[0.53]	[1.08]	[0.37]	[0.66]	[0.10]	[0.74]
Hyperactivity score	0.007	0.012	0.005	0.009**	−0.012	−0.007	−0.034**	−0.089***	−0.032**	0.012**
	[0.80]	[0.93]	[1.26]	[2.44]	[1.49]	[0.70]	[2.35]	[3.08]	[1.98]	[2.18]
Antisocial/Aggression score	0.011	0.065**	0.005	−0.003	−0.007	−0.047**	−0.007	−0.039	−0.010	−0.002
	[1.39]	[2.50]	[1.29]	[0.45]	[0.90]	[2.01]	[0.53]	[0.82]	[0.67]	[0.44]
Depressed/Emotional disorder score	−0.001	0.011	0.007	0.001	0.004	−0.004	0.004	0.053	−0.003	−0.006
	[0.15]	[0.83]	[1.64]	[0.25]	[0.46]	[0.31]	[0.27]	[1.57]	[0.17]	[1.08]
R^2	0.75	0.93	0.70	0.86	0.80	0.95	0.86	0.94	0.86	0.78
Number of observations	3,203	2,625	3,565	5,594	2,476	2,494	2,554	2,293	2,554	2,713

Notes: The absolute value of each t-statistic (clustered at the household level for OLS) is in brackets. Covariates included in these regressions are the same as those in the OLS regressions shown in the appendix.

***Significant at the 1 percent level.

**Significant at the 5 percent level.

*Significant at the 10 percent level.

worse academic outcomes, though perhaps surprisingly, there is little effect on delinquency once household fixed effects are included in the model (compare models 3 and 4). In Canada, this appears to be because the standard error rises in the fixed effects models, but in the U.S., the coefficient also falls substantially. A one unit change in the hyperactivity score increases the probability of grade repetition by very similar amounts in Canada and the United States (0.8 to 1 percentage point) and reduces math scores by 4 to 7 percent of a standard deviation. Where they can be compared, the estimates in the United States and Canada are quite similar. The U.S. estimates also show that hyperactivity increases the probability that the child is in special education by about 1 percentage point, and reduces standardized reading scores. The similarity between the OLS and fixed effects estimates suggests that measurement error is not driving the estimates, as discussed previously.[13] In fact, the fixed effects estimates often exceed the OLS ones.

One way to think about the size of these effects is to compare them with the effect of income, which has consistently significant effects. Appendix table 4A.1 shows all of the coefficient estimates for OLS models that included the overall behavior problem index. They show that each $100,000 increase in permanent income would decrease the probability of grade repetition by 1.9 percentage points, which is only slightly larger than the effect of reducing the hyperactivity score by one point, according to our estimates. On the other hand, the estimated effect of having a mother with greater than a high school education is consistently larger than $100,000 in permanent income. At the mean BPI score of 6.8, the effect of behavior problems is much larger than the effect of either education or income (see models 1 and 2).

In Canada, each $100,000 worth of permanent income is associated with a 7 percentage point decrease in the probability that a child repeats a grade between 1994 and 2002. Having a mother with more than a high school education is associated with a decrease in the probability of repeating a grade of approximately 5 percentage points. But a Canadian child with a score of only 4 out of 16 on the BPI index (around the mean) would be 8 percentage points more likely to have repeated a grade. Thus, in both the American and Canadian samples, the effect of behavior problems is large relative to the effect of income or mother's education.

Models 5 and 6 of table 4.4 show results for conduct disorder. In OLS models, conduct disorders have negative effects across the board. In models using sibling fixed effects, the effects remain statistically significant for delinquency, grade repetition, and test scores in the United States. In Canada, the "aggression" measure is marginally significant (at the 10 percent level) for grade repetition, and is significant at conventional levels for the probability

---

13. Random measurement error would be expected to reduce the size of the fixed effects estimates relative to the OLS estimates. Correlated errors (for example, if the mother tended to consistently exaggerate reports of a particular behavior for both children) would lead to much larger fixed effects estimates. If, on the other hand, parents exaggerate differences between siblings, the fixed effects estimates could theoretically be smaller than the OLS estimates.

that a youth sixteen to nineteen is in school. Because conduct disorder covers a broader spectrum of behaviors than "aggression," it is possible that this accounts for the different results.

Models 7 and 8 of table 4.4 examine the effects of anxiety/depression. High depression scores increase the probability of grade repetition in both the United States and Canada, although since there is no effect on test scores, this appears to be through some mechanism other than impairing a child's cognitive functioning.

Models 9 and 10 of table 4.4 show estimates from models that include all of the mental health scores. This specification demands a lot of the data, but allows for the fact that the incidence of different mental health problems tends to be correlated across individuals. The fixed effects coefficients are less precisely estimated, but are broadly consistent with the estimates discussed previously. In the United States, hyperactivity is estimated to reduce test scores and increase special education. In Canada, hyperactivity also reduces test scores, and increases the probability of grade repetition. In the United States, conduct disorder appears to have little effect once the other measures are included, while in Canada, aggression increases the probability of delinquency and reduces the probability that a sixteen- to nineteen-year-old child is in school. Finally, in the United States, the depression score predicts grade repetition (although it is only marginally significant even at the 10 percent level). The total behavior problem index is not statistically significant in these models, suggesting that the overall effect of behavior problems is accounted for by the information in the three included subscales, especially hyperactivity.

The analysis in table 4.4 suggests that if our aim was only to identify young children who were at risk of future problems because of mental health conditions, then the overall behavior problems index would be a sensible initial indicator. Hence, in the remainder of the chapter we focus on this measure.

An important question about the interpretation of the results in table 4.4 concerns whether we think that early mental health conditions matter because they predict later mental health conditions, or whether they have effects independent of a child's future mental health status. Table 4.5 shows models that include both the overall score for 1990 to 1994, and the score for 1998 to 2004. These models are estimated only for the United States, because the Canadian sample had too few children with scores available for both periods. The estimates suggest that for schooling attainment, early mental health problems matter mostly because they predict later mental health problems. However, for cognitive test scores, early mental health problems have large significant effects even controlling for later problems. Hence, these estimates indicate that early mental health problems have significant and lasting effects on children's cognitive achievements, even if they do not lead to grade repetition and special education.

Table 4.6 shows that the results are unchanged if we also control for

Table 4.5 The persistence of behavioral scores: OLS vs. fixed effects (US)

	Young adult delinquency	Grade repetition	In school	Standardized math score	Standardized reading score	Special education
1. OLS						
Total/Combined score (1990–1994)	−0.002	0.000	0.011***	−0.007	−0.022***	0.003
	[0.34]	[0.17]	[2.71]	[0.94]	[2.58]	[0.88]
Total/Combined score (1998–2004)	0.024***	0.011***	−0.023***	−0.040***	−0.043***	0.018***
	[5.47]	[4.22]	[5.67]	[5.26]	[4.82]	[6.20]
R^2	0.10	0.07	0.13	0.23	0.20	0.08
Number of observations	2,337	2,662	1,743	2,485	2,485	2,673
2. Fixed effects						
Total/Combined score (1990–1994)	−0.004	0.008	0.011	−0.029**	−0.036**	0.004
	[0.37]	[1.44]	[1.15]	[2.09]	[2.30]	[0.83]
Total/Combined score (1998–2004)	0.01	0.013***	−0.023***	−0.044***	−0.030**	0.023***
	[1.39]	[2.63]	[2.62]	[3.39]	[2.06]	[4.85]
R^2	0.81	0.76	0.86	0.86	0.86	0.80
Number of observations	2,349	2,680	1,754	2,502	2,502	2,692

Notes: Correlation between 1990–1994 BPI scores and 1998–2004 BPI scores are as follows: total score = 0.625; hyperactivity = 0.547; antisocial = 0.522; anxious/depressed = 0.475.

***Significant at the 1 percent level.

**Significant at the 5 percent level.

*Significant at the 10 percent level.

Table 4.6   Behavioral scores vs. learning disabilities

	Young adult delinquency		Grade repetition		In school		Standardized math score		Standardized reading score	Special education
	U.S.	Canada	U.S.	Canada	U.S.	Canada	U.S.	Canada	U.S.	U.S.
1. OLS										
Learning disability	−0.038	0.005	0.024	0.158***	0.028	−0.10**	−1.088***	−0.83***	−0.970***	0.539***
	[0.70]	[0.08]	[0.64]	[4.12]	[0.57]	[2.30]	[7.00]	[5.12]	[6.70]	[7.93]
R^2	0.09	0.07	0.06	0.07	0.12	0.20	0.25	0.09	0.21	0.13
Number of observations	3,203	2,185	3,565	5,594	2,467	2,493	2,558	2,293	2,558	2,714
2. Fixed effects										
Learning disability	0.009	−0.040	0.004	0.111**	0.015	−0.246**	−0.743***	−0.386	−0.840***	0.422***
	[0.11]	[0.21]	[0.07]	[2.43]	[0.20]	[2.12]	[3.33]	[0.80]	[3.33]	[5.62]
R^2	0.75	0.93	0.69	0.86	0.80	0.95	0.86	0.94	0.86	0.79
Number of observations	3,225	2,185	3,591	5,594	2,484	2,493	2,576	2,293	2,576	2,735
3. OLS										
Total/Combined score	0.016***	−0.056	0.007***	0.119***	−0.006**	−0.084**	−0.023***	−0.795***	−0.040***	0.010***
	[4.92]	[0.93]	[3.83]	[3.07]	[2.04]	[1.99]	[3.85]	[4.82]	[5.94]	[4.83]
Learning disability	−0.038	0.025***	0.024	0.017***	0.028	−0.01	−1.088***	−0.01	−0.970***	0.539***
	[0.70]	[4.23]	[0.64]	[6.97]	[0.57]	[1.30]	[7.00]	[1.17]	[6.70]	[7.93]
R^2	0.09	0.08	0.06	0.08	0.12	0.20	0.25	0.09	0.21	0.13
Number of observations	3,203	2,185	3,565	5,594	2,467	2,493	2,558	2,293	2,558	2,714
4. Fixed effects										
Total/Combined score	0.007	−0.077	0.013***	0.082*	−0.006	−0.240**	−0.044***	−0.177	−0.044***	0.011**
	[0.87]	[0.39]	[3.17]	[1.77]	[0.73]	[2.03]	[3.43]	[0.36]	[2.99]	[2.31]
Learning disability	−0.002	0.021	−0.017	0.014***	0.024	−0.003	−0.684***	−0.075*	−0.781***	0.406***
	[0.02]	[1.01]	[0.32]	[3.05]	[0.31]	[0.26]	[3.08]	[1.93]	[3.10]	[5.40]
R^2	0.75	0.93	0.69	0.86	0.80	0.95	0.86	0.94	0.86	0.79
Number of observations	3,225	2,185	3,591	5,594	2,484	2,493	2,576	2,293	2,576	2,735

Note: See table 4.4 notes.

***Significant at the 1 percent level.

**Significant at the 5 percent level.

*Significant at the 10 percent level.

Table 4.7   Behavioral scores vs. chronic conditions (Canada)

	Adult delinquency	Grade repetition	In school	Standardized math score
1. OLS				
Chronic conditions 1994	−0.010	0.000	0.00	−0.03
	[0.49]	[0.06]	[0.30]	[0.74]
R^2	0.07	0.06	0.20	0.09
Number of observations	2,185	5,594	2,493	2,293
2. Fixed effects				
Chronic conditions 1994	0.079	0.036**	0.012	−0.143
	[1.02]	[2.18]	[0.25]	[1.05]
R^2	0.93	0.86	0.95	0.94
Number of observations	2,185	5,594	2,493	2,293
3. OLS				
Chronic conditions 1994	−0.015	−0.003	0.006	−0.033
	[0.73]	[0.31]	[0.38]	[0.73]
Combined score 1994	0.024***	0.019***	−0.01*	−0.02*
	[4.17]	[7.86]	[1.80]	[1.66]
R^2	0.08	0.07	0.20	0.09
Number of observations	2,185	5,594	2,493	2,293
4. Fixed effects				
Chronic conditions 1994	0.081	0.037**	0.012	−0.148
	[1.03]	[2.22]	[0.24]	[1.10]
Combined score 1994	0.020	0.016***	−0.008	−0.079**
	[0.97]	[3.50]	[0.63]	[2.09]
R^2	0.93	0.86	0.95	0.94
Number of observations	2,185	5,594	2,493	2,293

Note: See table 4.4 notes.
***Significant at the 1 percent level.
**Significant at the 5 percent level.
*Significant at the 10 percent level.

the presence of other learning disabilities (even though these disabilities have large independent effects, especially on test scores). We have estimated similar models (not shown) that include birth weight, and this also has little effect on the estimated effect of mental health problems. Table 4.7 compares the effects of mental health conditions to those of chronic physical health problems. This analysis is conducted only with the Canadian data, since the U.S. data does not ask every child about the presence of chronic conditions. The estimated effects of mental health conditions are almost exactly the same as those in table 4.4. Chronic physical conditions have a large effect on grade repetition, but no effect on test scores.

Table 4.8 shows several specification checks. First, we try excluding children with other diagnosed learning disabilities. Second, we exclude treated children. Third, we impute a high (ninetieth percentile) BPI score to treated children. For the most part, these alternative ways of handling the

Table 4.8   Fixed effects robustness checks of the effects on behavioral scores on various outcomes

	Young adult delinquency		Grade repetition		In school		Standardized math score		Standardized reading score	Special education	Child delinquency
	U.S.	Canada	U.S.	Canada	U.S.	Canada	U.S.	Canada	U.S.	U.S.	Canada
1. Dropping children diagnosed with learning disabilities											
Total/Combined score	0.006	0.015	0.014***	0.013***	-0.005	0.006	-0.043***	-0.067*	-0.043***	0.011**	0.013
	[0.81]	[0.65]	[3.37]	[2.89]	[0.58]	[0.41]	[3.28]	[1.70]	[2.93]	[2.32]	[0.72]
R^2	0.75	0.93	0.71	0.87	0.81	0.95	0.86	0.94	0.86	0.78	0.92
Number of observations	3,141	2,110	3,504	5,452	2,410	2,401	2,532	2,272	2,532	2,683	2,260
2. Excluding treated children											
Total/Combined score	0.010	0.001	0.007	0.015***	-0.012	0.006	-0.042***	-0.077**	-0.047***	0.009*	0.006
	[1.11]	[0.02]	[1.44]	[3.18]	[1.29]	[0.41]	[2.87]	[2.00]	[2.90]	[1.70]	[0.31]
R^2	0.62	0.94	0.55	0.87	0.71	0.95	0.80	0.94	0.80	0.67	0.92
Number of observations	1,825	2,046	2,050	5,338	1,411	2,337	1,515	2,231	1,515	1,603	2,219
3. Assigning treated children the 90th percentile score											
Total/Combined score	0.005	0.007	0.010***	0.014***	-0.005	-0.003	-0.047***	-0.093**	-0.042***	0.010**	0.007
	[0.70]	[0.31]	[2.60]	[3.11]	[0.74]	[0.24]	[3.73]	[2.54]	[2.91]	[2.14]	[0.38]
R^2	0.75	0.93	0.69	0.86	0.80	0.95	0.86	0.94	0.86	0.79	0.92
Number of observations	3,225	2,185	3,591	5,594	2,484	2,493	2,576	2,293	2,576	2,735	2,283

Note: The absolute value of each t-statistic is in brackets.

***Significant at the 1 percent level.

**Significant at the 5 percent level.

*Significant at the 10 percent level.

Table 4.9   Means table for sample of children with all behavioral scores nonmissing,
                   sibling samples

	U.S.		Canada		U.S.		Canada	
					Mom HS +	Mom < HS	Mom HS +	Mom < HS
	Nonpoor	Poor	Nonpoor	Poor				
U.S./Canada behavioral scores (1994)								
Total/Combined	6.428	7.456	3.784	4.146	6.543	7.835	3.749	4.265
Hyperactivity	4.547	5.734	4.323	4.805	4.741	6.004	4.217	5.222
Antisocial/Aggression	4.417	5.722	1.460	1.718	4.565	6.243	1.431	1.823
Depressed/Emotional disorder	4.203	5.084	2.366	2.678	4.273	5.520	2.334	2.789
Outcomes								
Young adult delinquency	0.423	0.506	0.360	0.336	0.447	0.499	0.359	0.348
Grade repetition	0.041	0.140	0.070	0.140	0.057	0.173	0.062	0.167
In school	0.896	0.757	0.889	0.717	0.874	0.713	0.886	0.763
Standardized math score	0.241	−0.347	0.313	−0.005	0.151	−0.534	0.356	−0.165
Standardized reading score	0.406	−0.215	n.a.	n.a.	0.320	−0.460	n.a.	n.a.
Enrolled in special education	0.054	0.135	n.a.	n.a.	0.072	0.142	n.a.	n.a.

Note: n.a. = not applicable.

treated children produce estimates that are very similar to those shown in table 4.4. The main exception is that excluding treated children results in an insignificant coefficient on BPI in the equation for grade repetition in the NLSY, suggesting that, at least in the United States, the children who are treated are also the most likely to have repeated a grade.

4.6   Impacts on the Disadvantaged

Finally, we ask whether the impact of mental health problems is greater for disadvantaged children. Table 4.9 shows that differences in the prevalence of these conditions are apparent in our data, though they are relatively small. For example, the score on the overall behavior problems index is 6.4 for nonpoor children compared to 7.5 for poor children in the United States, and the corresponding scores for the ADHD subscale are 4.5 and 5.7. In Canada the scores differ by less than 1 point between poor and nonpoor. But it is also possible that the same mental health problems have more severe effects on poor children, since many physical health problems have stronger impacts on more disadvantaged children (Currie and Lin 2007), so it is of interest to see if that pattern is also true for mental health problems.

Table 4.10 reports estimates of equation (3), which includes interactions between BPI scores and income. Given that we are using permanent income,

Table 4.10   Interactions of income and mother's education with total/combined behavioral score

	Young adult delinquency		Grade repetition		In school		Standardized math score		Standardized reading score	Special education
	U.S.	Canada	U.S.	Canada	U.S.	Canada	U.S.	Canada	U.S.	U.S.
1. OLS–Income										
Income · Total/Combined score	-0.004	-0.017	-0.007***	-0.034***	0.001	-0.010	0.022*	0.001	0.030**	-0.006**
	[0.56]	[1.07]	[3.32]	[5.83]	[0.35]	[0.82]	[1.66]	[0.04]	[2.42]	[2.27]
Total/Combined score	0.017***	0.034***	0.011***	0.040***	-0.006	-0.001	-0.039***	-0.020	-0.060***	0.016***
	[3.82]	[3.02]	[4.35]	[7.81]	[1.58]	[0.10]	[4.55]	[0.92]	[6.47]	[5.34]
Income	0.034	0.089	0.019	0.051**	0.052*	0.120***	0.112	0.359***	0.061	0.010
	[0.75]	[1.47]	[1.60]	[2.57]	[1.85]	[2.71]	[1.43]	[2.83]	[0.85]	[0.69]
R^2	0.09	0.08	0.06	0.08	0.12	0.20	0.22	0.09	0.20	0.06
Number of observations	3,204	2,185	3,566	5,594	2,467	2,493	2,559	2,293	2,559	2,715
2. Fixed effects–Income										
Income · Total/Combined score	0.009	0.061	-0.005	-0.015	0.005	-0.03	0.005	0.102	-0.007	-0.003
	[0.60]	[0.96]	[0.68]	[0.99]	[0.40]	[0.73]	[0.21]	[0.85]	[0.24]	[0.34]
Total/Combined score	0.003	-0.024	0.015***	0.025**	-0.008	0.012	-0.049***	-0.131*	-0.043**	0.015**
	[0.29]	[0.48]	[2.80]	[2.40]	[0.78]	[0.40]	[2.79]	[1.79]	[2.19]	[2.30]
R^2	0.75	0.93	0.69	0.86	0.80	0.95	0.86	0.94	0.86	0.79
Number of observations	3,209	2,185	3,572	5,594	2,471	2,493	2,563	2,293	2,563	2,719
3. OLS–Mother less than HS										
Mother less than HS · Total/Combined score	-0.005	0.017	0.002	0.010*	0.004	-0.001	-0.002	0.022	-0.005	0.000
	[0.67]	[1.40]	[0.50]	[1.65]	[0.66]	[0.07]	[0.13]	[0.79]	[0.35]	[0.05]
Total/Combined score	0.017***	0.019***	0.007***	0.016***	-0.007**	-0.007	-0.027***	-0.024*	-0.043***	0.013***
	[4.60]	[2.84]	[3.58]	[6.42]	[2.26]	[1.60]	[4.10]	[1.85]	[5.66]	[5.56]
Mother less than HS	0.038	-0.064	0.053	0.040	-0.117**	-0.086**	-0.237**	-0.385***	-0.336***	0.029
	[0.66]	[1.20]	[1.44]	[1.55]	[2.13]	[1.97]	[2.06]	[3.17]	[2.66]	[0.67]
R^2	0.09	0.08	0.06	0.07	0.12	0.20	0.23	0.09	0.20	0.06
Number of observations	3,204	2,185	3,566	5,594	2,467	2,493	2,559	2,293	2,559	2,715

(continued)

Table 4.10 (continued)

	Young adult delinquency U.S.	Young adult delinquency Canada	Grade repetition U.S.	Grade repetition Canada	In school U.S.	In school Canada	Standardized math score U.S.	Standardized math score Canada	Standardized reading score U.S.	Special education U.S.
4. Fixed effects–Mother less than HS										
Mother less than HS · Total/Combined score	-0.030*	0.008	-0.003	0.002	-0.008	0.005	0.006	-0.090	-0.029	0.000
	[1.77]	[0.19]	[0.37]	[0.24]	[0.49]	[0.19]	[0.20]	[1.07]	[0.84]	[0.01]
Total/Combined score	0.015	0.017	0.014***	0.015***	-0.003	-0.010	-0.048***	-0.056	-0.041**	0.013**
	[1.63]	[0.69]	[2.92]	[2.87]	[0.32]	[0.64]	[3.27]	[1.33]	[2.48]	[2.41]
R^2	0.75	0.93	0.69	0.86	0.80	0.95	0.86	0.94	0.86	0.79
Number of observations	3,221	2,185	3,586	5,594	2,480	2,493	2,573	2,293	2,573	2,732
5. OLS–Poverty										
Poverty · Total/Combined score	0.002	0.010	0.003	0.022***	0.012**	0.001	-0.003	-0.010	0.002	0.002
	[0.26]	[0.79]	[0.83]	[3.41]	[2.12]	[0.07]	[0.23]	[0.43]	[0.14]	[0.32]
Total/Combined score	0.015***	0.021***	0.006***	0.014***	-0.011***	-0.007*	-0.026***	-0.017	-0.045***	0.013***
	[3.55]	[3.34]	[2.65]	[5.59]	[3.32]	[1.75]	[3.46]	[1.22]	[5.18]	[4.98]
Poverty	0.028	-0.069	0.013	-0.061**	-0.135***	-0.018	-0.105	0.066	-0.174	0.020
	[0.57]	[1.19]	[0.50]	[2.33]	[3.19]	[0.36]	[1.08]	[0.56]	[1.60]	[0.62]
R^2	0.09	0.08	0.06	0.08	0.12	0.20	0.23	0.09	0.20	0.06
Number of observations	3,159	2,185	3,517	5,594	2,431	2,493	2,534	2,293	2,534	2,686
6. Fixed effects–Poverty										
Poverty · Total/Combined score	-0.019	-0.039	0.000	0.019	0.000	-0.016	0.048*	-0.109	0.064**	-0.008
	[1.28]	[0.49]	[0.05]	[1.64]	[0.00]	[0.32]	[1.88]	[1.16]	[2.25]	[0.83]
Total/Combined score	0.018	0.022	0.012**	0.012**	-0.004	-0.007	-0.071***	-0.057	-0.079***	0.017**
	[1.64]	[1.05]	[2.16]	[2.54]	[0.36]	[0.54]	[3.93]	[1.37]	[3.88]	[2.53]
R^2	0.75	0.93	0.69	0.86	0.80	0.95	0.86	0.94	0.86	0.78
Number of observations	3,164	2,185	3,523	5,594	2,435	2,493	2,538	2,293	2,538	2,690

Note: The absolute value of each t-statistic (clustered at the household level for OLS) is in brackets.

***Significant at the 1 percent level.

**Significant at the 5 percent level.

*Significant at the 10 percent level.

the interaction terms in these fixed effects models are identified by the fact that BPI scores vary within families. What the interaction term tells us is whether the difference between the high and low BPI score children within a family is bigger in a low income household than in a high income household. That is, if the high income household is able to do a better job assisting the high BPI score child than the low income household, then the interaction will be significant.

The first panel of table 4.10 shows that in OLS models using the NLSY, the interactions with income are of the expected sign (that is, higher income appears to mitigate the effects of behavior problems in the equations for grade repetition, reading scores, and special education). However, in the fixed effects models the interactions are not even consistently negative. The standard errors are also much larger so that none of the interactions are statistically significant. The same is true for interactions between mental health scores and whether the mother is a high school dropout.

The last panel of table 4.10 shows that if we use poverty rather than a continuous income measure, the interaction terms for U.S. math and reading scores are positive and statistically significant and largely offset the negative main effects of having a high screener score. It is possible that this result reflects the fact that poor children have the lowest scores on these tests to begin with so that perhaps it is hard for mental illness to lower them further (that is, this result may reflect a "floor" on the tests).

In any case, there is little evidence that maternal education or family income mitigate the negative effects of childhood mental health conditions, in sharp contrast to the large literature suggesting that higher income does mitigate the negative effects of physical health conditions. This is not just a function of large standard errors on the interactions, because the interactions with socioeconomic status also tend to be small, and of inconsistent sign.

4.7   Discussion and Conclusions

Children with mental health problems suffer large negative consequences in terms of their achievement test scores and schooling attainment. Hyperactivity appears to have the broadest, and most consistently negative effects, followed by conduct disorders. A one unit change in the hyperactivity score increases the probability of grade repetition by very similar amounts in Canada and the United States (0.8 to 1 percentage point) and reduces math scores by 4 to 7 percent of a standard deviation. Conduct disorders have effects of roughly half this size. These effects are large relative to the effects of family income, which is known to be an important predictor of child outcomes. Effects of mental health conditions are also large relative to those of chronic physical health conditions.

These results are consistent with previous research suggesting that "externalizing" behavior problems are more likely to lead to negative outcomes than "internalizing problems." We do, however, find that anxiety/depression increases the probability of grade repetition by as much as 1 percentage point, which is again a large effect. Since, however, depression does not appear to affect math and reading test scores, it is possible that depression affects academic outcomes via a different mechanism.

While it is interesting to examine the impact of specific problems, our results also suggest that if one merely wanted to identify children at risk of bad outcomes because of their mental health problems, then an index such as the overall Behavior Problems Index would be as good if not better than the individual subscales.

Our estimates also indicate that mental health conditions in early childhood are predictive of future outcomes both because mental health conditions are likely to persist, and because early mental health problems have independent and persistent negative effects on children's future test scores. Our results are very robust and hold when we include indicators for other learning disabilities in our models, when we exclude children with other learning disabilities, when we include birth weight, and whether we exclude children who are treated for mental health problems, or impute a "pretreatment" mental health score to these children.

Finally, we find surprisingly little evidence that higher income protects against the negative effects of mental health conditions, though poor children are somewhat more likely to be affected by these problems than richer ones. This is surprising in that one might expect richer children to have access to superior treatment as well as other advantages. This result may speak to the fact that treatment for most childhood mental health problems is in its infancy, so that it is not at all clear that richer parents are able to identify, let alone purchase, the most effective treatments.

Table 4A.1   OLS: Effects of total/combined behavioral score on various outcomes

	Young adult delinquency		Grade repetition		In school		Standardized math score		Standardized reading score	Special education
	U.S.	Canada	U.S.	Canada	U.S.	Canada	U.S.	Canada	U.S.	U.S.
Total/Combined score	0.016***	0.023***	0.007***	0.019***	-0.005**	-0.007*	-0.028***	-0.019*	-0.045***	0.013***
	[4.88]	[4.13]	[3.97]	[7.86]	[1.97]	[1.78]	[4.69]	[1.66]	[6.68]	[5.95]
Permanent income (/$100,000)	0.013	0.030	-0.019**	-0.066***	0.061***	0.085***	0.230***	0.364***	0.222***	-0.023***
	[0.61]	[1.02]	[2.56]	[6.89]	[4.74]	[4.44]	[4.80]	[5.56]	[5.35]	[3.27]
Mother is immigrant	-0.042	0.061	-0.045***	-0.034***	0.073**	0.030	-0.031	0.018	-0.025	-0.043**
	[1.12]	[1.65]	[2.66]	[2.84]	[2.54]	[1.25]	[0.40]	[0.20]	[0.28]	[2.19]
Male child	-0.073***	0.182***	0.031**	0.037***	0.033*	-0.030**	-0.463***	0.084**	-0.378***	0.003
	[3.18]	[8.88]	[2.53]	[4.89]	[1.68]	[2.10]	[9.68]	[2.03]	[6.75]	[0.18]
Firstborn child	0.052**	0.014	0.037***	-0.013	-0.035	0.038**	-0.330***	0.026	-0.104*	-0.004
	[2.01]	[0.58]	[2.83]	[1.49]	[1.64]	[2.33]	[6.52]	[0.56]	[1.74]	[0.25]
Ln(Family size)	0.153***	0.072	0.034***	-0.012	-0.026*	-0.049	0.115***	-0.069	-0.040	0.058***
	[9.05]	[1.37]	[3.96]	[0.55]	[1.81]	[1.23]	[3.49]	[0.61]	[1.05]	[5.45]
Two-parent household	-0.092***	-0.036	-0.021**	-0.038**	0.054***	0.072**	0.159***	0.068	0.270***	-0.025**
	[4.85]	[0.98]	[2.17]	[2.12]	[3.29]	[2.47]	[4.34]	[0.89]	[6.65]	[2.05]
Mother's age at child's birth	-0.091***	0.002	-0.023	-0.001	-0.002	-0.001	-0.066	0.018***	-0.116	0.004
	[3.28]	[0.73]	[1.25]	[0.89]	[0.06]	[0.39]	[0.97]	[3.45]	[1.50]	[0.16]
Child born to teenage mother	-0.031	-0.095*	-0.039**	-0.016	0.054**	-0.040	0.060	0.040	0.082	-0.026
	[1.22]	[1.86]	[2.25]	[0.66]	[2.27]	[0.93]	[1.11]	[0.39]	[1.26]	[1.33]
Mother has less than high school education	-0.010**	0.004	-0.003	0.082***	0.009**	-0.089***	0.028***	-0.294***	0.022**	0.000
	[2.20]	[0.17]	[1.36]	[6.52]	[2.42]	[4.40]	[3.41]	[5.62]	[2.31]	[0.16]
Mother depressed or has activity limitation	-0.019	0.007	0.008	0.016	0.067	-0.035*	0.078	-0.077	0.164	-0.026
	[0.40]	[0.26]	[0.26]	[1.28]	[1.59]	[1.69]	[0.52]	[1.31]	[0.62]	[0.43]
Black (U.S.)	0.007		0.083***		-0.088***		-0.338***		-0.451***	0.037**
	[0.31]		[5.59]		[4.11]		[7.16]		[7.76]	[2.02]
Hispanic (U.S.)	0.033		-0.003		-0.060***		-0.158***		-0.112**	0.031*
	[1.55]		[0.28]		[3.05]		[3.47]		[2.02]	[1.81]

(continued)

Table 4A.1

	Young adult delinquency		Grade repetition		In school		Standardized math score		Standardized reading score	Special education
	U.S.	Canada	U.S.	Canada	U.S.	Canada	U.S.	Canada	U.S.	U.S.
Adult respondent is female (Canada)		0.066 [1.54]		0.016 [1.07]		-0.026 [1.05]		-0.313*** [2.99]		
Imputation dummy (Canada)		-0.055* [1.76]		0.005 [0.50]		-0.033*** [2.60]		-0.020 [0.43]		
Age 4	-0.293*** [5.93]		0.036 [1.59]	-0.048*** [3.10]			-0.066 [0.77]		-0.036 [0.39]	0.043 [1.62]
Age 5	-0.232*** [5.70]		0.050** [2.14]	-0.012 [0.71]			-0.011 [0.13]	0.001 [0.01]	-0.022 [0.24]	0.042* [1.72]
Age 6	-0.177*** [4.61]		0.033 [1.59]	-0.002 [0.14]	0.083*** [3.05]	0.288*** [10.41]	-0.030 [0.39]	-0.144*** [2.60]	-0.026 [0.31]	-0.001 [0.06]
Age 7	-0.117*** [3.20]	0.036 [0.35]	-0.009 [0.46]	0.004 [0.26]	0.050* [1.78]	0.335*** [8.12]	0.019 [0.25]	0.221*** [3.79]	-0.038 [0.46]	0.026 [1.20]
Age 8	-0.086** [2.45]	0.117*** [3.19]	-0.016 [0.83]	0.029 [1.59]	-0.121*** [3.94]	0.352*** [15.66]	-0.057 [0.79]	0.324* [1.81]	-0.037 [0.45]	0.043* [1.91]
Age 9	-0.076** [2.32]	0.121*** [3.46]	-0.005 [0.29]	0.030* [1.71]	0.023 [0.84]	0.315*** [13.23]	-0.040 [0.55]		-0.029 [0.37]	-0.020 [1.01]
Age 10	-0.075** [2.28]	0.093*** [3.53]	0.002 [0.10]	0.030* [1.83]	-0.137*** [4.67]	0.135*** [5.21]				
Constant	0.823*** [6.89]	-0.065 [0.53]	0.132** [2.00]	0.092** [2.05]	0.617*** [5.79]	0.680*** [7.70]	-0.353 [1.49]	-0.122 [0.50]	0.128 [0.47]	-0.036 [0.48]
R^2	0.09	0.08	0.06	0.07	0.12	0.20	0.22	0.09	0.19	0.06
Number of observations	3,204	2,185	3,566	5,594	2,467	2,493	2,559	2,293	2,559	2,715

Note: The absolute value of each t-statistic (clustered at the household level) is in brackets.

***Significant at the 1 percent level.

**Significant at the 5 percent level.

*Significant at the 10 percent level.

References

American Psychiatric Association. 1994. *Diagnostic and statistical manual of mental disorders, 4th ed.* Arlington, VA: American Psychiatric Press.

Blanden, J., P. Gregg, and L. Macmillan. 2006. Explaining intergenerational income persistence: Non-cognitive skills, ability, and education. Centre for Market and Public Organisation (CMPO) Working Paper no. 06/146, Department of Economics, University of Bristol, April.

Campell, S., S. Spieker, M. Burchinal, M. Poe, and the NICHD Early Child Care Research Network. 2006. Trajectories of aggression from toddlerhood to age 9 predict academic and social functioning through age 12. *Journal of Child Psychology and Psychiatry,* 47 (8): 791–800.

Caspi, A., B. Wright, T. Moffitt, and P. Silva. 1998. Early failure in the labor market: Childhood and adolescent predictors of unemployment in the transition to adulthood. *American Sociological Review* 63 (3): 424–51.

Cullen, J. B. 2003. The impact of fiscal incentives on student disability rates. *Journal of Public Economics* 87 (7–8): 1557–89.

Cuffe, S., C. Moore, and R. McKeown. 2003. ADHD symptoms in the national health interview survey: Prevalence, correlates, and the use of services and medication. Poster presented at the 50th Anniversary Meeting of the American Academy of Child and Adolescent Psychiatry, Miami Beach, FL, 15 October.

Currie, J., and M. Stabile. 2006. Child mental health and human capital accumulation: The case of ADHD. *Journal of Health Economics* 25 (6): 1094–118.

Currie, J., and L. Wanchuan. 2007. Chipping away at health: More on the relationship between income and child health. *Health Affairs* 26 (2): 331–44.

Curtis, L., M. Dooley, E. Lipman, and D. Feeny. 2001. The role of permanent income and family structure in the determination of child health in the Ontario Child Health Study. *Journal of Health Economics* 10 (4): 287–302.

Dooley, M., and J. Stewart. 2003. Family income, parenting styles and child behavioural-emotional outcomes. Working Paper. McMaster University, Hamilton, Ontario, Canada.

Farmer, E. 1993. Externalizing behavior in the life course: The transition from school to work. *Journal of Emotional and Behavioral Disorders* 1 (3): 179–88.

———. 1995. Extremity of externalizing behavior and young adult outcomes. *Journal of Child Psychology and Psychiatry* 36 (4): 617–32.

Garrett, A. B. 1996. *Essays in the economics of child mental health.* PhD diss. Columbia University.

Glied, S., C. Hoven, A. B. Garrett, R. Moore, P. Leaf, H. Bird, S. Goodman, D. Regier, and M. Alegria. 1997. Measuring child mental health status for services research. *Journal of Child and Family Studies* 6 (2): 177–90.

Gregg, P., and S. Machin. 1998. Child development and success or failure in the youth labour market. Center for Economic Performance, London School of Economics Discussion Paper 0397, July.

Heckman, J., J. Stixrud, and S. Urzua. 2006. The effects of cognitive and noncognitive abilities on labor market outcomes and social behavior. NBER Working Paper no. 12006. Cambridge, MA: National Bureau of Economic Research, January.

Kessler, R., C. Foster, W. Saunders, and P. Stang. 1995. Social consequences of psychiatric disorders, I: Educational attainment. *American Journal of Psychiatry* 152:1026–32.

Kim-Cohen, J., L. Arseneiault, A. Caspi, M. Tomas, A. Taylor, and T. Moffitt. 2005. Validity of DSM-IV conduct disorder in 41/2–5-year-old children: A longitudinal epidemiological study. *American Journal of Psychiatry* 162 (June): 1008–1117.

Korenman, S., J. Miller, and J. Sjaastad. 1995. Long-term poverty and child development in the United States: Results from the NLSY. *Children and Youth Services Review* 17 (1–2): 127–55.

Lipman, E., D. R. Offord, and M. H. Boyle. 1994. Economic disadvantage and child psycho-social morbidity. *Canadian Medical Association Journal* 151:431–37.

Mannuzza, S., and R. Klein. 2000. Long-term prognosis in attention-deficit/hyperactivity disorder. *Child and Adolescent Psychiatric Clinics of North America* 9 (3): 711–26.

McLeod, J. D., and K. Kaiser. 2004. Childhood emotional and behavioral problems and educational attainment. *American Sociological Review* 69 (October): 636–58.

McLeod, J. D., and M. J. Shanahan. 1993. Poverty, parenting and children's mental health. *American Sociological Review* 58 (3): 351–66.

Miech, R., A. Caspi, T. Moffitt, B. E. Wright, and P. Silva. 1999. Low socioeconomic status and mental disorders: A longitudinal study of selection and causation during young adulthood. *American Journal of Sociology* 104 (4): 1096–1131.

Nagin, D., and R. E. Tremblay. 1999. Trajectories of boys' physical aggression, opposition, and hyperactivity on the path to physically violent and nonviolent juvenile delinquency. *Child Development* 70 (5): 1181–96.

Offord, D., M. Boyle, P. Szatmari, N. I. Rae-Grant, P. S. Links, D. T. Cadman, J. A. Byles, J. W. Crawford, H. M. Blum, C. Byrne, H. Thomas, and C. A. Woodward. 1987. Ontario child health study: II. Six-month prevalence of disorder and rates of service utilization. *Archives of General Psychiatry* 44 (9): 832–36.

Phipps, S., and L. Curtis. 2003. Social transfers and the health status of mothers in Norway and Canada. *Social Science and Medicine* 58 (12): 2499–2507.

Puzzanchera, C. 2000. Self-reported delinquency by 12-year-olds, 1997. Office of Juvenile Justice and Delinquency Prevention, U.S. Department of Justice, Fact Sheet no. 3, February.

Shaffer, D., P. Fisher, M. K. Dulcan, M. Davies, J. Piacentini, M. E. Schwab-Stone, B. B. Lahey, et al. 1996. The NIMH diagnostic interview schedule for children version 2.3 (DISC-2.3): Description, acceptability, prevalence rates, and performance in the MECA study. Methods for the epidemiology of child and adolescent mental disorders study. *Journal of the American Academy of Child and Adolescent Psychiatry* 35 (7): 865–77.

U.S. Department of Health and Human Services. 1999. *Mental health: A report to the surgeon general.* Rockville, MD: U.S. Dept. of Health and Human Services.

Wigal, T., J. Swanson, R. Regino, M. Lerner, I. Soliman, K. Steinhoff, S. Gurbani, and S. Wigal. 1999. Stimulant medications for the treatment of ADHD: Efficacy and limitations. *Mental Retardation and Developmental Disabilities Research Reviews* 5 (3): 215–24.

5

Childhood Disadvantage and Obesity
Is Nurture Trumping Nature?

Patricia M. Anderson, Kristin F. Butcher, and
Diane Whitmore Schanzenbach

5.1 Introduction

Obesity has been one of the fastest growing health concerns among children, particularly among disadvantaged children. Childhood obesity has risen starkly over the last three decades. For children overall, obesity rates have tripled from 5 percent in the early 1970s to about 15 percent by the early 2000s. For disadvantaged children, the rates of obesity are even higher. For example, in the years 1999 to 2004, nearly 18 percent of low income children qualified as obese.

Obesity carries with it both short-term and long-term consequences. Obese children have higher incidences of type II diabetes, for example, and lower quality of life scores. In addition, obese children are much more likely than normal weight children to become obese adults, and obese adults are more likely to suffer disability during their prime working years, and have adverse health outcomes like hypertension, heart attack, and cancer. While the precise impact of obesity on mortality remains a matter of debate, there is little debate that obesity increases morbidity and its attendant health care costs. Since disadvantaged children and adults have higher rates of obesity

Patricia M. Anderson is a professor of economics at Dartmouth College and a faculty research fellow of the National Bureau of Economic Research. Kristin F. Butcher is a professor of economics at Wellesley College. Diane Whitmore Schanzenbach is an assistant professor in the Harris School of Public Policy at the University of Chicago.

This research was funded in part by the Annie E. Casey Foundation. We thank them for their support but acknowledge that the findings and conclusions presented in this report are those of the authors alone, and do not necessarily reflect the opinions of the Foundation. We thank Chris Rogers at NCHS for help accessing the confidential NHANES data, Qing Chang and Pauline Yu for helpful research assistance, and Jon Gruber, John Cawley, Doug Staiger, Bruce Sacerdote, and participants in the Disadvantaged Youth Conference for helpful comments.

than other segments of the population, they suffer more of the short-term and long-term consequences of this condition.

Understanding the increase in childhood obesity is important for devising policies to deal with this health problem. Although recent research and policy activity surrounding this issue has focused particularly on the food available to children through schools, there is a gap in our knowledge when it comes to the impact of home environment on children's obesity. To address this question, we ask, how does parental obesity relate to children's obesity? Is this different for disadvantaged families? Have these relationships changed over time? Parental obesity is very closely tied to children's obesity, for reasons of both nature and nurture. First, there is a strong genetic component to body composition. Second, parents and children share many environmental characteristics. Additionally, parents have a great deal of influence over what their children, particularly their young children, eat and how much energy they expend. Since genetics are unlikely to have changed dramatically over the past thirty years, if the correlation between parents' and children's obesity has changed over time, then it is likely that the environment and/or parental behavior has changed. If the overall correlation has increased over time, it suggests that something in the common environment (or decisions made by the family) is affecting all family members. On the other hand, if the correlation has decreased over time, then it suggests a larger role for something unique to the environment that children—but not their parents—face; for example, in child care settings and public schools.

In addition, there may be important differences in the relationship between parents' and children's obesity for disadvantaged children. For example, if the parent-child correlation is lower for the disadvantaged, then it suggests that the child-specific environmental factors may be relatively more important for disadvantaged children. Again, if the relationship is changing over time, it provides clues as to changes in the environment that may be contributing to the changes in obesity. Thus, this chapter focuses on a fundamental component of health status—obesity—for which disadvantaged children have particularly poor outcomes. It sheds light on how parents' health status is related to children's health status, and how that relationship differs for disadvantaged and advantaged children, and how the relationship changes over time.

We find that the parent-child correlation in weight outcomes has increased substantially since the early 1970s. This suggests that the importance of the shared family environment or genetic-environmental interactions has increased over time. Despite the fact that disadvantaged groups have higher obesity rates, parent-child weight outcomes are similar for advantaged and disadvantaged groups. On average, the observed increase in parents' body mass index[1] (BMI) can explain about 37 percent of the increase in children's

1. Weight in kilograms divided by height in meters squared.

BMI since the early 1970s. Thus, for advantaged and disadvantaged groups, genetic tendencies toward obesity and how these tendencies interact with the common environment are important, and increasingly so as obesity rates have risen over time. Nonetheless, for both advantaged and disadvantaged children an important role in their health status is played by child-specific environments, which suggests that policies affecting schools, day cares, playgrounds, and the like may have an effect on children's obesity.

5.2   Previous Research in this Area

Economic research on obesity has focused on changes in the (implicit) prices of food and exercise that have increased caloric intake and reduced energy expenditure (Cutler, Glaeser, and Shapiro 2003; Lakdawalla and Philipson 2002). While this work is important, it is not clear how well it applies to children, especially young children, who typically do not select the menu of food presented to them, nor do they have complete control over how they spend their time. Thus, work on childhood obesity has focused on changes in children's environment that may have tilted their energy balance toward consuming more calories and expending less energy. For example, work has focused on changes in maternal employment (Anderson, Butcher, and Levine 2003b), changes in the food available to children through schools (Anderson and Butcher 2006b; Schanzenbach 2005), and how these changes in the two institutions—families and schools, in which children spend most of their time—may have affected obesity.

There is, of course, a substantial literature outside economics on childhood obesity. Much of this focuses on whether children who consume more of specific types of foods (e.g., fast food, soda) or engage in particular activities (e.g., television watching, video game playing) are more likely to be obese (see Anderson and Butcher [2006a] for a summary of this literature). In addition, there is a large literature documenting that children from disadvantaged backgrounds are more likely to have weight problems than others (see, e.g., Strauss and Pollack 2001). Finally, there is a large literature documenting that there is an important genetic component of obesity (see, e.g., Stunkard et al. 1990).

5.3   Our Approach

What we believe is missing is a better understanding of whether the obesity epidemic in children is simply part and parcel of the obesity epidemic in adults, or whether it represents a related, but separate, phenomenon. If we see a high correlation between children's and parents' weight outcomes, then it suggests that increases in parents' weight—or the same factors that led to parents' weight gain—can explain a large fraction of the increase in children's weight. This would be consistent with an explanation for the rise in children's obesity where both parents and children are faced with an adverse environment that leads to more obesity, or that parents have always made determining choices about food and exercise that have affected their own and their children's weight (and in recent years these choices have been poor choices).

On the other hand, if we see that children's weight outcomes are not highly correlated with their parents, then it suggests that there are other, nonshared, factors that determine children's weight outcomes. At any given point in time, there may be differences between advantaged and disadvantaged children in how closely related children's weight is to parents' weight. For example, a parent who lives in a well-off neighborhood may walk to work for exercise and may encourage her children to walk to school as well. On the other hand, a parent in a disadvantaged neighborhood may feel comfortable walking to work herself, but may be less comfortable with her children walking to school due to safety concerns (traffic safety or criminal activity, for example). We would expect parents and children in the well-off neighborhood to have more similar weight outcomes, while in the disadvantaged neighborhood, parents and children would have less closely linked weight outcomes. Parent-child correlations may change over time, and these changes may also differ between advantaged and disadvantaged children. For both advantaged and disadvantaged children, we will discuss how much of the change in children's weight outcomes can be explained by parents' weight outcomes, given the correlation between the two in a given time period.

To address the question of how the parent-child correlation in BMI has changed over time for disadvantaged and nondisadvantaged groups, we rely on data from the National Health and Nutrition Examination Survey (NHANES). The nationally representative data were collected in 1971 to 1974 (NHANES 1), 1976 to 1980 (NHANES 2), and 1988 to 1994 (NHANES 3). Beginning in 1999, the NHANES became a continuously running survey collected in two-year panels. We pool the surveys from 1999 to 2000, 2001 to 2002, and 2003 to 2004 and refer to them (for comparison's sake) as "NHANES 4." (See data appendix for more details.)

The NHANES are the most frequently used data for tracking obesity trends in the U.S. population. The data collection procedures include an examination component, so the children in our sample were weighed and measured by trained personnel. These measurements go into our calculation of BMI for children. For each of the first three NHANES, reported height and weight is consistently available for the parents of examined children under age twelve. Thus, we focus on children two to eleven years old. In addition to the restrictions imposed by data availability, questions about the impact of parental choices on children's BMI may be particularly germane for this group since adults are likely to have a greater influence over these children's food and exercise options than would be the case for teenagers.

In the fourth NHANES, reported parental height and weight are not available. However, for both the third and fourth NHANES there are enough children in the sample who have an adult household member who is also in the sample that we can match children and adults within households and use measured heights and weights for both children and adults.[2] The data appendix describes more fully how we do the within-household matching and how this matched sample compares with the parental report sample in NHANES 3, where both are available.

5.4   Changes in Obesity and BMI

5.4.1   Measures of Obesity

Obesity for adults is typically defined as having a BMI of 30 or above. Children are classified as obese if they have a BMI above the ninety-fifth percentile of an age-sex specific BMI distribution (calculated with data that predates the current increase in obesity).[3]

One can also examine obesity using alternative measures of body composition. Body mass index does have drawbacks—in particular, muscular individuals may have a higher BMI than someone of the same build who is less muscular, and higher BMI in this case presumably does not indicate a poor health outcome. Ideally, one would like a measure of "fatness" that we know is related to poorer health outcomes both within and across individuals. Alternative measures to BMI—for example, subscapular skinfold measurements—are available in the NHANES. While the levels of obesity sometimes differ by these different measures, the trends in obesity over time show similar increases regardless of the measure chosen to define obesity (Burkhauser, Cowley, and Schmeiser 2007).

Most researchers have chosen to focus on BMI since there tend to be very high correlations between obesity rates as measured by any of the available outcomes, and BMI is relatively easily measured in surveys. A recent study on measuring obesity in children found no additional information was gleaned from subscapular skinfold measurements once BMI was accounted for (Mei et al. 2007). Thus, we focus on BMI and obesity rates as defined by BMI in our analysis following.[4]

---

2. We can also match children to adults within the household in the first two waves of the NHANES, but this results in losing about three-fourths of our sample.
3. The nomenclature in the medical literature is different for children and adults. Children whose BMI is above the ninety-fifth percentile for their age-sex distribution are called "overweight" and those above the eighty-fifth percentile are called "at-risk-for-overweight." In order to simplify the discussion, we will use the adult terminology for both children and adults.
4. We have also conducted many of our analyses using subscapular skinfold measurements and get very similar results for the effect of disadvantage and for our parent-child correlations in outcomes.

5.4.2   Measures of Disadvantage

Disadvantage is difficult to define, but has many correlates. Our approach is to examine BMI and obesity outcomes by several different potential measures of disadvantage. We examine differences in weight outcomes between race and ethnic groups, by educational attainment of adults in the household, and by income-to-poverty line measures. In general, these measures give similar pictures of obesity levels and trends, and the parent-child correlation in BMI for advantaged and disadvantaged children.

5.4.3   Trends in Obesity

Before turning to our investigation of children's weight outcomes, it is worth establishing how quickly adult obesity has been spreading throughout the United States. Figure 5.1 shows maps for 1990, 1995, and 2005 created by the Centers for Disease Control and Prevention using data from the Behavioral Risk Factor Surveillance System (Centers for Disease Control and Prevention 2007). In 1990, in almost all states less than 15 percent of the adult population was obese. By 2005, many states have more than 25 percent of their adult population that is obese. Given our interest in the role of disadvantage, it is important to note that states known to have a relatively large poor population appear to be the leading edge of the obesity wave. In 1990, it is states such as West Virginia, Louisiana, and Alabama that have over a 15 percent obesity rate. Similarly, by 2005, these same states, along with their neighboring states, have exceeded a 25 percent obesity rate.

Turning now to children, figure 5.2 uses NHANES data to illustrate the

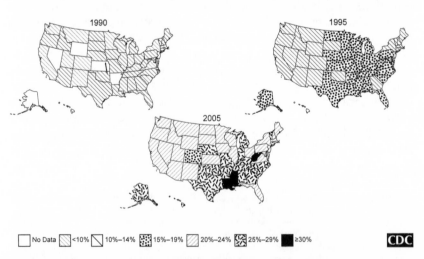

Fig. 5.1   Changes over time in adult obesity rates, by state. Obesity trends among U.S. adults (BMI ≥ 30, or about 30 lbs. overweight for 5′4″ person)
Source: Behavioral Risk Factor Surveillance System (BRFSS), CDC, 1990, 1995, and 2005.

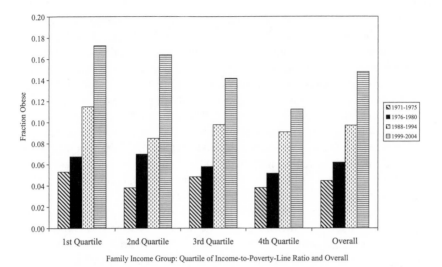

Fig. 5.2   Fraction obese by year and quartile of income-to-poverty ratio: Children 2 to 11 years old

differences across time in obesity rates for children age two to eleven (the focus of our study), as well as demonstrating the differences by the level of disadvantage for each time period. Here we are using the income-to-poverty line ratio as our indicator of level of disadvantage, examining obesity rates for children from families who fall into each quartile of the income-to-poverty-line ratio.[5] This figure clearly demonstrates the increase in obesity among children between 1971 and 1975 and 1999 and 2004. As seen in the last set of bars, the overall percentage obese almost triples from 5 percent in the earliest years to about 15 percent in the more recent years. We can also see that this increase over time applies to children in all family income groups. Although children in each of the family income groupings have increased their obesity rates, the gains have not all been the same. By the last period there is a clear gradient to children's obesity, with the lowest family income group having the highest fraction obese and children in the highest family income group having the lowest fraction obese. However, this gradient is not as clear in the earlier years.

Focusing on the fraction obese may mask some important features of changes in obesity, though. While an adult will be labeled as obese with a BMI greater than or equal to 30, it seems unlikely that someone with a BMI of 30.1 will have much worse health outcomes than someone with a BMI

5. Information on family income itself is only available in bracketed form, but a continuous income-to-poverty ratio measure is available in each year, which is a measure of reported family income relative to the poverty line. Thus, anything above one indicates the family's income is above the poverty line for that time period, and as it increases, families are better off.

of 29.9. Thus, if the increase in obesity is driven solely by small increases in BMI that push individuals across a (somewhat) arbitrary threshold that labels obesity, then we might not worry much about the future health consequences of these changes. Since children's obesity status is determined by a similar comparison to a (in this case age- and gender-specific) threshold, we want to examine what is happening to BMI among the obese, not just to the fraction of children whose BMI is above the cutoff.

In fact, the obesity epidemic is generally characterized by an increase in weight among those who are already heavy (Cutler, Glaeser, and Shapiro 2003; Anderson, Butcher, and Levine 2003a). Figure 5.3 shows how average BMI among obese children has changed over time and by family income groups. Average BMI among all obese children increased from 22.5 to 23.6 during this time period (about a 5 percent increase). In addition, by the later period we see a family income gradient emerge in average BMI among the obese. In the first period, there is if anything a reverse gradient—that is, the average BMI of the more advantaged obese children is higher than that of disadvantaged obese children. In the middle years, there is little systematic difference in the BMI between advantaged and disadvantaged obese children. By the later period, though, obese children in the poorer families are heavier than obese children in wealthier families. As differences in BMI get larger between the obese and the nonobese, we expect that long term health outcomes between them will also get larger. It is important to keep in mind, however, that differences in the age and sex composition across these groups and over time could be driving to these changes in BMI levels. In the next section we turn to regression analysis that allows us to hold constant age

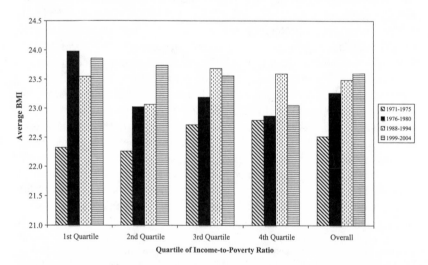

Fig. 5.3   Average BMI among the obese by year and quartile of income-to-poverty ratio: Children 2 to 11 years old

and gender as we examine the changes in BMI by different measures of disadvantage.

5.4.4   Changes in BMI over Time by Measures of Disadvantage

We first present simple regressions of children's log BMI on various measures of disadvantage for our four time periods. These regressions control for a cubic in age, gender, and interactions between these variables.[6] This should account for the fact that as children age, we expect their BMI to increase, and to increase at different rates for boys and girls. We control for age and gender in the regressions so that differences in BMI by measures of disadvantage will not be due to differences in the age-sex composition across these groups. Heteroskedasticity-robust standard errors are in parenthesis below the estimated coefficients.

The top panel of table 5.1 presents regressions of log BMI on racial and ethnic categories. The second panel shows regressions of log BMI on the highest grade of the household reference person.[7] The third panel shows the results for the income-to-poverty ratio. The fourth panel includes all measures of disadvantage simultaneously. In all years, there is some evidence that disadvantaged children are heavier, although the strength of that correlation varies with the measure and the time period. For example, black children do not have significantly higher BMIs than white children prior to 1999, although in the 1988 to 1994 wave of the NHANES the point estimate implies black children have an almost 1.0 percent higher BMI. By the 1999 to 2004 wave, that difference had increased to 2.1 percent and was statistically significant. Currently, the median eight-year-old girl stands at 4′2″ and weighs fifty-six pounds, so we would expect her to be 1.2 pounds heavier if she were black. Hispanic children have significantly higher BMIs than white non-Hispanic children in all but the first time period, and in the time periods when the difference is statistically significant it is stable at about 3.5 percent. For the same median eight-year-old girl then, we would expect her to be about two pounds heavier if she were Hispanic.

Being from a household where the reference person has a higher level of education is statistically significantly negatively correlated with BMI in all four time periods, increasing from a 0.2 percent lower BMI for each additional year of parental education in the early 1970s to a 0.6 percent reduction for each additional year by the early 2000s. Prior to 1980, children from families with higher income-to-poverty ratios did not have significantly lower BMIs. After 1988, however, that correlation is negative and statisti-

---

6. Note that sample sizes do not match those from later tables, as for these regressions we use all possible data. Regressions run on consistent samples are not substantively different from those shown here.

7. For NHANES 4, we define the reference person as the father, if present; otherwise, it is the mother. For the other three panels, the reference person is defined within the NHANES. See the data appendix for more details.

Table 5.1   Disadvantage and children's log BMI

	NHANES 1 1971–1975 (1)	NHANES 2 1976–1980 (2)	NHANES 3 1988–1994 (3)	NHANES 4 1999–2004 (4)
	Race on log BMI			
Black	−0.008	0.001	0.008	0.021
	(0.006)	(0.007)	(0.006)	(0.006)**
Hispanic	0.016	0.034	0.037	0.035
	(0.009)	(0.010)*	(0.006)**	(0.006)**
Other Nonwhite	0.006	−0.016	0.004	−0.002
	(0.020)	(0.014)	(0.012)	(0.013)
Observations	4,374	4,781	7,694	5,586
R^2	0.16	0.18	0.17	0.20
	Education on log BMI			
Highest grade for reference person	−0.002	−0.004	−0.003	−0.006
	(0.001)**	(0.001)**	(0.001)**	(0.002)**
Observations	4,260	4,688	7,582	2,869
R^2	0.16	0.18	0.17	0.18
	Poverty on log BMI			
Income/Poverty line ratio	0.002	−0.002	−0.006	−0.008
	(0.002)	(0.002)	(0.002)**	(0.002)**
Observations	4,276	4,637	7,095	5,142
R^2	0.16	0.17	0.17	0.20
	All 3 on log BMI			
Black	−0.009	−0.003	0.003	0.004
	(0.007)	(0.008)	(0.006)	(0.009)
Hispanic	0.011	0.026	0.024	0.033
	(0.009)	(0.011)*	(0.008)**	(0.009)**
Other Nonwhite	0.000	−0.018	−0.003	0.016
	(0.024)	(0.014)	(0.012)	(0.019)
Highest grade for reference person	−0.002	−0.005	−0.002	−0.001
	(0.001)*	(0.001)**	(0.001)*	(0.003)
Income/Poverty line ratio	0.005	0.006	−0.002	−0.007
	(0.002)*	(0.003)*	(0.003)	(0.003)*
Observations	4,175	4,567	7,011	2,646
R^2	0.16	0.19	0.17	0.19

Notes: All models also include a cubic in child's age fully interacted with gender. BMI is measured. Standard errors are in parentheses. Sample is limited to children age two to eleven.
***Significant at the 1 percent level.
**Significant at the 5 percent level.
*Significant at the 10 percent level.

cally significantly different from zero, and becoming steeper over time. By the last period, a girl from a family with income at the poverty line would be about 2.4 percent heavier than one with income three times the poverty line, compared to just 1.8 percent heavier in the previous period.

When we include all measures of disadvantage simultaneously, we find that once the income-to-poverty ratio and education are held constant, being black is no longer significantly positively correlated with BMI in any of the years, but being Hispanic is still associated with a higher BMI in all but the first period. Each additional year of education of the household reference person is associated with a 0.1 to 0.5 percent reduction in BMI, but the effect is no longer increasing over time, and in fact is not significantly different from zero in the final period. Finally, in all but the third wave, the income-to-poverty ratio is significantly correlated with children's BMI; however, in the first two periods the effect is positive. Overall, then, these regressions show that disadvantaged children are generally heavier, using a variety of measures of disadvantage. Additionally, for most of these measures, the effect of disadvantage has been growing over time.

5.5   Parent's and Children's Weight Outcomes

5.5.1   Mothers and Fathers

Parents and children share common genetics, and, if they live together, share a common environment. Thus, we expect to see a strong correlation between the BMI of parents and children. Note that the literature on nature versus nurture typically uses the standard behavioral genetics model to carry out a decomposition of these two effects by assuming that an outcome is a linear combination of the independent effects of genetics, shared family environment, and unexplained factors. Given that, in fact, genetics and the shared environment are unlikely to be independent, it is typical to interpret the genes component as incorporating both the direct effect of genes and the effect of the gene-environment interaction (Sacerdote 2007). Thus, while we do not expect that the underlying genetic predisposition toward obesity will have changed over the twenty or so years that childhood obesity has been increasing, examining changes in the parent-child correlation in BMI should give us insight into the ways in which the environment that parents and children share has affected children's body mass, or into how the interaction of shared genes and the environment has changed.

We investigate the parent-child correlation in BMI by running regressions of log(Child's BMI) on log(Parent's BMI). The coefficient on log(Parent's BMI) tells us the elasticity of children's BMI with respect to their parents—a one percent change in parent's BMI is correlated with what percent change in children's BMI. A larger elasticity implies a greater role for the common environment and genes that parents and children share; a smaller elasticity implies a greater role for environments that children do not share with their parents.

Table 5.2 presents regressions of the log of child's BMI on his or her mother's log BMI (column [1]), his or her father's BMI (column [2]), and both simultaneously (column [3]). These regressions control for race, ethnicity,

Table 5.2   **Intergenerational BMI elasticity**

	(1)	(2)	(3)
NHANES 1: 1971–1975			
log Mother's BMI	0.142		0.131
	(0.014)**		(0.015)**
log Father's BMI		0.141	0.126
		(0.016)**	(0.016)**
Observations	3,918	3,609	3,552
R^2	0.20	0.19	0.22
F test: Mom = Dad			0.04
Prob > F			0.843
NHANES 2: 1976–1980			
log Mother's BMI	0.141		0.120
	(0.016)**		(0.018)**
log Father's BMI		0.180	0.152
		(0.021)**	(0.021)**
Observations	4,402	4,173	4,116
R^2	0.22	0.22	0.24
F test: Mom = Dad			1.05
Prob > F			0.305
NHANES 3: 1988–1994			
log Mother's BMI	0.206		0.178
	(0.020)**		(0.022)**
log Father's BMI		0.208	0.150
		(0.023)**	(0.022)**
Observations	6,555	6,016	5,817
R^2	0.24	0.22	0.26
F test: Mom = Dad			0.66
Prob > F			0.415
NHANES 4: 1999–2004			
log Mother's BMI	0.196		0.188
	(0.019)**		(0.025)**
log Father's BMI		0.201	0.126
		(0.030)**	(0.029)**
Observations	2,249	1,770	1,394
R^2	0.27	0.23	0.30
F test: Mom = Dad			1.95
Prob > F			0.163

Notes: Dependent variable is the log of the child's measured BMI. Parental BMI data are reported for NHANES 1 through 3, and measured and matched for NHANES 4 (see data appendix for details). All models also control for race, highest grade completed by the household reference person, the household income-to-poverty ratio, and a cubic in child's age fully interacted with gender. Standard errors are in parentheses.

***Significant at the 1 percent level.

**Significant at the 5 percent level.

*Significant at the 10 percent level.

education of the reference person, the family's income-to-poverty ratio, and a cubic in the child's age fully interacted with gender.[8] The results in the first panel show that a 10 percent increase in either mother's or father's BMI is correlated with about a 1.4 percent increase in child's BMI. When both parents' BMI measures are in the regression the individual coefficients decline somewhat—as is to be expected since mother's and father's BMI are correlated as well—but both are statistically significant. If children, on average, shared the same amount of common genetics with their mothers and their fathers but shared more common environment with their mothers, we might expect that mothers' BMI would be more important in explaining children's BMI than fathers'—as mothers' BMI would pick up both the effect of common genetics and common environment. These results suggest that the common environment shared by mothers and their children and fathers and their children is similar. One caveat to this is that fathers' reported BMI is more likely to be missing than mothers'. Thus, one might say that the parent-child correlation in BMI is about the same for fathers and mothers, *when the father is present.* Since including fathers' BMI in the regression does not make much difference to the estimated mother-child correlation in BMI and we lose observations when we require nonmissing father BMI data (and those children who are missing fathers' BMI data are more likely to be disadvantaged), we focus on mother-child BMI elasticities in the analyses that follow.

Looking down the panels in table 5.2 we can see how the mother-child BMI elasticity has changed over time. Between the first and second wave of the NHANES, recall that children's obesity rates and BMIs do not change very much. Here we see that the mother-child BMI elasticity is nearly identical in these two periods as well, implying that a 10 percent increase in mothers' BMI is correlated with a 1.4 percent increase in children's BMI. In the third wave of the NHANES, the mother-child elasticity has grown larger. Now, a 10 percent increase in mothers' BMI is correlated with a 2.1 percent increase in children's BMI. In the fourth wave, the mother-child elasticity remains larger than in the earlier periods, with a 10 percent increase in mothers' BMI being correlated with about a 2 percent increase in children's BMI.

We can use the parent-child elasticity to estimate how much of the increase in children's average BMI over time would be predicted, given the mothers' average increase over the same time. We use the average BMI for mothers and children shown in appendix table 5A.1 to calculate the percentage change in children's BMI and the percentage change in mothers' BMI between the first and fourth period. Using the standard midpoint formula, this would imply that mothers' BMI grew 13.7 percent and the children's BMI grew 7.3

---

8. Results look similar if the child's own birth weight is included as a control variable.

percent.[9] However, even using the larger, later period, elasticity, the growth in mothers' BMI would imply less than a 3 percent growth in children's BMI.[10] The growth in mothers' BMI can explain 37.5 percent of the increase in children's BMI between the beginning and the end periods. Clearly, there are other factors besides the shared genetic-environmental factors of mothers and children that are driving the increase in children's BMI.

5.5.2   Interpreting the BMI Elasticity

As noted previously, the parent-child BMI elasticity cannot be used to isolate pure genetic and pure environmental determinants of weight status. The observed increase in mother-child BMI elasticity is best interpreted as reflecting an increase in the shared environment of mothers and their children, or the effect of the interaction of shared genes with the environment.[11] Using a sample of adult adopted and genetic siblings collected in 2004, Sacerdote (2007) estimates that the shared environment explains 30.8 percent of the variance in BMI, genes (and their correlation with the environment) explain 11.5 percent, and the rest (57.7 percent) is unexplained. Interestingly, this decomposition is very close to the one he calculates for family income, even though this is an outcome that typically might not be considered to be as genetically determined as BMI. That said, the role of genetics in the mother-child BMI elasticity is made clear when comparing estimates using the adopted children to those using the biological children.[12] Running a regression similar to that shown in column (1) of table 5.2 using these data,[13] one obtains an elasticity (standard error) for the biological children of 0.221 (0.045), but only 0.025 (0.025) for the adoptees. Thus, the elasticity for biological children for this sample is similar to our later elasticities, but it is unlikely to reflect current shared environment. The implication is that the interaction of shared genes and the general, not just the intrahousehold, environment is likely very important. Thus, suppose that some parents and children are predisposed to eat too much junk food, and vending machines go from being rare in the early period to being ubiquitously available in the later period both at work and in schools. We would observe an increase in BMI in both parents and children for the genetically predisposed that we would attribute to shared genetic-environmental factors. However, it is not

9. This is obtained by dividing the change between the first and last period by the average of the two periods.

10. Percentage change in children's BMI = (elasticity · percentage change in mothers' BMI) = (0.2 · 13.7 percent).

11. One concern is whether the increase in elasticity is real, or an artifact of changes in measurement error in BMI over time. We find that changes in measurement error would have to be implausibly large to be the underlying driver of the observed increase in parent-child BMI elasticities. See data appendix for a more detailed explanation.

12. Recall that these "children" are actually adults—the average age is twenty-eight for the adoptees and thirty-two for the biological children. Thus, it is unlikely that mother and child are literally sharing an environment at this point.

13. We thank Bruce Sacerdote for making his data available to us.

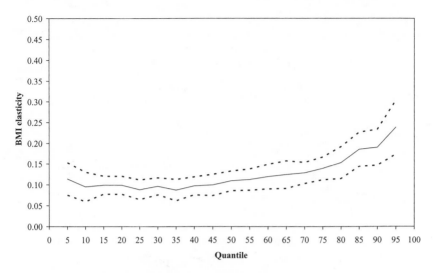

Fig. 5.4   NHANES 1 Mother-child log(BMI) relationship

necessarily the case that these shared environmental factors are solely within the walls of the household.

Finally, recall that although BMI has increased for everyone, the BMI for the obese has increased more than for the median person, which corresponds to a model of obesity such that there may be some people who are particularly susceptible to weight gain when the environment is right, and in the last two decades, the environment has been right.[14] Thus, the impact of common genetic and environmental factors may be different for children who occupy different points in the BMI distribution. Given that we have seen that disadvantaged kids are heavier, it is important to investigate whether the mother-child elasticity is constant throughout the BMI distribution or not. Thus, we estimate models identical to column (1) from table 5.2, but using quantile regression rather than OLS. We estimate elasticities that fit at each of 20 quantiles of the BMI distribution (versus OLS, which fits at the mean).

Figures 5.4 through 5.7 plot these quantile regression estimates and 95 percent confidence intervals for the mother-child BMI elasticity for NHANES 1 through 4. First, we see that the elasticity is generally higher at higher quantiles of the BMI distribution, suggesting that for heavier children, the shared environmental-genetic component captured by mothers' BMI is more important in determining their BMI. Second, this relationship seems

---

14. Note that how this all works is far from settled science. Recent evidence suggests that the obese may have different body chemistry such that for a given number of calories ingested, their digestive tract can extract more calories for use (Weill Medical Center 2007).

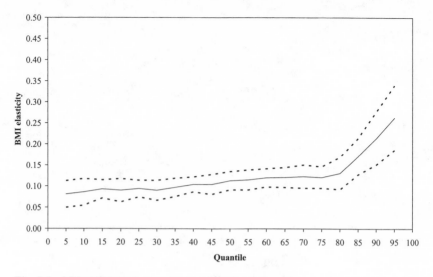

Fig. 5.5   NHANES 2 Mother-child log(BMI) relationship

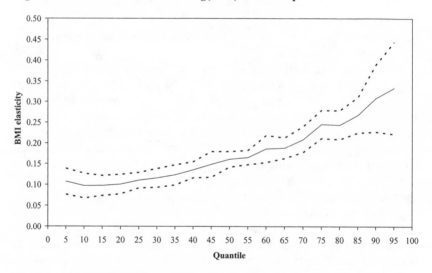

Fig. 5.6   NHANES 3 Mother-child log(BMI) relationship

to have gotten steeper over time. That is, while the elasticity is around 10 percent for the lowest quantiles in all periods, in the earlier periods it does not rise much above that level until increasing sharply at about the eightieth percentile. By contrast, in the later periods the elasticity rises smoothly throughout the quantiles.[15] The heavier the child, the more important the

15. Note, of course, that children at the middle quantiles in NHANES 3 and 4 have BMIs that would have placed them farther up the quantile distribution in the earlier year, but since

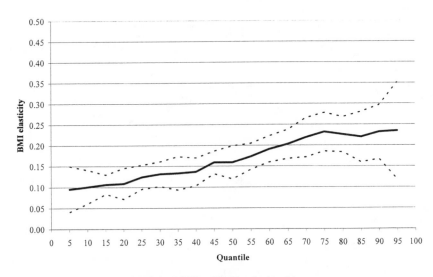

Fig. 5.7 NHANES 4 Mother-child log(BMI) relationship

common family genes and environment appear to be in determining his or her weight outcomes.

5.5.3 Differences in Mother-Child Elasticities by Measures of Disadvatages

Since disadvantaged children are heavier, the results in the preceding section might lead one to believe that parent-child elasticities would be higher for disadvantaged groups. Table 5.3 investigates whether the mother-child elasticity, which has increased on average, has changed in similar ways for advantaged and disadvantaged groups. The regressions control for a cubic in age fully interacted with gender, and all measures of disadvantage. Interactions between mother's log BMI and specific measures of disadvantage are entered separately. The top panel shows the interaction of log of mothers' BMI with race/ethnicity; the second panel shows the interaction with the reference person's highest grade completed; the third panel shows the interaction with the income-to-poverty-line ratio. The results for the different waves of the NHANES are reported in the four columns.

Looking down the panels we see, in general, that there is little consistent role for disadvantage in terms of its effect on the mother-child elasticity.[16] In the first panel, the majority of the point estimates imply that the mother-child elasticity for blacks and for Hispanics is smaller than for white

we are using ln(BMI) the shift is not as stark as it would be in levels. Thus, across NHANES 2 and 3, median ln(BMI) only increases from 2.77 to 2.78, while seventy-fifth percentile ln(BMI) increases from 2.85 to 2.88.

16. There continues to be no significant interaction effect when using quantile regression.

Table 5.3   **Interactions between disadvantage and mother's BMI**

	NHANES 1 1971–1975 (1)	NHANES 2 1976–1980 (2)	NHANES 3 1988–1994 (3)	NHANES 4 1999–2004 (4)
Race on log BMI				
log Mother's BMI	0.155	0.146	0.211	0.190
	(0.016)**	(0.019)**	(0.031)**	(0.025)**
Black	0.156	0.036	0.162	−0.064
	(0.122)	(0.120)	(0.112)	(0.126)
Hispanic	0.181	0.004	0.040	0.130
	(0.172)	(0.238)	(0.127)	(0.164)
Other race	−0.569	0.379	−0.155	−0.529
	(0.435)	(0.189)*	(0.177)	(0.316)
log Mother's BMI * Black	−0.054	−0.015	−0.053	0.014
	(0.035)	(0.038)	(0.035)	(0.038)
log Mother's BMI * Hispanic	−0.056	0.006	−0.010	−0.026
	(0.054)	(0.075)	(0.040)	(0.049)
log Mother's BMI * Other race	0.180	−0.125	0.045	0.173
	(0.140)	(0.059)*	(0.056)	(0.098)
Observations	3,918	4,402	6,555	2,249
R^2	0.20	0.22	0.24	0.27
Education on log BMI				
log Mother's BMI	0.172	0.177	0.172	0.371
	(0.053)**	(0.060)**	(0.077)*	(0.135)**
Highest grade for reference person	0.008	0.006	−0.011	0.048
	(0.015)	(0.016)	(0.022)	(0.036)
log Mother's BMI * Highest grade	−0.003	−0.003	0.003	−0.014
	(0.005)	(0.005)	(0.007)	(0.011)
Observations	3,918	4,402	6,555	2,249
R^2	0.20	0.22	0.24	0.27
Poverty on log BMI				
log Mother's BMI	0.119	0.101	0.171	0.217
	(0.025)**	(0.030)**	(0.029)**	(0.031)**
Income/Poverty line ratio	−0.034	−0.065	−0.055	0.031
	(0.036)	(0.045)	(0.051)	(0.036)
log Mother's BMI * Income/Poverty line	0.013	0.023	0.018	−0.010
	(0.012)	(0.014)	(0.016)	(0.011)
Observations	3,918	4,402	6,555	2,249
R^2	0.20	0.22	0.24	0.27

Notes: See notes to table 5.2.

***Significant at the 1 percent level.

**Significant at the 5 percent level.

*Significant at the 10 percent level.

non-Hispanics, but the estimates are not significantly different from zero and are not consistently negative in all periods. In the second panel, using the household reference person's education as a measure of disadvantage, there is again no real impact on the elasticity. In the final panel, when we use perhaps the most straightforward measure of disadvantage—the income-to-poverty-line ratio—the majority of the point estimates imply a lower elasticity for the disadvantaged, but again the difference is not significantly different from zero.

Nonetheless, table 5.4 uses the point estimates from table 5.3 to calculate the implied mother-child BMI elasticity for different groups. Doing this calculation makes clear that this elasticity has increased over time for most groups, but indicates that it may have decreased slightly (albeit not significantly) for the more advantaged groups in the last period. Recall from table 5.1 that the effect of disadvantage on children's BMI was positive and growing over time. That is, that the disadvantaged were increasingly heavier than the nondisadvantaged. However, it does not appear that this increasing effect of disadvantage can be attributed to differences in the shared genetic-environmental factors of these mothers and their children.

These results are somewhat puzzling when contrasted with the quantile regression results in the previous section. We expected that since heavier children show higher parent-child BMI elasticities, and disadvantaged children tend to be heavier, that we would find higher parent child elasticities for the disadvantaged. However, the quantile regression results suggest that common genetic-environment factors play a larger role for heavier children, and that this difference is better captured by one's place in the log BMI distribution itself than by coarse measures of disadvantage that are simply correlated with one's place in the BMI distribution.

Table 5.4   Mother-child BMI elasticity by group

	NHANES 1 1971–1975 (1)	NHANES 2 1976–1980 (2)	NHANES 3 1988–1994 (3)	NHANES 4 1999–2004 (4)
White	0.155	0.146	0.211	0.190
Black	0.101	0.131	0.158	0.204
Hispanic	0.336	0.150	0.251	0.320
Other race	−0.414	0.525	0.056	−0.339
Reference person's education = 10	0.142	0.147	0.202	0.231
Reference person's education = 12	0.136	0.141	0.208	0.203
Reference person's education = 16	0.124	0.129	0.220	0.147
Income-to-poverty ratio = 1st quartile cutoff	0.135	0.126	0.188	0.207
Income-to-poverty ratio = 2nd quartile cutoff	0.144	0.142	0.206	0.198
Income-to-poverty ratio = 3rd quartile cutoff	0.155	0.165	0.226	0.181

Notes: Calculations based on elasticities reported in table 5.4.

5.6   Common Parent-Child Environmental Factors

The previous analysis suggests that, overall, common parent-child factors are becoming increasingly important in determining weight outcomes. Ideally, we would like to be able to observe the factors that determine BMI—caloric intake and expenditure—and correlate these underlying factors for both adults and children. We would like to be able to do this for different measures of disadvantage in order to see whether it is differences in food consumed or exercise that determines differences in BMI across disadvantaged groups. Further, we would ideally be able to observe the environments in which the advantaged and disadvantaged live and examine whether these differences affect caloric intake or expenditure. In this section, we present some evidence on these environmental factors, while also discussing the many challenges in examining these direct determinants of BMI.

5.6.1   Caloric Intake by Disadvantage

Because we know that BMI is higher for disadvantaged groups, it seems likely we should find that caloric intake is higher for these groups or energy expended is lower. However, it is very difficult to find evidence of these differences. First, over time, relatively small caloric imbalances can result in a relatively large amount of weight gain. In fact, Cutler, Glaeser, and Shapiro (2003) estimate that the weight gain observed for the median adult male between the early 1970s and the early 2000s can be entirely accounted for by just a daily 150-calorie imbalance. Thus, just one extra twelve ounce can of nondiet soda per day is sufficient to cause the increase in the median man's weight gain seen in recent years. Even fewer excess calories can explain the increase in obesity for children (Schanzenbach 2005). Second, good data on caloric intake and expenditure are difficult to obtain. While food diary data (as is available in the NHANES), is generally considered fairly reliable, the caloric intake is still likely measured with error. Caloric expenditure data tends to be more problematic, since accurately describing the intensity of exercise can be difficult. As a result, analyses of caloric imbalance will likely have difficulty precisely estimating differences in calorie intake that are as small as those required to explain a great deal of weight gain over time.

Nonetheless, we will use the food diary data from the NHANES to try to get a feel for eating patterns over time and by disadvantage status. We will investigate caloric intake overall, and from a set of food types that may be markers of better or worse nutritional habits. In particular, we focus mainly on food away from home, fast food, and fruits and vegetables. Table 5.5 presents a regression of log(calories + 1) for each of these food types on the income-to-poverty ratio along with a cubic in age fully interacted with gender.[17] Thus, these models are identical to those shown in the third panel

---

17. We add one to all of the calorie counts so as not to have to drop observations with no consumption in a specific food group. See the data appendix for further details.

Table 5.5   **Calorie intake among children age 2 to 11**

	log(Total calories + 1) (1)	log(Calories from fruits and vegetables + 1) (2)	log(Calories eaten away from home + 1) (3)
	NHANES 1: 1971–1975		
Income/Poverty line ratio	0.006	0.080	0.002
	(0.005)	(0.022)**	(0.037)
Observations	4,092	4,092	4,092
R^2	0.11	0.01	0.09
	NHANES 2: 1976–1980		
Income/Poverty line ratio	0.011	0.081	0.065
	(0.006)*	(0.030)**	(0.052)
Observations	4,466	4,466	4,466
R^2	0.14	0.01	0.05
	NHANES 3: 1988–1994		
Income/Poverty line ratio	−0.009	0.066	0.284
	(0.006)	(0.025)**	(0.040)**
Observations	7,046	7,046	7,046
R^2	0.16	0.01	0.09
	NHANES 4: 1999–2004		
Income/Poverty line ratio	0.000	−0.026	0.357
	(0.006)	(0.024)	(0.042)**
Observations	3,099	3,099	3,099
R^2	0.11	0.02	0.08

Notes: Other covariates include a cubic in age fully interacted with gender. BMI is measured. Standard errors are in parentheses.
***Significant at the 1 percent level.
**Significant at the 5 percent level.
*Significant at the 10 percent level.

of table 5.1, but using calories instead of BMI in the dependent variable. The regressions using total calories show an inconsistent pattern in the correlation between the income-to-poverty line ratio and total calories. In the first wave, the relationship is positive, but insignificant. In the second wave, it is positive and significant—meaning that children from wealthier families report consuming more calories. In the third wave it is negative and insignificant; in the fourth, it is very small and insignificant. Thus, if anything, we observe a change between NHANES 2 and 3 in which disadvantage no longer implies fewer calories (rather, more calories), but that in more recent years, all children have similar caloric intake.

While total calories (if well-measured) are what ought to matter for weight gain or loss, we also examine calorie intake from fruits and vegetables and calories consumed away from home. Consumption of fruits and vegetables may be viewed as a "marker" of healthful eating habits, and thus may give us some insight into how disadvantage may correlate with poor nutrition. Similarly, we examine calories from food consumed away from home. One popular explanation for the rise in obesity is that consumption of food from fast food and other restaurants has increased. The notion is that with professionally prepared food individuals are less aware of the calorie content of what they are eating, have less control over portion size, and may find the food more palatable than food prepared at home. Note that French fries are included in this measure of fruits and vegetables—for some of the years we can separate out certain food types and food venders and we will do that when we examine parent-child correlations in calorie consumption.

For now, note that the second column of table 5.5 indicates that in the first three NHANES, higher income is associated with significantly more calories from fruits and vegetables. In the last two NHANES, higher incomes are associated with significantly more calories consumed away from home. Thus, there is some evidence that advantaged and disadvantaged children consume calories from different sources, and that these relationships may have changed over time. However, with these broad measures of caloric intake it is hard to see how this may translate into differences in BMI.

5.6.2   Mother-Child Calorie Elasticies

Having seen that the intrahousehold correlation in BMI has increased over time, but with no real pattern by disadvantaged, we now turn to looking more closely at intrahousehold correlations in eating patterns. With NHANES 3 and 4, we have enough data to look at children matched to an adult household member. The matched data looks very similar to the total data that are both available for NHANES 3. Appendix table 5A.2 repeats the relevant panel of table 5.5, and then replicates it using the matched data. Additionally, the more detailed food codes allow us to remove French fries and potato chips from the fruit and vegetable category, and to identify fast food consumption. The final columns, then, reflect these two additional food groups. Note that without French fries and chips, the effect of disadvantage on fruit and vegetable consumption becomes more important. Similarly, while the more advantaged do eat more fast food, the effect is much smaller than for the broader food-away-from-home category, and is not significantly different from zero.

Having seen that the matched data is similar to the full data, we now use NHANES 3 and 4 data to estimate intrahousehold calorie elasticities in a manner identical to those calculated for BMI in table 5.2. For each of the five food groups (i.e., total calories, fruit and vegetable calories, calories away from home, fruit and vegetable calories without fries and chips, and fast food calories), we regress the child's log(calories + 1) on first the mother's log(calories + 1), then the father's log(calories + 1), and then both. The results are in table 5.6. For total calories, the results show patterns that are similar to the BMI estimates. That is, both the mother and the father matter, estimates are similar whether the parents are included together or separately, and there is no significant difference between mother and father.

Table 5.6   **Relationship between parent and child calorie intake**

	NHANES 3 (1988–1994)			NHANES 4 (1999–2004)		
	(1)	(2)	(3)	(4)	(5)	(6)
	log (Total calories + 1)					
log(Mom's total calories)	0.101		0.101	0.150		0.116
	(0.021)**		(0.030)**	(0.029)**		(0.037)**
log(Dad's total calories)		0.147	0.131		0.120	0.071
		(0.034)**	(0.034)**		(0.038)**	(0.038)
Observations	3,342	1,859	1,859	1,229	994	748
R^2	0.17	0.18	0.19	0.14	0.15	0.15
F test: Mom = Dad			0.39			0.70
Prob > F			0.532			0.403
	log (Calories eaten away from home + 1)					
log(Mom's calories away from home)	0.288		0.202	0.329		0.292
	(0.027)**		(0.035)**	(0.034)**		(0.043)**
log(Dad's calories away from home)		0.179	0.145		0.244	0.196
		(0.042)**	(0.042)**		(0.040)**	(0.047)**
Observations	3,342	1,859	1,859	1,229	994	748
R^2	0.16	0.11	0.15	0.23	0.19	0.29
F test: Mom = Dad			0.92			1.73
Prob > F			0.339			0.189
	log (Calories from fruits and vegetables + 1)					
log(Mom's fruit/veg calories)	0.246		0.248	0.111		0.099
	(0.036)**		(0.049)**	(0.039)**		(0.048)*
log(Dad's fruit/veg calories)		0.237	0.179		0.077	0.009
		(0.047)**	(0.049)**		(0.041)	(0.044)
Observations	3,342	1,859	1,859	1,229	994	748
R^2	0.07	0.08	0.13	0.05	0.03	0.04
F test: Mom = Dad			0.79			1.67
Prob > F			0.375			0.197
	log (Calories from fruits and vegetables, less french fries + 1)					
log(Mom's fruit/veg calories, no fries)	0.263		0.270	0.165		0.158
	(0.029)**		(0.042)**	(0.040)**		(0.048)**
log(Dad's fruit/veg calories, no fries)		0.229	0.146		0.132	0.080
		(0.038)**	(0.042)**		(0.041)**	(0.046)
Observations	3,342	1,859	1,859	1,229	994	748
R^2	0.09	0.09	0.16	0.06	0.04	0.07
F test: Mom = Dad			2.98			1.24
Prob > F			0.084			0.266
	ln (Calories from fast food + 1)					
log(Mom's fast food calories)	0.375		0.319	0.506		0.447
	(0.038)**		(0.046)**	(0.037)**		(0.049)**
log(Dad's fast food calories)		0.229	0.151		0.353	0.204
		(0.041)**	(0.035)**		(0.038)**	(0.042)**
Observations	3,342	1,859	1,859	1,229	994	748
R^2	0.19	0.10	0.21	0.29	0.18	0.35
F test: Mom = Dad			6.99			9.67
Prob > F			0.008			0.002

Notes: Data are for the matched NHANES 3 (1988–1994) and NHANES 4 (1999–2004) samples. Other covariates include a cubic in age fully interacted with gender, race, income-to-poverty ratio, and head's education level.

***Significant at the 1 percent level.

**Significant at the 5 percent level.

*Significant at the 10 percent level.

Additionally, unlike for the BMI elasticity, the point estimate of the calorie elasticity increases somewhat between the two later periods.

For the specific food groups, the mother elasticity is always larger, and is sometimes significantly different from the father elasticity when included together. In the earlier period, while mother is not significantly different from father for all fruits and vegetables, once we remove French fries and chips there is a marginally statistically significant difference. When looking specifically at fast food, the maternal elasticity of 0.319 is twice the size of the paternal elasticity of 0.151. This finding is consistent with a story where fathers have opportunities to eat fast food that do not include their children—for example, lunch on a workday. In the second period, however, only the elasticity of calories from fast food shows a statistically significant difference between the mother and father.

Some interesting patterns emerge when comparing the food subgroup results across periods. For the main markers of poor diet—food away from home and fast food, the calorie elasticity increases over time, while for both measures of fruits and vegetables, the calorie elasticity decreases, as does the total calorie elasticity. This pattern holds for both the mothers and the fathers. Recall that the data with which we can calculate parent-child calorie elasticities come from only the last two NHANES. In these data, the parent-child BMI elasticity was higher than in the earlier two periods, but about the same between these two years. Thus, it is not necessarily a conflict that we do not see an increase in, for example, the total calorie elasticity between these two years.

While it appears that both mother's and father's eating patterns influence children, mothers seem to play the dominant role. Thus, as was the case with the BMI elasticities, we will just focus on the maternal elasticity when investigating the role of disadvantage.

Table 5.7 is parallel to the bottom panel of table 5.3, in that it uses the income-to-poverty ratio as the measure of disadvantage, and interacts it with the maternal log(calorie + 1) measure. Here, each column is a different food group. Looking first at column (1), we see that the elasticity of total calories is larger for the more disadvantaged, but this difference is only marginally statistically significant in the last period. This point estimate may be due to the fact that by this time period advantaged mothers are more likely to work (and work longer hours) than disadvantaged mothers (Anderson, Butcher, and Levine 2003b). Advantaged mothers may thus be spending more time away from their children than disadvantaged mothers, leading to a lower elasticity in calories consumed. Overall, though, as was the case with table 5.3, there is little evidence of a statistically significant difference in the mother-child calorie elasticity for the disadvantaged.

6.6.3   Other Environmental Factors

Previously we examined reported caloric intake patterns for insight into the shared environment between mothers and their children that might affect

Table 5.7   Relationship between calories, disadvantage, and mother's calories

	log (Total calories + 1) (1)	log (Calories from fruits and vegetables + 1) (2)	log (Calories eaten away from home + 1) (3)	log (Calories from fruit/veg, no fries + 1) (4)	log (Calories from fast food + 1) (5)
		A. NHANES 3 (1988–1994)			
log(Mother's calories)	0.162	0.224	0.310	0.267	0.360
	(0.039)**	(0.064)**	(0.042)**	(0.049)**	(0.063)**
log(Mother's calories) * Income/ Poverty line ratio	−0.030	0.011	−0.011	−0.002	0.007
	(0.019)	(0.030)	(0.019)	(0.021)	(0.026)
Observations	3,342	3,342	3,342	3,342	3,342
R^2	0.17	0.07	0.16	0.09	0.19
		B. NHANES 4 (1999–2004)			
log(Mother's calories)	0.229	0.120	0.341	0.243	0.502
	(0.048)**	(0.064)	(0.059)**	(0.068)**	(0.063)**
log(Mother's calories) * Income/ Poverty line ratio	−0.041	−0.004	−0.003	−0.038	0.002
	(0.019)*	(0.029)	(0.021)	(0.029)	(0.023)
Observations	1,229	1,229	1,229	1,229	1,229
R^2	0.15	0.05	0.22	0.06	0.29

Notes: See table 5.6.

***Significant at the 1 percent level.

**Significant at the 5 percent level.

*Significant at the 10 percent level.

their BMI. This intake is clearly a small subset of the complex environmental factors that affect body mass, however. One would clearly like information on calories expended as well as calories consumed. The measurement problems that attend collecting information on calories consumed are increased for calories expended—not only does one need information on the number of minutes spent running, for example, but the intensity of that activity. Carefully controlled medical studies are able to document how calories expended and consumed affect BMI; however, these necessarily give us little insight into who chooses to participate in different caloric intake and expenditure behavior and why they make those different decisions.

In order to explain differences in body mass between the advantaged and disadvantaged, many social science researchers have turned to documenting differences in the living environment that each group faces. We examined county business pattern data for 1980 to 1986 and 1988 to 1994 (years that roughly correspond to the second and third waves of the NHANES data— the period when we see an initial jump in children's obesity rates) in order to see whether the environments in which the disadvantaged live have changed differentially from the environments in which the advantaged live in ways that are likely to affect body mass. The results showed no consistent pattern between changes in the availability of restaurants, grocery stores, or recreation outlets and various measures of disadvantage.

There are several problems with this approach. First, the establishment definitions are coarse; for example, many types of restaurants are grouped together. Growth in the count of restaurants in an advantaged area may represent growth in establishments that cater to a health-conscious crowd, while in a disadvantaged area it may represent growth in fast food restaurants. Thus, it is perhaps not surprising that we found no consistent pattern in changes in establishment types over time by county level measures of disadvantage.

A second problem is more fundamental, and would be a problem even if we had very detailed and accurate measures of establishment type linked to specific geographic areas. Ideally, we would like to examine whether an exogenous increase in concentration of fast food restaurants, for example, increases caloric intake and increases body mass. Similarly, we would like to know whether an exogenous increase in recreational space, for example, increases exercise and reduces weight. Without that exogenous variation, it is very hard to say whether fast food restaurants cause people to eat unhealthful foods, or whether restaurant owners simply open franchises near where they perceive their customers to live—for example, obese individuals would likely consume fast food whether or not there is one around the corner, but franchise owners, in an attempt to get customers into their *particular* store, may try to locate very close to the customers. Given the importance for policy purposes of understanding whether location of fast food restaurants, for example, has a *causal* impact on obesity, research with a design that credibly answers this question is a high priority.

5.7   Conclusion

Designing good policies to affect childhood obesity will require an understanding of how the environment that children face is related to their body mass. Although our attempts to directly measure changes in the food and exercise environments faced by advantaged and disadvantaged children were not very fruitful, our earlier results on child-parent BMI elasticity indirectly suggest that shared environment/genetics do play an important role. In fact, we find that the shared mother-child component of BMI became increasingly important over this time period, reflected in the increase in the mother-child BMI elasticity. However, if the only determinants of children's body mass were their genes and the environment they share with their parents, we would expect to find that increases in parents' BMI can go a long way toward explaining the increases we have seen in children's BMI over the last few decades. Instead, on average, based on our estimates of the mother-child BMI elasticity, the 13.7 percent increase in mothers' average BMI over the thirty-year period we examine can explain, at most, 40 percent of the 7.3 percent increase in children's average BMI.

The title of this chapter asks whether in determining children's obesity, "nurture" is trumping "nature" and whether that is different for disadvantaged children. While we find that common parent-child factors are becoming more important in determining children's weight outcomes, this result is consistent with *both* an increasing role for "nurture" *and* an increasing role for "nature." For example, there is either an increasing role for the shared environments that affect both parents' and children's body mass, or an increasing role of the overall environment for certain genetic profiles (which may be shared by parents and their children). The former situation might fit what we loosely mean by "nurture"—parental choices that involve such things as increasingly sharing meals and snacks made up of unhealthful foods or sharing more sedentary, rather than vigorous, activities. The latter situation might fit what we loosely think of as "nature"—or at least how one's natural susceptibility toward obesity interacts with one's environment—and might include eating increasingly available unhealthful foods in separate environments (say at school for children, at work for parents) that have similar effects on those with the same genetic susceptibility to weight gain. Note that Anderson and Butcher (2006b) finds evidence for a different effect of "environment" on those with a genetic susceptibility toward weight gain since that study finds that the availability of junk food in schools results in higher weights only for those adolescents who have an overweight parent.

Overall, it appears that the parent-child elasticity is similar for advantaged and disadvantaged children, for both it has increased over time, but, as noted previously, changes in parents' BMI still does not explain most of the change in children's BMI. Regardless of whether one wants to interpret the finding that the elasticity has increased as evidence for increasing importance of parental choices for children ("nurture") or the increasing importance of the environment for both children and parents who share a similar genetic susceptibility to weight gain ("nature" interacting with the environment), there appear to be different factors that affect parents' and children's body mass. Child-specific environments like schools, child care facilities, and playgrounds may play an important role in determining children's weight outcomes. This is an important implication since it suggests policies targeted at changing children's environment outside the family, rather than solely targeting parental choices, may be an effective way to address childhood obesity.

Data Appendix

Variable Definitions and Parent-Child Match

All of the data used in the chapter are from the National Health and Nutrition Examination Survey (NHANES). Most of these data are publicly available from the National Center for Health Statistics (NCHS), Centers for Disease Control and Prevention (CDC), at their website (http://www.cdc.gov/nchs/nhanes.htm). We use four waves of this survey. The first, known as NHANES 1, was collected between 1971 and 1975; the second, NHANES 2, was collected between 1976 and 1980, while the third, NHANES 3, was collected between 1988 and 1994. With sampling weights, these data are representative of the U.S. population at the midpoint of the survey years. For each of these three waves, we extract publicly available information from the youth examination files on professionally measured body mass index (BMI) for all children age two to eleven. For each of these children reported BMI is also publicly available for each of their resident parents, along with basic demographics such as age, gender, and race/ethnicity. For an adult household reference person, we also have completed education in years, and for the family as a group we have the ratio of family income to the poverty line for a family of that size in that year.

Also publicly available for the children is information from a twenty-four-hour recall food diary. Each food item consumed is separately recorded, giving the food category, along with key nutritional information such as calories. The exact food codes used differ slightly over the waves, but we can always identify whether the food item was consumed at home or away, and the major food group (e.g., fruits and vegetables, dairy products, etc.). For consistency across waves, we choose to look at total calories, calories from the major category, "all fruits and vegetables," and calories consumed away from home. For each individual, then, we aggregate the calories from food items in those categories to obtain a per-person measure of total calories consumed, calories consumed from fruits and vegetables, and calories consumed away from home. We then add one to each of these aggregates. While one calorie is fairly incidental in an individual's diet, this addition allows us to take logs of our calories subgroups, even if an individual did not eat any calories from that group in the twenty-four hours captured by the diary.

The fourth wave is slightly different from the first three. First, what we will refer to as NHANES 4 is actually made up of three separate sub-waves named NHANES 1999–2000, NHANES 2001–2002, and NHANES 2003–2004. These data can be pooled and appropriate six-year sample weights computed such that the data are also representative of the U.S. population at the midpoint of the survey years. As with the other waves, we extract publicly available data on professionally measured BMI for children age two to eleven, along with basic demographics such as age, gender, and race/ethnicity. Also available for each child is the income-to-poverty line ratio for the child's family. Unfortunately, the reported parental BMI is not available in these data. As a result, we must create a "matched" data set using a confidential household identifier to compute intrahousehold BMI elasticities. Because NHANES 3 is also large enough to create a similar matched data set (using the publicly available household identifier), we can evaluate the importance of this alternate approach.

Based on results from NHANES 3, which determined that 89 percent of households had only one adult (age twenty to fifty) male and 88 percent had only one adult female, we settled on a very simple matching algorithm. For each household, the adult females age twenty to fifty, adult males age twenty to fifty, and children age two to eleven were separated out and sorted by age. The first adult female in the household was then assigned to be the child's "mother" and the first adult male was assigned to be the "father." Based on the reported parental information in NHANES 3, it appeared that only 4 percent of the matched mothers had a BMI and age that were inappropriate. As a result, models identical to those in tables 5.2 and 5.3 run using the matched NHANES 3 data looked very much like those presented using the larger data set with reported parental BMI.

Unfortunately, with NHANES 4, we cannot make this same comparison, but again, given the large number of households with only one adult female or adult male, we feel confident that the results are reliable. A few other differences in NHANES 4 are potentially problematic. First, education was not reported for the household reference person. Thus, we must use the matched "mother" and "father" to determine the reference person's education. When we have education for a "father" in the household, we choose that as the reference person's education. Otherwise, we use the "mother" in the household. Second, in NHANES 4, education is not recorded as years completed, but rather is categorical—less than high school, high school graduate, and beyond high school. To maintain consistency with the previous waves, we code these categories as ten years of education, twelve years,

Table 5A.1   Summary statistics

	(1) NHANES 1 1971–1975	(2) NHANES 2 1976–1980	(3) NHANES 3 1988–1994	(4) NHANES 4 1999–2004
BMI	16.41	16.58	17.05	17.65
	(2.29)	(2.61)	(3.02)	(3.52)
Mother's BMI	24.14	23.93	24.90	27.68
	(4.96)	(4.91)	(5.54)	(6.89)
Father's BMI	28.68	25.62	26.12	27.86
	(5.30)	(3.65)	(4.05)	(5.39)
Black	0.14	0.15	0.16	0.10
	(0.34)	(0.36)	(0.36)	(0.30)
Hispanic	0.07	0.08	0.08	0.19
	(0.25)	(0.27)	(0.28)	(0.39)
Other race	0.01	0.03	0.10	0.05
	(0.10)	(0.16)	(0.30)	(0.23)
Female	0.49	0.49	0.49	0.49
	(0.50)	(0.50)	(0.50)	(0.50)
Highest grade of reference person	11.54	11.87	12.60	12.49
	(3.16)	(3.25)	(3.05)	(1.61)
Income/Poverty line ratio	2.12	1.99	2.21	2.35
	(1.22)	(1.09)	(1.42)	(1.55)
Observations	4,092	4,594	7,124	2,870

Note: Standard deviations in parentheses.

and fourteen years, respectively. The results obtained when approximating continuous years of education in this way do not differ substantively from results obtained when including the categorical dummies. Appendix table 5A.1 presents summary statistics for the variables used in our main analyses for all four waves of the NHANES.

As noted previously, the twenty-four-hour food recall diaries (used in our secondary analyses) are available for everyone, making it possible to examine the effect of disadvantage on eating patterns for all waves of the NHANES. However, within-household correlations can only be computed when children are matched to adults in the household. While we can follow the matching procedures previously outlined for NHANES 1 and 2, the resulting sample sizes are too small to provide useful estimates. Thus, we limit our in-depth analysis of intrahousehold eating behaviors to the NHANES 3 and 4.

Across these two waves, we try to maintain as much consistency in the definition of food groups as possible. One area where this is not entirely possible is in the definition of fast food calories. In NHANES 3, calories are coded based on the item being described using a set of detailed codes for branded products (e.g., Burger King Whopper, Wendy's Frosty, etc.). Thus, "fast food calories" implies having consumed any kind of food from a fast food restaurant, no matter where it was consumed. In NHANES 1999–2000, we can

Table 5A.2   **Comparing reported and matched NHANES 3 samples**

	log (Total calories + 1) (1)	log (Calories from fruits and vegetables + 1) (2)	log (Calories eaten away from home + 1) (3)	log (Calories from fruit/veg, no fries + 1) (4)	log (Calories from fast food + 1) (5)
		NHANES III: Overall sample			
Income/Poverty line	−0.009	0.066	0.284	0.117	0.035
ratio	(0.006)	(0.025)**	(0.040)**	(0.026)**	(0.028)
Observations	7,046	7,046	7,046	7,046	7,046
R^2	0.16	0.01	0.09	0.01	0.00
		NHANES III: Matched sample			
Income/Poverty line	−0.002	0.039	0.251	0.081	0.044
ratio	(0.010)	(0.043)	(0.059)**	(0.042)	(0.043)
Observations	3,365	3,365	3,365	3,365	3,365
R^2	0.15	0.00	0.07	0.01	0.00

Note: See table 5.6.
**Significant at the 5 percent level.

identify that a food item was eaten at a fast food establishment, but if it was brought home and eaten, it will not be coded as "fast food." In NHANES 2003–2004, we can identify that a food item was obtained from a fast food restaurant, no matter where it was consumed, while in NHANES 2001–2002 we cannot identify fast food at all. As a result, for NHANES 4, "fast food calories" implies calories from food items that were either eaten at a fast food restaurant in the early years or obtained from a fast food restaurant in the later years.

Implications for Estimated Elasticity of Changing Measurement Error in BMI

While it appears that between the 1971 to 1980 and 1988 to 2004 periods there was a marked increase in the parent-child BMI elasticity, a concern with this conclusion may be that, in fact, the true elasticity has not changed, but rather the amount of measurement error in BMI has fallen, allowing us to estimate this true elasticity more precisely (e.g., the signal-to-noise ratio has risen). If one makes the assumption of a constant true elasticity, one can use the estimated elasticities, along with the variance in log mothers' BMI, to estimate what combination of constant elasticity and error variance would be consistent with these estimated elasticities. The result is an implausibly large error variance of 0.030 combined with a constant elasticity of 0.52. Note that in NHANES 3, since we have both reported and measured maternal BMI, we can calculate an alternate measure of the error variance (and thus of the true elasticity) from a regression of the measured BMI on the reported BMI. This exercise implies a true elasticity of 0.23, with an error variance of just 0.004 in NHANES 3. Thus, we conclude that it is very unlikely that a simple measurement error story is behind the increase in the estimated elasticity, and that there has indeed been an increase in the true elasticity.

References

Anderson, P. M., and K. F. Butcher. 2006a. Causes of the increase in childhood overweight and obesity. *The Future of Children: Childhood Obesity* 16 (1): 19–46.

———. 2006b. Reading, writing and refreshments: Are school finances contributing to children's obesity? *Journal of Human Resources* 41 (3): 467–94.

Anderson, P. M., K. F. Butcher, and P. B. Levine. 2003a. Economic perspectives on childhood obesity. Federal Reserve Bank of Chicago, *Economic Perspectives* 27 (3): 30–48.

———. 2003b. Maternal employment and overweight children. *Journal of Health Economics* 22:477–504.

Burkhauser, R. V., J. Cawley, and M. D. Schmeiser. 2007. Prevalence of adult obesity based on skinfold thickness in the United States, 1959–2004. Cornell University, Unpublished Manuscript.

Centers for Disease Control and Prevention. 2007. Obesity trends among U.S. adults between 1985 and 2004. Powerpoint presentation available at: http://www.cdc.gov/nccdphp/dnpa/obesity/trend/maps/.

Cutler, D. M., E. L. Glaeser, and J. M. Shapiro. 2003. Why have Americans become more obese? *Journal of Economic Perspectives* 17 (3): 93–118.

Lakdawalla, D. N., and T. J. Philipson. 2002. The growth of obesity and technological change: A theoretical and empirical examination. NBER Working Paper no. 8946. Cambridge, MA: National Bureau of Economic Research, May.

Mei, Z., L. M. Grummer-Strawn, J. Wang, J. C. Thornton, D. S. Freedman, R. N. Pierson, Jr., W. H. Dietz, and M. Horlick. 2007. Do skinfold measurements provide additional information to body mass index in the assessment of body fatness among children and adolescents? *Pediatrics* 119 (6): 1306–13.

Sacerdote, B. 2007. How large are the effects from changes in family environment? A study of Korean American adoptees. *Quarterly Journal of Economics* 122 (1): 119–58.

Schanzenbach, D. W. 2005. Do school lunches contribute to childhood obesity? University of Chicago, Harris School of Public Policy Studies, Working Paper no. 0513.

Strauss, R. S., and H. A. Pollack. 2001. Epidemic increase in childhood overweight, 1986–1998. *Journal of the American Medical Association* 286 (22): 2845–48.

Stunkard, A. J., J. R. Harris, N. L. Pedersen, and G. E. McClearn. 1990. The body-mass index of twins who have been reared apart. *New England Journal of Medicine* 322 (21): 1483–87.

Weill Medical School of Cornell University. 2007. Body weight and body chemistry: Obesity is not just lack of willpower or exercise, but body chemistry gone awry—but you can outsmart the system. *Food and Fitness Advisor* February.

Socioeconomic Disadvantage
and Early Childbearing

Melissa S. Kearney and Phillip B. Levine

6.1 Introduction

Each year, roughly five percent of teenagers give birth in the United States, a level that is considerably higher than that in any other developed country (United Nations 2006). This point-in-time statistic masks higher cumulative rates of childbearing as women pass through their teen years. As we show subsequently, in the United States between 7 and 10 percent of women will give birth before the age of eighteen and roughly 20 percent will give birth before the age of twenty.

Concern is often expressed regarding the potential harm that teen childbearing imposes on the mother, the child, and potentially to society more broadly. The National Campaign to Prevent Teen Pregnancy (2007) has summarized many of the statistics that are often used to support arguments about the potential pitfalls associated with teen childbearing. They highlight the fact that women who give birth as teens tend to subsequently have lower educational attainment and higher rates of welfare receipt. Their children are more likely to be born with low birth weight and have weaker performance in school. Although it is difficult to determine the extent to which the teen birth is the causal reason for these poor outcomes, these relationships

Melissa S. Kearney is an assistant professor of economics at the University of Maryland and a faculty research fellow of the National Bureau of Economic Research. Phillip B. Levine is the Class of 1919 Professor at Wellesley College and a research associate of the National Bureau of Economic Research.

This paper was prepared for the conference meeting, "An Economics Perspective on the Problems of Disadvantaged Youth." The authors thank conference participants for very helpful comments and Dubravka Colic and Rebecca Vichniac for very helpful research assistance. This research was funded by the Annie E. Casey Foundation. We thank them for their support but acknowledge that the findings and conclusions presented in this report are those of the authors alone, and do not necessarily reflect the opinions of the Foundation.

are both sufficiently strong and alarming that they receive a great deal of attention.

If early childbearing is associated with poor outcomes for both mothers and their children, then why do women give birth at such an early age? Public discussions directed at answering this question have focused on a number of potential explanations: the incentives of the welfare system, poor labor market outcomes for teens, lack of access to affordable contraception, poor parental and peer influences, and socioeconomic disadvantage, among others. In this chapter we focus on the last potential contributor.

Socioeconomic disadvantage can lead to early childbearing through a number of different mechanisms. The poor may lack the resources available to know about the different opportunities available to them or to take advantage of those opportunities. This could hinder their ability to make optimal choices regarding contraceptive use, educational attainment, labor market training, and the like. Alternatively, those at the bottom of the economic ladder may have given up hope of improving their economic conditions or those of their offspring. Schools and/or labor market conditions in their communities may be so weak that staying in school and avoiding early motherhood might not be seen as offering any material benefit. In addition, some evidence suggests that those who grow up in disadvantaged situations have a stronger "taste" for children. Edin and Kafalas (2005) argue that "the daily stresses of an impoverished adolescence . . . breed a deep sense of need for something positive to 'look to'" (205).

Our goal in this chapter is to examine the empirical relationship between socioeconomic disadvantage and rates of early childbearing. We begin by exploring past research in different disciplines that posit factors that may lead to early childbearing, focusing on the role that socioeconomic disadvantage may play. We then extend our literature review to discuss related empirical research that may inform our discussion. We continue our analysis by offering our own empirical exercises. First, we use micro-level data from the Panel Study of Income Dynamics (PSID) to provide a descriptive analysis of the relationship between socioeconomic disadvantage and early childbearing. Second, we aggregate Vital Statistics microdata from 1968 through 2003 to conduct a cohort-based analysis of the relationship between rates of socioeconomic disadvantage of a birth cohort and the cohort's subsequent early childbearing experiences.[1] We proxy for disadvantage at birth with four alternate factors, all based on the mother's characteristics: having been born

---

1. To be clear, we do not investigate what it is about socioeconomic disadvantage that leads young women to have children before the age of eighteen or twenty. Our empirical approach does not allow us to separately identify which aspects of socioeconomic disadvantage—such as poor schools, peer influences, living arrangements, or lack of optimism about future labor market opportunities—are driving this relationship. Yet, as we clarify in our literature review, the state of knowledge regarding the broader relationship is sufficiently limited that we can make a substantial contribution focusing on that alone.

to a mother with a low level of education, to an unmarried mother, or to a teen or minor mother.

Our cohort-based analysis allows us to answer the following hypothetical question: if we reduce the rate of socioeconomic disadvantage among a birth cohort of women, then what impact does that have on their subsequent rate of early childbearing? Asked differently, to what extent is early childbearing driven by socioeconomic disadvantage and its associated environmental factors? We know from previous studies that women who grow up "disadvantaged" are much more likely to give birth as teens. Our PSID analysis confirms this strong correlation at the individual level. Our cohort level analysis implies an even tighter intergenerational correlation between rates of background disadvantage and early childbearing. But, when our analysis econometrically controls for fixed state and year of birth effects in the model to account for cultural and other differences across cohorts, the relationship between rates of disadvantage and early childbearing is found to be quite modest. For example, the elasticity of early childbearing rates by age eighteen with respect to the probability of being born to a mother under age eighteen is only 0.05. This suggests that broader, societal forces are far more important in determining rates of early childbearing than rates of socioeconomic disadvantage per se.

The remainder of the chapter proceeds as follows. Section 6.2 presents some theoretical considerations that are designed to help think about what we might expect regarding the relationship between socioeconomic disadvantage and early childbearing. Section 6.3 describes the results of past research that may help guide our thinking. In section 6.4, we present our analysis of PSID data, providing a descriptive analysis of this relationship. Section 6.5 reports the details of our cohort-based analysis using aggregated Vital Statistics natality data. We conclude in section 6.6.

6.2   Theoretical Considerations

Noneconomists typically attribute early childbearing to be the result of myriad influences that affect a youth's development and fall outside the control of a rational decision-making process (e.g., Brooks-Gunn and Furstenberg 1989; Hardy and Zabin 1991; Brooks-Gunn and Paikoff 1997). Brooks-Gunn and Furstenberg (1989) consider five perspectives on adolescent sexual behavior: (a) biological perspectives; (b) parental influences; (c) peer influences; (d) academic perspectives; and (e) social cognitive perspectives. In stark contrast to the economic model of rational decision making, the authors note that "most teens do not consciously plan to become sexually active, and they often do not foresee their first sexual experience. As such, it frequently is not experienced as a decision but rather as something that 'happened,'" citing Chilman (1983, 251) on this last point.

A focus on *biological perspectives* emphasizes the role of hormonal factors in driving the onset of sexual activity.[2] In their consideration of *parental influences* the authors highlight research suggesting that teens who have good communication with their parents, teens who have feelings of "connectedness and supportiveness" with their parents, and teens with relatively more parental supervision tend to have later onset of intercourse. In discussing *peer influences,* the authors cite work suggesting that perceptions about what is normative in one's peer group are more strongly associated with sexual behavior than the actual behavior of one's peers. But the authors suggest that the presumed effects of parental and peer influences on teenage sexual behavior are stronger than the available research evidence indicates. A focus on *academic perspectives* emphasizes the observation that teenagers with lower academic success or aspirations are more likely to have sex as teenagers. And finally, their consideration of *social cognitive* abilities raises questions about the ability to "integrate domain-specific knowledge into a coherent system" (i.e., into an understanding of "where babies come from"). Other social cognitive processes that the authors point to as relevant and in need of greater research understanding include self-definitions, self-efficacy, and social comparisons; that is, how a teenage girl determines what it means to be a mature woman.

A more recent article by Brooks-Gunn and Paikoff (1997) moves even further from the traditional economic approach to the issue by suggesting that the study of adolescent sexuality must consider not only behaviors, but also feelings. They write that though insightful, the framework that they and others have used to consider adolescent sexual behavior, namely in the contexts of family, peer, neighborhood, biological, and cognitive characteristics, has been limiting. They propose four key topics that need to be explored in order to understand adolescent sexuality: (a) sexual well-being and developmental transitions; (b) the gendered nature of sexuality; (c) decision making and sexuality, and (d) the meaning of sexuality to youth.

Economists generally do not attempt to model parental behavior or the effect of feelings directly. But that does not mean that we ignore that these factors are potentially very important, perhaps crucial, to determining whether a young woman will engage in sexual activity and give birth as a teenager. Indeed, it is the correlation of these "other" factors with observable characteristics such as childhood poverty and growing up in a single-mother household that leads us to worry that the empirical associations between such background characteristics and early childbearing cannot be

---

2. The authors are quick to note that social and contextual effects will interact with the onset of hormonal changes: "So while very early sexual initiations may be in part hormonally mediated, by the time that behavior is normative, social factors may account for sexual initiation" (251). They cite research indicating that initiation of sexual behavior is highly associated with what is perceived as normative in one's peer group. They further purport that racial differences in the initiation of intercourse prior to puberty speak to the importance of social and contextual factors on sexual behavior.

interpreted as causal. For example, if single mothers tend to be the type of women who would be less likely to supervise or communicate with their adolescent daughters regardless of marital status, then it is the not the fact of being born to a single mother per se that leads daughters from single-parent homes to have relatively higher rates of early childbearing.

Work in other social sciences on this topic has tended to group the theoretical linkages between background characteristics and teen nonmarital childbearing into four categories, as helpfully summarized by An, Haveman, and Wolfe (1993): (a) the lifestyle characteristics of the parents; (b) information and network effects; (c) stressful childhood events; and (d) a utility maximization perspective. The first perspective emphasizes the intergenerational transmission of a culture of "welfare dependence." The idea is that a girl growing up in a mother-only family where welfare receipt is the norm will develop preferences and behaviors that lead her to repeat such a lifestyle for herself. The second perspective holds that girls who grow up in poverty or without connections to the labor market will be more likely to engage in early childbearing than girls who grow up with economic resources and connections to a world that engenders career or educational ambitions. The third perspective is borne from research in sociology suggesting that stressful and unsettling events during childhood or early youth, such as changes in family structure, may lead to feelings of insecurity in young women. These types of feelings might lead a young girl to desire a baby or family of her own and therefore give birth as a teenager.

The fourth perspective, emphasizing a rational choice framework, tends to be the approach taken by economists who have written in this area (see, e.g., Leibowitz, Eisen, and Chow 1986; Duncan and Hoffman 1990; Lundberg and Plotnick 1995). This literature builds on the seminal work of Becker (1960) and Ward and Butz (1980) by modeling fertility as a decision-making process determined by economic factors. While Becker (1960) and Ward and Butz (1980) focus on the fertility of married women, their insight can easily be applied to the decision facing unmarried teenage women. Duncan and Hoffman (1990) is an early example of a study modeling the choice to have a nonmarital birth as a rational comparison of the income outcomes associated with the choice, modeled by these authors as welfare benefits versus expected income returns from career and a higher probability of marriage.

Recent work by behavioral economists offers some important modifications that may help synthesize a rational choice model with the perspectives of other social scientists. Work in this field argues that the rational-choice model is inaccurate in some systematic and important ways. A key insight for the issue of early childbearing is that when modeling decisions to undertake actions that involve immediate gratification and future costs—such as sex or smoking—otherwise rational individuals might exhibit "present-biased preferences" (e.g., O'Donahue and Rabin 1999; Laibson 1994). Such preferences are characterized by "excessive myopia," whereby individuals put additional weight on the present period relative to all future periods. When we talk about the actions of teens, such a model implies that teens might engage in too much risky behavior (say, unprotected sex) because they attach too little weight to their well-being as adults. In other words, they overly discount long-term consequences relative to short-term gratification. Economists tend to be uncomfortable normatively declaring that people's behaviors are not in their best interest; but if individuals make decisions based on present-biased preferences, that is tantamount to them making decisions about present actions that they will regret later in life. Such preferences might also be considered a reflection of self-control problems. If an otherwise rational decision maker who is considering the costs and benefits of early childbearing has such present-biased preferences, or has self-control problems, then she might make decisions that lead to early childbearing, even if it is not in her long-term best interest.

O'Donoghue and Rabin (2001) review insights and issues raised by behavioral economists and psychologists that are relevant to modeling risky behavior by adolescents, including behaviors leading to unprotected sex and potentially early childbearing. Their reading of the behavioral/psychological evidence is that adolescents are similar to adults in terms of their ability to carry out the decision-making process but, importantly, that youths are less able to recognize the consequences associated with given actions. If minors are not fully capable of predicting the consequences of early childbearing—either for themselves or their children—they might initiate childbearing earlier than would be optimal from their own fully-informed perspective.

6.3   Relevant Empirical Literatures

Our analysis of the impact of socioeconomic disadvantage on early childbearing is related to several empirical literatures. Some are directly on point while others address different, albeit related, questions and can help inform our discussion and analysis. This section describes each of these related areas and what we can learn from them regarding the relationship between socioeconomic disadvantage and early childbearing.

6.3.1   The Costs of Teenage Childbearing

There is a fairly large literature in economics examining the consequences of giving birth at an early age. This literature has separately focused on the costs to the teen mother herself in the form of inferior subsequent outcomes (e.g., lower completed schooling and earned income) and the costs to her offspring (e.g., lower cognitive ability, higher rates of child poverty, and, potentially, early childbearing). Recent analyses have focused on methods designed to separately identify the role that early childbearing plays in altering these outcomes, abstracting from all of the other differences that exist between women who give birth at an early age and those who delay childbearing. Analysts have used approaches including examining differences in later-life outcomes between siblings who did and did not have a teen birth (Geronimus and Korenman 1992 and Geronimus, Korenman, and Hillemeier 1994); between teens who gave birth to those who were pregnant but miscarried (Hotz, McElroy, and Sanders 2005); and between teens who gave birth to twins to those who gave birth to singletons (Grogger and Bronars 1993). The motivation for these approaches is to find a relevant comparison group for teenage mothers whose average outcomes might reasonably be considered a proxy for what the average teen mother would have experienced had she not given birth before the age of eighteen or twenty. These studies generally find that the inferior outcomes observed for women who give birth as teens are largely due to underlying unobserved heterogeneity, as opposed to the teen birth itself.[3]

It is important to recognize that these studies are in some sense examining the reverse causal relationship from the one we address in this chapter. The studies previously described are designed to identify the impact of early childbearing on subsequent rates of disadvantage. Our analysis attempts to identify the link between early childhood disadvantage and the propensity to give birth at an early age. In fact, the studies described deliberately hold constant measures of childhood disadvantage in order to isolate the impact of teen childbearing from any confounding influence of disadvantage. This is precisely *not* what we try to do with our empirical analysis described following.

6.3.2 The Determinants of Teenage Childbearing

Two distinct literatures in economics focus directly on the determinants of teen childbearing. One focuses on the impact of policies and social conditions in a woman's state of residence and the other examines the impact of personal characteristics. The policy-related literature is methodologically stronger, applying quasi-experimental methods designed to identify causal estimates of a policy's impact on teen childbearing. Moffitt (1992, 1998, 2003) reviews the extensive literature on the effects of welfare policy on the incidence of female-headed households.[4] Economists have also explored the role that abortion policy, and particularly parental involvement laws and Medicaid funding restrictions, play in teen fertility behavior (e.g., Levine, Trainor, and Zimmerman 1996; and Levine 2003). Kearney and Levine (2007) examine the cost of contraception, finding that publicly-funded

---

3. Ribar (1994) and Klepinger, Lundberg, and Plotnick (1999) use the age at menarche as an instrument for teen pregnancy, based on the observation that an earlier age at menarche leads to more years at risk of becoming pregnant. Ribar (1994) finds that this approach eliminates any negative effect of teen births on high school completion; Klepinger, Lundberg, and Plotnick (1999) find a negative causal effect.
4. Female-headed households are not necessarily headed by women who initiated childbearing as a teen, but there is a strong correlation between the two.

family planning can significantly reduce teen birth rates. The role of labor market conditions also has been examined (e.g., Dehejia and Lleras-Muney 2004; Levine 2001). Despite the methodological advantages of this work, the focus on specific policies and their impact on early childbearing is different than our goal of examining the role of socioeconomic disadvantage. But, these literatures do help guide our choice of other factors that are important to control for in our model.

The literature that is perhaps most closely aligned with our goals examines the impact of personal background characteristics on early childbearing outcomes. Haveman and Wolfe (1995) review a large number of studies in this area, highlighting the key contributions in this area of Duncan and Hoffman (1990), An, Haveman, and Wolfe (1993), and Lundberg and Plotnick (1995). An important contribution since this review is Duncan et al. (1998). These studies examine the relationship between factors related to economic disadvantage (including family income, parental education, and family structure) and the likelihood of giving birth at a young age and/or outside a marital union. Given that there are almost surely unobserved factors correlated with both an individual's observed characteristics and her propensity for a teen or nonmarital birth, these individual-level studies are limited in their ability to identify a causal link between disadvantage per se and early childbearing.[5] Two recent studies exploit arguably exogenous variation in female educational attainment in order to identify the causal link between education and teen childbearing (Black, Devereux, and Salvanes 2004; McCrary and Royer 2006).[6] These studies are somewhat further removed from the focus of our analysis, as they concentrate on a woman's own level of education. We are interested in the environment into which a young girl is born and are therefore interested in relating her mother's level of education to her own likelihood of giving birth as a teen.

6.3.3   The Intergenerational Transmission of Income

As we describe following, our empirical analysis relates early childbearing as the outcome of interest to childhood disadvantage, which we define as being born to a mother with certain characteristics. When we use being born to a young mother as our measure of disadvantage and examine its links to early childbearing, we are conducting an exercise very similar in spirit to that considered in the literatures on intergenerational transmission of personal characteristics like income, education, and health. (For a

---

5. The methodological considerations of these studies tend to focus more on issues such as correlated errors in joint decision processes that include teen childbearing and welfare receipt, rather than on finding exogenous variation in measures of economic disadvantage.

6. Black, Devereux, and Salvanes (2004) uses variation in compulsory schooling laws and McCrary and Royer (2006) uses age-at-school-entry policies to identify exogenous differences in the amount of education received by women.

review of these literatures, see Solon [1999].) These literatures examine the extent to which a parent's characteristic is transmitted to his or her child. The earlier economics literature on this question almost always focused on the intergenerational transmission of income from fathers to sons. In a regression framework where son's income is the dependent variable, the coefficient on father's income represents the intergenerational correlation. The methodological issue frequently grappled with in this literature is how to appropriately measure income (say, by using multiple years of earnings) in order to reduce attenuation bias due to measurement error.[7] More recent studies of intergenerational income correlation have considered the relationship between father's or family income and daughter's earnings or family income. These studies have addressed conceptual issues such as assortative mating (Chadwick and Solon 2002) and the transmission of gender preferences for work (Altonji and Dunn 2000).

More recent work in this area has focused on trying to identify the mechanisms for intergenerational correlations, asking whether the intergenerational correlation in income is attributable to an intergenerational correlation in health or education, for instance (e.g., Currie and Moretti 2007; Black, Devereaux, and Salvanes 2005). If one views part of our analysis as the intergenerational correlation in early childbearing, then this may be thought of as one of the mechanisms generating an intergenerational correlation in income.[8]

6.4   Evidence from the Panel Study of Income Dynamics (PSID)

We begin our exploration of the empirical linkages between socioeconomic disadvantage and early childbearing with an examination of data from the Panel Study of Income Dynamics (PSID). The PSID is a longitudinal survey of a representative sample of U.S. individuals and their households. It was conducted annually from 1968 to 1997 and biannually since then. We study the cohort of women age twenty to thirty-five in the 2003 survey and observe particular circumstances of their births using information contained in the 1968 through 1983 survey files. We focus on five measures of disadvantage at birth: being born to a mother of age less than twenty or less than eighteen, being born to a single mother, being born to a mother who has not completed high school, and being born into a family whose income is at or below the federal USDA poverty threshold. We also consider two measures of socioeconomic disadvantage during adolescence:

---

7. In our work on early childbearing, measurement issues are less of a concern, particularly in our analysis of Vital Statistics data.

8. This would depend upon the extent to which early childbearing is causally related to low income. As we described earlier, this proposition is not perfectly clear on the basis of past research.

not living with married parents (or stepparents) at age fifteen and living in poverty at age fifteen.[9]

Our PSID sample consists of 1,797 women age twenty to thirty-five observed in the 2003 survey and back to the year of their birth. Table 6.1 reports rates of disadvantage and rates of teen childbearing by disadvantage factor. Among our sample of women, 24 percent gave birth before age twenty.[10] The rates of teen childbearing are dramatically higher for women who were born with each of our four measures of disadvantage. Forty-six percent of women born to teen mothers give birth as teenagers themselves; 43 percent of women are born to an unmarried mother; 44 percent of women are born to a mother with less than a high school degree (including teenagers); and 49 percent of women are born into poverty. Similar increases in the likelihood of giving birth by age eighteen are also observed for women from disadvantaged backgrounds.

One interesting finding in table 6.1 is that the heightened propensity to give birth as a teen relative to the full sample is about the same for any of the disadvantage factors considered. In particular, being born to a teen mother, an unmarried mother, or a less-educated mother has about the same impact on rates of early childbearing as does being born to a poor mother, which is perhaps the measure that is most closely associated with the notion of childhood disadvantage. This is important to keep in mind when we move to our cohort-based analysis, where poverty status at birth is something that we are unable to measure.

We also use these data to estimate raw intergenerational correlations in teen childbearing in a manner consistent with past research on intergenerational correlations in economic outcomes. In particular, we run simple regressions of own teen childbearing behavior on an indicator variable for whether each woman was born to a teen mother. We conduct an analogous exercise for births before age eighteen. It is important to recognize that these simple models are only designed to identify correlations; results should not necessarily be interpreted as causal.

The results of this exercise are reported in the top panel of table 6.2. They indicate that women who were born to teen mothers are 25 percentage points more likely to go on to give birth as teens themselves; given that the mean

9. In our exploration of linkages between background factors and early childbearing in the PSID, we do attempt to be as exhaustive in our set of variables considered as the PSID analyses of either An, Haveman, and Wolfe (1993) or Duncan et al. (1998), which look at much larger sets of demographic characteristics for earlier cohorts of young women. We merely look to the PSID for descriptive purposes. In the attempt to uncover causal relationships, we rely primarily on a cohort-based analysis of vital statistics natality data.

10. One potentially confusing finding in these data is that 24 percent of women gave birth to children before age twenty, but only 14 percent of them were born to mothers under twenty years old. The reason for the discrepancy is that not all of the women in our PSID sample are firstborn children. So, the number of women born to teen mothers understates the number of women in that older cohort who actually had a *first* birth during their teen years.

Table 6.1   Rates of early childbearing by disadvantage factor

	% with disadvantage	% gave birth before age 20	% gave birth before age 18
All	—	0.24	0.12
Born to mother less than age 20	0.14	0.46	0.26
(n = 1,797)			
Born to mother less than age 18	0.04	0.43	0.24
(n = 1,797)			
Born to unmarried mother	0.28	0.45	0.23
(n = 1,743)			
Born to mother with less than HS degree	0.28	0.44	0.26
(n = 1,266)			
Born into poverty	0.13	0.49	0.26
(n = 1,611)			
Not living with married parents at age 15	0.45	0.39	0.21
(n = 1,412)			
Living in poverty at age 15	0.04	0.53	0.38
(n = 1,553)			

Notes: The sample is comprised of women age twenty to thirty-five in the 2003 PSID. Estimates are similar when we use a uniform sample size across measures.

rate of teen childbearing is 24 percent, this is roughly a doubling of the odds. The results for births by age eighteen are not statistically significant, likely due to the very small number of children born to mothers under age eighteen in the sample.

The remainder of table 6.2 reports the results of multivariate regression specifications where the dependent variable is defined as giving birth before the age of twenty and giving birth before the age of eighteen, and combinations of measures of disadvantage are included as explanatory variables. The results from these models can be interpreted as descriptive only, but they establish a form of "horse race" between disadvantage factors that provide at least one gauge of their relative importance. The six measures of socioeconomic disadvantage examined include the following: born to a teen mother, born to an unmarried mother, born to a mother with less than a high school degree, born into poverty, not living with married parents at age fifteen, and living in poverty at age fifteen. The coefficient estimates from these specifications imply statistically significant and substantial increases in rates of early childbearing among young women associated with most of these measures of disadvantage, even after controlling for the other correlated measures of disadvantage.

It is important to keep in mind that all of the results reported so far are purely descriptive in nature, representing correlations, and are not designed to tease out causal findings. The next section of this chapter will move more in that direction.

Table 6.2   Relationship between early childbearing and measures of disadvantage

	Dependent variable Gave birth by age 20		Dependent variable Gave birth by age 18	
	(1)	(2)	(3)	(4)
Born to mom < 20 (col. [1] and [2]) or 18 (col. [3] and [4])	0.250 (0.041)	—	0.043 (0.061)	—
Born to mom < 20 (col. [1] and [2]) or 18 (col. [3] and [4])	0.014 (0.045)	−0.001 (0.049)	−0.108 (0.061)	−0.122 (0.067)
Born to single mom	0.186 (0.031)	0.092 (0.037)	0.112 (0.024)	0.059 (0.029)
Born to mom < HS grad	0.198 (0.030)	0.191 (0.033)	0.146 (0.023)	0.135 (0.025)
Born into poverty	0.075 (0.041)	0.112 (0.028)	0.049 (0.032)	0.075 (0.035)
Age 15—Not living w/ married parents	—	0.112 (0.028)	—	0.053 (0.022)
Age 15—Living in poverty	—	0.093 (0.068)	—	0.121 (0.054)
Constant	0.138 (0.014)	0.112 (0.017)	0.056 (0.011)	0.046 (0.014)
Sample size	1,213	1,022	1,213	1,022
Adjusted R^2	0.116	0.117	0.0823	0.083

Notes: Estimates are the results from linear probability models that include no other covariates besides those listed.

6.5   Analysis of Vital Statistics Birth Data

In this section of the chapter, we use Vital Statistics birth data to explore the relationship between early childbearing among a birth cohort compared to the share of the cohort that was born to young mothers. One advantage that a cohort-based approach has compared to an analysis of a woman's own childbearing experiences relative to her mother is that a lot of the unobserved heterogeneity across women is averaged out. This is a property that will assist our analysis using these data, as described in more detail subsequently.

6.5.1   Data Description

We now turn to an exploration of data from the Vital Statistics Natality Detail Files between 1968 and 2003. These data represent individual records on births that took place in the United States.[11] We use data from 1968 to

11. These data are first available starting in 1968 and 2003 is the last year currently available. From 1985 onward, these data represent a complete count of births. Prior to 1972, births were sampled at a 50 percent rate nationwide. In the intervening period, some states sampled at a 50 percent rate and others included all births. In our analysis, we applied appropriate weights to provide estimates of all births.

1986 to identify the number of women born in each state and year along with the proportion of those births that can be classified as "disadvantaged." The alternative measures of disadvantage for those women born in these years include having a mother who is a high school dropout, unmarried, or under age eighteen or twenty at the time of giving birth.[12] These data provide us with rates of "disadvantage" for the women born in these birth cohorts and also provide us with a denominator for a measure of the rate of early childbearing that these women subsequently experience.

To get the numerator for this early childbearing statistic, we use data from the 1980 through 2003 Vital Statistics file to tally births born to women less than age eighteen or age twenty.[13] These data allow us to assign every birth that takes place in the United States to the mothers' state and year of birth.[14] From these data, we tally all first births that occur to women less than age eighteen or twenty from that state/year of birth cohort. Dividing this count by the size of that cohort provides a measure of the rate of early childbearing.

Consider, for instance, the 1970 birth cohort from New York. We use the 1970 Vital Statistics natality file to tally the total number of females born in that state and year, which becomes the denominator for our early childbearing statistic. That data file also allows us to identify the number born to teen/minor mothers, to unmarried mothers, and to mothers with less than a high school degree. We use this information to construct the rates of "disadvantage" in this cohort. To calculate the numerator for our early childbearing statistic, we sum the number of first births in 1983 to thirteen-year-old mothers born in New York, the number of first births in 1984 to fourteen-year-old mothers born in New York, and so on through the 1989 file, when the 1970 birth cohort would have been age nineteen. That sum represents the number of girls born in New York in 1970 who gave birth by age twenty.

The ability to link births to mothers' birth cohorts is crucial for our purposes. In effect, we are linking three generations: we look at birth records in a given year and identify the age—and birth cohort—of the mother. We then look to the birth records for that cohort of teenage mothers and identify the characteristics of their mothers. The completeness of Vital Statistics birth

12. We also experimented with a measure of the poverty rate, but decided not to include it in our analysis because of data limitations. Poverty rates by state and year are not available for the birth cohorts in our sample. Instead, we tried using county level data from the 1970 Census, attaching to each birth cohort the poverty rate that existed in the relevant county of birth. As the geographic composition of births changed over time within a state, this measure would provide some within state variation in poverty. Unfortunately, we found that this variation was insufficient to provide robust parameter estimates.

13. When we consider births before age twenty, we can only use birth cohorts through 1984.

14. For a very small number of births, this information is missing. These births are not included in the analysis.

records substantially reduces measurement error in our estimated rates of early childbearing. Nevertheless, the data are not perfect. First, our identification of a teen mother's birth cohort relies on the reporting of a mother's age on the birth record; the natality data does not report the exact year in which the mother was born. We simply subtract the mother's age from the year she gave birth to determine her birth year, so there may be a misclassification by up to one year in the mother's birth cohort associated with an early birth.[15]

Another important limitation of these data is that information on mother's education and marital status is not complete in the years in which we are measuring the size of birth cohorts and recording their rates of disadvantage. First, data on maternal education is not available at all for the 1968 birth cohort and they exist for only a subset of states for the years between 1969 and 1979. To balance the panel when we use this variable, we include in our analysis just the thirty-six states for which these data are available in all years. Similarly, direct information on marital status of the mother is only available in all years for thirty-seven states; we focus our attention on just those states in analyses regarding marital status.[16]

6.5.2   Descriptive Analysis

Figures 6.1 through 6.4 provide a description of these data, separately considering the conditions at birth for these cohorts of women along with their subsequent rates of early childbearing. Figure 6.1 displays trends in the percentage of each birth cohort that exhibit each form of disadvantage. The first conclusion that one can draw from this figure is that there are very distinct trends over time that differ across measures of disadvantage. The percentage of birth cohorts that are born to less-educated mothers (defined as not having completed high school) has fallen rather consistently from slightly more than 31.7 percent among the 1969 birth cohort to 20 percent for the 1986 birth cohort. The fraction of a birth cohort born to a mother less than age twenty has likewise fallen from a high of 19.7 percent among the 1973 birth cohort to 12.5 percent among the 1986 birth cohort. On the other hand, the fraction of each birth cohort born to an unmarried mother has risen continuously over this period (and beyond). In the youngest birth cohort we study, nearly one in four women (23.1 percent) were born to unmarried mothers, compared to roughly one in ten among the oldest birth cohort. These secular changes over time, driven by other social

15. Another minor limitation of these data is that births to women who were born in the United States but gave birth in another country would not be captured in these data. It is our impression that this is a very infrequent event and we ignore it here.

16. The set of states with missing information on maternal education is the following: AL, AR, CA, CT, DE, DC, FL, GA, ID, MD, NM, OR, PA, TX, and WA. The set of states with inadequate data on marital status is: CA, CT, GA, ID, MD, MA, MT, NM, NY, OH, VT, MI, NV, and TX.

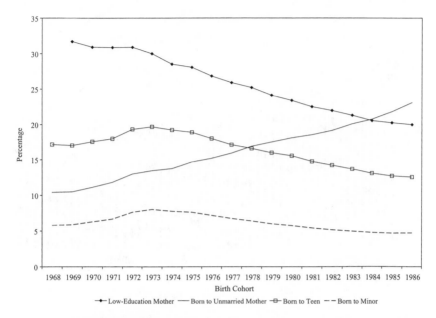

Fig. 6.1   **Trends in conditions at birth**

forces (cohort fixed effects), are the type of variation in the data that needs to be held constant in an analysis trying to identify the causal impacts of disadvantage.

Similar variation exists in these measures of disadvantage across states at a point in time. Figure 6.2 displays one representative measure, the percentage of a birth cohort born to teen mothers, across states. Among the 1969 birth cohort, over 20 percent were born to teen mothers in Mississippi and Alabama, but less than half that percentage in Massachusetts and Minnesota. Clearly, at least a portion of this gap may be attributable to different social customs that exist across these states. This is apparent in the fact that most states that have rates of births to teen mothers in 1969 also have relatively high rates in 1983. Again, these long-standing differences in state attitudes toward fertility (state fixed effects) need to be held constant if we are going to attempt to identify the causal impact of disadvantage.

It is interesting to note in figure 6.2 that the change between 1969 and 1983 within states in the percentage of a birth cohort born to teen mothers varies considerably across states. This rate fell in every state over the fourteen-year period, but it fell by more in some states than others. For instance, Rhode Island and New Mexico experienced a trivial drop, but the percentage of a birth cohort born to teen mothers fell by roughly one-third in Washington and Kansas. Although it is not clear that the variation in changes in measures of birth cohort disadvantage—such as being born to a teen mother—

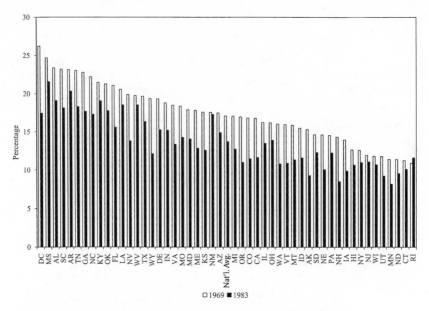

Fig. 6.2   Cross-sectional variation in percentage of birth cohorts born to teen mothers

over time between states is purely exogenous to preferences/tastes for early childbearing (as we will discuss later), focusing on these within-state, across-birth-cohort changes as our identifying source of variation removes the confounding influences of secular changes that occurred over time nationally and long-standing cross-sectional variation across states.

Figures 6.3 and 6.4 provide analogous information about the patterns in early childbearing for women in these birth cohorts. Figure 6.3 displays the aggregate trend over time.[17] It shows that the percentage of women giving birth either before age eighteen or before age twenty rose somewhat among women born for the early 1970s birth cohorts, but then fell subsequently. This pattern roughly corresponds to the aggregate trends in annual teen childbearing rates, which spiked in the late 1980s and early 1990s. Figure 6.4 displays cross-sectional variation in the percentage of women giving birth by age twenty (similar patterns exist for births by age eighteen). Again, there is substantial cross-sectional variation in early childbearing rates. Among women in the 1969 birth cohort, about 30 percent in Mississippi and the District of Columbia gave birth by age twenty. The comparable figure for women born in Massachusetts and Connecticut is closer to 10 percent. For women born in most states, the rate of early childbearing fell somewhat between the 1969 and 1983 birth cohorts. Importantly, there is considerable

17. No data is available for births by age nineteen beyond the 1984 birth cohort because 2003 is the most current Vital Statistics data available.

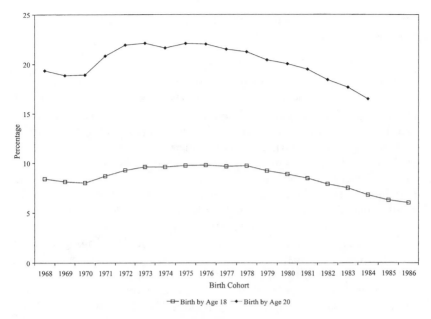

Fig. 6.3 Trends in rates of early childbearing

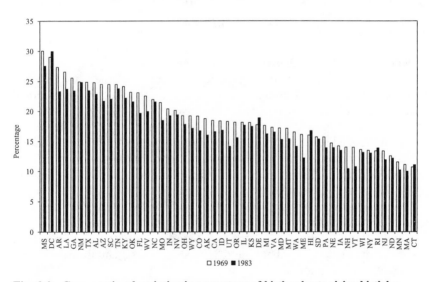

Fig. 6.4 Cross-sectional variation in percentage of birth cohorts giving birth by age 20

variation across states in the extent of the reduction in rates of early child-bearing between 1969 and 1983.

6.5.3   Econometric Specification

Our empirical approach relates the variation in state-year birth cohort teen childbearing rates to the variation in state-year birth cohort rates of disadvantage. The thought experiment that corresponds to this econometric exercise is the following: if we could reduce the amount of socioeconomic disadvantage among a birth cohort of women, what impact would that have on their rates of early childbearing down the road? If that impact were large, we would infer that early childbearing is in large part a consequence of being born into socioeconomic disadvantage, as so measured. If that impact were small in magnitude, however, we would conclude that teen childbearing is driven only in small measure by childhood disadvantage.

In our more formal econometric discussion, we develop our thinking regarding the models that we estimate and report, highlighting their strengths and limitations as well as appropriate interpretations. Let us begin by considering the following cross-sectional, individual-level model. The outcome variable is a binary indicator for early childbearing (EC). It is modeled as a function of some measure of economic disadvantage in the individual's past (D) and other personal characteristics ($\mathbf{X}_1$) for individual i.

$$(1) \qquad ECi = \beta_0 + \beta_1 D_i + \mathbf{\Gamma}_1 \mathbf{X}_{1i} + v_i.$$

This equation is a simplification of the approaches reviewed in Haveman and Wolfe (1995), emphasizing the cross-sectional nature of the variation in the data available. The estimate of coefficient β_1 is interpretable as the relationship between the disadvantage measure and early childbearing, conditional on the control variables included in the $\mathbf{X}$-vectors.

The main limitation of equation (1) is that there are likely to be factors that are related to both the measure of disadvantage and the early child-bearing outcome that are not controlled for and may even be very difficult or impossible for the researcher to observe. As such, they lead to omitted variable bias that precludes assigning a causal interpretation to β_1. Suppose, for instance, that a woman's own values lead her to have a child early and to instill those values in her daughters, leading them to have children early as well. If those values are related to lower socioeconomic outcomes, then we may erroneously attribute the relationship in early childbearing across generations to economic disadvantage.

We can move closer to identifying a causal relationship between D and EC by controlling for state and cohort fixed effects in the model. For instance, early childbearing outcomes for women who reached age twenty in 1996 are likely to be different than their counterparts who reached age twenty in 1986, due to differences in the cultural climates in the years in which they were developing values and making relevant choices. Likewise, there are cultural differences across communities that exert influence on individual decisions and behaviors. We thus augment the model as follows:

(2) $EC_{ics} = \beta_0 + \beta_1 D_{ics} + \Gamma_1 X_{1ics} + \gamma_c + \gamma_s + \eta_{ics}.$

In this specification, each individual i is identified by her "community" (state in this example, denoted by s) and period (or cohort—denoted by c). This approach eliminates two possible forms of unobservable heterogeneity. To the extent that rates of disadvantage vary by cohort and by state, and to the extent that time and place matter to early childbearing decisions, the inclusion of these controls in the model will alleviate some of the omitted variable bias.

We can go one step further in removing individual-level heterogeneity by estimating this model at the aggregate level. This has the effect of averaging out differences across individuals within cohorts/states. There is sure to be a great deal of variation in individual values that may be related to disadvantage and early childbearing decisions and this variation is greatly reduced when aggregated. So, instead of estimating equation (2) with individual-level data, we estimate this relationship at the level of a state/year birth cohort:

(3) $EC_{cs} = \beta_0 + \beta_1 D_{cs} + \Gamma_1 X_{1cs} + \gamma_c + \gamma_s + \eta_{cs}.$

This differs from equation (2) in the subscripts, indicating the aggregated nature of the data within cohorts. Each variable is now the average over individuals within the state/birth cohort cell.

We control for a set of X variables that varies at the level of state/year birth cohort. At the cohort level, rates of childbearing will vary with the average demographic composition of a cohort. We explicitly control for marital status, age, racial/ethnic composition, and level of educational attainment among women fifteen to forty-four in the state/year cohort. Any remaining demographic differences are captured with cohort fixed effects, to the extent that those differences are geographically uniform at a point in time. The vector of control variables in equation (3) also includes a set of variables that are designed to measure environmental conditions around the time that early childbearing decisions are being made. The specific variables we include are the unemployment rate, to capture economic conditions, and an extensive set of policy variables, including abortion restrictions, welfare benefit levels and reform indicators, and State Children's Health Insurance Program (SCHIP) implementation.[18] Further details regarding the specific

18. Specifically, these variables include indicators for Temporary Assistance for Needy Families (TANF) implementation, the presence of a welfare family cap, maximum Aid to Families with Dependent Children (AFDC)/TANF benefits for a family of three, SCHIP implementation, Medicaid coverage of abortion, abortion parental notification requirements, and abortion delay rules. We also control for cohort size, although the results are virtually unchanged when cohort size is excluded from the model.

variables used and their sources are available in Kearney and Levine (2007). We simplify the measurement of these variables by including their values at the time each birth cohort was age seventeen or age nineteen in specifications in which our measure of early childbearing is births by age eighteen and births by age twenty, respectively.

How should we interpret the results of estimating equation (3)? As stated previously, the thought experiment captured by this cohort specification is the following: if we were to "shock" the amount of socioeconomic disadvantage (D) of a birth cohort of women, what impact would that have on cohort rates of early childbearing (EC)? Two points of comparison and contrast with equation (2) are important. First, equation (2) relates a particular background characteristic, say being born in poverty, and early childbearing outcomes. As discussed, the existence of omitted variable bias in such equations almost surely make a causal interpretation inappropriate. We have not completely surmounted this issue of omitted variable bias with our cohort specification. There might be remaining unobserved differences across state/year birth cohorts that correlate with both our measures of disadvantage and early childbearing outcomes. For example, it is possible that values change within states across birth cohorts in a way that is correlated with both economic disadvantage and early childbearing. As we note following, a comparison of results from the estimation of various specifications of equation (3) suggest that these possibilities are probably not that important.[19]

The second important issue relevant to the interpretation of the coefficient, β_1, is that when estimating this equation at the cohort level, β_1 incorporates spillover or peer effects. When we "shock" the amount of disadvantage in a state/year birth cohort, that might have a general effect on sexual behavior and fertility outcomes even for those women whose own background characteristic is not changed. Consider the possibility that the tastes and values of girls born to married women are to some extent influenced by the proportion of girls in their cohort born to unmarried mothers. We remain agnostic as to how such spillover or peer effects operate in this context.

In general, we cannot fully characterize the complexities of the mechanism by which socioeconomic disadvantage may affect early childbearing.

---

19. One methodological approach that would, in principle, be useful to eliminate this remaining source of unobservable heterogeneity is instrumental variables. To implement this approach, one would need instruments that are correlated with our measures of disadvantage without being correlated with the residual in early childbearing. The difficulty in identifying such an instrument is that any variable that shifts the characteristics of a birth cohort, like the fraction born to teen mothers, is likely to alter other characteristics of that cohort, like its values/tastes. For instance, we experimented with using variation in abortion legalization across states and over time in the early 1970s, like Ananat et al. (2004). The problem with this is that if abortion legalization changed the selection process determining who is born (like the percentage to teen mothers), it is likely also to affect attributes of that birth cohort other than their socioeconomic disadvantage (like their tastes/values). Without any other obvious suitable instruments, we have chosen not to pursue this estimation strategy.

When we define D in equation (3) as, say, the proportion of a state/year birth cohort born to a teen mother, we are estimating the relationship between the prevalence of this factor and cohort rates of early childbearing. This does not identify the isolated impact of teen childbearing itself; when we "shock" teen childbearing, we necessarily shock all associated factors that are not directly controlled for in the model, such as the values of the women, their parenting styles, their career aspirations, their relationship formations, and so forth. So, we do not purport to get inside the black box of what it is about a particular characteristic that leads to changes in teen childbearing propensities; we claim only to empirically estimate the broader relationship.

6.5.4   Results

The results of our analysis using Vital Statistics data are reported in tables 6.3 and 6.4. The left panel of these tables uses data from the 1968 through 1986 birth cohorts and considers a dependent variable measuring their rate of early childbearing, defined as giving birth before age eighteen. The mean value of this early childbearing rate across states and birth cohorts is 8.4 percent. The right panel uses data from the 1968 through 1984 birth cohorts and is comparable, but defines early childbearing to be that occurring before age twenty; the mean of this rate is 20.1 percent.

The first row of table 6.3 presents sample means for each measure of disadvantage at birth for the relevant subset of birth cohorts. These data indicate that about 26 percent of the women in these birth cohorts were born to mothers who had not yet completed high school, about 16 percent to mothers who were not yet married, over 16 percent to mothers who were teens, and over 6 percent to mothers who were minors.

The first panel of regression results in table 6.3 reflects estimates from simple regressions where the dependent variable is the relevant rate of early childbearing for the birth cohort and the sole independent variable is the rate of economic disadvantage at birth among that state/year female birth cohort. These results show a very strong intergenerational linkage between disadvantage at birth and subsequent rates of early childbearing. These figures indicate that a birth cohort with an additional 1 percentage point higher rate of children in it born to minors is associated with about a 1 percentage point higher rate of childbearing as minors themselves. A similar result is obtained for births by age twenty as a function of the proportion of the cohort born to teen mothers.

This estimated relationship of a nearly one-to-one correspondence in rates of teen childbearing across generations stands in contrast to the estimated relationship at the individual level in the PSID. Recall that in that analysis we found that having been born to a teen mother increases one's likelihood of having a teen birth by 25 percentage points. This comparison suggests that early childbearing is much more tightly linked across generations in the *aggregate*. We interpret these findings as suggesting that the

Table 6.3   Estimates of the impact of alternative measures of economic disadvantage on early childbearing

Measure of disadvantage	Dependent variable: Proportion of cohort giving birth by age 18 (mean = 0.084)				Dependent variable: Proportion of cohort giving birth by age 20 (mean = 0.201)			
	Mother with low education	Unmarried mother	Born to teen	Born to minor	Mother with low education	Unmarried mother	Born to teen	Born to minor
Proportion w/ disadvantage	0.257	0.162	0.163	0.061	0.264	0.154	0.167	0.063
	No other covariates							
Coefficient/standard error	0.261	0.184	0.550	1.097	0.478	0.327	1.062	2.037
	(0.021)	(0.040)	(0.033)	(0.059)	(0.035)	(0.078)	(0.061)	(0.124)
R^2	0.635	0.168	0.746	0.776	0.588	0.153	0.792	0.783
	State and birth cohort fixed effects							
Coefficient/standard error	0.106	0.060	0.122	0.250	0.095	0.137	0.172	0.292
	(0.022)	(0.053)	(0.063)	(0.114)	(0.038)	(0.071)	(0.088)	(0.164)
R^2	0.982	0.968	0.974	0.974	0.988	0.984	0.985	0.985
	State and birth cohort fixed effects along with additional policy and demographic control variables							
Coefficient/standard error	0.137	0.057	0.129	0.272	0.161	0.155	0.187	0.342
	(0.022)	(0.040)	(0.056)	(0.095)	(0.036)	(0.065)	(0.074)	(0.128)
R^2	0.983	0.974	0.98	0.98	0.989	0.985	0.985	0.986
Number of observations	612	666	918	918	576	629	867	867

Notes: Additional policy and demographic control variables include the unemployment rate, indicator variables for the implementation of a welfare waiver (pre-TANF) or TANF, and the implementation of a welfare family cap, log maximum welfare benefits for a family of three, an indicator for SCHIP implementation, abortion policy indicators including the presence of a Medicaid funding restriction, parental notification law and mandatory delay law, and aggregate demographic characteristics of women of childbearing age, including the percent married, percent white, percent Hispanic, and the percent who are high school dropouts, high school graduated, and have attended some college. All these variables are measured in the year the cohort turned age eighteen (left panel) or twenty (right panel).

culture or environment that supports teen childbearing is more deterministic of early childbearing outcomes than the specific influence of the individual's mother and her childbearing experiences.[20] This is an example of what we referred to earlier as spillover or peer effects that may lead to differences in results based on aggregate data as opposed to microdata.

The remainder of table 6.3 provides additional evidence that cultural factors play a very important role in explaining early childbearing. In the second panel of the table, we report ordinary least squares (OLS) estimates in models that are augmented by state and birth cohort fixed effects, but with no other covariates. In these models, the estimated coefficient on the relevant measure of disadvantage is greatly attenuated compared to the results from the simple regression models. Although considerably smaller in magnitude, many of the estimates still are statistically significant, at least at the 10 percent level.

The coefficient on the proportion of a state/year birth cohort born to a minor in a model where the dependent variable is defined as giving birth before age eighteen falls from 1.097 (standard error of 0.059) to 0.250 (standard error of 0.114). This estimate implies that a cohort with a 1 percentage point higher rate of being born to a minor (a 16 percent increase from a 6.1 percent base) will, net of state and birth year fixed effects, have a roughly 0.25 percentage point higher rate of childbearing as minors themselves. With a mean rate of childbearing as minors of 8.4 percent, this is a very small impact for a sizeable intervention.

Similarly, the estimated coefficient on the proportion of a state/year birth cohort born to mothers without a high school degree (base rate of 25.7 percent) in the model focusing on births by age eighteen falls from 0.261 (standard error of 0.021) to 0.106 (standard error of 0.022). This means that if the rate of less educated mothers fell from 25.7 percent to, say, 20.7 percent, then the rate of early childbearing by age eighteen would fall by about half a percentage point. Again, given that the mean rate of childbearing before age eighteen is 8.4 percent, this is not a very large impact for a substantial reduction in the rate of socioeconomic disadvantage.

Table 6.4 replicates the analysis in table 6.3, reporting models of the form described by equation (3), but in log-log form so that the coefficients can

---

20. One reason that we would expect the intergenerational correlation in early childbearing to be smaller in microdata is that outcomes are determined by probabilities even if behavior is changed with certainty. As an extreme example to clarify the point, suppose that all children born to young mothers are willing to engage in unprotected sexual intercourse at a young age themselves. Yet because of the uncertainties associated with finding a partner, having sex, getting pregnant, and carrying the pregnancy to term, one would not expect all of these women to have children at an early age themselves. One could imagine a larger impact in aggregate data if communities in which more women became mothers at an early age change the social norms of behavior for all teens. In that case, the hypothesized changes in behavior among more young women could lead to larger changes in outcomes even after factoring in all the relevant probabilities.

Table 6.4   Elasticity estimates of the impact of alternative measures of economic disadvantage on early childbearing

Measure of disadvantage	Dependent variable: Log proportion of cohort giving birth by age 18				Dependent variable: Log proportion of cohort giving birth by age 20			
	Mother with low education	Unmarried mother	Born to teen	Born to minor	Mother with low education	Unmarried mother	Born to teen	Born to minor
No other covariates								
Coefficient/standard error	0.852	0.256	1.115	0.861	0.623	0.227	0.915	0.669
	(0.055)	(0.076)	(0.059)	(0.041)	(0.050)	(0.063)	(0.052)	(0.040)
R^2	0.646	0.095	0.78	0.799	0.557	0.127	0.803	0.792
State and birth cohort fixed effects								
Coefficient/standard error	0.252	0.103	0.101	0.049	0.196	0.000	0.124	0.054
	(0.120)	(0.067)	(0.100)	(0.082)	(0.075)	(0.041)	(0.055)	(0.042)
R^2	0.983	0.981	0.979	0.979	0.988	0.985	0.985	0.985
State and birth cohort fixed effects along with additional policy and demographic control variables								
Coefficient/standard error	0.282	0.052	0.129	0.054	0.229	0.002	0.140	0.065
	(0.088)	(0.055)	(0.092)	(0.063)	(0.056)	(0.036)	(0.046)	(0.029)
R^2	0.987	0.985	0.984	0.984	0.99	0.987	0.987	0.987
Number of observations	612	666	918	918	576	629	867	867

Notes: All measures of disadvantage are included in the right-hand side as the log of the proportion in the cohort with each disadvantage. Standard errors are clustered at the state level. Additional policy and demographic control variables include the unemployment rate, indicator variables for the implementation of a welfare waiver (pre-TANF) or TANF, and the implementation of a welfare family cap, log maximum welfare benefits for a family of three, an indicator for SCHIP implementation, abortion policy indicators including the presence of a Medicaid funding restriction, parental notification law and mandatory delay law, and aggregate demographic characteristics of women of childbearing age, including the percent married, percent white, percent Hispanic, and the percent who are high school dropouts, high school graduated, and have attended some college. All these variables are measured in the year the cohort turned age eighteen (left panel) or twenty (right panel). Standard errors are clustered at the state level. Regressions are weighted by cohort size.

be interpreted as elasticities. Once we include fixed effects, we see that a 10 percent decrease in the proportion born to a mom with less education than a high school degree is associated with a 2.5 percent reduction in the rate of childbearing by age eighteen. The analogous decrease in the proportion born to a teen mom is also associated with a decrease of approximately 2 percent. These are the two largest elasticities that we observe and they are not that large. Other elasticities are considerably smaller. For instance, a 10 percent reduction in the proportion of a cohort born to minors only reduces the rate of childbearing by age eighteen in that cohort by about 0.5 percent.

It is interesting to note that once the model controls for state and birth year fixed effects, there no longer appears to be a statistically significant relationship between the percentage of a birth cohort born to unmarried mothers and childbearing by age eighteen (it still has a statistically significant impact on childbearing by age twenty in levels, but not in logs). Nevertheless, this may indicate that mother's marital status may not be as good an indicator of socioeconomic disadvantage as mother's age or educational attainment. One might even expect that it would become an even poorer measure of disadvantage at birth as we go forward since the last birth cohort we are analyzing here is from 1986. As nonmarital childbearing continues its steady growth, it is reasonable to assert that it has become less selective on economic disadvantage.

The remaining panel of tables 6.3 and 6.4 includes a large array of variables controlling for differences in population characteristics (age/race/educational attainment/marital status) in each state/year at the time each birth cohort reached age seventeen or nineteen as well as differences in relevant policies (abortion, welfare, Medicaid) in place and labor market conditions at those times. As we discussed earlier, including birth cohort and state fixed effects helps control for important elements of heterogeneity that may introduce bias, but they do not solve the problem. In particular, omitted variables that reflect differences across cohorts in different locations may still result in bias. Although we recognize the possibility of unobservable factors that have this feature, we incorporate these additional variables here as an attempt to reduce the problem.

The results reported in the bottom panel of the tables are very similar to those reported in the middle panel, from models that include no additional covariates besides the state and birth year fixed effects. Among the additional variables included, the unemployment rate at about the time that early childbearing would take place is estimated to be positively related to early childbearing. Similarly, when the population of women fifteen to forty-four in a state/year is comprised of more high school dropouts, the rate of early childbearing at that time in that location tends to be higher. Other than that, all other factors tend to be statistically insignificant. The fact that adding these observable factors that vary by birth cohort/state had so little impact on the disadvantage coefficient estimates may provide a glimmer of hope that much of the unobservable heterogeneity has been eliminated. Of course, it would be imprudent to rely on this proposition too heavily.

6.6   Conclusions

This chapter has addressed the relationship between socioeconomic disadvantage and early childbearing. After presenting a review of relevant theoretical and empirical literatures from economics as well as other disciplines, we provided a descriptive analysis from the PSID of the relationship between socioeconomic disadvantage and early childbearing at the individual level. Confirming what many previous studies have shown, we find that growing up disadvantaged is associated with substantially higher rates of teen childbearing.

The main empirical contribution of this chapter is a cohort-based analysis of the relationship between rates of socioeconomic disadvantage among women at birth and their subsequent rates of early childbearing. This analysis is conducted at the level of a state and year female birth cohort. We initially use these cohort-based data to estimate an intergenerational correlation in early childbearing, relating the percentage of a birth cohort that gives birth at a young age to the percentage of the cohort born to young mothers. Unlike the intergenerational transmission of early childbearing propensities between mothers and daughters, the intergenerational *cohort-level* correlation includes the impact of peer and spillover effects generated by a shared culture or environment. The results of our analyses suggest that the correlation of early childbearing across generations is much stronger in the aggregate than at the individual level. This suggests that community characteristics and the culture of teen childbearing may be more important than whether or not one's own mother gave birth at an early age.

We obtain similar results when we take advantage of the panel nature of the cohort-based data and estimate the relationship between early childbearing and measures of disadvantage at birth. With these data, we can econometrically capture cultural/environmental differences that are long-standing in nature across states as well as geographically uniform changes that take place over time. When these elements are accounted for with state and year fixed effects, the estimated relationship between disadvantage at birth and subsequent early childbearing is greatly attenuated. This suggests that the observed relationship is almost entirely driven by broader changes in social conditions. For each of our four measures of socioeconomic disadvantage, our estimates imply that a 10 percent reduction in the proportion of a cohort with that particular proxy characteristic would lead to a decline of less than about 2.5 percent in the proportion who give birth by age eighteen or age twenty. Our results lead us to conclude that the impact of a fairly large shock to socioeconomic disadvantage would have only a modest impact on rates of early childbearing. Other broader societal forces seem to play a larger role in determining early childbearing rates.

References

Altonji, J. G., and T. A. Dunn. 2000. An intergenerational model of wages, hours, and earnings. *Journal of Human Resources* 35 (2): 221–58.

Ananat, E. O., J. Gruber, and P. B. Levine. 2004. Abortion legalization and lifecycle fertility. NBER Working Paper no. 10705. Cambridge, MA: National Bureau of Economic Research, August.

An, C.-B., R. Haveman, and B. Wolfe. 1993. Teen out-of-wedlock births and welfare receipt: The role of childhood events and economic circumstances. *The Review of Economics and Statistics* 75 (2): 195–208.

Becker, G. S. 1960. An economic analysis of fertility. In *Demographic and economic change in developed countries*, 225–56. Princeton, NJ: Princeton University Press.

Black, S. E., P. J. Devereaux, and K. G. Salvanes. 2004. Fast times at Ridgemont High? The effect of compulsory schooling laws on teenage births. NBER Working Paper no. 10911. Cambridge, MA: National Bureau of Economic Research, November.

———. 2005. Why the apple doesn't fall far: Understanding the intergenerational transmission of education. *American Economic Review* 95 (1): 437–49.

Brooks-Gunn, J., and F. F. Furstenberg, Jr. 1989. Adolescent sexual behavior. *American Psychologist* 44 (2): 249–57.

Brooks-Gunn, J., and R. Paikoff. 1997. Sexuality and developmental transitions during adolescence. In *Health risks and development transitions during adolescence*, ed. J. Schulenberg, J. L. Maggs, and K. Hurrelmann, 190–245. Cambridge, England: Cambridge University Press.

Chadwick, L., and G. Solon. 2002. Intergenerational income mobility among daughters. *American Economic Review* 92 (1): 335–44.

Chilman, C. S. 1983. *Adolescent sexuality in a changing American society: Social and psychological perspectives for the human services professions, 2nd ed.* New York: Wiley.

Currie, J., and E. Moretti. 2007. Biology as destiny? Short- and long-run determinants of intergenerational transmission of birth weight. *Journal of Labor Economics* 25 (2): 231–64.

Dehejia, R., and A. Lleras-Muney. 2004. Booms, busts and babies' health. *Quarterly Journal of Economics* 119 (3): 1091–1130.

Duncan, G., and S. Hoffman. 1990. Welfare benefits, economic opportunities, and out-of-wedlock births among black teenage girls. *Demography* 27 (November): 519–36.

Duncan, G., W. J. Yeung, J. Brooks-Gunn, and J. R. Smith. 1998. How much does childhood poverty affect the life chances of children? *American Sociological Review* 63 (3): 406–23.

Edin, K., and M. Kefalas. 2005. *Promises I can keep: Why poor women put motherhood before marriage.* Berkeley, CA: University of California Press.

Geronimus, A. T., and S. Korenman. 1992. The socioeconomic consequences of teen childbearing reconsidered. *Quarterly Journal of Economics* 107 (4): 1187–1214.

Geronimus, A. T., S. Korenman, and M. M. Hillemeier. 1994. Does young maternal age affect child development? Evidence from cousin comparisons in the United States. *Population and Development Review* 20 (3): 585–609.

Grogger, J., and S. Bronars. 1993. The socioeconomic consequences of teen childbearing: Findings from a natural experiment. *Family Planning Perspectives* 25 (July–August): 156–61.

Hardy, J. B., and L. Schwab Zabin. 1991. *Adolescent pregnancy in an urban environment.* Washington, D.C.: Urban Institute Press.

Haveman, R., and B. Wolfe. 1995. The determinants of children's attainments: A review of methods and findings. *Journal of Economic Literature* 33 (December): 1829–78.

Hotz, V. J., S. W. McElroy, and S. G. Sanders. 2005. Teenage childbearing and its life cycle consequences: Exploiting a natural experiment. *Journal of Human Resources* 40 (3): 683–715.

Kearney, M. S., and P. B. Levine. 2007. Subsidized contraception, fertility, and sexual behavior. NBER Working Paper no. 13045. Cambridge, MA: National Bureau of Economic Research, April.

Klepinger, D., S. Lundberg, and R. Plotnick. 1999. Teen childbearing and human capital: Does timing matter? Discussion Papers in Economics at the University of Washington 0057, October.

Laibson, D. 1997. Golden eggs and hyperbolic discounting. *Quarterly Journal of Economics* 62 (May): 443–77.

Leibowitz, A., M. Eisen, and W. K. Chow. 1986. An economic model of teenage pregnancy decisionmaking. *Demography* 23 (1): 67–78.

Levine, P. B. 2001. The sexual activity and birth control use of American teenagers. In *An economic analysis of risky behavior among youths,* ed. J. Gruber, 167–218. Chicago: University of Chicago Press.

———. 2003. Parental involvement laws and fertility behavior. *Journal of Health Economics* 22 (5): 861–78.

Levine, P. B., A. Trainor, and D. J. Zimmerman. 1996. The effect of state Medicaid funding restrictions on pregnancy, abortion, and births. *Journal of Health Economics* 15 (5): 555–78.

Lundberg, S., and R. D. Plotnick. 1995. Adolescent premarital childbearing: Do economic incentives matter? *Journal of Labor Economics* 13 (2): 177–200.

McCrary, J., and H. Royer. 2006. The effect of female education on fertility and infant health: Evidence from school entry policies using exact date of birth. NBER Working Paper no. 12329. Cambridge, MA: National Bureau of Economic Research, June.

Moffitt, R. A. 1992. Incentive effects of the U.S. welfare system: A review. *Journal of Economic Literature* 30 (1): 1–61.

———. 1998. The effect of welfare on marriage and fertility. In *Welfare, the family, and reproductive behavior: Research perspectives,* ed. R. A. Moffitt, 50–97. Washington, D.C.: National Academy Press.

———. 2003. The temporary assistance for needy families program. In *Means-tested transfer programs in the U.S.,* ed. R. A. Moffitt, 291–364. Chicago: University of Chicago Press.

National Campaign to Prevent Teen Pregnancy. 2007. *Why it matters.* Available at: http://www.teenpregnancy.org/wim/default.asp.

O'Donoghue, T., and M. Rabin. 1999. Doing it now or later. *American Economic Review* 89 (1): 103–24.

———. 2001. Risky behavior among youths: Some issues from behavioral economics. In *Risky behavior among youths,* ed. J. Gruber, 29–68. Chicago: University of Chicago Press.

Riber, D. 1994. Teenage fertility and high school completion. *Review of Economics and Statistics* 76 (3): 413–24.

Solon, G. 1999. Intergenerational mobility in the labor market. In *Handbook of labor economics,* ed. O. Ashenfelter and D. Card, 1761–96. Amsterdam: Elsevier.

United Nations, Department of Economic and Social Affairs. 2006. *Demographic yearbook.* New York: United Nations.

Ward, M. P., and W. P. Butz. 1980. Completed fertility and its timing. *The Journal of Political Economy* 88 (5): 917–40.

III

Contextual Influences

7

Parental Income Shocks and Outcomes of Disadvantaged Youth in the United States

Marianne Page, Ann Huff Stevens, and Jason Lindo

Government policies that increase the incomes of poor families have been promoted as a way of improving children's life chances on the grounds that children who grow up in rich families tend to have better socioeconomic outcomes as adults than children who grow up in poor families. Yet the process that generates the relationship between parents' incomes and those of their children, though well documented, is not well understood. One possibility is that differences in family income lead to differences in parents' monetary investments in their children. Another is that differences in family income reflect differences in parents' innate characteristics that are passed on to their children.

Understanding which factors contribute to the intergenerational transmission of socioeconomic status is crucial to the development of public policies that improve youths' outcomes. If, for example, disadvantaged children have poor outcomes because their parents have less money, then the effects of public policies on family income should be a central consideration when evaluating their costs and benefits. On the other hand, if children's outcomes are mostly determined by innate parental characteristics that are correlated with income, then social policy should be less concerned with income redistribution and focus more on addressing deficits in the other characteristics.

Marianne Page is an associate professor of economics at the University of California, Davis, and a faculty research fellow of the National Bureau of Economic Research. Ann Huff Stevens is associate professor of economics at the University of California, Davis, and a faculty research fellow of the National Bureau of Economic Research. Jason Lindo is an assistant professor of economics at the University of Oregon.

This research was funded by the Annie E. Casey Foundation. We thank them for their support but acknowledge that the findings and conclusions presented in this report are those of the authors alone, and do not necessarily reflect the opinions of the Foundation.

An extensive literature documents that children raised in low-income families have significantly lower levels of education, earnings, and family income as adults than children who grew up in affluent families (see, e.g., Solon's 1999 survey). However, whether these relationships result from the effects of income per se or whether they reflect other family background characteristics is a subject of debate. Although some studies have found that the association does not disappear even after controlling for a variety of parental characteristics (e.g., Corcoran et al. 1999; Hill and Duncan 1987), one cannot be sure that observable family background variables sufficiently capture all of the familial conditions that affect children's long-term outcomes. Finding a way of comparing youth whose family characteristics would be identical except for the differences in their incomes has proven to be a challenge. The handful of studies (Blau 1999; Duncan et al. 1998; Dahl and Lochner 2005; Duncan and Brooks-Gunn 1997; Haveman and Wolfe 1995; Levy and Duncan 1999; Shea 2000) that have attempted to do so have produced mixed results. Even Susan Mayer (1997), who has devoted an entire book to this question, acknowledges that none of the five empirical strategies that she uses to tease out the causal effect of income would be convincing by itself.

This research attempts to shed some light on these questions by analyzing the effects of unexpected job loss on the next generation's socioeconomic outcomes. Jacobsen, Lalonde, and Sullivan (1993) and Stevens (1997) have documented that displaced workers experience substantive long-lasting reductions in earnings, and they argue that layoffs and firm closings can be thought of as exogenous employment shocks after conditioning on predisplacement earnings. Our estimation strategy compares groups of individuals whose families had the same levels of permanent income prior to a period when some of the family heads were displaced. In order to implement this approach, we require data on the economic outcomes of both parents and their children. We use longitudinal data from the Panel Study of Income Dynamics (PSID), which contains detailed information on both generations over many years. A disadvantage of the PSID is that sample sizes are small. As a result, our estimates are often imprecise and must be interpreted cautiously.

Nevertheless, the patterns we observe generate three broad conclusions. First, estimates of the intergenerational effects of parental job loss are sensitive to the definition of displacement. Specifically, we estimate large, statistically significant effects on the next generation's income and earnings when displacements include layoffs, but not when they are restricted to firm closures. This dichotomy suggests that individuals who are selected for layoffs may have unobserved characteristics that are correlated with their children's outcomes. Second, although we find no evidence that firm closings have intergenerational effects on average, there is evidence that such events impose long-term costs on disadvantaged children. Finally, the effects of exogenous income shocks (from business closings) are largest among children who are young at the time of the income shock.

7.1   Empirical Strategy

Our analysis is conducted in two parts. First, we use methods taken from the displacement literature to demonstrate that displacement has a substantive and long-lasting effect on a family's resources. The purpose of this part of the analysis is to make a convincing case that displacement produces a significant exogenous shock to family income over many years. Second, we estimate the effects of this shock on children's outcomes as young adults.

7.1.1   Estimating the Effect of Displacement on a Family's Resources

We begin by following the empirical strategy introduced by Jacobson, LaLonde, and Sullivan (1993)—henceforth, JLS—to demonstrate that displacement has a large, persistent effect on a family's monetary resources. For simplicity, in this section we refer to "displacement" without distinguishing between business closings and layoffs. In the results that follow we will further distinguish results by the nature of the job displacement. We start by regressing annual measures of (log) family income and head's earnings on displacement indicators, age squared,[1] and calendar year effects.

$$(1) \qquad \ln I_{it} = \mathbf{D}_{it}\delta + \beta_1 age_{it}^2 + \mathbf{Y}\gamma_t + \alpha_i + u_{it},$$

where $\ln I_{it}$ is the log of family i's resources in year t, and $\mathbf{D}_{it}$ is a vector of dummy variables indicating that a displacement has taken (or will take) place in a future, current, or previous year; $\mathbf{Y}$ is a vector of calendar year dummies. In addition, we control for family-specific fixed effect, α_i. Because the model includes fixed effects, characteristics of the family head that do not vary over time, such as race and education, are not included.

The vector of displacement indicators ($\mathbf{D}_{it}$) contains three types of variables: dummy variables that equal one in the years prior to the displacement, a dummy variable equal to one in the year that the family head loses his job, and a series of dummy variables indicating that a displacement took place in a previous year. The first set of indicator variables captures the possibility that the head's wages may begin to deteriorate prior to the actual displacement. This might happen if wages are cut when the firm hits difficult times. Failure to include these dummies would lead to a biased estimate of the effect of the displacement. Our model, therefore, includes a dummy variable for each of the two years before the job loss occurs. The dummy variable indicating the year of the displacement captures its immediate effect on family resources, whereas the coefficients on the set of variables indicating

---

1. We do not control directly for the head's age because its effects on family income cannot be separately identified from year effects when family-specific fixed effects are included.

that a displacement occurred in a previous year will reflect the persistence of the displacement effect over time. We include individual post-displacement controls for five years, along with an indicator for whether a displacement occurred six or more years ago.

By including family-specific fixed effects, we control for unobserved, time-invariant characteristics of the parents in our sample (which are potentially correlated with the probability of displacement). This means that the estimated displacement effects summarize the long-term effects of an income shock on a family's resources, and are not contaminated by permanent differences in family background. In the main part of our analysis we use this displacement shock as a source of variation in children's resources.

7.1.2   Estimating the Effect of Displacement on Children's Outcomes

The next step is to regress a measure of the child's economic well-being during early adulthood on average parental income three to five years before the job loss, some additional controls for family background, and an indicator for whether the head of the child's family was ever displaced:

(2) $O_i = a + bAvgInc_{3-5} + cFamilyCharacteristics_{it} + dDisplaced_i + \varepsilon_i,$

where O_i represents an economic outcome for child i. Since layoffs and firm closures are thought to be exogenous events, the estimated coefficient on the *Displaced* dummy is not expected to reflect parental characteristics that are correlated with income. The key to this identification strategy is the assumption that, among families with similar incomes, displacement is not correlated with unobservables that could affect children's outcomes. We examine the claim that displacements are independent of family background by including in some specifications controls for observable parental characteristics. If displacements are truly random then the inclusion of family background variables should not alter the estimated effect of displacement on children's outcomes.

7.2   Data

We use data from the 1968 to 2003 waves of the Panel Study of Income Dynamics (PSID), focusing on the displacement experiences of households that include children ages fifteen and younger. We later observe these children as young adults. Displacement is initially defined as a job separation that occurs as the result of a firm closure or layoff. Because we are more confident that job losses due to business closures are uncorrelated with unobserved characteristics of the families, in subsequent specifications we eliminate children whose parents were displaced via a layoff, and focus on the effects of firm closures only. The children whose parents were displaced and are exposed to the income shock are referred to as our treatment group.

Children without a displacement in their family history serve as a control group.

Our primary treatment group consists of children whose parent, specifically the head of household, experienced a displacement sometime before the child turned sixteen. Children over age sixteen are increasingly likely to live in independent households where exposure to their parents' monetary circumstances will be mitigated. As children age, the number of years over which they are exposed to the consequences of the income shock diminish.[2] We must also eliminate children whose parents do not have income observations three, four, or five years prior to the displacement, so that we can compute a three-year average of family income prior to the job loss.

To be included in the sample for the income and earnings outcomes, each child must be observed as the head or spouse of their own household for at least three years.[3] For other outcomes, such as completed education and labor force status, we require only a single year of observation. We focus on the first displacement experienced by a family, since subsequent displacements for a given family may not be independent events. With this in mind, we do not include in the sample any children whose parent experienced a displacement prior to the child's birth. Effectively, this means that the displacements we observe occur between 1971 and 1987, with a median displacement year of 1974. The treatment group consists of individuals whose parents experienced a displacement during this period, and the control group consists of children whose parent did not experience a displacement. The children affected are observed as heads and wives between 1975 and 2003, with a median year of 1992.

Because we want to control for family income or earnings prior to a job loss, it is necessary to choose a set of years over which we will measure income prior to the shock. While this is straightforward for those individuals who are displaced, it is less clear what income observations should be used for the control group. To solve this problem while preserving the sample size, we randomly assign children in the control group a "reference age" using the distribution of ages associated with the first displacement in our treatment group.[4] This allows us to include income three to five years prior

2. We have replicated our analysis using the displacement experiences of households including children up to age eighteen to see whether there are particular effects when the displacement occurs close to the time of college attendance decisions. The results are virtually identical to those reported here.

3. This helps to reduce measurement error in the dependent variable, which is particularly likely given the young ages at which the children's earnings are observed.

4. For example, because 8.1 percent of the displaced children have a parental displacement at age eight, controls are assigned age eight as the reference age with a probability of .081. We then use the first year in which a child is observed at the reference age as the reference year. For a control child not observed at his or her assigned reference age, we use the earliest age at which he or she is observed. If a control child is not in the survey at the assigned reference age or earlier, he or she is dropped.

to either first displacement (for the treatment group) or three to five years prior to the reference year (for the control group) in our regressions.[5] Finally, to be in our analysis sample, we require children to have the same head of household in either the year of displacement (for the treatment group) or the reference year (control group) and the five preceding years. This helps ensure that displacements are exogenous conditional on predisplacement income, while maintaining consistent sample requirements for the treatment and control groups.

To ensure that our predisplacement income measure is not driven by parent's gender or age, or by business cycle effects, we adjust parental income for these characteristics prior to including it in equation (3). We regress the natural log of parent's income on dummy variables indicating the year income is observed, and the head of household's gender and age. We then use the average of the residuals from these regressions three to five years prior to displacement (or the reference year) to control for predisplacement income.

7.4   Results

7.4.1   Summary Statistics

Sample summary statistics are shown in table 7.1. Our sample contains nearly 1,800 children, 673 of whose fathers lost their jobs due to a layoff or firm closing sometime when the children were under age fifteen, and 242 of whose fathers lost their jobs due to a firm closing. We show separate statistics for our treatment and control groups. Note that the earnings and family income of heads who will eventually be displaced are somewhat lower than among parents who do not experience a job loss. Average earnings three to five years before the displacement (reference) year are $41,499 among heads in the treatment group, and $52,325 among heads in the control group. The difference in average predisplacement earnings is much smaller when heads who experienced layoffs are eliminated from the sample: $51,396 among those who will eventually lose their jobs to a firm closure, and $53,089 among those who will not. Predisplacement income is similarly lower for the treatment group. These differences highlight the fact that displacements are not randomly distributed throughout the population: instead we assume that they are random *conditional* on predisplacement income. The legitimacy of this assumption will be discussed in section 7.4.3.

There are also substantial differences in the educational distributions

5. We have also replicated our results using a simpler design, which uses average income when the child is between ages zero and four as the control variable for both groups. This results in a smaller sample since it requires all children to be observed at age one rather than requiring that they be observed five years prior to displacement or reference year. This sample produces very similar estimates.

Table 7.1   **Sample means by parent's displacement status**

	Using all displacements			Using only closures		
	Displaced	Control	All	Displaced	Control	All
	Parents					
Earnings	35,379	48,193	43,778	42,956	48,762	47,872
3 to 5 years prior to displacement (reference) year	41,499	52,325	48,591	51,396	53,089	52,830
3 to 5 years after displacement (reference) year	38,540	55,490	49,722	45,976	55,329	53,891
Family income	58,242	76,510	70,216	69,313	77,623	76,349
3 to 5 years prior to displacement (reference) year	53,589	66,311	61,928	65,878	67,564	67,306
3 to 5 years after displacement (reference) year	60,989	83,462	75,893	72,378	84,146	82,374
Education < HS	0.44	0.27	0.33	0.33	0.27	0.28
Education = HS	0.25	0.29	0.28	0.29	0.29	0.29
Education > HS	0.31	0.44	0.40	0.38	0.44	0.43
Displacement (reference) year	1976	1976	1976	1977	1976	1976
Age	39.1	41.8	40.9	41.3	41.9	41.8
Kid's age	10.7	11.6	11.3	11.6	11.9	11.9
	Children					
Age	28.6	28.9	28.6	29.3	29.0	29.3
Average earnings	27,374	30,868	29,668	33,161	31,116	31,430
Earnings at ages 25 to 27	22,899	25,021	24,312	26,991	24,967	25,257
Average income	48,585	54,884	52,714	59,389	54,942	55,628
Family income at ages 25 to 27	43,673	46,842	45,782	50,570	46,368	46,969
Working	0.89	0.88	0.88	0.92	0.89	0.89
Education < HS	0.39	0.10	0.13	0.13	0.10	0.11
Education = HS	0.41	0.33	0.35	0.35	0.33	0.33
Education > HS	0.35	0.57	0.51	0.53	0.57	0.56
Ever received UI	0.35	0.25	0.28	0.31	0.26	0.27
Received UI in a given year	0.08	0.06	0.07	0.07	0.06	0.06
Ever received AFDC/TANF	0.15	0.10	0.12	0.16	0.09	0.10
Received AFDC/TANF in a given year	0.06	0.04	0.04	0.05	0.04	0.04
Had teenage pregnancy	0.25	0.20	0.22	0.16	0.21	0.20
N (Number of individuals)	673	1,117	1,790	242	1,202	1,444
N (total person-years)	7,124	12,395	19,519	2,479	13,421	15,900

Notes: Means are weighted using the individual weight in last year the individual is observed with a nonzero weight. The sample of parents is defined by the children's head of household in the first displacement year or reference year. Children of interest are observed as adults if they are heads/wives in households at ages greater than age twenty-three. Money variables are measured in 2002 dollars. Means for AFDC and teen pregnancy are calculated for women only.

of parents who do and do not suffer displacements. Approximately one-third of the treatment group parents have more than a high school education, whereas 44 percent of the control parents have obtained some post-secondary schooling. These differences narrow when we drop parents who were laid off, but they are not eliminated, which suggests that while the event of a firm closing is likely to be exogenous with respect to individual characteristics, the likelihood of working in a job that is "susceptible" to closings is higher for less skilled workers. We will address this issue in the regression analysis by including a number of family background characteristics, and by showing that once we control for predisplacement income, the additional characteristics have little impact on the estimated effect of losing a job due to a firm closure.

Table 7.1 also shows dramatic post-reference year differences in head's earnings and family income between children whose parents were displaced and those whose parents were not. Average family income three to five years after displacement is approximately $61,000, while average family income among those with no parental displacement is more than $83,000. This suggests that firm closings and layoffs produce substantial shocks to a child's financial resources.

Table 7.1 also shows that treatment and control children have somewhat different labor market outcomes as adults. For example, average family income between ages twenty-five and twenty-seven is about $44,000 among those whose parents experienced a job loss and about $47,000 for those whose parents did not. Similarly, treatment children have lower levels of education and higher rates of Unemployment insurance (UI) receipt than the controls. Given the predisplacement differences in parents' earnings, income, and other characteristics, it is impossible to say whether this reflects any causal effect of job loss on children's outcomes. This is the focus of the regression analysis in the next section.

7.4.2 The Monetary Costs of Displacement

We begin by showing that displacement leads to a substantial long-term reduction in a family's monetary resources. Table 7.2 presents the results from regressions of heads' annual earnings and family income on the displacement dummies. The left half of the table provides results for the sample that includes all displacements, and the right half of the table shows the estimates produced by the sample that restricts displacements to those resulting from firm closures. Like previous studies, we find that family resources decline substantially when a job loss occurs. For example, when all displacements are followed, head's earnings fall by 36 percent and family income falls by 21 percent[6] in the year after displacement.[7] Family resources recover somewhat over time, but even six years later head's earnings are approximately 26 percent lower than they would have been if the displacement had not occurred. Similarly, family income is reduced by 20 percent. These estimates are all

6. The percentage effect on earnings is computed as $e^\delta - 1$.

7. A firm closure can occur anytime during the year. The fathers in our sample may, therefore, lose their job anytime between early January and late December. As a result, spells of unemployment and earnings losses may be larger in the year following the displacement than in the displacement year itself.

Table 7.2   **Estimated effects of first displacements on parent's log earnings and log family income**

Dependent variable	All displacements		Only closures	
	Ln earnings (1)	Ln family income (2)	Ln earnings (3)	Ln family income (4)
3 years prior to displacement	−0.039	−0.040	−0.040	−0.043
	(0.035)	(0.026)	(0.045)	(0.035)
2 years prior to displacement	−0.055	−0.052**	−0.027	−0.061*
	(0.038)	(0.026)	(0.046)	(0.036)
1 years prior to displacement	−0.122**	−0.086***	−0.141**	−0.139***
	(0.048)	(0.031)	(0.066)	(0.050)
Year of displacement	−0.314***	−0.206***	−0.242***	−0.189***
	(0.057)	(0.040)	(0.092)	(0.068)
1 year after displacement	−0.441***	−0.239***	−0.391***	−0.240***
	(0.062)	(0.041)	(0.080)	(0.060)
2 year after displacement	−0.295***	−0.202***	−0.237***	−0.182***
	(0.055)	(0.038)	(0.079)	(0.056)
3 year after displacement	−0.369***	−0.242***	−0.333***	−0.268***
	(0.070)	(0.043)	(0.092)	(0.066)
4 year after displacement	−0.331***	−0.204***	−0.319***	−0.220***
	(0.067)	(0.044)	(0.092)	(0.070)
5 year after displacement	−0.418***	−0.206***	−0.305***	−0.187***
	(0.101)	(0.046)	(0.087)	(0.063)
6 or more years after displacement	−0.295***	−0.220***	−0.262***	−0.233***
	(0.055)	(0.041)	(0.072)	(0.056)
Number of individuals	985	985	830	830
Person-year observations	20,180	20,180	17,310	17,310
R^2	0.593	0.639	0.59	0.628

Notes: Individual-clustered standard error estimates are shown in parentheses. Regressions are weighted using the individual weight in last year the individual is observed with a nonzero weight. Regression includes individual fixed effects, year dummies, and age-squared.

***Significant at the 1 percent level.

**Significant at the 5 percent level.

*Significant at the 10 percent level.

statistically significant, and indicate that displacement produces substantive and persistent economic losses, similar to those produced by JLS (1993). The results based on firm closures display the same pattern.[8] The first two rows of table 7.2 also show small declines in family income even before the displacement occurs, consistent with previous work on the effects of displacement (Stevens 1997).

8. We have also estimated the relationship between displacement and parental earnings and income including an individual-specific trend, along with the individual fixed effect. Results for fathers' earnings are similar, although results for family income produce smaller long-run effects when individual trends are included. This may partially reflect the difficulty of identifying the individual-trend model in a relatively small data set.

7.4.3   Intergenerational Effects of Displacement—Income and Earnings

Having established that displacement substantially reduces family resources, we now investigate its intergenerational effects. Table 7.3 displays the results from the second part of our analysis. The dependent variables are based on the child's responses to the survey beginning at age twenty-four and for each year thereafter. Specially, we consider the average of adjusted log earnings and the average of adjusted log family income. As in table 7.1, the left side of the table shows the results for the full sample, and the right side of the table focuses only on displacements caused by firm closures.

Beginning with the full sample, column (1) shows the results from an ordinary least squares (OLS) regression of the log of the child's income in adulthood on the log of average family income three to five years before the "displacement" year. The estimated coefficient of 0.37 is consistent with estimates from the intergenerational correlations literature, which generally finds that the correlation between fathers' and sons' earnings is about 0.40 (Solon 1992; Zimmerman 1992). Sample variation in this variable is likely to reflect variation in other family background characteristics that are correlated with income, however, so it is inappropriate to conclude that family income has a causal effect on child's future resources.

In the next column we add a dummy variable indicating whether the father lost his job due to a layoff or firm closing. This variable is clearly correlated with the next generation's income, which is 9.2 percent lower than the average family income of those whose parents were not displaced. Next, we add a set of observable family background variables to the regression, specifically measures of the head's educational attainment, state of residence, and industry. If displacements are truly random after controlling for parental income, then the inclusion of these variables should have no impact on their estimated effect. In fact, the magnitude of the estimated displacement effect declines substantially when other family background characteristics are included, suggesting that the estimate in column (2) may partly reflect the impact of other parental attributes. Most of the change in the magnitude of the point estimates is driven by the inclusion of parental education.

The last three columns of table 7.3 provide displacement estimates for a sample that restricts treatment children to those whose parents lost their job via a firm closure. Eliminating parents who experienced a layoff from the analysis has virtually no impact on the estimated income correlation, but does reduce the point estimate on the displacement dummy to nearly zero. The standard error estimates are so large that we cannot reject the possibility that plant closings have moderately sized intergenerational effects; nevertheless, the decline in the coefficient estimate is intriguing since firm closures are more likely to be exogenous with respect to other parental characteristics.

The bottom panel of table 7.3 shows the effects of parental job loss on

Table 7.3   **Estimated effects of parental displacement on family income and earnings as adults**

	All displacements			Only closures		
	(1)	(2)	(3)	(4)	(5)	(6)
Average adjusted adult family income						
Avg. adj. log parent's	0.366***	0.359***	0.176***	0.339***	0.339***	0.162***
famioy income	(0.055)	(0.054)	(0.047)	(0.059)	(0.059)	(0.051)
Displaced (= 1 if yes)		−0.097**	−0.070		−0.006	0.002
		(0.044)	(0.044)		(0.061)	(0.060)
Parent less than HS			−0.406***			−0.432***
graduate			(0.064)			(0.074)
Parent has exactly HS			−0.137**			−0.121*
education			(0.060)			(0.063)
Parent industry fixed						
effects			X			X
Parent state fixed effects			X			X
Observations	1,623	1,623	1,623	1,314	1,314	1,314
R^2	0.075	0.078	0.193	0.065	0.065	0.191
Average adjusted adult earnings						
Avg. adj. log parent's	0.342***	0.335***	0.131**	0.296***	0.296***	0.104*
family income	(0.063)	(0.062)	(0.058)	(0.063)	(0.063)	(0.056)
Displaced (= 1 if yes)		−0.112**	−0.095*		−0.007	0.020
		(0.050)	(0.051)		(0.072)	(0.076)
Parent less than HS			−0.450***			−0.437***
graduate			(0.071)			(0.082)
Parent has exactly HS			−0.176***			−0.128*
education			(0.068)			(0.071)
Parent industry fixed						
effects			X			X
Parent state fixed effects			X			X
Observations	1,597	1,597	1,597	1,301	1,301	1,301
R^2	0.048	0.052	0.148	0.038	0.038	0.150

Notes: Standard error estimates are shown in parentheses. Regressions are weighted using the individual weight in last year the individual is observed with a nonzero weight. Earnings and income are adjusted for age, year, and sex. "X" indicates that parent industry fixed effects and/or parent state fixed effects are included in the regression.
***Significant at the 1 percent level.
**Significant at the 5 percent level.
*Significant at the 10 percent level.

adult earnings. As in the top half of the table, children whose parents were displaced appear to have lower earnings as adults than children whose parents were not displaced. Specifically, children whose parents experienced a job loss have adult earnings that are about 9 percent lower than children whose parents did not, even after controlling for family background characteristics other than income. The magnitude of this estimate again changes substantially (and is very close to zero) when the sample of displacements is restricted to those resulting from a firm closure, however.

What explains the difference in the magnitude of the estimates across the different definitions of displacement? One possibility is that workers who are selected for layoffs have unobserved traits that affect both their probability of being laid off and their children's outcomes. Such concerns are less likely if we focus on firm closures, since a firm shut-down leads to job losses for *all* workers at the firm.[9] The results from table 7.2 lend weight to our concern that layoffs may be correlated with unobserved parental attributes, since the magnitude of the income and earnings shocks are very similar across the different definitions of displacement; it is not the case that layoffs and firm closures have different effects on the family's financial resources. Table 7.3 also shows that the estimated displacement coefficient is more sensitive to the inclusion of additional family background variables when the treatment group includes layoffs. Because firm closures are more plausibly exogenous, the estimated coefficient on the broader definition of displacement (including layoffs) should be thought of as an upper bound on the causal effect of income, which may also contain the effects of unobservable characteristics that lead to the layoff, but which are not captured adequately by predisplacement income. For this reason, in the rest of the chapter, we focus on displacements that occur only as the result of business closings. Results including both layoffs and closures are included in the appendix for comparison. Including the layoffs consistently produces larger and more often significant effects of job loss on the children's outcomes. This may be the result of unobservable factors that both contribute to the probability of layoff and negatively affect children's outcomes. Layoffs may be associated with poorer outcomes among the affected children, but we are less comfortable in making causal statements about this connection.

Intergenerational Effects of Displacement—Other Outcomes

Table 7.4 shows the estimated relationship between parental job loss due to business closures and other measures of socioeconomic success. Specifically, we analyze indicators for whether the child had at least a high school education, or more than a high school education, dummy variables indicating whether the child filed for unemployment benefits, Aid to Families with Dependent Children (AFDC) benefits (females only), indicators for experiencing a teen pregnancy (females only), and a variable indicating the fraction of years in which the child was working when observed at age twenty-four and later. First we consider the effect of firm closures on the next generation's completed schooling. While the estimates in the first two rows of table 7.4 are not very precise, they are of the expected sign, and suggest that children whose parents lose their jobs via a firm closure are less likely to complete

---

9. Firm closures do not entirely eliminate the possibility of selection based on individual characteristics, since more able workers may leave prior to the actual firm closure and possibly avoid some of the impact of an involuntary job change.

Table 7.4   **Estimated effects of firm closures during childhood on additional adult outcomes**

	(1)	(2)
Complete at least high school		
Displaced (= 1 if yes)	–0.030	–0.019
	(0.026)	(0.020)
Attended some college		
Displaced (= 1 if yes)	–0.042	–0.015
	(0.044)	(0.048)
Ever receive unemployment insurance		
Displaced (= 1 if yes)	0.068	0.056
	(0.043)	(0.045)
Ever receive AFDC (women only, N = 746)		
Displaced (= 1 if yes)	0.056	0.049
	(0.037)	(0.038)
Teen pregnancy (women only, N = 746)		
Displaced (= 1 if yes)	–0.043	–0.061
	(0.043)	(0.042)
Working		
Displaced (= 1 if yes)	0.031*	0.049***
	(0.016)	(0.018)
Observations	1,444	1,444

Notes: Standard error estimates are shown in parentheses. Estimated marginal effects are based on probit models using the individual weight in last year the individual is observed with a nonzero weight. Column (1) controls for parent's average adjusted income. Column (2) adds controls for parent's education, industry, and state.
***Significant at the 1 percent level.
**Significant at the 5 percent level.
*Significant at the 10 percent level.

high school and less likely to attend college. The next row shows the estimated effect of parental displacement on the probability of receiving UI benefits, which is positive but not statistically significant. The next two rows of table 7.4 display the estimated impact of firm closings on welfare receipt and teen pregnancy. Neither set of estimates is statistically significant. The final row of table 7.4 shows the probability that the child is working after age twenty-four. Here, the surprising result is that individuals are significantly more likely to be working if their father experienced a job loss.

7.4.4   Intergenerational Effects of Displacement—by Subgroups

Our estimates provide little evidence that, on average, income shocks have long-term effects on the next generation's socioeconomic status. By focusing on average effects, however, we may miss important differences across groups. For example, the effect of a job loss on financial constraints (and associated stress) are likely to be larger for low socioeconomic status (SES) families, so we might expect the intergenerational impact on children growing up in such families to be larger.[10] In order to explore this possibility we have estimated displacement coefficients for different subgroups of children according to their poverty status, family structure (both measured prior to displacement), parental education, and race.

Table 7.5 summarizes the results of this exercise. The first column shows the average effect of displacement on the child's financial resources, and, for purposes of comparison, the first row of the table repeats estimates for the full sample from tables 7.3 and 7.4. The first column of table 7.5 summarizes the effect of the job loss on parental household income (as shown in table 7.2); subsequent columns show the effects on children's adult outcomes.

Moving from the full sample to subsamples of children who are disadvantaged prior to any job loss changes the nature of these results. Among families with income below the poverty line before the job loss, there is a somewhat larger than average impact of displacement on family income in the parent's generation. These effects on household income during childhood seem to carry over into some statistically and economically significant effects on the next generation when we focus on disadvantaged subsamples. The family incomes of poor children whose parents experienced a plant closing are 34 percent below that of the control group. While the estimate is quite imprecise, it does stand in contrast to the very small point estimates generated for the full sample. Earnings of these children are also substantially reduced, and this estimate is statistically different from zero. When we increase the sample size by including all children with household income below 1.5 times the poverty line (in the years before job loss) we continue to find strong evidence of negative effects on children's family income and earnings as young adults. Results are similar, though somewhat weaker, when we include families with incomes up to two times the poverty line.

In contrast, row 5 shows no evidence of negative effects of parental displacement on income or earnings among those with incomes well above the poverty line. This pattern suggests that the overall lack of effects of job loss summarized in tables 7.3 and 7.4 obscures substantial effects among children who are disadvantaged prior to the parental job loss. Among children whose parental financial resources are already limited, parental job loss and the associated income shock generates substantial negative effects on their earnings and income as adults. This seems to occur only among disadvantaged families, despite the fact that closures produce substantial declines in monetary resources across the income distribution.

This concentration of negative effects among those at the bottom of the family income distribution prior to displacement is confirmed when we look

10. For example, Coelli (2005) finds that low income teenagers whose parents experience a job loss are less likely to attend college, and virtually all of this affect is concentrated among parents with only a high school education or less. Similarly, Oreopoulos, Page, and Stevens (2006) find that the effects of firm closures on children are largely concentrated among children whose family income is in the bottom quartile.

Table 7.5   Estimated long-term effects of firm closures for specific groups

Sample	Average effect of closure on log parental income (1)	Effect of closure on children's adult outcomes							
		Family income (2)	Earnings (3)	Completed high school (4)	Attended some college (5)	Received unemployment insurance (6)	Received AFDC (7)	Teen pregnancy (8)	Working (9)
(1) Full sample	-0.222***	0.002	0.020	-0.019	-0.015	0.056	0.049	-0.061	0.049***
(N = 1,444)	(0.050)	(0.060)	(0.076)	(0.020)	(0.048)	(0.045)	(0.038)	(0.042)	(0.018)
(2) Parent's income < Poverty line	-0.289***	-0.422	-0.456*	-0.282*	-0.116	-0.218*	-0.004	-0.489***	0.004
(N = 206)	(0.108)	(0.279)	(0.263)	(0.152)	(0.108)	(0.124)	(0.212)	(0.152)	(0.073)
(3) Parent's income < 1.5x Poverty line	-0.288***	-0.496***	-0.358*	-0.360***	-0.160***	-0.031	0.285	0.104	-0.019
(N = 393)	(0.081)	(0.166)	(0.200)	(0.105)	(0.052)	(0.106)	(0.186)	(0.144)	(0.051)
(4) Parent's income < 2x Poverty line	-0.206***	-0.274**	-0.135	-0.073	-0.078	0.006	0.048	0.032	0.013
(N = 589)	(0.067)	(0.121)	(0.127)	(0.075)	(0.064)	(0.078)	(0.101)	(0.102)	(0.035)
(5) Parent's income > 2x Poverty line	-0.219***	0.136*	0.059	-0.017	0.009	0.052	-0.021	-0.048	0.065***
(N = 855)	(0.058)	(0.070)	(0.097)	(0.020)	(0.055)	(0.057)	(0.032)	(0.050)	(0.023)
(6) Single parent	-0.327*	-0.304	-0.019	0.017	0.024	0.067	0.450*	0.318	-0.088
(N = 157)	(0.169)	(0.324)	(0.314)	(0.080)	(0.152)	(0.157)	(0.270)	(0.245)	(0.111)
(7) Black	-0.131	-0.171	-0.263	-0.152*	-0.179**	0.184*	0.084	-0.036	0.032
(N = 476)	(0.082)	(0.149)	(0.179)	(0.073)	(0.080)	(0.096)	(0.115)	(0.117)	(0.076)
(8) Parent has < High school education	-0.186***	-0.158	-0.004	-0.003	0.017	0.001	0.207**	-0.085	0.014
(N = 545)	(0.060)	(0.130)	(0.171)	(0.071)	(0.077)	(0.077)	(0.098)	(0.072)	(0.036)

Notes: Standard error estimates are shown are in parentheses. Regressions are weighted using the individual weight in last year the individual is observed with a nonzero weight. Columns (4) through (8) show estimated marginal effects based on probit models. Earnings and income are adjusted for age, year, and sex. Estimated impacts on children's adult outcomes control for parent's education, industry, and state.

***Significant at the 1 percent level.

**Significant at the 5 percent level.

*Significant at the 10 percent level.

at other outcomes. Children with family income below 1.5 times the poverty line and whose parents experienced a job loss are 36 percentage points less likely to have completed high school than poor children whose parents were not displaced, and 16 percentage points less likely to have attended some college. There are positive estimated effects of parental displacement on both receiving welfare and experiencing a teen pregnancy among this group, though these effects are not statistically significant. There is a surprisingly strong and negative effect on teen pregnancy among those with income below the poverty line. This is an unexpected and implausibly large result, but is based on a very small sample of females.[11]

The next row of table 7.5 summarizes results for the cohort of children who were living with a single parent prior to job loss. There are few significant effects here, probably because the sample is extremely small. Those from single parent households are the only group for which there is a positive and significant effect of displacement on being a teen parent. Again, however, the small samples suggest caution in drawing conclusions from this group, and the estimated magnitude of the point estimate and standard errors are large enough to warrant some caution.

The next row displays the estimated effects of parental job loss on black children. The point estimates for income and earnings are negative and larger in magnitude than they are when the entire sample is included, but they are not statistically significant. There are negative and significant effects of parental job losses on college attendance among black children. There is also a significantly increased probability of receiving UI among black children whose parents lost jobs.

Finally, table 7.5 provides only limited evidence that the consequences of parental displacement may be larger for children of less-educated parents than for the population as a whole. Family income of the adult children is negatively affected by parental job loss, but this estimate is not statistically significant. Only the probability of receiving welfare is significantly higher among the children of less-educated parents.

In table 7.6 we focus on a different type of heterogeneity; specifically, whether the effects of parental job loss vary depending on the age at which the income shock occurs. This exercise is motivated by recent work in both child development and economics (summarized by Cunha et al. 2006), which suggests that (a) early childhood interventions may be more effective at reducing ability gaps than interventions undertaken at later ages, and (b) credit constraints operating in early life have a larger effect on adult outcomes than credit constraints encountered when children approach their late teens. To investigate this possibility, we add an interaction term between the displacement dummy and a variable indicating whether the child was under age seven at the time of the income shock to our basic regression. While

---

11. There are 112 girls in this subsample, and forty-six of them experience a teen pregnancy.

Table 7.6   Estimated long-term effects of firm closures by age at displacement

	Family income		Earnings		Completed high school		Attended some college		Received unemployment insurance		Received AFDC		Teen pregnancy		Working	
	(1)	(2)	(3)	(4)	(5)	(6)	(7)	(8)	(9)	(10)	(11)	(12)	(13)	(14)	(15)	(16)
Avg. adj. log parent's family income	0.339***	0.162***	0.296***	0.104*	0.076***	0.029***	0.223***	0.112***	-0.042*	-0.051*	-0.075***	0.002	-0.128***	-0.034	0.012	0.009
	(0.059)	(0.051)	(0.063)	(0.056)	(0.017)	(0.010)	(0.050)	(0.040)	(0.023)	(0.027)	(0.023)	(0.024)	(0.033)	(0.036)	(0.012)	(0.013)
Displaced (= 1 if yes)	0.011	0.013	0.030	0.047	-0.025	-0.014	-0.030	-0.002	0.063	0.047	0.041	0.031	-0.049	-0.072*	0.033**	0.051***
	(0.065)	(0.064)	(0.077)	(0.079)	(0.028)	(0.020)	(0.047)	(0.049)	(0.045)	(0.047)	(0.038)	(0.037)	(0.047)	(0.043)	(0.017)	(0.019)
Displaced at age ≤ 6 (= 1 if yes)	-0.123	-0.077	-0.269	-0.194	-0.030	-0.037	-0.076	-0.083	0.033	0.068	0.093	0.170	0.066	0.148	-0.014	-0.017
	(0.149)	(0.151)	(0.171)	(0.173)	(0.068)	(0.060)	(0.116)	(0.129)	(0.107)	(0.121)	(0.104)	(0.147)	(0.113)	(0.156)	(0.046)	(0.051)
Parent has less than HS education		-0.432***		-0.435***		-0.142***		-0.435***		0.063		0.150***		0.107*		-0.018
		(0.074)		(0.082)		(0.031)		(0.043)		(0.043)		(0.050)		(0.057)		(0.024)
Parent has exactly HS education		-0.119*		-0.121*		-0.021		-0.172***		-0.035		0.089**		0.043		0.03
		(0.064)		(0.071)		(0.021)		(0.046)		(0.037)		(0.040)		(0.055)		(0.020)
Parent industry fixed effects		X		X		X		X		X		X		X		X
Parent state fixed effects		X		X		X		X		X		X		X		X
Observations	1,314	1,314	1,301	1,301	1,428	1,367	1,428	1,418	1,409	1,390	722	590	746	690	1,317	1,317

Notes: Standard error estimates are shown in parentheses. Regressions are weighted using the individual weight in last year the individual is observed with a nonzero weight. Columns (5) through (14) show estimated marginal effects based on probit models. Earnings and income are adjusted for age, year, and sex. "X" indicates that parent industry fixed effects and/or parent state fixed effects are included in the regression.

***Significant at the 1 percent level.

**Significant at the 5 percent level.

*Significant at the 10 percent level.

none of the estimated coefficients on the interaction terms are statistically significant, their magnitudes and the overall pattern suggests that the negative effects of family income shocks may be larger when the shocks are experienced at young ages. Every one of the interaction effects between parental displacement and the child being under seven at the time of displacement have the expected sign if the impact of displacement is worse at younger ages. Nearly all of the estimated coefficients on the interaction terms are an order of magnitude greater than the estimate on the displacement dummy. For example, the point estimates suggest that children under seven whose parents have experienced a job loss have adult earnings that are 18 percent lower than older children whose parents have been displaced, and an 8 percentage point lower probability of getting post-secondary schooling. While one cannot make too much of such imprecise estimates, the systematic pattern across all outcomes is striking. Such a pattern could be explained by the fact that younger children are exposed to the income shock for a longer period of time, but would also be consistent with theories suggesting that early childhood interventions have bigger impacts.

Taken as a whole, our results have important elements in common with two previous, and closely related, studies. First, using an administrative data set from Canada, Oreopoulos, Page, and Stevens (2006) show that there are large effects of firm closures on children's adult outcomes. Like our study, it shows that virtually all of these effects are driven by families in the lowest quartile of the income distribution. While our current study is based on a much smaller sample, and therefore produces estimates that are much less precise, both studies suggest that income, if it plays a role in children's success, is probably most important among those children with other forms of disadvantage. Second, work by Shea (2000) also using the PSID finds limited evidence of effects of parental income on children's adult outcomes for the full sample, but does find effects for those in the poverty subsample. Shea uses an instrumental variable strategy, including industry, union, and firm closures as the key instruments to isolate the role of parental income. Our estimates have the advantage of controlling for income prior to job loss, and then looking at the effects of job loss, which Shea acknowledges may be more exogenous than some of his other instruments. The fact that our results are qualitatively similar to Shea's suggests that the implied effects of income disruptions hold up, even after conditioning on the prior level of income.

Before concluding, we return to the literature on intergenerational correlations in income. How do our results fit in to this literature? Solon (1992) and Zimmerman (1992) find that the correlation in earnings between fathers and sons is approximately .40. If the income shock from displacement is exogenous, and if displacement does not produce long-run effects on children's outcomes through mechanisms other than income, we can use our estimates to measure how much of this .40 correlation reflects a causal effect. The point estimates for our full sample are close to zero and this is consistent with none of the correlation being driven by a causal relationship from parental to kids' income. On the other hand, this zero point estimate is sufficiently imprecise that we also cannot rule out the possibility that all of the .40 correlation is due to causal effects.[12]

The more important message from this chapter with respect to estimated intergenerational correlations, however, is that nonlinearities in the relationship between parental income and kids' outcomes may be very important. The pattern of results in table 7.5 suggests that disadvantaged children are far more likely to experience negative effects from parental job losses than are children from households with average or higher income. Thus, simple correlations based on the entire income distribution cannot be easily decomposed into causal and other effects for the entire sample.

7.5 Conclusions

The question that motivates this chapter is whether family income itself, as opposed to the many family characteristics that are correlated with income, plays an important role in determining disadvantaged children's long-run socioeconomic success. Our strategy for answering this question is to focus on job displacement as an exogenous income shock. We compare outcomes among children whose families are very similar except that some families experienced a job loss. When we restrict the treatment group to families who lost jobs via a firm closure, we find little evidence that such shocks have long run effects on the next generation. Evidence of long-run negative effects is stronger when we include families who experienced a layoff, but we believe that layoffs are less likely to be exogenous events, so estimates based on this sample may reflect unobserved characteristics of the parents, rather than the effect of the income loss itself.

Although we find little evidence that income shocks affect the next generation's long-run socioeconomic success, on average, we do find evidence that such shocks have negative impacts on children who were already disadvantaged. In particular, we find that displacement substantially reduces the adult income of children whose parental income was already below the poverty line. We also find suggestive evidence that children whose parents are less educated, black, or unmarried suffer negative consequences, although these estimates are not typically statistically significant. The pattern of point estimates among the less advantaged samples suggests that these groups experience larger long-run losses when a parent loses his job, in spite of the fact that the magnitude of the income shock is similar across more and less advantaged groups.

Finally, the evidence that income affects children's long-term outcomes is

12. The lower end of a 95 percent confidence interval around our main effect on kids' income of .002 is –0.12. Dividing this effect of displacement on kids' income by the effect of displacement on parental income (–0.22) gives an estimate of the effect of parental income of –0.12/–0.22, or .54, which is slightly larger than typical estimates of the overall intergenerational correlation.

strongest when the income shocks occur early in childhood. This may simply reflect the fact that, because firm closures have permanent effects on family income, an earlier shock will result in a larger total loss in income over the course of childhood. Alternatively, it may reflect a differential importance of financial resources early in childhood, as has been suggested by James Heckman and others.

Disruptions to family income do seem to compound the difficulties disadvantaged children will face as adults. There is little evidence that such disruptions have measurable negative effects on children who are otherwise relatively advantaged. This may help to explain one reason that the causal role of income on children's well-being has been difficult to establish in empirical research; such effects may only exist for certain subpopulations who face other obstacles or barriers to economic success as adults.

Appendix

Table 7A.1   Estimated effects of all displacements during childhood on additional adult outcomes

	(1)	(2)
Completed at least high school		
Displaced (= 1 if yes)	–0.086***	–0.047***
	(0.021)	(0.017)
Attended some college		
Displaced (= 1 if yes)	–0.127***	–0.082**
	(0.031)	(0.034)
Ever receive unemployment insurance		
Displaced (= 1 if yes)	0.104***	0.099***
	(0.029)	(0.031)
Ever receive AFDC (women only, N = 957)		
Displaced (= 1 if yes)	0.044*	0.021
	(0.026)	(0.023)
Teen pregnancy (women only, N = 957)		
Displaced (= 1 if yes)	0.031	0.010
	(0.034)	(0.035)
Working		
Displaced (= 1 if yes)	0.005	0.007
	(0.014)	(0.014)
Observations	1,790	1,790

Notes: Standard error estimates are shown in parentheses. Estimated marginal effects are based on probit models using the individual weight in last year the individual is observed with a nonzero weight. Column (1) controls for parent's average adjusted income. Column (2) adds controls for parent's education, industry, and state.

***Significant at the 1 percent level.

**Significant at the 5 percent level.

*Significant at the 10 percent level.

Table 7A.2   Estimated long-term effects of all displacements for specific groups

| | Average effect of closure on log parental income (1) | Effect of closure on children's adult outcomes | | | | | | | |
Sample		Family income (2)	Earnings (3)	Completed high school (4)	Attended some college (5)	Received unemployment insurance (6)	Received AFDC (7)	Teen pregnancy (8)	Working (9)
(1) Full sample	−0.218***	−0.070	−0.095*	−0.047***	−0.082**	0.099***	0.021	0.010	0.007
(N = 1,790)	(0.034)	(0.044)	(0.051)	(0.017)	(0.034)	(0.031)	(0.023)	(0.035)	(0.014)
(2) Parent's income < poverty line	−0.194*	−0.237	−0.299**	−0.217**	−0.098	−0.123	−0.112	−0.111	−0.142***
(N = 320)	(0.113)	(0.181)	(0.150)	(0.089)	(0.064)	(0.094)	(0.126)	(0.171)	(0.048)
(3) Parent's income < 1.5x poverty line	−0.283***	−0.198**	−0.004	−0.124**	−0.068	−0.005	0.162**	0.218**	−0.001
(N = 584)	(0.074)	(0.096)	(0.133)	(0.062)	(0.049)	(0.064)	(0.081)	(0.089)	(0.035)
(4) Parent's income < 2x poverty line	−0.213***	−0.134	−0.056	−0.075*	−0.066	0.026	0.097	0.130**	−0.007
(N = 846)	(0.053)	(0.082)	(0.090)	(0.044)	(0.047)	(0.048)	(0.062)	(0.065)	(0.026)
(5) Parent's income > 2x poverty line	−0.221***	0.008	−0.099	−0.031*	−0.054	0.125***	0.007	−0.060	0.021
(N = 944)	(0.040)	(0.056)	(0.069)	(0.017)	(0.044)	(0.044)	(0.038)	(0.041)	(0.018)
(6) Single parent	−0.176*	−0.223	−0.120	0.059	0.120	0.035	−0.149	0.124	−0.065
(N = 210)	(0.105)	(0.232)	(0.218)	(0.064)	(0.103)	(0.119)	(0.176)	(0.172)	(0.068)
(7) Black	−0.151**	−0.155	−0.166	−0.080*	−0.072	0.075	−0.026	−0.001	−0.037
(N = 622)	(0.074)	(0.112)	(0.122)	(0.045)	(0.059)	(0.056)	(0.074)	(0.078)	(0.045)
(8) Parent has < High school education	−0.226***	−0.167**	−0.151	−0.120**	−0.085*	0.060	0.116**	0.089	−0.021
(N = 769)	(0.051)	(0.074)	(0.100)	(0.049)	(0.045)	(0.050)	(0.056)	(0.066)	(0.026)

Notes: Standard error estimates are shown in parentheses. Regressions are weighted using the individual weight in last year the individual is observed with a nonzero weight. Columns (4) through (8) show estimated marginal effects based on probit models. Earnings and income are adjusted for age, year, and sex. Estimated impacts on children's adult outcomes control for parent's education, industry, and state.

***Significant at the 1 percent level.

**Significant at the 5 percent level.

*Significant at the 10 percent level.

Table 7A.3 Estimated long-term effects of all displacements by age at displacement

	Family income		Earnings		Completed high school		Attended some college		Received unemployment insurance		Received AFDC		Teen pregnancy		Working	
	(1)	(2)	(3)	(4)	(5)	(6)	(7)	(8)	(9)	(10)	(11)	(12)	(13)	(14)	(15)	(16)
Avg. adj. log parent's family income	0.359***	0.175***	0.335***	0.129**	0.109***	0.050***	0.277***	0.154***	-0.031	-0.033	-0.080***	-0.031	-0.158***	-0.066*	0.024*	0.014
	(0.054)	(0.047)	(0.061)	(0.058)	(0.021)	(0.015)	(0.056)	(0.045)	(0.022)	(0.028)	(0.021)	(0.022)	(0.034)	(0.037)	(0.013)	(0.013)
Displaced (= 1 if yes)	-0.081*	-0.048	-0.082	-0.059	-0.078***	-0.042**	-0.114***	-0.071*	0.117***	0.113***	0.048*	0.03	0.023	-0.01	0.002	0.004
	(0.047)	(0.048)	(0.055)	(0.055)	(0.022)	(0.018)	(0.034)	(0.036)	(0.031)	(0.033)	(0.027)	(0.025)	(0.036)	(0.037)	(0.015)	(0.015)
Displaced at age ≤ 6 (= 1 if yes)	-0.076	-0.110	-0.140	-0.177**	-0.033	-0.019	-0.053	-0.046	-0.055	-0.061	-0.018	-0.034	0.043	0.106	0.017	0.014
	(0.078)	(0.069)	(0.086)	(0.087)	(0.039)	(0.030)	(0.060)	(0.063)	(0.051)	(0.051)	(0.041)	(0.027)	(0.071)	(0.082)	(0.025)	(0.026)
Parent has less than HS education		-0.406***		-0.450***		-0.180***		-0.410***		0.066*		0.162***		0.165***		-0.031
		(0.064)		(0.071)		(0.032)		(0.040)		(0.040)		(0.042)		(0.055)		(0.021)
Parent has exactly HS education		-0.133**		-0.170**		-0.034		-0.166***		-0.023		0.138***		0.099*		0.021
		(0.060)		(0.069)		(0.026)		(0.043)		(0.037)		(0.045)		(0.059)		(0.019)
Parent industry fixed effects		X		X		X		X		X		X		X		X
Parent state fixed effects		X		X		X		X		X		X		X		X
Observations	1,623	1,623	1,597	1,597	1,772	1,728	1,772	1,764	1,748	1,725	933	825	957	891	1,626	1,626

Notes: Standard error estimates are shown in parentheses. Regressions are weighted using the individual weight in last year the individual is observed with a nonzero weight. Columns (5) through (14) show estimated marginal effects based on probit models. Earnings and income are adjusted for age, year, and sex. "X" indicates that parent industry fixed effects and/or parent state fixed effects are included in the regression.

***Significant at the 1 percent level.

**Significant at the 5 percent level.

*Significant at the 10 percent level.

References

Blau, D. M. 1999. The effect of income on child development. *Review of Economics and Statistics* 81 (2): 261–76.

Coelli, M. B. 2005. Parental income shocks and the education attendance of youth. University of Melbourne, Department of Economics Working Paper.

Corcoran, M., R. Gordon, D. Laren, and G. Solon. 1992. The association between men's economic status and their family and community origins. *The Journal of Human Resources* 27 (4): 575–601.

Cunha, F., J. J. Heckman, L. J. Lochner, and D. V. Masterov. 2006. Interpreting the evidence on life cycle skill formation. In *Handbook of the economics of education,* ed. E. A. Hanushek and F. Welch, 697–812. Amsterdam: North-Holland.

Dahl, G., and L. Lochner. 2005. The impact of family income on child achievement. NBER Working Paper no. 11279. Cambridge, MA: National Bureau of Economic Research, April.

Duncan, G. J., and J. Brooks-Gunn. 1997. *Consequences of growing up poor.* New York: Russell Sage Foundation.

Duncan, G. J., W. Yeung, J. Brooks-Gunn, and J. Smith. 1998. How much does childhood poverty affect the life chances of children? *American Sociological Review* 63 (June): 406–23.

Haveman, R., and B. Wolfe. 1995. The determinants of children's attainments: A review of methods and findings. *Journal of Economic Literature* 33 (4): 1829–78.

Hill, M., and G. Duncan. 1996. Parental family income and the socioeconomic attainment of children. *Social Science Research* 16 (1): 37–73.

Jacobson, L. S., R. J. LaLonde, and D. G. Sullivan. 1993. Earnings losses of displaced workers. *The American Economic Review* 83 (4): 685–709.

Levy, D., and G. Duncan. 1999. Using sibling samples to assess the effect of childhood family income on completed schooling. Northwestern University/University of Chicago Joint Center for Poverty Research Working Paper.

Mayer, S. E. 1997. *What money can't buy: Family income and children's life chances.* Cambridge, MA: Harvard University Press.

Oreopoulos, P., M. E. Page, and A. H. Stevens. 2008. The intergenerational effects of worker displacement. *Journal of Labor Economics* 26 (3): 455–83.

Shea, J. 2000. Does parents' money matter? *Journal of Public Economics* 77 (2): 155–84.

Solon, G. 1992. Intergenerational income mobility in the United States. *American Economic Review* 82 (3): 393–408.

———. 1999. Intergenerational mobility in the labor market. In *Handbook of labor economics,* ed. O. Ashenfelter and D. Card, 1761–96. Amsterdam: Elsevier.

Stevens, A. H. 1997. Persistent effects of job displacement: The importance of multiple job losses. *Journal of Labor Economics* 15 (1): 165–88.

Zimmerman, D. 1992. Regression towards mediocrity in economic stature. *American Economic Review* 82 (June): 409–29.

The Role of Religious and Social Organizations in the Lives of Disadvantaged Youth

Rajeev Dehejia, Thomas DeLeire, Erzo F. P. Luttmer, and Josh Mitchell

8.1 Introduction

This chapter examines whether religious and social organizations benefit youth by offsetting the long-term consequences of growing up in a disadvantaged environment. Disadvantages suffered during childhood not only impose an immediate cost on children and families, but have also been shown to impose harm that lasts well into adulthood. Research in economics and other social sciences has documented that children who grow up in poverty have worse physical health, lower levels of cognitive ability, lower levels of school achievement, more emotional and behavioral problems, and higher teenage childbearing rates. Other sources of disadvantage include growing up with a single or less educated parent, parental job loss, divorce, or death, and growing up in a poor neighborhood. Moreover, the consequences of a disadvantaged upbringing may be compounded by weak ties to the community and the family.

Not all children who grow up disadvantaged suffer negative outcomes to

Rajeev Dehejia is an associate professor of economics at Tufts University and a faculty research fellow of the National Bureau of Economic Research. Thomas DeLeire is an associate professor of public affairs and population health sciences at the University of Wisconsin-Madison. Erzo F. P. Luttmer is an associate professor at the Kennedy School of Government, Harvard University, and a faculty research fellow of the National Bureau of Economic Research. Josh Mitchell is a PhD. student in the department of Economics, Harvard University.

This research was funded by the Annie E. Casey Foundation. We thank them for their support but acknowledge that the findings and conclusions presented in this report are those of the authors alone, and do not necessarily reflect the opinions of the Foundation. Luttmer also gratefully acknowledges funding from the National Institute on Aging through Grant Number T32-AG00186 to the National Bureau of Economic Research. We thank Jon Gruber, Dan Hungerman, Chris Ellison, and conference participants for useful suggestions and helpful discussions. All errors are our own.

the same extent. Families and children can adopt strategies to try to minimize the negative impacts of their surroundings. In this chapter, we examine one such strategy: engagement with religious and other social organizations. The link between poverty and poor outcomes has been hypothesized to be partially due to deficiencies in parenting, home environments, and neighborhoods. Religious and social organizations could therefore make up for some of this lost social capital by providing counseling, social services, income support, or a network of social contacts. Our previous research (Dehejia, DeLeire, and Luttmer 2007) has found that religious organizations enable adults to partially insure their consumption and happiness against income shocks. This chapter builds on those results by examining whether involvement with religion or social organizations mitigates the long-run negative effects on youth of growing up in a disadvantaged environment.

In particular, we examine whether, by adulthood (thirteen to fifteen years later), children whose parents were involved with religious and social organizations suffered less harm from growing up in a disadvantaged environment than children whose parents were less involved. We consider fourteen measures of disadvantage in childhood: family income and poverty (measured by household income relative to the poverty line, the poverty rate in the census tract where the child resides, and by whether the child's household received public assistance); family characteristics (measured by the mother's level of education, by whether the child's parent was unmarried, by whether the parents' marriage broke up, and by an indicator for nonwhite households[1]); and child characteristics (parental assessments of the child, whether the child has repeated a grade, and an index of disciplinary problems). We consider twelve outcome measures in adulthood to capture whether these disadvantages had lasting detrimental consequences: the child's level of education, household income relative to the poverty line, whether the child receives public assistance, and measures of risky behavior (measured by smoking, age of first sex, and health insurance coverage) and psychological well-being (measured by subjective happiness and locus of control). Thus, in total, we test for buffering of religious participation in 168 (= 14 × 12) possible combinations of a measure of youth disadvantage and a measure adult outcome.

We find that religious organizations provide buffering effects that are statistically significant at the 5 percent level for 38 out of a total of 168 disadvantage-outcome combinations examined. We can formally reject at the 1 percent level that this number of significant effects could arise by pure chance, and we conclude that religious organizations play an important buffering role against disadvantage experienced during youth. Of course, it is

---

1. While we do not consider being nonwhite to be a disadvantage per se, it may be associated with disadvantages (such as experiencing racism or discrimination) that we are unable to capture in our other measures.

quite plausible that religious organizations also provide buffering effects for many of the disadvantage-outcome combinations that were not significant in our analysis. In those cases, we simply do not have the statistical power to prove or disprove buffering effects.[2] The buffering effects of religious organizations are most often statistically significant when outcomes are measured by high school graduation or nonsmoking and when disadvantage is measured by family resources or maternal education, but we also find statistically significant buffering effects for a number of other outcome-disadvantage pairs. Our data do not allow us to determine to what extent the buffering effects are driven by religious organizations actively intervening in the lives of disadvantaged youth (through tutoring, mentoring, or financial assistance) as opposed to providing the youth with motivation, values, or attitudes that lead to better outcomes. We find suggestive evidence that leisure groups also provide some buffering against youth disadvantage. Other types of social organizations do not appear to provide buffering, but this lack of findings could be due to the fact that the buffering effects of social organizations are not very precisely estimated.

Because participation in a religious or social organization is a choice that a child's parents actively make, we must be cautious in interpreting the buffering effect of religion as a causal effect of religious participation. For example, the effect of participation could be confounded with other coping strategies that families adopt in response to disadvantage, leading our estimated buffering effect to capture the combined effect of all of these strategies. Reverse causality is less of a concern since outcomes for disadvantaged youth are observed thirteen to fifteen years after we measure involvement with religious and social organizations and whether the child had a disadvantaged upbringing.

We believe our results show that religious organizations play an important role in shaping the lives of disadvantaged youth by mitigating at least some of the long-term consequences of disadvantage. We view our research as a first step in the important task of understanding whether—and through what mechanisms—disadvantaged youth benefit from participating in religious organizations.

8.2   Literature Review

The consequences of growing up in disadvantaged circumstances have been extensively documented in the academic research literature. In this section, we provide a brief overview of three aspects of this literature: the sources of disadvantage, the consequences of growing up in disadvantaged circumstances, and adaptive behaviors that families may adopt to protect

---

2. None of the 168 estimates of buffering effects is even marginally significantly negative, so we cannot reject the hypothesis of a positive buffering effect for any disadvantage-outcome combination at the 10 percent level.

themselves, in part, from these disadvantages. Finally, we review the less extensive economic literature on the role of religion in the lives of youth.

8.2.1   Sources of Disadvantage for Youth

Children can be disadvantaged if they grow up in poverty or if they experience any one of a large number of other circumstances. Collectively, researchers have considered a large number of potential disadvantages when examining consequences for youth. These include low family income and poverty (e.g., Duncan and Brooks-Gunn 1997), growing up in a single-parent family (McLanahan and Sandefur 1994), having a less educated mother (Currie and Moretti 2003; Black, Devereux, and Salvanes 2005; Oreopoulos, Page, and Stevens 2006), having a parent on public assistance (Antel 1992; Page 2004), having obese parents (Anderson, Butcher, and Schanzenbach 2007), and poor parenting behaviors (Currie and Hyson 1999; Bitler and Currie 2004).

8.2.2   Consequences of Growing up Disadvantaged

Many studies have documented the correlation between poverty and youth outcomes (inter alia Brooks-Gunn and Duncan 1997; Duncan and Brooks-Gunn 1997). Growing up in poverty is related to having worse physical health (Korenman and Miller 1997), lower levels of cognitive ability, lower levels of school achievement, and a greater number of emotional or behavioral problems (Smith, Brooks-Gunn, and Klebanov 1997). Low income is unlikely to be causally responsible for all of these outcomes. Longitudinal analysis has suggested that omitted parental characteristics that are correlated with income are likely responsible for many of these negative outcomes (Mayer 1997). However, there is also evidence from social experiments (Currie 1997) and sibling fixed effects models (Duncan et al. 1998), suggesting that income does at least partially matter. Shea (2000), Dahl and Lochner (2005), Oreopoulos, Page, and Stevens (2005), and Page, Stevens, and Lindo (2007) use plausibly exogenous income variation due to industry shocks, changes in Earned Income Tax Credit (EITC) rules, and worker layoffs. These studies generally find effects of parental income on subsequent educational and labor market outcomes for the youths, and in many cases the effects are strongest for disadvantaged youths.

Having an unmarried parent has also been found to be associated with a range of negative outcomes for youth. McLanahan and Sandefur (1994, 3) argue that "growing up with only one biological parent frequently deprives children of important economic, parental, and community resources, and that these deprivations ultimately undermine their chances of future success." Their analysis suggests that roughly one-half of the deficit associated with having a single parent is due to low income, and one-half is due to inadequate parental guidance and a lack of ties to community resources. Other research has also suggested that parenting behavior is an important determinant of child outcomes (Hanson, McLanahan, and Thomson 1997).

Parental education also matters. In addition to being associated with higher levels of family income, research has shown that parents' level of education has a strong, causal effect on children's health (Currie and Moretti 2003) and children's educational attainment (Black, Devereux, and Salvanes 2005). Other parental behaviors can influence children's outcomes as well. Even otherwise positive behaviors can have negative consequences. For example, Anderson, Butcher, and Levine (2003) find a causal relationship between maternal employment and the likelihood that a child is overweight.

Growing up in a poor neighborhood may also have a negative effect on outcomes later in life. Identifying these effects is complicated by the likely correlation of neighborhood conditions with unobserved parental characteristics and behaviors. Moreover, it is difficult to even sign the bias stemming from this correlation, as parents who live in poor neighborhoods may have unobservable characteristics that lead to worse outcomes for their children or, alternatively, parents in poor neighborhoods may invest more in compensating activities to partially alleviate those effects. A number of studies have sought to overcome these biases to identify the effects of growing up in a poor neighborhood on children's outcomes using sibling fixed effects models (e.g., Aaronson 1997) or instrumental variables (Case and Katz 1991; Evans, Oates, and Schwab 1992).

8.2.3   Strategies to Minimize the Consequences of Disadvantage

Families and children can adopt strategies to mitigate the negative impacts of their surroundings. For example, single mothers can improve the educational outcomes and reduce the delinquency of their children by living with their own parents in multigenerational households (DeLeire and Kalil 2002). Guralnick (2004) describes how parents of children with developmental challenges adopt strategies—including expanding their networks of social support—in order to best meet the needs of their children. These strategies to mitigate the negative impact of disadvantage may or may not have value in and of themselves. While some adaptive strategies may be intrinsically valuable, others, such as not venturing outdoors in response to living in a dangerous neighborhood, may not.

8.2.4   Economic Consequences of Religion

In an overview of the growing literature on the economics of religion, Iannaccone (1998) discusses a range of studies on the economic consequences of religious participation—for example, Freeman's (1986) finding that black youth who attend church are less likely to smoke, drink, or engage in drug use. More recent studies have also focused on the consequences of religious participation, but it has been difficult to determine whether the consequences are causal or driven by omitted variables. Gruber (2005) succeeds in credibly establishing causality by instrumenting own religious attendance by the religious market density of other ethnic groups sharing the same denomination. He finds that increased religious participation leads to higher educational attainment and income, less dependence on social insurance programs, and greater levels of marriage. Gruber and Hungerman (2006) use variation in "blue laws" to find causal evidence that religious attendance reduces drug use and heavy drinking. Lillard and Price (2007) show a strong association between religious participation among youth and criminal and delinquent behavior, smoking, drug use, and drinking. Moreover, they use a variety of methods including propensity score matching, instrumental variables (using the "blue laws" instrument described previously), and Altonji, Elder, and Taber's (2005) method of using selection on observables to infer the degrees of selection on unobservables to suggest that at least some of their observed associations between religious participation and outcomes are indeed causal relationships.

There is also a large literature showing that religiosity correlates with health outcomes and subjective well-being. Studies show a relationship between religion (variously measured by self-reported "religious coping" or religious activity including prayer) and a range of health outcomes (including depression, mortality, and immune system responses). These are exclusively correlation studies (see, e.g., McCullough et al. 2000). Similarly, there is widespread evidence that religiosity is correlated with measures of subjective well-being (see inter alia Diener, Kahneman, and Schwarz [1999] and the meta-analyses by Parmagent [2002] and Smith, McCullough, and Poll [2003]).

A number of papers study the buffering effects of religion on subjective well-being in the context of traumatic life events. Using cross-sectional data from the General Social Survey, Ellison (1991) finds that people with stronger religious beliefs have higher well-being and are less affected by traumatic events. Strawbridge et al. (1998) find nonuniform buffering effects using cross-sectional data from California. They find that religiosity buffers the effects of nonfamily stressors (e.g., unemployment) on depression but exacerbates the effects of family stressors (e.g., marital problems). This finding dovetails with Clark and Lelkes (2005), who find that religiosity may dampen or exacerbate the happiness effect of a major life shock depending on the denomination and the type of shock. Dehejia, DeLeire, and Luttmer (2007) find that religion buffers subjective well-being against income shocks. Moreover, in that paper we document that religious involvement also insures consumption against income shocks; that is, religion provides more than spiritual support alone.

8.3   Data Description

8.3.1   The National Survey of Families and Households

We use three waves of the National Survey of Families and Households (NSFH), a panel data set collected by demographers (Sweet, Bumpass, and

Call 1988; Sweet and Bumpass 1996, 2002). The NSFH contains detailed information on participants' family structure, living arrangements, educational attainment, religiosity, and economic and psychological well-being.

The first wave of interviews took place from 1987 to 1988 and was conducted in a face-to-face setting with respondents taking self-administered questionnaires for more sensitive topics. The sample consists of 13,007 individuals, and is nationally representative of individuals age nineteen or older, living in households, and able to speak English or Spanish. If these "main respondents" lived in a household with children age nineteen or younger, one of these children was chosen at random to be the "focal child." The respondent answered a series of questions about this focal child, including questions about the child's behavior and school performance. Wave 1 contains information on 5,684 focal children. A second wave of interviews with the main respondents took place from 1992 to 1994. This allows our analysis to consider changes in variables of interest over the first two waves, such as whether the household experienced a marital break up.

The third wave of interviews took place in 2001 to 2003. This wave included interviews both with the main respondents and with people who were focal children in wave 1 (for convenience we continue to refer to them as "focal children," though by wave 3 they are adults). We use the information from these grown-up focal children to construct our outcome measures. The NSFH conducted telephone interviews with eligible focal children, namely those aged eighteen to thirty-four in wave 3 (and who were age three to nineteen in wave 1). The NSFH originally identified 4,128 focal children as eligible but were only able to locate and successfully interview 1,952 of them; this raises issues of sample attrition, which we discuss in section 8.5.5. These interviews asked about the focal child's educational attainment, income, risky behaviors, and subjective measures of well-being.

The NSFH granted us permission to use a limited-access version of the data set that contains characteristics of the respondent's neighborhood from the 1990 Census at the tract level. A census tract is a local area that is fairly homogenous and typically contains between 2,500 and 8,000 people. We use log median household income and the poverty rate as tract level measures of disadvantage.

8.3.2   Data Description and Choice of Variables

The full sample of wave 3 interviewees who were focal children in wave 1 includes 1,952 observations. In some specifications, we restrict the sample to individuals older than twenty-five in wave 3. This sample consists of 1,125 observations. The age restriction is useful for outcomes that are best measured in adulthood (for example, education or income). Table 8.1 provides a snapshot of the samples. Households are mostly white (with 8 percent black, 5 percent Hispanic, and 1 percent other nonwhite). Of the wave 1 adult respondents, 91 percent are biological parents (for convenience we

Table 8.1   Characteristics of parents and children in our sample

	Children: All ages				Children: Ages 25+ in wave 3			
	Mean	Standard deviation	Minimum	Maximum	Mean	Standard deviation	Minimum	Maximum
Characteristics of children								
Age at wave 1	11.02	4.51	3	19	14.38	2.58	9	19
Age at wave 3	25.95	4.54	18	34	29.34	2.55	25	34
Black	0.08	0.27	0	1	0.07		0	1
Hispanic	0.05	0.21	0	1	0.04		0	1
Other nonwhite	0.01	0.11	0	1	0.01		0	1
Female	0.53	0.50	0	1	0.51		0	1
Wave 3 interview in 2001	0.07	0.25	0	1	0.06		0	1
Wave 3 interview in 2002	0.76	0.43	0	1	0.75		0	1
Characteristics of parent respondent								
Age at wave 1	38.96	8.05	19	71	42.19	7.56	24	71
Biological parent	0.91	0.29	0	1	0.88		0	1
Female	0.55	0.50	0	1	0.56		0	1
Married at wave 1	0.87	0.34	0	1	0.86		0	1
Wave 1 interview in 1987	0.90	0.30	0	1	0.91		0	1
Number of Observations			1,952				1,125	

refer to both biological parents and guardians as "parents"). Parents' ages range from nineteen to seventy-one in wave 1, with an average age of thirty-nine.

We use a range of variables to measure household disadvantage in wave 1 of the data. Summary statistics for household disadvantage are presented in table 8.2 for the full sample as well as for parents who are above and below the median religious attendance frequency in our sample. Our first set of measures is based on family resources or poverty: log household income relative to the poverty line, an indicator for household income less than 200 percent of the poverty line (21 percent of the full sample), log median household income in the census tract, the poverty rate at the census-tract level (11 percent of the full sample), and an indicator for the household receiving

Table 8.2   Measures of childhood disadvantage

	All		Attendance > Median		Attendance < Median	
	Mean	Standard deviation	Mean	Standard deviation	Mean	Standard deviation
Family resources/Poverty						
Log household income / Poverty line	1.17	0.82	1.19	0.77	1.16	0.86
Household income less than 200 percent of poverty line	0.21	0.41	0.21	0.40	0.21	0.41
Log median household income in census tract	10.35	0.43	10.34	0.43	10.35	0.42
Poverty rate in census tract	0.11	0.11	0.11	0.11	0.11	0.10
Received public assistance in prior year	0.05	0.21	0.04	0.19	0.06	0.12
Family characteristics						
Nonwhite	0.14	0.34	0.16	0.36	0.12	0.32
Unmarried parent	0.13	0.34	0.10	0.30	0.16	0.37
Marital breakup between wave 1 and wave 2[a]	0.10	0.30	0.09	0.28	0.12	0.32
Mother is a high school dropout	0.11	0.31	0.08	0.27	0.14	0.34
Mother has high school education or less	0.52	0.50	0.48	0.50	0.55	0.50
Child characteristics						
Parent does not expect child to graduate from college[b]	0.34	0.47	0.29	0.45	0.40	0.49
Parent says focal child is difficult to raise[b]	0.08	0.27	0.07	0.25	0.09	0.29
Focal child repeated a grade[b]	0.08	0.26	0.05	0.21	0.10	0.31
Composite of discipline trouble[bc]	0.09	0.29	0.10	0.30	0.09	0.28

Note: Attendance measures the number of times per year the parent attends religious services (expressed as percentile).

[a]Sample restricted to children age three to twelve with married parents at wave 1.

[b]Sample restricted to children age three to twelve.

[c]Parent reports any of the following: disciplinary meeting with teacher or principal, child suspended or expelled from school, child in trouble with police.

public assistance in wave 1 (5 percent of the full sample). The second set of disadvantage measures is based on family characteristics, namely indicators for: nonwhite parents (14 percent of the full sample), an unmarried parent (13 percent of the full sample), a break up of the parents' marriage (divorce or separation) occurring between wave 1 and wave 2 (10 percent of the sample, conditional on having married parents at wave 1), a mother with less than a high school education (11 percent of the full sample), and a mother with high school education or less (52 percent of the full sample).

The third set of disadvantage measures is based on child characteristics: indicators for whether the parent thinks the focal child is unlikely to graduate from college or is difficult to raise; an indicator for the focal child having repeated a grade; and a composite measure of discipline difficulties. Some child characteristics reflect the parent's perception of the child, and as such must be interpreted with great care. For example, if religious parents systematically assess their children differently than nonreligious parents, then our estimates of buffering could be spurious.[3]

Tables 8.3 and 8.4 summarize measures of participation in religious and social organizations and religious affiliation. Table 8.3 summarizes the measure of religious participation that we use in this chapter: the parent's percentile rank in the wave 1 distribution of attendance at religious services.[4] We see that the distribution is substantially skewed to the right: the parent at the tenth percentile never attends, the median parent attends twice per month (twenty-four times per year), and the parent at the ninetieth percentile attends twice per week (104 times per year). We also examine the robustness of our results to alternative specifications of parental religious attendance. In table 8.4, we see that most youth have parents that participate in a social organization (where such organizations include community, work-related, leisure, and religious groups; note that here religious groups refer to nonworship activities). Approximately 90 percent of the sample provides information about a religious denomination, with the most common denominations being Catholic and Baptist.

Finally, table 8.5 summarizes our wave 3 outcome measures for the adult focal child. We examine measures of educational attainment (indicators for having a high school education or more, some college or more, and being a college graduate) and income (the age-specific percentile rank of a household's income to poverty line ratio, an indicator for a household's being above the twenty-fifth percentile in the age-specific distribution of the income to poverty line ratio, and an indicator for receiving public assistance).

3. If religious parents have a lower threshold for saying that the child is in trouble (e.g., skipping church qualifies as trouble), then "troubled" children of religious parents have on average less severe trouble than "troubled" children of nonreligious parents. As a result, we would expect troubled children of religious parents to have better outcomes later in life even if religion does not directly help youth overcome the negative consequences of being in trouble.
4. We use the religious attendance of the parent who was selected as the "main respondent" by the NSFH.

Table 8.3   Distribution of parent religious attendance

Percentile (%)	Times/Year
1	0
5	0
10	0
25	1
50	24
75	52
90	104
95	156
99	156
Mean	36.5
Standard deviation	46.7
Number of observations	1,911

Note: Based on the self-reported frequency of attendance of the parent respondent in wave 1.

Table 8.4   Religious affiliation and participation in nonprofit organizations

	Mean	Standard deviation
Participation in the following types of social organizations		
Community organizations	0.28	0.45
Work-related organizations	0.35	0.48
Leisure groups	0.66	0.47
Church-based social organizations	0.53	0.50
Religious affiliation		
No religion	0.08	0.27
Catholic	0.25	0.44
Jewish	0.02	0.15
Baptist	0.18	0.38
Episcopalian	0.02	0.14
Lutheran	0.06	0.24
Methodist	0.11	0.31
Mormon	0.05	0.21
Presbyterian	0.04	0.19
Congregational	0.02	0.13
Protestant, no denomination	0.05	0.23
Other Christian	0.10	0.30
Other religious/missing	0.02	0.14

Notes: Community organizations is a dummy variable indicating any participation in fraternal groups, service clubs, veterans' groups, or political groups. Work-related organizations is a dummy variable indicating any participation in labor unions, farm organizations, or professional/academic societies. Leisure groups is a dummy variable indicating any participation in sports groups, youth groups, hobby or garden clubs, or literary/art groups. Church-based social organizations is a dummy variable indicating any participation in church-affiliated groups (other than attending religious service). Religious affiliation is the self-reported religious affiliation of the parent respondent in wave 1.

Table 8.5   Adult outcomes measures (wave 3)

	All		Attendance > Median		Attendance < Median	
	Mean	Standard deviation	Mean	Standard deviation	Mean	Standard deviation
Education, income, public assistance						
High school education or more (includes GED)	0.94	0.25	0.96	0.19	0.91	0.29
Some college or more[a]	0.65	0.48	0.71	0.45	0.59	0.49
College graduate[a]	0.24	0.43	0.39	0.49	0.29	0.46
Percentile household income/ poverty line[ab]	0.51	0.29	0.52	0.28	0.49	0.30
Household income/poverty line above twenty-fifth percentile[ab]	0.76	0.43	0.77	0.42	0.73	0.44
Received public assistance in prior year	0.06	0.23	0.05	0.22	0.07	0.26
Behavior and health						
Nonsmoker (smoked < 1 cigarette per day in last month)	0.71	0.45	0.77	0.42	0.65	0.48
Age of first sex 16 or over (includes never)	0.75	0.43	0.83	0.38	0.68	0.47
Normal weight (18.5 ≤ Body Mass Index < 25.0)	0.51	0.50	0.52	0.50	0.50	0.50
Covered by health insurance	0.77	0.42	0.79	0.40	0.74	0.44
Subjective happiness (scale from 1–10)	7.39	1.50	7.46	1.44	7.32	1.56
Composite locus of control (scale from 1–5)[c]	3.81	0.75	3.85	0.73	3.78	0.76

Note: Attendance measures the number of times per year the parent attends religious services (expressed as percentile).

[a]Sample restricted to those age 25+ in wave 3.

[b]Percentiles are within age categories.

[c]Composite Locus of Control is average of responses to three questions (each on scale from 1–5): whether or not focal child feels pushed around, whether or not focal child can solve problems, and whether or not focal child has control over situation.

We also include measures of behavior and psychological well-being: an indicator for being a nonsmoker, an indicator for whether the child's age at first having sex was sixteen or older, an indicator for a normal body mass index[5], an indicator for being covered by health insurance, a measure of overall happiness, and a composite measure of locus of control (i.e., the extent to which someone perceives himself or herself to be in control of his or her environment).

5. Body mass index (BMI) is defined as weight in kilograms divided by height in meters squared. We followed the National Heart, Lung, and Blood Institute (part of the National Institutes of Health) in defining a healthy body weight as 18.5 ≤ BMI < 25.0.

8.4 Empirical Strategy

In this section we present our empirical strategy, and discuss related identification and econometric issues.

8.4.1 Specification

To examine whether religious and other organizations help to attenuate the effect of a disadvantaged upbringing, we estimate models of the form:

$$
\begin{aligned}
(1) \qquad Outcome_{it} = {}& Disadvantaged_{i,t-1}\beta_1 + Religious_{i,t-1}\beta_2 \\
& + Disadvantaged_{i,t-1} \times Religious_{i,t-1}\beta_3 \\
& + X_{i,t-1}\beta_4 + \alpha_{it} + \delta_t + \varepsilon_{it},
\end{aligned}
$$

where $Outcome_{it}$ is a particular youth outcome in wave 3, $Disadvantaged_{i,t-1}$ is an indicator of a disadvantaged household in wave 1 of the survey, and $Religious_{i,t-1}$ is a measure of parents' religiosity in wave 1 (or a measure of the parents' participation in other social organizations); $X_{i,t-1}$ is a set of controls for the characteristics of the household in which the youth grew up as well as the race/ethnicity and gender of the youth; α_{it} is a set of dummies for the age of the youth at the time of the wave 3 interview; δ_t is a set of year-of-interview dummies for the wave 1 and wave 3 interview; and ε_{it} are error terms.

Based on the literature, we expect to find a negative β_1 (disadvantage leads to worse outcomes in adulthood) and a positive β_2 (growing up with religious parents is generally associated with better outcomes). However, since any measure of disadvantage is likely correlated with several omitted measures of disadvantage, β_1 merely measures an association. Similarly, since parental religious participation is a choice and is likely to be correlated with many other omitted characteristics that have a beneficial effect on later outcomes, the effect of parental religious participation is unlikely to be causal. Our main coefficient of interest is β_3, which measures the extent to which children of religious parents are less affected by growing up under disadvantaged conditions. Thus, we take a positive β_3 as suggestive evidence of the buffering effect of religion.

Despite omitted variables problems that bias β_1 and β_2, it is possible, under strong assumptions, to give a causal interpretation to β_3. The key condition for identification is that omitted characteristics are correlated with religious attendance to the same degree for disadvantaged and nondisadvantaged households. However, we prefer to interpret the estimates of β_3 as associations rather than as causal evidence of buffering because we are concerned that this identification condition does not hold in practice. In particular, it is possible that parental religious involvement is more strongly associated with omitted characteristics that affect later outcomes for disadvantaged children than it is for nondisadvantaged children. For example, it is possible that parents who participate in religious activities out of concern for their children's growing up in a disadvantaged environment might also decide to enroll their children in after-school activities that could mitigate the effects of disadvantage. We could fully address this issue if we had an instrument for parental participation in religion, but unfortunately no such variable is available in our data.[6] We also acknowledge that the disadvantaged religious families form a selected sample for which religious participation did not succeed in overcoming their disadvantage in the first wave of our data. Thus, our estimated buffering effect should be interpreted as the average buffering given the selected nature of the sample in wave 1. We are less worried about reverse causation because we measure disadvantage in wave 1 of the survey and outcomes in wave 3, thirteen to fifteen years later.

8.4.2   Joint Significance of the Buffering Effects

Given the large number of effects we investigate (fourteen measures of disadvantage and twelve outcomes), we would expect to find some statistically significant buffering effects of religion simply as a matter of chance. It would be problematic, indeed data mining, only to present the significant effects. Furthermore, there is a danger of ex-post theorizing to justify the particular pattern of effects we find. We deal with this issue in two ways. First, we present our results—both significant and insignificant—for a range of disadvantage and outcome measures that we believe reasonably spans the data available to us. Second, we show the whole distribution of t-statistics on the buffering effects of all disadvantage-outcome pairs and compare this with a simulated distribution of t-statistics under the null hypothesis of no true buffering effect; that is, we test whether we observe more statistically significant effects than would be expected by chance if religious organizations did not buffer at all against disadvantage.

8.5   Results

8.5.1   Direct Effects of Wave 1 Disadvantage on Wave 3 Outcomes

We begin by examining the direct effect of our measures of disadvantage in wave 1 on outcomes in wave 3. These results are present in table 8.6, panels A and B. With the exception of the log of the ratio of household income to the poverty line, log median household income in the census tract, and the indicator for public assistance (the first and third rows and the sixth column, which are shaded), disadvantage measures and outcomes are scaled so that a negative coefficient corresponds to a worse outcome for the child.

---

6. An instrumental variable for religion has been suggested by Gruber (2005), namely the percent of individuals in the same locality who, based on their ethnic background, are predicted to share the respondent's religious denomination. For our relatively small sample, however, this instrument yielded estimates that were so imprecise that they did not provide evidence either way on whether our main results can be interpreted causally.

Table 8.6 **Effect of youth disadvantage on adult outcomes: Coefficient on disadvantage**

	High school or more	Some college or more (age 25+)	College graduate (age 25+)	Household income/ poverty line	Household income/ poverty line above 25th percentile	Public assistance
			A. Outcomes in wave 3: Education, income, and public assistance			
Family resources/Poverty						
Log household income / Poverty line	0.04***	0.13***	0.15***	0.08***	0.06***	−0.02**
Household income less than 200 percent of poverty line	−0.09***	−0.19***	−0.22***	−0.15***	−0.10***	0.03**
Log median household income in census tract	0.06***	0.19***	0.22***	0.14***	0.16***	−0.03**
Poverty rate in census tract	−0.25***	−0.62***	−0.59***	−0.50***	−0.65***	0.23***
Received public assistance	−0.12***	−0.28***	−0.25***	−0.16***	−0.17**	0.05*
Family characteristics						
Nonwhite	−0.07***	−0.19***	−0.16***	−0.15***	−0.20***	0.05***
Unmarried parent	−0.12***	−0.12***	−0.15***	−0.06**	−0.08*	0.04***
Marital breakup between waves 1 and 2	−0.02	−0.03	−0.07	−0.05	−0.12**	0.06***
Mother is a high school dropout	−0.07***	−0.26***	−0.20***	−0.16***	−0.21***	0.03
Mother has high school education or less	−0.05***	−0.23***	−0.29***	−0.12***	−0.11***	0.02*
Child characteristics						
Not expected to graduate college	−0.12***	−0.40***	−0.30***	−0.06	−0.07	0.04***
Difficult to raise	−0.10***	−0.21***	−0.14*	−0.04	−0.09	0.02
Repeated a grade	−0.17***	−0.34***	−0.19***	−0.22***	−0.20***	0.13***
Composite of discipline trouble	−0.07**	−0.16**	−0.22***	−0.06	−0.03	0.04*

(continued)

Table 8.6 (continued)

			B. Outcomes in wave 3: Absence of problem behavior			
	Nonsmoker	Age first sex ≥ 16	Normal weight	Health insurance	Subjective happiness	Locus of control
Family resources/Poverty						
Log household income / Poverty line	0.04**	0.04***	0.06***	0.08***	-0.05	0.08***
Household income less than 200 percent of poverty line	-0.06*	-0.08***	-0.07**	-0.17***	0.05	-0.09*
Log median household income in census tract	0.06**	0.10***	0.07**	0.12***	0.05	0.20***
Poverty rate in census tract	-0.09	-0.39***	-0.28**	-0.49***	-0.70*	-0.66***
Received public assistance	-0.13***	-0.15***	-0.06	-0.17***	-0.41**	-0.19**
Family characteristics						
Nonwhite	0.08**	-0.06**	-0.12***	-0.12***	-0.16	-0.01
Unmarried parent	-0.10***	-0.13***	-0.05	-0.15***	-0.12	-0.01
Marital breakup between waves 1 and 2	-0.07*	-0.14***	-0.07	-0.12***	-0.34**	-0.10
Mother is a high school dropout	-0.03	-0.05	-0.13***	-0.17***	-0.09	-0.12**
Mother has high school education or less	-0.05**	-0.07***	-0.11***	-0.09***	0.01	-0.15***
Child characteristics						
Not expected to graduate college	-0.12***	-0.09***	-0.02	-0.15***	-0.19*	-0.22***
Difficult to raise	-0.10*	-0.08	-0.19***	-0.14***	-0.25	0.03
Repeated a grade	-0.10*	-0.13**	-0.17***	-0.18***	0.03	-0.24**
Composite of discipline trouble	-0.12**	-0.08*	-0.12**	-0.18***	-0.10	0.03

Notes: Each cell contains the coefficient on disadvantage when we regress outcome (column) on disadvantage (row), percentile of parent's religious attendance, and controls. Controls include race, sex, and age dummies, an indicator of whether the focal child is a biological child, and year of interview dummies. Shaded cells indicate entries where we expect the value to be positive (due to reverse coding of the measure of disadvantage or the outcome).

***Significant at the 1 percent level.

**Significant at the 5 percent level.

*Significant at the 10 percent level.

Table 8.6, panel A, depicts the effects of our disadvantage measures on education, income, and public assistance in wave 3. Regressions include controls for parental religious participation, parental race-ethnicity dummies, a dummy for whether the guardian is a biological parent, a dummy for the gender of the focal child, age dummies for the focal child, and year of interview dummies. In columns (1) and (2), we see that each measure of disadvantage (other than parents' marital breakup) has a negative and significant effect (at the 1 or 5 percent levels) on a dummy for high school or more education as well as on the dummy for some college or more education. The same holds for the college graduation variable, except that the effect of "difficult to raise" is now only marginally significant. The next two columns examine the effect of disadvantage on two measures of income. As with education, we find uniformly significant effects of family income and resource measures of disadvantage, and many significant effects among family characteristics. The effects of child characteristics are more equivocal. Finally, in column (6) we note that most measures of disadvantage have a significant positive effect on an indicator for receiving public assistance in wave 3.

Table 8.6, panel B, depicts the effects of wave 1 disadvantage on wave 3 behavior, well-being, and health-related outcomes. We find the most uniform effects for the health insurance indicator, followed by the normal weight indicator, smoking, and age at first sex. We find fewer significant effects for subjective well-being and locus of control.

Overall, these results show a significant ongoing association between childhood disadvantage and outcomes in adulthood. It must be emphasized that, although it is appealing to interpret these results causally, they are fundamentally correlations. From other studies (especially Currie 1997; Duncan et al. 1998; Currie and Moretti 2003; and Black, Devereux, and Salvanes 2005) we know that at least part of the effect of the family resource and poverty measures is causal. For child characteristics—particularly parental assessments of whether the child is expected to graduate from college or is difficult to raise—the scope for omitted variable bias is higher because both these assessments and the future outcome may depend on factors that are known to the parents but not to the researcher.

8.5.2   Religion and Buffering

Before examining the full set of religion-disadvantage interactions, we begin by examining in detail the results for a single specification, the effect of having a mother with a high school degree or less (measured in wave 1) on the adult child's having some college or more education in wave 3. In table 8.7, we present both ordinary least squares (linear probability model) and probit results. Columns (1) and (3) show the direct effect of having a mother with no more than a high school education on the adult child's level of education in wave 3. In both specifications, there is a negative effect that is significant at the one percent level. In the ordinary least squares (OLS)

Table 8.7 The effect of wave-1 maternal education (high school graduate or less) on focal child's wave-3 education (some college or more)

Specification	OLS		OLS		Probit		Probit	
	Coefficient	Standard error	Coefficient	Standard error	Marginal effect	Standard error	Coefficient	Standard error
Mother a high school graduate or less	-0.23***	0.03	-0.38***	0.06	-0.25***	0.03	-1.08***	0.21
Parental religious participation	0.16***	0.05	0.01	0.07	0.17**	0.07	0.03	0.28
High school grad or less × Religious participation			0.29***	0.10			0.78**	0.37
Parent black	-0.10*	0.06	-0.10*	0.06	-0.11*	0.06	-0.31**	0.15
Parent hispanic	-0.20***	0.07	-0.22***	0.07	-0.21***	0.08	-0.59***	0.20
Parent other race	-0.33*	0.17	-0.34	0.17	-0.40***	0.19	-1.04*	0.56
Focal child male	-0.11***	0.03	-0.12***	0.03	-0.12***	0.04	-0.35***	0.10
Guardian is biological parent	0.18***	0.04	0.17***	0.04	0.20***	0.06	0.51***	0.14
Age dummies for focal child	Yes		Yes		Yes		Yes	
Interview year dummies	Yes		Yes		Yes		Yes	
(Pseudo) R^2	0.14		0.14		0.11		0.11	
Buffering effect								
(A) Effect of parent a high school grad or less at twenty-fifth percentile of religious participation			-0.31***	0.04			-0.89***	0.13
(B) Effect of parent a high school grad or less at seventy-fifth percentile of religious participation			-0.16***	0.04			-0.50***	0.14
(C) Difference (A–B)			-0.15***	0.05			-0.39**	0.19
(D) Buffering (C/A)			0.48***	0.13			0.44***	0.17

Note: The buffering effects for the Probit in column (4) refer to effects in "latent variable space," not to effects expressed in terms of probabilities. "Parent white" is omitted race category. OLS = ordinary least squares.

specification, having a mother with no more than a high school education reduces the probability that the adult child has at least some college in wave 3 by 23 percentage points, relative to a mean of 65 percent. The direct effect of religious participation is positive and significant at the 1 percent level in both specifications. Moving from the twenty-fifth to the seventy-fifth percentile of parental religious participation is associated with an 8 percentage point increase in the adult child's probability of having some college or more education in wave 3.

In columns (2) and (4), we see that the interaction of religious participation and mother's education is positive and significant at the 1 percent level for OLS and at the 5 percent level for the probit specification. The lower half of the table expresses this interaction coefficient in terms of the buffering effect that religious participation provides against the measure of disadvantage. Row A shows that having a mother with no more than a high school degree reduces the probability that the child has at least some college by 31 percentage points if the parent was at the twenty-fifth percentile of religious participation (i.e., the typical nonparticipant). Row B shows that this effect is reduced to 16 percentage points if the parent was at the seventy-fifth percentile of religious attendance (i.e., the typical active participant). The difference between rows A and B, 15 percentage points, is shown in row C. We refer to this difference, expressed as a fraction of row A, as the buffering effect of religion. In this case, we find that religious involvement buffers $(31 - 16)/31 = 48$ percent of the negative effect of having a mother with no more than a high school degree on the adult child's probability of having some college or more education in wave 3. The results for the probit specification are very similar.[7]

We next examine the extent to which religious participation can buffer the long-term effects of a disadvantaged childhood for our full set of measures of disadvantage and our full set of outcome variables. For simplicity, we present the results for the OLS specifications, but we show that results are similar for probit specifications when we check the robustness of the results in table 8.11. Table 8.8, panels A and B, present the t-statistics of the buffering effects of religion while table 8.9, panels A and B, present the magnitude of the buffering effects.

Table 8.8, panel A, column (1), shows whether measures of youth disadvantage have less of a detrimental impact on the high school graduation rates of youths with religious parents than on youths whose parents do not

---

7. It is also clear from table 8.7 that the direct effect of religious participation declines in magnitude and loses significance when moving from specifications (1) and (3) to (2) and (4). However, this is not typically the case. In fact, the direct effect of religion remains positive and significant in a clear majority of outcome-disadvantage combinations. We stress again that our hypothesis does not concern whether greater religious participation itself leads to better outcomes but whether it alleviates the effects of disadvantage on those outcomes. Furthermore, the direct effect cannot be interpreted causally due to the likely presence of omitted variables.

Table 8.8   Buffering effect of religious participation

			Outcomes in wave 3: Education, income, and public assistance			
t-statistics for buffering effect	High school or more	Some college or more (age 25+)	College graduate (age 25+)	Household income/ poverty line	Household income/ poverty line above 25th percentile	Public assistance
Family resources/Poverty						
Log household income / Poverty line	1.99**	0.19	0.81	-1.24	-0.87	-0.61
Household income less than 200 percent of poverty line	3.54***	1.72*	-0.07	-0.96	-0.61	-0.37
Log median household income in census tract	3.68***	0.89	0.47	0.96	1.58	1.11
Poverty rate in census tract	4.04***	0.09	-0.84	0.31	1.11	1.57
Received public assistance	5.50***	2.24**	-0.17	0.52	0.99	0.03
Family characteristics						
Nonwhite	3.81***	0.03	-0.56	-0.27	-0.31	1.27
Unmarried parent	1.00	0.73	0.04	0.13	-0.53	1.76*
Marital breakup between wave 1 and 2	0.14	-0.07	0.43	2.38**	3.50***	-0.09
Mother is a high school dropout	4.37***	-0.73	0.20	0.17	0.33	0.86
Mother has high school education or less	3.10***	3.66***	2.12**	1.99**	0.37	-0.16
Child characteristics						
Not expected to graduate college	1.19	2.13**	2.09**	1.85*	1.90*	2.49**
Difficult to raise	-0.58	-0.68	0.13	1.73*	-0.19	2.05**
Repeated a grade	1.34	3.27***	3.14***	1.05	2.51**	4.37***
Composite of discipline trouble	-0.56	0.26	-0.32	0.01	-0.06	-0.12

Outcomes in wave 3: Absence of behavioral problems

t-statistics for buffering effect	Nonsmoker	Age first sex	Normal weight	Health insurance	Subjective happiness	Locus of control
Family resources/Poverty						
Log household income/Poverty line	2.43**	1.88*	−0.72	−1.43	1.69*	−0.79
Household income less than 200 percent of poverty line	2.56**	2.30**	0.63	0.82	1.41	−0.22
Log median household income in census tract	3.79***	−0.54	−0.65	0.90	1.86*	−0.19
Poverty rate in census tract	2.36**	−0.33	−0.61	−0.20	2.72***	−0.17
Received public assistance	1.99**	−0.79	−0.27	0.53	0.06	1.51
Family characteristics						
Nonwhite	−0.37	0.53	−0.12	−0.83	0.18	3.05***
Unmarried parent	2.05**	−0.43	−0.49	0.13	1.27	0.09
Marital breakup between wave 1 and 2	0.22	−0.90	−0.17	2.06**	2.89***	0.80
Mother is a high school dropout	1.92*	1.23	0.06	−0.78	−0.04	−0.45
Mother has high school education or less	2.08**	1.16	0.01	1.43	1.57	1.29
Child characteristics						
Not expected to graduate college	1.70*	1.37	0.12	0.85	−0.21	0.11
Difficult to raise	1.91*	1.79*	−0.64	0.64	4.01***	0.35
Repeated a grade	1.81*	2.10**	−0.84	0.93	1.70*	1.89*
Composite of discipline trouble	2.09**	1.98***	−0.35	−0.11	1.95*	1.04

Note: Each cell contains the t-statistic for the buffering effect when we regress outcome (column) on disadvantage (row), percentile of parent's religious attendance, the interaction of disadvantage and religious attendance, and controls. Controls include race, sex, and age dummies, an indicator for whether the focal child is a biological child, and year of interview dummies.

***Significant at the 1 percent level.

**Significant at the 5 percent level.

*Significant at the 10 percent level.

frequently attend religious services. For all measures of family resources and poverty and for most measures of family characteristics, we find statistically significant buffering effects. However, we find no significant buffering effects with respect to any of the child characteristics. Table 8.9, panel A, column (1), shows that the magnitude of the buffering effect ranges between 42 and 113 percent for the significant effects.[8] It is notable that we do not find many significant effects when education is measured using an indicator for having some college or more or using an indicator for being a college graduate in columns (2) and (3). This suggests that the buffering effects of religion are concentrated on the high school dropout margin. It is also notable that we do not find a uniformly statistically significant buffering effect for any of our income measures, including those that might be expected to pick up the effect of high school or more versus less than high school education (such as the indicators for being above the twenty-fifth percentile of the ratio of household income to the poverty line and for being on public assistance). One potential explanation for this puzzling result is that annual income is a noisy measure of permanent income in the age range at which we observe respondents in wave 3.

The most uniformly significant buffering effect of religion against disadvantage as measured by child characteristics is for the public assistance indicator, with significant buffering effects for "not expected to go to college," "difficult to raise," and repeated a grade. In table 8.9, panel A, we see that among disadvantages associated with child characteristics, the significant buffering effects range from 35 to 130 percent.

Tables 8.8 (panel B) and 8.9 (panel B) present the t-statistics and the magnitudes of the buffering effects for behavior and psychological well-being. We find the most uniform buffering effects for the indicator for being a nonsmoker. We find buffering effects of religiosity for all family resource measures of disadvantage, some family characteristic measures of disadvantage, and one of the child characteristics. For the significant effects, the degree of buffering ranges between 71 and 181 percent. For other behavior and psychological well-being outcomes we do not find any uniformly significant buffering effects.

8.5.3   Joint Significance of the Buffering Hypothesis

Although our discussion thus far has examined the buffering effect of religion for each disadvantage-outcome combination, we have not yet addressed the overarching hypothesis of the chapter, that participation in religious activities buffers disadvantaged youth later in life. Overall we

---

8. The magnitude of the buffering effects is generally reasonable (between 0 and 1) for the significant buffering effects. However, estimates of buffering effects sometimes become unreasonably large when the direct effect of disadvantage on the outcome measure is small because this direct effect enters in the denominator of the formula for buffering effects. However, the resulting unreasonably large buffering effects are never statistically significant.

Table 8.9   **Buffering effect of religious participation**

			Outcomes in wave 3: Education, income, and public assistance			
Value of buffering effect	High school or more	Some college or more (age 25+)	College graduate (age 25+)	Income/Poverty line percentile (age 25+)	Income/Poverty line above 25th percentile	Public assistance
Family resources/Poverty						
Log household income/Poverty line	0.42**	0.05	0.15	−0.57	−1.14	−1.72
Household income less than 200 percent of poverty line	0.56***	0.41*	−0.02	−0.39	−0.87	−0.39
Log median household income in census tract	0.69***	0.22	0.11	0.21	0.40	0.49
Poverty rate in census tract	0.78***	0.04	−0.70	0.10	0.33	0.45
Received public assistance	0.99***	0.62**	−0.10	0.24	0.53	0.03
Family characteristics						
Nonwhite	0.68***	0.02	−0.70	−0.14	−0.18	0.46
Unmarried parent	0.22	0.36	0.02	0.10	−1.21	0.75*
Marital breakup between wave 1 and 2	13.8	−10.2	0.53	1.51**	1.42***	−0.06
Mother is a high school dropout	1.13***	−0.29	0.08	0.06	0.12	0.70
Mother has high school education or less	0.66***	0.48***	0.28**	0.37**	0.15	−0.20
Child characteristics						
Not expected to graduate college	0.22	0.35**	0.42**	0.99*	1.11*	0.74**
Difficult to raise	−5.41	−1.30	0.13	1.38*	−0.48	1.30**
Repeated a grade	0.35	0.78***	1.13***	0.34	0.94**	0.99***
Composite of discipline trouble	−1.54	0.20	−0.25	0.02	−0.35	−0.15

(continued)

Table 8.9 (continued)

Value of buffering effect		Outcomes in wave 3: Absence of behavioral problems				
	Nonsmoker	Age first sex ≥ 16	Normal weight	Health insurance	Subjective happiness	Locus of control
Family resources/Poverty						
Log household income/Poverty line	0.90**	0.61*	-0.43	-0.75	1.23*	-0.83
Household income less than 200 percent of poverty line	0.96**	0.70**	0.35	0.19	1.38	-0.27
Log median household income in census tract	1.08***	-0.29	-1.34	0.23	1.50*	-0.07
Poverty rate in census tract	1.45***	-0.18	-1.39	-0.08	1.02***	-0.09
Received public assistance	0.74**	-0.97	-1.10	0.21	0.04	0.70
Family characteristics						
Nonwhite	-0.51	6.48	-0.07	-1.12	12.0	1.81***
Unmarried parent	0.71**	-0.22	-2.18	0.04	1.06	8.67
Marital breakup between wave 1 and 2	15.8	-1.00	-11.7	0.67**	0.97***	0.60
Mother is a high school dropout	1.66*	0.87	0.03	-0.32	-0.11	-0.57
Mother has high school education or less	0.71**	0.37	0.00	0.38	1.80	0.37
Child characteristics						
Not expected to graduate college	0.47*	0.47	12.1	0.22	-0.24	0.04
Difficult to raise	0.86*	0.95*	-0.72	0.35	1.43***	3.86
Repeated a grade	1.06*	0.90**	-3.33	0.39	3.16*	0.81*
Composite of discipline trouble	0.71**	0.81*	-0.48	-0.06	1.27*	2.47

Note: Each cell contains the value of the buffering effect when we regress outcome (column) on disadvantage (row), the interaction of disadvantage and religious attendance, and controls. Controls include race, sex, and age dummies, an indicator of whether the focal child is a biological child, percentile of parent's religious attendance, and year of interview dummies.

***Significant at the 1 percent level.
**Significant at the 5 percent level.
*Significant at the 10 percent level.

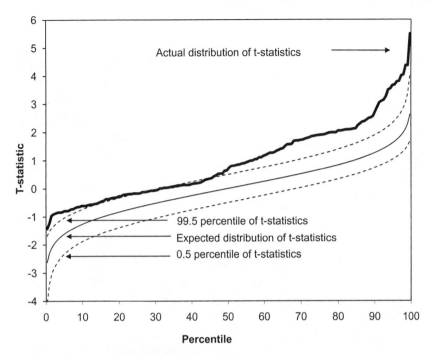

Fig. 8.1   The actual and predicted percentiles of the distribution of *t*-statistics

Notes: The figure shows the actual distribution of *t*-statistics of the buffering effect (thick line). In addition, it shows the expected distribution and the 0.5th and 99.5th percentile of the ordered distribution of *t*-statistics under the null hypothesis of no true buffering effect (thin lines).

find that just over 20 percent of the buffering effects from all disadvantage-outcome combinations are significant at the 5 percent level, and we find no cases of a significantly negative buffering effect. Given the number of coefficients in question, is this statistically significantly more than we would expect by chance?

Figures 8.1 to 8.3 test this formally. We order the 168 *t*-statistics of the buffering effects estimated in table 8.8, panels A and B, from smallest to largest. The thick line in figure 8.1 shows these ranked *t*-statistics, with the smallest (first percentile) having a value of about −1.5 and the largest (ninety-ninth percentile) having a value of about 5.5. In addition, we plot the expected value (and the 99 percent confidence interval) of each percentile of ranked *t*-statistics under the null hypothesis of no buffering effect in any disadvantage-outcome pair (the thin lines).[9] Comparing the actual

9. Under the null hypothesis of no effect, the observed *t*-statistics are a draw from a distribution with zero mean and unknown covariance structure. By bootstrapping our sample 10,000 times and recalculating the *t*-statistics of our 168 disadvantage-outcome combinations, we obtain the correlation matrix of our *t*-statistics. We then draw 100,000 vectors of 168 *t*-statistics

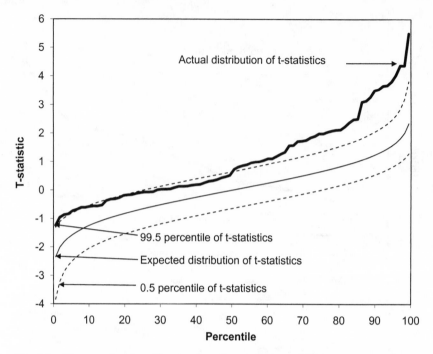

Fig. 8.2   The actual and predicted percentiles of the distribution of *t*-statistics for buffering of education and income outcomes

Notes: The figure shows the actual distribution of *t*-statistics of the buffering effect (thick line). In addition, it shows the expected distribution and the 0.5th and 99.5th percentile of the ordered distribution of *t*-statistics under the null hypothesis of no true buffering effect (thin lines).

with the expected distribution confirms that we observe significantly more significant buffering effects than would be expected by chance. In particular, at the critical values for the 5 percent and 1 percent levels of significance (1.96 and 2.57), the observed distribution of *t*-statistics lies not only above the expected distribution of *t*-statistics, it also lies above the 99 percent confidence interval for the expected distribution of *t*-statistics. Moreover, all *t*-statistics greater than 0.5 lie above the 99 percent confidence interval for ordered *t*-statistics. Thus, we are able to reject the joint null hypothesis of no buffering effect of religion across all outcomes.

Figures 8.2 and 8.3 present the same test for the subsets of education and income *t*-statistics and for behavior and mental and physical health *t*-statistics. In both cases, we can also reject the null hypothesis of no sig-

from a distribution with mean zero and this correlation matrix. This creates a probability distribution for each percentile of the distribution of *t*-statistics, which we summarize by the mean and 0.5 and 99.5 percentiles.

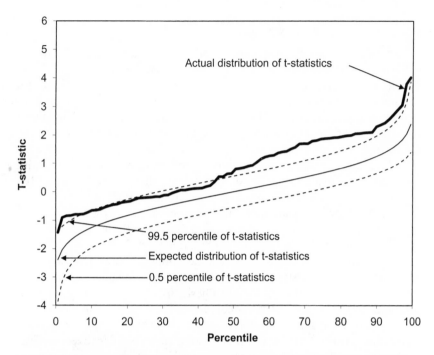

Fig. 8.3   The actual and predicted percentiles of the distribution of *t*-statistics for behavior and mental and physical health outcomes

Notes: The figure shows the actual distribution of *t*-statistics of the buffering effect (thick line). In addition, it shows the expected distribution and the 0.5th and 99.5th percentile of the ordered distribution of *t*-statistics under the null hypothesis of no true buffering effect (thin lines).

nificant effects at the 1 percent level, but the distribution for the education and income *t*-statistics lies further above the confidence interval than the distribution for the behavior and mental and physical health *t*-statistics. Thus, the evidence for buffering is stronger for education and income outcomes. Overall, we observe significantly more significant effects than would be expected by chance alone, which allows us to reject the hypothesis of no overall buffering effect.

In tables 8.10 to 8.13, we present additional specifications that explore whether social organizations also provide buffering effects, the robustness of the buffering results to changes in specification, likely mechanisms for buffering effects, and heterogeneity in the buffering effects by youth demographics. Space constrains us from showing the buffering effects for all 168 disadvantage-outcome combinations for these additional specifications. Instead, for the additional specifications, we present five disadvantage-outcome combinations that are broadly representative of the significant buffering effects in the baseline specification.

8.5.4   Buffering Effects of Social Organizations

In table 8.10 we consider whether other social organizations provide buffering effects that are comparable to those associated with religious participation. In particular, we examine the effects of parental involvement with community groups, work-related organizations, leisure clubs, and church-related social organizations. This last category refers to church-related social groups rather than worship per se. For the five selected adult outcome-disadvantage combinations, we measure the effects of indicators for each of these additional measures of social ties, both directly and interacted with the selected disadvantage measures. In the final column, we examine all 168 possible outcome-disadvantage combinations and report the number that show statistically significant buffering. We compare this to the religious participation baseline where we find significant positive buffering in thirty-eight of the 168 outcome-disadvantage combinations.

While the point estimates suggest that there might be some buffering effect associated with participating in community and work-related organizations, those effects are typically not statistically significant. For community organizations, only ten out of 168 outcome-disadvantage combinations show significant positive buffering, while for work-related organizations, there are zero instances of positive buffering and four instances of negative buffering. However, given the relatively large standard errors on our estimates, we cannot rule out that these groups do provide sizeable buffering in many of the insignificant cases. For leisure clubs, on the other hand, we find significant positive buffering for twenty-seven of the outcome-disadvantage combinations and no significant negative buffering for any of the outcome-disadvantage combinations. This suggests that parental involvement with leisure groups may also mitigate the effects of growing up in a disadvantaged environment.

The buffering effects of church-based social organizations are similar to the buffering effects of religious attendance. While participation in religious worship and other social groups are sufficiently correlated that it would be difficult to identify both effects simultaneously, it is striking that the consistent buffering effects that we find are from religious worship and church-based social organizations, with the important caveat that leisure clubs also seem to confer substantial buffering.

8.5.5   Robustness Checks and Attrition

Table 8.11 presents a range of robustness checks of our baseline specification, which is reproduced in the first row. In the second row, we use an alternative measure of religiosity, the raw attendance scale rather than the percentile of religious attendance. We continue to find significant buffering effects. In row three, we instead use an indicator for attendance greater than the median. Again, in most specifications, we continue to find significant

Table 8.10 The buffering effect of social organizations

Outcome measure/ Measure of disadvantage	Some college or more/Mother high school graduate or less		High school graduate or more/Poverty rate in census tract		Received public assistance/Focal child repeated grade		Nonsmoker/ Household income below 200 percent poverty line		Subjective happiness/ Marital break up between wave 1 and 2		All outcome-disadvantage pairs: statistically significant buffering	
	Effect	Standard error	Effect	Standard error	Effect	Standard error	Effect	Standard error	Effect	Standard error	Number positive	Number negative
Baseline buffering effect of religious participation (from table 8.9)	0.48***	0.13	0.78***	0.19	0.99***	0.23	0.96**	0.38	0.97***	0.34	38	0
Buffering effect of participation in community organizations	−0.22	0.31	0.96***	0.30	0.05	0.24	1.01	0.92	0.67	0.51	10	1
Buffering effect of participation in work-related organizations	0.19	0.27	0.70*	0.37	−0.30	0.24	1.35	1.08	−0.52	0.93	0	4
Buffering effect of participation in leisure groups	0.04	0.25	0.38	0.28	0.33***	0.12	−0.38	1.65	0.29	0.44	27	1
Buffering effect of participation in church-based social organizations	0.50***	0.14	0.80***	0.17	0.64***	0.17	0.74	0.48	0.63**	0.32	27	0

Notes: Each specification measures the value and standard error of the buffering effect of participating in the social organization and is analogous to the baseline specification. We regress outcome on disadvantage, participation in the social organization, the interaction of disadvantage and the social organization, and controls. Controls include percentile of parents' religious attendance, race, sex, and age dummies, an indicator of whether the focal child is a biological child, and year of interview dummies. The rightmost column, "All Outcome-Disadvantage Pairs," counts the number of statistically significant (at 5 percent level) positive and negative buffering effects of social organizations found for the full set of outcome-disadvantage pairs (total of 168 pairs).

***Significant at the 1 percent level.

**Significant at the 5 percent level.

*Significant at the 10 percent level.

Table 8.11   Robustness checks on buffering effects

Outcome measure/Measure of disadvantage	Some college or more/Mother high school graduate or less		High school graduate or more/Poverty rate in census tract		Received public assistance/Focal child repeated grade		Nonsmoker/Household income below 200 percent poverty line		Subjective happiness/Marital break up between wave 1 and 2	
	Effect	Standard error	Effect	Standard error	Effect	Standard error	Effect	Standard error	Effect	Standard error
Baseline (from table 8.9)	0.48***	0.13	0.78***	0.19	0.99***	0.23	0.96**	0.38	0.97***	0.34
Attendance scale	0.44***	0.12	0.78***	0.18	0.63*	0.35	1.02***	0.37	0.87***	0.33
Attendance > Median	0.55***	0.13	0.76***	0.19	0.75***	0.22	0.80*	0.42	0.77**	0.39
Avg. of parents' attendance	0.44***	0.13	0.70***	0.20	0.99***	0.23	0.82**	0.41	0.92**	0.36
Max. of parents' attendance	0.44***	0.13	0.72***	0.21	0.98***	0.22	0.87*	0.67	1.00***	0.34
Min. of parents' attendance	0.44***	0.13	0.62***	0.21	0.94***	0.23	0.77***	0.37	0.44	0.52
Cut by median attendance										
(A) Effect of disadvantage (Attendance < Median)	-0.33***	0.04	-0.42***	0.10	0.20***	0.04	-0.08**	0.04	-0.55***	0.20
(B) Effect of disadvantage (Attendance > Median)	-0.14***	0.04	-0.07***	0.07	0.00	0.04	-0.03	0.04	-0.13	0.20
Buffering (A − B)/A	0.57***	0.13	0.83***	0.16	0.98***	0.22	0.61	0.53	0.76**	0.38
Probit	0.44**	0.17	0.45	0.36	1.01**	0.51	0.97**	0.45	n.a.	n.a.
Additional controls	0.31***	0.10	1.02***	0.29	1.09***	0.23	0.84**	0.41	0.97***	0.35

Notes: Attendance Scale measures attendance on a six-point scale (never, few times a year, once a year, once a month, two to three times a month, once a week, two or more times a week). "Average Parents' Attendance," "Max. of Parents' Attendance," and "Min. of Parents' Attendance" uses both main parent and spousal responses. If the spouse is absent, the main parent's value is used alone. "Cut by Median Attendance" takes the standard specification but runs separate regressions conditioning on parent percentile attendance being above and below the median. Additional Controls consist of three maternal education dummies (high school grad, some college, college grad), three region dummies (northeast, north central, south) and four wave 1 household size dummies (three, four, five, six or more persons). All specifications also include the standard controls: percentile of parent's religious attendance (or one of the above alternative measures of attendance), race, sex, and age dummies, an indicator of whether a biological child, and year of interview dummies. n.a. = not applicable.

***Significant at the 1 percent level.

**Significant at the 5 percent level.

*Significant at the 10 percent level.

effects at the 5 percent level, and, in the one case where we do not, our estimate loses precision but continues to correspond to plausible buffering effects.

We are also concerned that our measure of religious participation of the main parent may not reflect the level of involvement of the entire family. For households where a spouse is present we try alternative measures of religious participation: the average, the maximum, and the minimum attendance of both parents (again expressed as percentile in the attendance distribution). If there is no spouse present or if religious participation information is missing for the spouse, we use the main parent information alone. Results in rows four, five, and six indicate that buffering effects are robust to these alternative family religious participation measures.[10]

In row seven, we run separate regressions for those with an attendance frequency above and below the median. This is equivalent to adding interaction terms between the indicator of attendance above the median and each of the controls to our row three specification. We again find substantial buffering in most cases and this suggests that our baseline results are not simply picking up omitted effects of our controls that differ by degree of religious participation. In row eleven, we use a probit specification rather than a linear probability model, and continue to find significant buffering effects for most outcomes. Finally, in row twelve we add additional controls for Census region, maternal education, and household size to our baseline specification; our results remain robust.

Since just over half the sample of focal children in wave 1 are not reinterviewed in wave 3, we explore whether attrition might bias our estimates of buffering effects. We find that attrition is not random—youth from disadvantaged backgrounds are more likely to attrit, and this effect is significant for all measures of disadvantage except those based on child characteristics. Moreover, treating attrition as an outcome variable, we find evidence of differential attrition by religious attendance: religious organizations buffer against attrition when disadvantage is measured by neighborhood income, the neighborhood poverty rate, or the mother's having a high school degree or less. Since disadvantaged youth are less likely to attrit if their parents have high attendance, disadvantaged youth will be overrepresented in the high attendance group relative to the low attendance group. To the extent disadvantage is fully measured by our variables, our control for the direct effect of disadvantage will correct for this and our estimate of buffering effects will not be biased by this differential attrition. However, to the extent that there are also unobservable components of disadvantage and there is also differential attrition on the unobservable component, unobservably disad-

---

10. Ultimately, we chose the main parent measure of attendance for our baseline specification because the religious attendance survey question for the main parent allows a more detailed response than does the corresponding survey question for the spouse.

vantaged youth will be overrepresented in the high attendance group, and the estimates of the buffering effect of religious organizations will therefore be biased down. Thus, it seems plausible that bias introduced by differential attrition causes our estimates to understate the true buffering effects provided by religious organizations.

8.5.6   Buffering Mechanisms

In table 8.12, we examine mechanisms that could plausibly account for the buffering effects of religion that we find. The first row reproduces our baseline estimates. In the second row, we use the grandparent's attendance of religious services as our measure of religiosity instead of using the parent's attendance.[11] If we were to continue to find significant effects, then it would bolster a causal interpretation of our results since the grandparent's religious attendance is more likely to be exogenous with respect to the child's outcomes. However, since the grandparent's religious attendance is only available for about 40 percent of our sample, the resulting estimates are much less precise. This plausibly explains why we find a significant buffering effect in only one of the five disadvantage-outcome combinations we examine. However, in no case can we rule out that the buffering effect is as large as in the baseline specification.

In the remaining rows, we run "horse races" between additional variables and religious attendance; that is, we add both the direct effect of these variables and their interaction with the measure of disadvantage to our main specification. As a result, these regressions contain two interaction terms: an interaction between disadvantage and religious attendance ("religious attendance interaction") and an interaction term between the additional variable and disadvantage ("horse race interaction"). In the third row, we run a horse race between actual attendance and attendance as predicted by covariates. The point estimates of buffering remain similar to those in the baseline specification, but only one estimate remains significant at the 5 percent level while the other four are now merely significant at the 10 percent level. Despite this decline in statistical significance, the robustness of the point estimates suggests that our estimates of buffering in our main specifications are due to actual religious attendance rather than the underlying covariates associated with religious attendance.

In the fourth row, we address the concern that people with higher levels of religious attendance might be living in neighborhoods that have peers, schools, or other institutions that provide buffering effects.[12] To disentangle

---

11. In wave 2, the NSFH randomly selected one of the parents of the main respondent for a telephone interview. Thus, the grandparent's religious attendance is measured at wave 2 rather than at wave 1.

12. However, the raw correlation between attendance and neighborhood quality (as measured by log median household income in the Census tract) is negative but not statistically significant.

Table 8.12   Possible mechanisms for the buffering effect

Outcome measure/Measure of disadvantage	Some college or more/Mother high school graduate or less		High school graduate or more/Poverty rate in census tract		Received public assistance/Focal child repeated grade		Nonsmoker/Household income below 200 percent poverty line		Subjective happiness/Marital break up between wave 1 and 2	
	Effect	Standard error	Effect	Standard error	Effect	Standard error	Effect	Standard error	Effect	Standard error
Baseline buffering effect of religious participation (from table 8.9)	0.48***	0.13	0.78***	0.19	0.99***	0.23	0.96**	0.38	0.97***	0.34
Buffering effect if participation is measured by grandparent's attendance ($N = 763$)	−0.28	0.57	0.68**	0.27	0.70*	0.39	1.34	1.28	98	6,841
Horse race with predicted attendance										
Religious attendance interaction	0.18**	0.12	0.61**	0.23	−0.20	0.12	0.14	0.11	0.80	0.60
Horse race interaction	0.07**	0.29	−1.32**	0.57	−0.62***	0.26	0.25	0.27	1.71	1.50
Buffering effect of religious participation	0.36*	0.21	0.82***	0.24	0.90*	0.46	0.78*	0.48	0.72*	0.42
Horse race with neighborhood income										
Religious attendance interaction	0.15**	0.07	0.66***	0.20	−0.38***	0.10	0.19**	0.10	1.11**	0.50
Horse race interaction	0.05	0.05	−0.24***	0.11	0.24***	0.07	−0.01	0.08	−0.72**	0.33
Buffering effect of religious participation	0.34**	0.14	0.73***	0.27	0.90***	0.21	1.07***	0.48	0.89***	0.32
Horse race with belief										
Religious attendance interaction	0.22**	0.12	0.52***	0.22	−0.33***	0.11	0.28**	0.11	1.18**	0.56
Horse race interaction	0.03	0.03	0.05	0.06	−0.07**	0.03	−0.07**	0.03	0.11	0.15
Buffering effect of religious participation	0.42**	0.18	0.68***	0.23	0.94***	0.26	1.61**	0.64	0.88**	0.32

Notes: Horse race adds a direct effect ("Predicted attendance," "Neighborhood income," "Belief") and its interaction with disadvantage to the baseline specification. Standard focal child controls along with maternal education, parent gender, region, household size, log of household income to poverty ratio, and four dummies for degree of agreement (scale from 1–5) for each response to four values statements are used to predict religious attendance, with R^2 of 0.17. These four statements are: (1) It is much better for everyone if the man earns the main living and the woman takes care of the home and family; (2) It's better for a person to get married than to go through life being single; (3) Preschool children are likely to suffer if their mother is employed; (4) In a successful marriage, the partners must have freedom to do what they want individually. Neighborhood Income is the log of median household income in the Census Tract. Belief is strength of religious belief as measured by degree of agreement (scale from 1–5) with following two statements: (1) The Bible is God's word and everything happened or will happen exactly as it says; (2) The Bible is the answer to all important human problems. Responses to these statements are averaged and standardized to have a mean of zero and standard deviation of one.

***Significant at the 1 percent level.

**Significant at the 5 percent level.

*Significant at the 10 percent level.

the buffering effects of religious attendance from the potential buffering effects of living in a better neighborhood, we run a horse race with neighborhood quality as measured by log median income in the Census tract. We find that religious attendance continues to have significant buffering effects, suggesting that our findings are not driven by selection of religiously active parents into higher income neighborhoods.

Finally, we run a horse race between religious attendance and religious beliefs (as measured by belief in religious doctrine and in the literal truth of the Bible). We continue to find a significant buffering effect of religious attendance, suggesting that attendance over and above belief buffers children against a disadvantaged upbringing. Taken together, the results from table 8.12 suggest that it is religious participation itself, rather than a likely correlate of religious participation, that provides the buffering effect against growing up in a disadvantaged environment.

8.5.7   Buffering Effects by Subpopulation

Table 8.13 displays how our baseline results for the five selected disadvantage-outcome combinations vary by the age, race, and sex of the child, the mother's level of education, the marital status of the parent, and religious denomination. While the estimates are not nearly as precise for these subpopulations, we generally find buffering effects of similar magnitude independently of the youth's sex, age, race, parental marital status, or maternal education. In fact, for none of the five disadvantage-outcome combinations do we find significant differences between the subpopulations defined by these demographic characteristics.

When we cut the results by religious denomination, we consistently find significant buffering effects for those belonging to evangelical Protestant denominations. Although we find almost no significant buffering effects for Catholics or mainline Protestant denominations, the difference in buffering effects across denominations is not statistically significant at the 5 percent level for any of the five disadvantage-outcome combinations.

A large literature (Altonji, Elder, and Taber 2005; Evans and Schwab 1995; Grogger and Neal 2000; Neal 1997) has examined whether Catholic school attendance increases educational attainment; many of these papers use self-reported Catholic denomination as an instrument for Catholic school attendance. The fact that we find relatively weak buffering effects among Catholics suggests that Catholic schooling is unlikely to account for the buffering effects we observe.

8.6   Conclusions and Discussion

We draw two conclusions from our results. First, there are significant long-term effects of childhood disadvantages on subsequent outcomes in adulthood. This is not surprising, given the large and expanding literature on intergenerational correlations in income, health, and education. Second,

Table 8.13   Buffering effects by subpopulation

Outcome measure/Measure of disadvantage	Some college or more/Mother high school graduate or less		High school graduate or more/Poverty rate in census tract		Received public assistance/Focal child repeated grade		Nonsmoker/Household income below 200 percent poverty line		Subjective happiness/Marital break up between wave 1 and 2	
	Effect	Standard error	Effect	Standard error	Effect	Standard error	Effect	Standard error	Effect	Standard error
Baseline, from table 8.9	0.48***	0.13	0.78***	0.19	0.99***	0.23	0.96**	0.38	0.97***	0.34
Gender of focal child										
Male (N = 1,037)	0.44***	0.15	−0.40	2.11	1.12***	0.21	1.09**	0.51	1.04***	0.35
Female (N = 894)	0.44	0.29	0.99***	0.15	1.15	0.77	0.82	0.63	1.04	0.78
Race										
White (N = 1,563)	0.49***	0.14	0.57***	0.22	1.19***	0.28	0.68*	0.39	0.91***	0.41
Nonwhite (N = 386)	0.44	0.32	1.34**	0.63	0.37	0.67	2.00**	0.81	1.11**	0.53
Maternal education										
High school graduate or less (N = 889)	—	—	1.15***	0.38	0.94***	0.33	−0.14	0.93	0.84	0.53
Some college or more (N = 1,059)	—	—	0.02	0.67	1.38***	0.52	1.57**	0.72	1.00**	0.47
Wave one age of focal child										
Age ≤ 12 (N = 792)	0.30	0.37	0.79***	0.30	—	—	0.93	0.64	0.87**	0.43
Age > 12 (N = 1,160)	0.51***	0.14	0.91**	0.23	—	—	0.90**	0.41	1.08*	0.61
Marital status of parent										
Married (N = 1,197)	−0.46	0.52	0.63	0.41	1.35	1.96	1.28*	0.65	—	—
Not married (N = 555)	0.76*	0.46	0.84**	0.30	0.34	0.43	0.10	0.90	—	—
Religious denomination										
Catholic (N = 452)	1.48	3.79	−0.66	1.14	0.12	0.67	−0.38	1.23	0.29	0.60
Mainline Protestant (N = 585)	−0.28	0.88	−0.40	0.60	0.48	1.20	−2.51	31.4	1.69**	0.71
Evangelical (N = 671)	0.98***	0.23	0.79***	0.16	0.97***	0.18	1.24**	0.49	1.33**	0.62

Notes: Dashes indicate that the sample cannot be or is already cut along those dimensions. All regressions include the standard controls: percentile of parent's religious attendance, race, sex, and age dummies, an indicator of whether a biological child, and year of interview dummies.

***Significant at the 1 percent level.

**Significant at the 5 percent level.

*Significant at the 10 percent level.

we find a substantial buffering effect of religion for a significant subset of outcomes. In particular, we find that religion buffers against a broad range of measures of disadvantage along the high school or more dimension. The buffering effect of religion on education, however, does not seem to translate into a buffering effect for income. In looking at behavior outcomes, we find some significant buffering effects for the likelihood of smoking. Finally, for health, health insurance, and psychological outcomes we find few systematic buffering effects of religion.

Overall, we believe that our results support the notion that religion plays an important role in how households respond to the disadvantages they face. Our results are especially strong when disadvantage is measured by maternal education and outcomes are measured by the youth's educational attainment. Given that education has been shown to have far-reaching consequences for a range of outcomes, including mortality, voting, and crime, we believe our results shed light on a potentially important mechanism that can mitigate the intergenerational transmission of disadvantage.

References

Aaronson, D. 1997. Sibling estimates of neighborhood effects. In *Neighborhood poverty, vol. II,* J. Brooks-Gunn, G. Duncan, and L. Aber, 80–93. New York: Russell Sage Foundation.

Altonji, J., T. Elder, and C. Taber. 2005. Selection on observed and unobserved variables: Assessing the effectiveness of Catholic schools. *Journal of Political Economy* 113 (1): 151–84.

Anderson, P. M., K. F. Butcher, and P. B. Levine. 2003. Maternal employment and overweight children. *Journal of Health Economics* 22 (3): 477–504.

Anderson, P. M., K. F. Butcher, and D. Whitmore Schanzenbach. 2007. Childhood disadvantage and obesity: Is nurture trumping nature? Dartmouth College, Unpublished Manuscript.

Antel, J. J. 1992. The intergenerational transfer of welfare dependency: Some statistical evidence. *The Review of Economics and Statistics* 74 (3): 467–77.

Brooks-Gunn, J., and G. Duncan. 1997. The effects of poverty on children. *The Future of Children* 7 (2): 55–71.

Bitler, M. P., and J. Currie. 2004. Does WIC work? The effect of WIC on pregnancy and birth outcomes. *Journal of Policy Analysis and Management* 24 (1): 73–91.

Black, S., P. J. Devereux, and K. G. Salvanes. 2005. Why the apple doesn't fall far: Understanding intergenerational transmission of human capital. *American Economic Review* 95 (1): 437–49.

Case, A., and L. F. Katz. 1991. The company you keep: The effects of family and neighborhood effects on disadvantaged youths. NBER Working Paper no. 3705. Cambridge, MA: National Bureau of Economic Research, May.

Clark, A., and O. Lelkes. 2005. Deliver us from evil: Religion as insurance. Paris School of Economics (PSE) Working Papers 2005-43.

Currie, J. 1997. Choosing among alternative programs for poor children. *The Future of Children* 7 (2): 113–31.

Currie, J., and R. Hyson. 1999. Is the impact of health shocks cushioned by socio-economic status? The case of birth weight. *American Economic Review* 89 (2): 245–50.

Currie, J., and E. Moretti. 2003. Mother's education and the intergenerational transmission of human capital: Evidence from college openings. *Quarterly Journal of Economics* 118 (4): 1495–1532.

Dahl, G. B., and L. Lochner. 2005. The impact of family income on child achievement. NBER Working Paper no. 11279. Cambridge, MA: National Bureau of Economic Research, April.

Dehejia, R., T. DeLeire, and E. F.P. Luttmer. 2007. Insuring consumption and happiness through religious organizations. *Journal of Public Economics* 91 (1–2): 259–79.

DeLeire, T., and A. Kalil. 2002. Good things come in threes: Single-parent multigenerational family structure and adolescent adjustment. *Demography* 39 (2): 393–412.

Diener, E., D. Kahneman, and N. Schwarz, eds. 1999. *Well-being: The foundations of hedonic psychology.* New York: Russell Sage Foundation.

Duncan, G. J., and J. Brooks-Gunn. 1997. *Consequences of growing up poor.* New York: Russell Sage Foundation.

Duncan, G. J., W. J. Yeung, J. Brooks-Gunn, and J. R. Smith. 1998. How much does childhood poverty affect the life chances of children? *American Sociological Review* 63 (3): 406–23.

Ellison, C. G. 1991. Religious involvement and subjective well-being. *Journal of Health and Social Behavior* 32 (1): 80–99.

Evans, W. N., W. E. Oates, and R. M. Schwab. 1992. Measuring peer group effects: A study of teenage behavior. *Journal of Political Economy* 100 (5): 966–91.

Evans, W. N., and R. M. Schwab. 1995. Finishing high school and starting college: Do Catholic schools make a difference? *Quarterly Journal of Economics* 110 (4): 941–74.

Freeman, R. B. 1986. Who escapes? The relation of churchgoing and other background factors to the socioeconomic performance of black male youths from inner-city tracts. In *The black youth employment crisis,* ed. R. B. Freeman and H. J. Holzer, 353–76. Chicago: University of Chicago Press.

Grogger, J., and D. Neal. 2000. Further evidence on the benefits of Catholic secondary schooling. *Brookings-Wharton Papers on Urban Affairs* 2000 (1): 151–93.

Gruber, J. 2005. Religious market structure, religious participation, and outcomes: Is religion good for you? *Advances in Economic Analysis and Policy* 5 (1): 1–30.

Gruber, J., and D. Hungerman. 2006. The church vs. the mall: What happens when religion faces increased secular competition? NBER Working Paper no. 12410. Cambridge, MA: National Bureau of Economic Research, August.

Guralnick, M. J. 2004. Family investments in response to the developmental challenges of young children with disabilities. In *Family investments in children's potential: Resources and parenting behaviors that promote success,* ed. A. Kalil and T. DeLeire, 119–39. Mahwah, NJ: Lawrence Erlbaum.

Hanson, T. L., S. McLanahan, and E. Thomson. 1997. Economic resources, parental practices, and children's well-being. In *Consequences of growing up poor,* ed. G. J. Duncan and J. Brooks-Gunn, 190–238. New York: Russell Sage Foundation.

Iannaccone, L. R. 1998. Introduction to the economics of religion. *Journal of Economic Literature* 36 (3): 1465–95.

Korenman, S., and J. E. Miller. 1997. Effects of long-term poverty on physical health of children in the national longitudinal survey of youth. In *Consequences of Grow-*

ing Up Poor, ed. G. J. Duncan and J. Brooks-Gunn, 70–99. New York: Russell Sage Foundation.

Lillard, D. R., and J. Price. 2007. The impact of religion on youth in disadvantaged families. Cornell University, Unpublished Manuscript.

Mayer, S. E. 1997. *What money can't buy: Family income and children's life chances.* Cambridge, MA: Harvard University Press.

McCullough, M. E., W. T. Hoyt, D. B. Larson, H. G. Koenig, and C. Thoresen. 2000. Religious involvement and mortality: A meta-analytic review. *Health Psychology* 19 (3): 211–22.

McLanahan, S., and G. Sandefur. 1994. *Growing up with a single parent.* Cambridge, MA: Harvard University Press.

Neal, D. 1997. The effects of Catholic secondary schooling on educational attainment. *Journal of Labor Economics* 15 (1): 98–123.

Oreopoulos, P., M. E. Page, and A. Huff Stevens. 2005. The intergenerational effects of worker displacement. NBER Working Paper no. 11587. Cambridge, MA: National Bureau of Economic Research, August.

———. 2006. The intergenerational effects of compulsory schooling. *Journal of Labor Economics* 24 (4): 729–60.

Page, M. E. 2004. New evidence on intergenerational correlations in welfare participation. In *Generational income mobility in North America and Europe,* ed. Miles Corak, 226–44. Cambridge: Cambridge University Press.

Page, M., A. Huff Stevens, and J. Lindo. 2007. Parental income shocks and outcomes of disadvantaged youth in the United States. University of California at Davis, Unpublished Manuscript.

Pargament, K. I. 2002. The bitter and the sweet: An evaluation of the costs and benefits of religiousness. *Psychological Inquiry* 13 (3): 168–81.

Shea, J. 2000. Does parents' money matter? *Journal of Public Economics* 77 (2): 155–84.

Smith, J. R., J. Brooks-Gunn, and P. K. Klebanov. 1997. Consequences of living in poverty for young children's cognitive and verbal ability and early school achievement. In *Consequences of growing up poor,* ed. G. J. Duncan and J. Brooks-Gunn, 132–89. New York: Russell Sage Foundation.

Smith, T. B., M. E. McCullough, and J. Poll. 2003. Religiousness and depression: Evidence for a main effect and the moderating influence of stressful life events. *Psychological Bulletin* 129 (4): 614–36.

Sweet, J. A., and L. L. Bumpass. 1996. The national survey of families and households—Waves 1 and 2: Data description and documentation. Center for Demography and Ecology, University of Wisconsin-Madison. Available at: http://www.ssc.wisc.edu/nsfh/home.htm.

———. 2002. The national survey of families and households—Waves 1, 2, and 3: Data description and documentation. Center for Demography and Ecology, University of Wisconsin-Madison. Available at: http://www.ssc.wisc.edu/nsfh/home.htm.

Sweet, J. A., L. L. Bumpass, and V. Call. 1988. The design and content of the National Survey of Families and Households. Center for Demography and Ecology, University of Wisconsin-Madison, NSFH Working Paper no. 1.

Strawbridge, W. J., S. J. Shema, R. D. Cohen, R. E. Roberts, and G. E. Kaplan. 1998. Religiosity buffers effects of some stressors on depression but exacerbates others. *Journal of Gerontology Series B: Psychological Sciences and Social Sciences* 53 (3): 118–26.

Neighborhood Violence
and Urban Youth

Anna Aizer

9.1 Introduction

In a 1997 survey nearly three quarters of American children reported having been exposed to neighborhood violence (Hill and Jones 1997; Boney-McCoy and Finkelhor 1996). These rates are highest among low-income urban youth. There have been numerous studies of the impact of exposure to violence on children that have linked exposure to violence with restricted emotional development, aggressive behavior, depression, anxiety, sleep disturbances, learning problems, and truancy.

However, the existing literature on neighborhood violence is characterized by a number of shortcomings. In a review of the literature, psychiatrist Joy Osofsky identifies a number of these shortcomings and calls for future research to address them.[1] One shortcoming relates to the difficulty defining or characterizing neighborhood violence, which leads to significant measurement error. Another is the fact that neighborhood violence is often correlated with high rates of domestic violence and other types of disadvantage (racial, income, and parental education) which in turn have been shown to have deleterious effects on child outcomes.[2] As such, research documenting

Anna Aizer is an assistant professor of economics at Brown University and a faculty research fellow of the National Bureau of Economic Research.

This research was funded by the Annie E. Casey Foundation. We thank them for their support but acknowledge that the findings and conclusions presented in this report are those of the author alone, and do not necessarily reflect the opinions of the Foundation. The author would also like to thank Jonathan Gruber and Jens Ludwig for very useful comments and Jeffrey Grogger, Goerge Tita and Bing-ru Teh for generously providing the LA crime data used in this chapter.

1. Osofsky (1999).

2. Research conducted in the early 1990s concluded that three to ten million children witness assaults against a parent by an intimate partner each year (Straus 1992). More recent work has

a relationship between neighborhood violence and poor child outcomes may overstate the relationship.

In this chapter we seek to answer the following questions: (a) In what other ways do violent neighborhoods differ from non-violent ones? (b) Who is exposed to neighborhood violence? Is exposure to violence random? and (c) Does exposure to violence affect child outcomes or does it reflect other poor circumstances or types of disadvantage?

This research contributes to the existing body of work on the impact of exposure to violence on child outcomes by examining this issue with new data that is well-suited to address many of the shortcomings of the existing work. Importantly, we use established econometric techniques (referred to as neighborhood and family fixed effects) that allow one to control for both observed and unobserved measures of neighborhood and family disadvantage that might be correlated with both exposure to violence and poor child outcomes, thereby enabling causal inference. The data come from the Los Angeles Family and Neighborhood Study (LA FANS), an individual survey of children and their families residing in sixty-five neighborhoods in Los Angeles, California. The survey contains information on child and parent characteristics including exposure to violence and association with violent peers as well as family characteristics and multiple measures of child well-being. Because all the children in the sample reside in one county, they are subject to the same macroeconomic conditions and government programs so that we can implicitly control for differences along these dimensions and focus on the impact of neighborhood differences on child well-being.

In addition, we utilize alternative measures of community or neighborhood violence. Typically, measures of neighborhood violence consist of police or crime reports available only at an aggregate level (such as the county or city) that is not truly representative of a child's neighborhood. In addition, they do not necessarily reflect true violence or victimization but rather a combination of underlying violence and police response to that violence. Instead, we use two alternative measures of violence designed to overcome these shortcomings. The first is the rate of hospitalizations for assault developed from California Hospital Discharge data, which is an administrative database consisting of all hospitalizations in the state. These data allow one to create measures of violence at the zip code (which is more local than the county or city) that are not subject to recall or self-reporting bias and do not reflect policing policies. The second source of data on neighborhood violence is based on police data for individual reporting districts in LA City. While these data are generated by the LA Police Department and therefore reflect both underlying violence and police reports, the data are

---

found that violence against pregnant women (most often perpetrated by an intimate partner) has a negative and significant impact on birth outcomes, which have been linked to worse economic outcomes later in life (Aizer 2007).

available at a very fine level of detail (the census tract) and therefore more closely approximate one's immediate neighborhood—even more so than a zip code.

Combining the individual level data from the LA FANS survey with measures of neighborhood violence and other neighborhood characteristics from the 2000 Census yields a data set with a wide range of information on child, family, and neighborhood characteristics. These data enable one to explore both the effects of exposure to violence on child well-being and how individual, family, and neighborhood characteristics affect one's exposure to violence. In addition, we employ econometric techniques, referred to as "fixed effects," (described in greater detail later) that allow us to control for underlying disadvantage at the neighborhood and family level that is unobserved by the researcher. In so doing, we can isolate the causal impact of exposure to violence, separate from underlying family and neighborhood disadvantage, on child outcomes. This research will help us to better understand the role of violence in the lives of disadvantaged children. It should be stressed that the focus of this work is estimating the impact of intermittent exposure to neighborhood violence on child outcomes. As such, these results are not generalizable to children who are the victims of repeated victimization such as child abuse.[3]

9.2   Literature Review

There have been numerous studies of the impact of exposure to violence on children, with most of the research conducted by psychologists, psychiatrists, and social workers. This research has linked exposure to violence with restricted emotional development, aggressive behavior, depression, anxiety, sleep disturbances, learning problems, and truancy.[4]

The earliest studies focused on single nonrecurring acts of violence such as sniper shootings in school playgrounds (Pynoos et al. 1987). These studies generally found posttraumatic stress symptom responses related to internalizing problems (anxiety and depression) that varied with proximity to the actual violence. However, it has since been noted that the clinicians in these studies were not blind to the subjects' exposure to violence, which some believe may have biased the findings (Cooley-Quille et al. 1995).

More recently, researchers have focused on exposure to chronic community violence. These studies have, in general, linked exposure to community violence to externalizing behavioral problems (Bell and Jenkins 1993). For example, in a study of thirty-seven school children age seven through twelve, Cooley-Quille et al. (1995) found that exposure to high levels of

3. For example, recent work by Currie and Tekin (2006) suggests that repeated child abuse and maltreatment leads to large and significant reductions in child well-being.
4. Fonagy, Target, Steele, and Steele 1997; Gorman-Smith and Tolan 1998; Jenkins 1995; Loeber et al. 1993; Schwab-Stone et al. 1995.

community violence was not related to internalizing behavior and disorders, but was associated with externalizing behavior problems, restlessness, and impaired social and behavioral functioning. However, the authors also note that "families of children with high exposure to community violence were characterized by high conflict and lack of cohesiveness." This leads the authors to conclude that "An important caution is needed in interpreting the relationship between exposure to violence and behavior problems. Because of the study's correlational nature, it cannot be determined whether one variable causes the other or whether both are mediated by a third factor" (1365).

In another (larger) survey of 2,248 sixth, eighth, and tenth graders in an urban public school system, Schwab-Stone et al. (1995) find that 40 percent of youth reported exposure to a shooting or a stabbing in the past year. Children exposed to high levels of violence were more likely to be black and/or Latino and more likely to receive free lunch. Using one-way Analysis of variance (ANOVA) to examine differences in child outcomes, they found that violence exposure was associated with greater willingness to use physical aggression, diminished perception of risk, lowered personal expectations for the future, dysphoric mood, antisocial activity, alcohol use, and diminished academic achievement. However, in their discussion, the authors also acknowledge the difficulty establishing a causal relationship, writing, "from the current study one cannot say that violence exposure or feeling unsafe causes any of the attitudes or aspects of adaptation that are significantly related, statistically speaking, to them" (1366).

Few economists have studied the impact of exposure to violence on child outcomes. The little work that does exist explicitly recognizes the difficulty of making causal inference, as exposure to violence may be correlated with other sources of disadvantage that may be responsible for the poor outcomes observed. Grogger (1998) estimates the impact of school violence on high school graduation rates based on a large survey of school children and their school administrators. School violence can affect graduation rates by reducing school attendance and/or the ability to concentrate when in school, thereby lowering the probability of graduation. A major problem estimating the impact of school violence on outcomes is that more violent schools may have lower graduation rates simply because violent students are less likely to complete high school. Grogger overcomes this problem by focusing on the high school graduation rates of nonviolent students. He finds that higher rates of school violence as reported by principals among one's peers was related to lower rates of graduation among the *nonviolent* students.

But it may still be the case that nonviolent children in violent schools differ in important ways from nonviolent children in nonviolent schools. Violent schools are more likely to be in poorer neighborhoods and parents who send their children to violent schools may suffer from other forms of disadvantage relative to parents who send their children to nonviolent schools. It may be these differences, not differences in school violence per se, that are responsible for these differences.

More recent work by Kling, Liebman, and Katz (2004) and Ludwig, Duncan, and Hirschfield (2001) based on the Moving to Opportunity (MTO) demonstration provides experimental evidence of the impact of neighborhoods on child well-being. In the MTO study, poor families were randomly selected to receive subsidies to move to higher income neighborhoods. The MTO study overcomes previous difficulties estimating the impact of environment on child well-being—because of the random assignment, families living in poor and nonpoor neighborhoods will not differ in significant ways. The analysis consisted of in-depth interviews with families followed by a quantitative analysis of how moving to a higher income neighborhood affected child outcomes. In the qualitative analysis, the authors found that fear of random violence caused parents to focus much of their time and energy on keeping their children safe and that parental monitoring declined when they moved to higher income neighborhoods.

In the quantitative analysis that followed, the authors found a positive and significant impact of moving to a higher income neighborhood on girls but no impact on boys (Kling and Liebman 2005). Females experienced improvements in education and mental health and were less likely to engage in risky behaviors. While the focus of the MTO study is to evaluate the impact of poor neighborhoods (and not violence specifically) on child outcomes, the authors find that families that move to higher income neighborhoods report lower rates of victimization, especially for females, but the reductions are not statistically significant. There are, however, significant differences between poor and nonpoor neighborhoods in the quality of the school environments, the presence of adult role models, and the health of the environment. Thus, while the qualitative analysis suggested that safety and lack of fear of random violence would explain improved outcomes associated with moving to a higher income neighborhood, the quantitative evidence does not appear to support this.

Finally, recent work by Ludwig and Kling (2007) investigates whether the findings of Ludwig, Duncan, and Hirschfield (2001)—that moving to a lower-poverty neighborhood reduces violent criminal behavior among youths—can be explained by reductions in exposure to criminal activity as measured by neighborhood crime rates. Ludwig and Kling (2007) find no support for the hypothesis that crime is "contagious." Rather, they find that neighborhood racial segregation appears to be a much more important factor than neighborhood crime rates in explaining youth crime. Although the focus of their work is criminal activity, crime and violence are highly correlated and these results provide further suggestive evidence that exposure to neighborhood violence may not have a strong causal impact on youth behavior or outcomes but that the underlying level of neighborhood disadvantage may be more important.

Thus, the existing literature on the impact of violence on child well-being appears to be mixed. While work by psychiatrists and psychologists has found an association between exposure to community violence and externalizing behavioral problems, there is also evidence that children exposed to more community violence are disadvantaged in other respects—they are poorer, more likely to be black, and their families suffer from "lack of cohesiveness." As such, it is difficult to make causal inferences regarding the relationship between exposure to violence and child well-being. Work by economists that has sought to overcome this difficulty through randomized assignment to neighborhood has found that moving out of poor neighborhoods does improve outcomes for girls, but cannot attribute the improvements to reductions in violence. In addition, they have found that the reductions in criminal activity associated with moving to a lower poverty neighborhood are not attributable to reductions in neighborhood crime but are more likely explained by improvements in other measures of neighborhood disadvantage—racial and income segregation (Ludwig and Kling 2007).

In the work presented here, we attempt to distinguish the impact of violence from other forms of disadvantage. In other words, we attempt to answer the question: does exposure to community violence cause child outcomes to worsen? Or rather, is it the case that disadvantaged youth are exposed to more violence, and it is the underlying disadvantage, not the violence, that is responsible for the worse child outcomes? We proceed in two stages. First, we include multiple controls for neighborhood and family disadvantage that are available in the data. Second, we employ neighborhood and family "fixed effects," which enable us to control for forms of neighborhood and family disadvantage that may be correlated with exposure to violence but not captured in the data. This method is described in greater detail in section 9.6.

9.3   Data

9.3.1   The Los Angeles Family and Neighborhood Study (LA FANS)

The LA FANS is a panel study of a representative sample of all neighborhoods in Los Angeles. Poor neighborhoods and children are oversampled and all analyses presented here are weighted using the survey weights, which are designed to provide estimates generalizable to the population of all children living in Los Angeles. While the survey is designed as a panel, only data for the first wave (conducted in 1999 to 2000) are currently available. In wave 1, an average of forty-one households within each neighborhood were randomly selected for interview. Sampled adults were asked questions about household economic status, health insurance, participation in welfare programs, and use of social services, as well as questions about their neighborhoods. Caregivers provided information on the home environment, children's behavioral problems, and school performance. Cognitive assessments were administered to children over three. Children older than nine were also asked about exposure to violence, their friends, and social interaction; as such, the analysis sample is limited to this older group of 785 children.

To compare the analysis sample with the overall population of children in the United States, we present descriptive statistics for this sample and for the sample of children living in Los Angeles and the nation from the 2000 Census in table 9.1. In column (1) are the unweighted means for the LA FANS sample; column (2) contains the weighted means. In column (3) are population means for families with at least one child between the ages often and nineteen in LA county from the 2000 Census and in column (4) are means for the entire U.S. population of families with at least one child between ten and nineteen.

The children included in this analysis are, on average, fifteen years old. Thirty six percent of mothers are high school dropouts, 67 percent are married, and 34 percent live below poverty. Eleven percent of the mothers receive cash welfare benefits. Given that the survey was conducted in Los Angeles, it is not surprising that 55 percent are Hispanic, 10 percent black, 27 percent white, and 8 percent Asian. If we compare the raw means in column (1)

Table 9.1   **Comparison of LA FANS with 2000 Census**

	LA FANS— Unweighted	LA FANS— Weighted	Census— LA county	Census— United States
Family/Child characteristics				
Maternal education (years)	11.99	12.37	11.14	12.77
Mother < high school	0.36	0.32	0.39	0.16
Black	0.10	0.12	0.08	0.11
Hispanic	0.55	0.51	0.49	0.12
White	0.27	0.27	0.34	0.65
Asian	0.08	0.11	0.14	0.04
Married	0.67	0.68	0.77	0.69
Family earnings (in thousands)	43.53	46.62	47.87	52.57
Below poverty	0.34	0.29	0.19	0.13
Welfare participation	0.11	0.11	0.09	0.04
SSI receipt	0.04	0.04	0.01	0.02
Maternal age	42.4	41.8	41.37	40.90
Child age	15.1	15.1	14.11	14.21
Male	0.51	0.51	0.51	0.51
Number of siblings	1.32	1.43	1.83	1.45
Violence measures				
Know gang members	0.21	0.20		
Witnessed shooting in past year	0.08	0.06		
Robbed in past year	0.11	0.11		
Family often hits	0.18	0.17		

with the weighted means in column (2), we see that when we weight the sample means, the children appear slightly less disadvantaged. When we compare the weighted means to those from the 2000 Census, we conclude that the LA FANS sample is slightly more disadvantaged relative to the LA county population (column [3]) in terms of race (LA FANS is more likely to include black and Hispanic children) as well as poverty (LA FANs includes more poor families and families that rely on welfare or Supplemental Security Income [SSI]). However, when we compare the average characteristics of children sampled in the LA FANS with those in the nation more generally, we find that the LA FANS children are much more disadvantaged in terms of income, race, and maternal education (column [4]). The fact that the analyses are based on a disadvantaged (and nonrepresentative) population of children should be taken into account when interpreting the results.

Exposure to violence in this sample is somewhat common. Twenty one percent of children in this sample report having violent peers as measured by whether they know a gang member (girls are as likely to report violent peers as boys in this sample). As for exposure to street violence, 11 percent reported being robbed and 8 percent witnessed a shooting in the past year.[5]

9.3.2   California Hospital Discharge Data

The LA FANS data, which contain the household census tract, are merged with measures of neighborhood violence developed from California's hospital discharge database. The hospital data is available at the zip code level. As such, for analyses involving these data, the child's neighborhood is defined as the zip code in which he or she lives. A zip code(s) is a far more precise measure of one's neighborhood than measures typically used (cities or counties) for the purpose of measuring neighborhood violence. Information on the number of individuals in each zip code (to compute an assault rate) as well as characteristics of the zip code (poverty rate, racial composition, share low skilled, etc.) comes from the 2000 Census. There is considerable variation in the number and rate of admissions for assault across LA's neighborhoods. For example, in South Central Los Angeles there were 501 admissions for assaults among those age fifteen to forty-four in 2000 (or forty-five per 10,000). In Compton there were 213 admissions (thirty-six per 10,000) and in Beverly Hills there were five (three per 10,000).[6]

The main advantage of using hospital discharge data to calculate measures of neighborhood violence is that it enables one to calculate much

---

5. Eighteen percent report exposure to family violence, as measured by reports of family members "often hitting." However, the characteristics of the families of children who report family violence differ considerably from the characteristics of violent families reported in other data, suggesting that this measure may be unreliable in the LA FANS. For this reason, we do not use this measure in the analysis. However, when we conduct the family fixed effect analysis (described later) we implicitly control for measures of domestic violence.

6. South Central includes zip codes 90001, 90002, 90003, 90047, and 90059; Compton 90220, 90221, and 90222; and Beverly Hills includes zip codes 90210, 90211, and 90212.

more local measures than other data sets and does not rely on self-reports or police reports.[7] In addition, the measures can be broken down by race and whether the violence involved a gun. But there are potential drawbacks to these data. First, they capture extreme acts of violence (though they are likely highly correlated with less severe violence). Second, because they are based on hospital utilization, they may capture violence perpetrated against those most likely to rely on hospitals as a source of medical care (those with fewer resources or those located closest to hospitals). However, the measure is based only on admission to the hospital, not emergency department utilization, and as there is less discretion in hospital admission, we believe that the potential for this measure to capture poverty is minimal and that it fairly accurately captures neighborhood violence. But in a conservative effort to limit any potential for bias we recalculate our measure of neighborhood violence not as a rate of assaults, but as the share of all hospitalizations for an injury that are due to assaults. The latter implicitly controls for greater reliance on hospitals for care in some zip codes relative to others.

9.3.3   Violent Crime by Census Tract for LA City

We can link information on violent crime by census tract (a smaller area than zip code) to the roughly 475 youth surveyed as part of the LA FANS and who reside in LA City (a subset of LA County). These data were first compiled by Grogger (2002).[8] As noted previously, while these data are based on police reports and thus capture not only violence but reports to the police, they are available at the finest level of detail possible—the census tract that includes on average 5,800 individuals in LA county, as opposed to a zip code that includes on average 67,000 individuals. These data are not available by race or age. Rates of violent crime for the year 1999 range from 0 to 1,910 per 10,000, with an average of 136, which is considerably lower than it was in the early 1990s. In 1992, the first year for which these data are available, the average rate of violent crime per census tract in Los Angeles was 275 per 10,000, representing a 50 percent decline in violent crime over an eight-year period.

The next three sections contain our analysis of the role of violence in the lives of urban youth. In the next section (section 9.4), we seek to answer the first of the three questions: in what other ways do violent neighborhoods differ from nonviolent ones? In section 9.5, we answer the second set of questions: who is exposed to neighborhood violence? Is exposure to violence

---

7. Calculations by the author based on the National Crime Victimization Survey (NCVS) of 2004 reveal that the vast majority of violent crime occurs near the victim's home. For example, among those age twelve to nineteen who were victim of an assault, 15 percent reported that the assault happened in or very near the home, 47.7 percent reported that it happened within one mile, and 76.2 percent reported that it occurred within five miles. This suggests that assault rates calculated from hospital discharge data that identify the patient's zip code of residence do accurately reflect violence in the zip code.

8. The data were subsequently updated by George Tita.

random or correlated with other forms of family disadvantage? Finally, in section 9.6, we answer the last of our three questions, does exposure to violence affect child outcomes or does it reflect other poor circumstances or types of disadvantage?

9.4   How Do Violent Neighborhoods Differ from Nonviolent Ones?

Our first measure of neighborhood violence is the share of all hospitalizations for an injury in a zip code that are the result of an assault. This measure should reduce, if not eliminate, any bias in the measures of violence that derives from one group's greater reliance on hospitals for care.[9] We also decompose the assault rate into gun and nongun assaults.

In figure 9.1 we present graphic evidence of a relationship between this measure of community violence and various community characteristics. As is evident from all graphs, there is a positive correlation between neighborhood violence among youths (those aged fifteen to nineteen) and neighborhood measures of disadvantage. Zip codes with higher levels of violence have a greater share of high school dropouts, individuals below poverty, households receiving welfare, black individuals, and a higher unemployment rate. These relationships persist for adults (age twenty-five to forty-four) as well.

The two most important predictors of violence are the share below poverty and the share black in a neighborhood. Among youths, if the share below poverty increases by a standard deviation (.104) then the assault rate (as a ratio) increases 15 percent of a standard deviation. If the share black increases by a standard deviation, then violence increases by 28 percent of a standard deviation. Among adults, poverty appears to have a greater impact than race in predicting violence.

In figures 9.2 and 9.3 the rates are decomposed into gun-related assaults and non-gun-related assaults, respectively. In Los Angeles, among those age fifteen to nineteen, gun violence is responsible for a large share of hospital admissions: 12 percent of all hospital admissions for an injury and 61 percent of all hospital admissions for an assault. As is evident from figures 9.2 and 9.3, the relationship between violence and neighborhood disadvantage is driven almost entirely by gun violence, and, as with the total assault rate, the share below poverty and the share black appear to be the most important predictors of neighborhood violence.

In figure 9.4 we present results from a similar exercise based on census tracts in LA City. The findings are similar: race (share black) is highly correlated with violent crime at the census tract level, as are the share receiving welfare and the share below poverty. Unlike the hospitalization data, the

---

9. Results based on the assault rate are very similar but tend to yield more "outlier" observations.

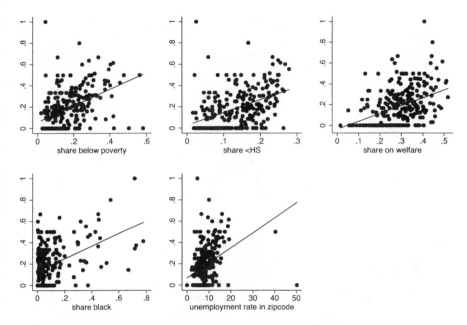

Fig. 9.1   Neighborhood characteristics and assaults / total injuries

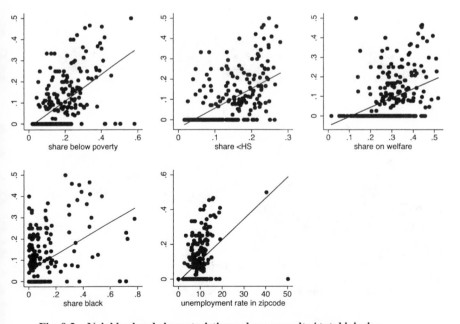

Fig. 9.2   Neighborhood characteristics and gun assaults / total injuries

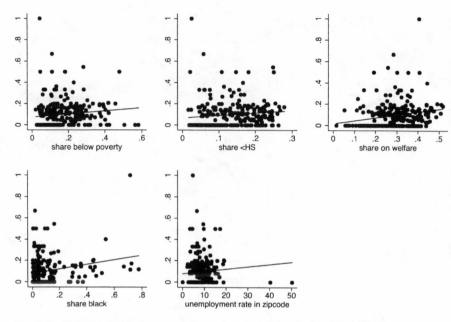

Fig. 9.3   Neighborhood characteristics and non-gun assaults / total injuries

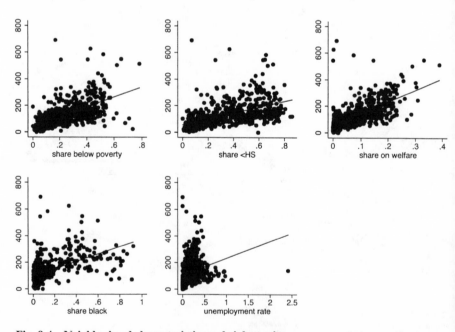

Fig. 9.4   Neighborhood characteristics and violent crime

crime data do not allow us to look at gun versus nongun crimes or differences by age.

Overall, this preliminary analysis based on aggregate data suggests that community violence (and gun violence, in particular) is correlated with multiple measures of disadvantage. This will affect our ability to attribute any negative relationship that we observe between violence and child well-being to violence and not the underlying disadvantage without adequately controlling for underlying sources of disadvantage.

9.5   Who Is Exposed to Violence? Are Children from Disadvantaged Families Exposed to More Violence?

What determines personal exposure to violence? Is living in a violent neighborhood the most important factor? How much do family characteristics matter? We begin to answer these questions by comparing hospitalization rates across races and age groups. In table 9.2 we see that hospitalization for assault is more common among youths age fifteen to nineteen than adults (age twenty-five to forty-four) and children (age zero to fifteen, not shown). The decline in violence by age is even more striking when we focus on gun violence (column [3]). In addition, blacks have much higher rates of assault than other groups: nearly 4 per 1,000 compared to .5 per 1,000 for whites and 1.4 for Hispanics. This is particularly true for gun assaults (column [3]). But the higher rates for blacks reflect, in part, their greater reliance on hospitals for care. In column (2) of table 9.2 we present the share of all hospitalizations for an injury that are the result of an assault, and in columns (4) and (5) the share of all hospitals for an assault and any injury that are the results of a

Table 9.2   Hospitalization for assaults by race and age—LA county 2000

	Assaults per 1,000	Assaults/ Total injuries	Gun assaults per 1,000	Gun assaults/ Total injuries	Gun assaults/ Total assaults	Population
			Age 15–19			
White	0.456	0.083	0.167	0.07	0.366	179,725
Black	3.913	0.415	3.203	0.267	0.819	70,533
Hispanic	1.390	0.270	0.889	0.147	0.639	390,588
Asian	0.374	0.131	0.054	0.025	0.144	85,587
Other	0.081	0.217	0.035	0.097	0.433	222,698
Total	1.002	0.221	0.649	0.119	0.647	949,131
			Age 25–44			
White	0.323	0.055	0.064	0.006	0.198	1,098,897
Black	2.638	0.262	1.077	0.077	0.408	307,807
Hispanic	0.698	0.150	0.226	0.042	0.324	1,551,054
Asian	0.133	0.063	0.023	0.009	0.172	419,679
Other	0.037	0.100	0.004	0.013	0.108	839,816
Total	0.554	0.115	0.180	0.027	0.325	4,217,253

Table 9.3   **Personal exposure to violence conditional on neighborhood violence and maternal vigilance**

	Nonviolent neighborhood	Violent neighborhood	All neighborhoods	
			Mother knows	Mother not know
Know gang member	0.16	0.23	0.126	0.18
Family hits	0.18	0.22	0.166	0.233
Witnessed shooting	0.04	0.14	0.048	0.078
Robbed	0.07	0.15	0.09	0.161
Mother often knows whereabouts	0.698	0.609		
Father often knows whereabouts	0.43	0.299		

gun assault, respectively. When we correct for the greater reliance on hospitals for care among some groups, we find that blacks still have the highest rate of assault (42 percent of all injuries are assaults as opposed to 8 percent for whites) but the gap is somewhat smaller. Interestingly, racial differences in assault rates are greater for youths than adults.

We follow the analysis based on aggregate data with an analysis of personal exposure to violence as reported in the LA FANS survey. In table 9.3 we present the probabilities of exposure to different types of violence by neighborhood type (columns [1] to [2]). Personal exposure to violence consists of exposure to violent peers and exposure to street violence. The former is defined as whether the child knows any gang members and the latter is defined in one of two ways—whether the person witnessed a shooting or was robbed in the past year.

A violent neighborhood is defined as one in the top one-third of the distribution of violence as measured by the hospitalization rate for assault and a nonviolent neighborhood is in the bottom third of the distribution of violence. Living in a violent neighborhood increases one's exposure to violence: those in violent neighborhoods are more likely to know a gang member, witness a shooting, or be robbed. However, certain parental characteristics are just as important in determining exposure to violence. For example, whether a child's mother often knows his or her whereabouts is just as predictive of exposure to violence as a violent neighborhood (columns [3] and [4]). In other words, watchful parents appear to be just as protective as safe neighborhoods. A more formal decomposition of the effects of family versus neighborhood on exposure to violence suggests that family characteristics explain more of the variation in exposure to violence than do neighborhood characteristics, and the degree of difference depends on the measure of violence. For example, neighborhood characteristics explain less than 13 percent of the variation in violence as measured by whether the child knows a gang member and family characteristics explain slightly more than 15

Table 9.4   The overlap in violence

	Know gang	Shooting	Robbed
Robbed	16.36	33.85	
Witnessed shooting	20.12		25
Family often hits	28.48	39.39	36.36
Know gang		50	31.03

Note: As an example of how to read this table, 16.36 percent of those who know a gang member were robbed.

percent. For witnessing a shooting, the difference is much greater: neighborhood characteristics explain 12 percent while family characteristics explain 36 percent. For being robbed, family (5 percent) and neighborhood (1.8 percent) characteristics appear to explain much less of the variation.

There is also considerable overlap in the types of violence to which children in this sample are exposed. Of the children who report knowing someone in a gang, 16.36 percent of them were also robbed, 20.12 percent witnessed a shooting, and 28.48 percent reported that family members "often hit." Likewise for those who witness a shooting, 33.85 report being robbed and 50 percent know someone in a gang, and for those who have been robbed, 25 percent witnessed a shooting and 31 percent knew someone in a gang (table 9.4).

In table 9.5 we present evidence that the family characteristics of those exposed to violence are significantly different from those not exposed. The table includes three panels. The first is based on the full sample, the second and third are based on nonviolent and violent neighborhoods, respectively. We find important differences in the family background characteristics of those who are exposed to violence in this sample, even when we control for the underlying level of neighborhood violence as we implicitly do in panels 2 and 3. Those personally exposed to violence are more disadvantaged than those who are not, even conditional on the level of neighborhood violence. The largest differences are observed for those who witnessed a shooting (versus those who did not) and those who know gang members. We find considerably smaller differences for those who were robbed versus those who were not, which may suggest that of the measures of violence considered here, being robbed may be the least reflective of family disadvantage and may include a greater random or exogenous component than the other measures.

These descriptive analyses yield a number of interesting findings with respect to the role of violence in the lives of urban youth. First, violent neighborhoods are correlated with higher exposure to violence, but families living in violent neighborhoods are poorer, less educated, and more likely to be black or Hispanic than those living in nonviolent neighborhoods. Second, violence does not appear to be random. Children exposed to street violence

Table 9.5 Personal exposure to violence and underlying family characteristics

	Witness shooting			Robbed			Peers (know gang)		
	Nonviolent	Violent	Difference	Nonviolent	Violent	Difference	Nonviolent	Violent	Difference
All neighborhoods									
Maternal education	12.32	10.05	2.27	12.26	11.76	0.51	12.31	11.22	1.09
Mother < High school	0.34	0.54	−0.21	0.34	0.39	−0.05	0.35	0.43	−0.09
Black	0.13	0.18	−0.05	0.13	0.16	−0.03	0.12	0.18	−0.05
White	0.29	0.13	0.16	0.28	0.29	−0.01	0.30	0.20	0.10
Hispanic	0.53	0.72	−0.19	0.54	0.54	0.00	0.52	0.66	−0.14
Asian	0.12	0.02	0.10	0.12	0.03	0.09	0.12	0.05	0.08
Male	0.51	0.59	−0.09	0.48	0.77	−0.29	0.54	0.52	0.02
Child age	15.05	15.24	−0.19	15.07	14.95	0.12	13.17	14.46	−1.28
Family earnings (in 1,000s)	46.92	15.59	31.33	46.20	36.35	9.85	45.88	32.87	13.01
Married	0.67	0.56	0.11	0.67	0.67	−0.01	0.69	0.55	0.14
Welfare receipt	0.10	0.33	−0.23	0.10	0.21	−0.11	0.10	0.24	−0.14
SSI receipt	0.04	0.06	−0.02	0.04	0.05	0.00	0.04	0.09	−0.05
Nonviolent neighborhoods									
Maternal education	13.80	10.79	3.01	13.86	12.28	1.58	13.69	12.55	1.13
Mother < High school	0.20	0.47	−0.27	0.19	0.37	−0.18	0.21	0.27	−0.06
Black	0.09	0.07	0.03	0.09	0.10	−0.01	0.08	0.13	−0.04
White	0.45	0.14	0.31	0.43	0.51	−0.09	0.47	0.34	0.13
Hispanic	0.43	0.79	−0.36	0.46	0.36	0.10	0.40	0.62	−0.23

Asian	0.15	0.00	0.15	0.16	0.00	0.16	0.13	0.10	0.03
Male	0.52	0.50	0.03	0.49	0.80	-0.31	0.56	0.53	0.03
Child age	15.03	15.06	-0.03	15.07	14.72	0.35	13.29	13.98	-0.70
Family earnings (in 1,000s)	61.73	16.50	45.23	61.03	50.35	10.68	61.90	41.70	20.20
Married	0.71	0.78	-0.07	0.71	0.78	-.07	0.77	0.54	0.23
Welfare receipt	0.03	0.41	-0.38	0.04	0.13	-0.09	0.04	0.19	-0.15
SSI receipt	0.03	0.03	0.00	0.03	0.04	-0.01	0.03	0.07	-0.05
Violent neighborhoods									
Maternal education	9.29	9.30	-0.01	9.06	10.47	-1.42	9.52	9.87	-0.35
Mother < High school	0.61	0.60	0.01	0.64	0.43	0.21	0.60	0.59	0.01
Black	0.20	0.31	-0.10	0.20	0.29	-0.09	0.19	0.27	-0.08
White	0.04	0.02	0.01	0.04	0.01	0.03	0.05	0.02	0.03
Hispanic	0.76	0.69	0.07	0.75	0.75	0.00	0.77	0.71	0.07
Asian	0.01	0.01	0.00	0.01	0.00	0.00	0.02	0.00	0.02
Male	0.48	0.67	-0.19	0.43	0.80	-0.36	0.53	0.53	0.00
Child age	14.92	15.47	-0.55	15.04	14.71	0.33	12.77	14.72	-1.95
Family earnings (in 1,000s)	25.53	12.21	13.32	24.43	21.56	2.87	23.41	19.04	4.37
Married	0.61	0.40	0.22	0.58	0.63	-0.05	0.62	0.47	0.15
Welfare receipt	0.17	0.36	-0.19	0.18	0.24	-0.06	0.17	0.38	-0.21
SSI receipt	0.04	0.06	-0.02	0.04	0.04	0.00	0.02	0.07	-0.05

(shootings and robbery) often associate with violent peers. In addition, even within violent neighborhoods, only some children report personal exposure to violence and those who do are more disadvantaged than those who do not. Together this preliminary evidence suggests that other forms of disadvantage, not simply neighborhood violence, may be responsible for the negative child outcomes associated with exposure to violence.

In order to determine whether it is exposure to violence itself or other characteristics that are correlated with violence and child outcomes, we must control for the underlying level of disadvantage as well as possible. For this we turn to regression analysis in the next section.

9.6   Does Exposure to Neighborhood Violence Affect Child Outcomes?

We pursue two empirical estimation strategies in order to determine whether it is exposure to violence that negatively affects child well-being or whether other types of disadvantage (income, educational, racial) may be correlated with violence that affect child outcomes. In the first, we conduct ordinary least squares (OLS) regression analysis of the impact of violence on child outcomes with and without controlling for other types of disadvantage. The first equation estimated is:

(1) $Y = \beta_0 + \beta_1 \text{Violence} + \varepsilon,$

where Y is cognitive test scores for reading comprehension and math. The cognitive test scores are a percentile (0 to 100), normed against other children of the same age and sex. We focus on cognitive test scores because they are objective measures of child cognitive achievement that have been shown to significantly affect a child's future economic success (Currie and Thomas 2001; Zax and Rees 2001; Murname, Levy, and Willett 2005). Previous studies of the impact of violence on child outcomes have examined cognitive scores, GPAs, psychological evaluations, and the Behavior Problems Index (BPI). We also look at the impact of violence on the BPI. However, both GPA and BPI have strong subjective components that can bias these measures, whereas cognitive test scores suffer no such bias.

Violence in equation (1) is one of five measures of violence. The first and second are measures of neighborhood violence—the rate of assaults among those aged fifteen to nineteen (or the ratio, as defined previously) in the neighborhood (zip code) in which the child lives and the level of violent crime in the census tract.[10] The third is peer violence, which is defined as whether the child knows any gang members. The fourth and fifth measures

---

10. The census tract of children in the LA FANS is known and matched to the corresponding zip code. Of the eighty-nine census tracts in the LA FANS, fifty-eight matched to only one zip code and thirty-one matched to two or three zip codes. For children in census tracts with more than one zip code, the average assault rate across all zip codes that comprise the census tract was used.

of violence in equation (1) are defined in one of two ways—whether the person witnessed a shooting or was robbed in the past year. The error term ε includes all child, family, and neighborhood characteristics not included in the regression that influence child outcomes. Finally, we redefine neighborhood violence as the natural log of the violent crime rate in the census tract.

In the top panel of table 9.6 are regression estimates of the impact of violence (neighborhood, peer violence, and street violence) on child outcomes without any additional controls (equation [1]). It appears that neighborhood violence, as measured by the rate of hospitalizations for assaults, has a large negative and significant impact on both reading and math test scores (columns [1] and [2]). If the level of violence in one's neighborhood were to increase by one standard deviation (13 assaults per 10,000), then reading and math scores would decline by 7 and 6 points, respectively (or 23 and 22 percent of a standard deviation). Violent neighborhoods are also associated with both internalizing and externalizing behavioral problems (columns [3] and [4]). Internalizing behavioral problems refer to all problems that are directed inwardly. They include low or restricted activity levels, being shy, timid and unassertive, withdrawing from social situations, and acting in a fearful manner. The BPI (internalizing index) ranges from zero to 20, with a mean and standard deviation of 3. Externalizing behavioral problems include such behaviors as aggression, delinquency, and hyperactivity. The BPI externalizing index ranges from zero to 31, with a mean and standard deviation of 6. A standard deviation increase in neighborhood violence is associated with a half-point increase in both the internalizing and externalizing BPI, or 17 and 8 percent of a standard deviation increase, respectively.

Personal exposure to violence is also associated with worse test scores and greater behavioral problems. Association with violent peers (columns [5] and [6]) results in an 11 and 16 point drop in reading and math scores, respectively (37 and 54 percent of a standard deviation), and a 1 point and 3 point increase in internalizing and externalizing behavioral problems, respectively (30 percent and 50 percent of a standard deviation). Witnessing a shooting is associated with 16 and 18 point drops in test scores (49 and 61 percent of a standard deviation), and with a 45 and 55 percent standard deviation increase in internalizing and externalizing behavioral problems. Finally, being robbed in the past year is associated with 10 and 6 point drops (35 and 23 percent of a standard deviation, respectively) in reading and math, and a small insignificant increase in internalizing behaviors and a small (15 percent of a standard deviation), but significant increase in externalizing behaviors.

However, these estimates may be biased. Recall that in equation (1) the error term ε includes all child, family, and neighborhood characteristics not included in the regression that influence child outcomes. These include all

Table 9.6   Impact of violence on child outcomes—Zip code level

	Reading	Math	BPI (int)	BPI (ext)
No controls				
Assault rate in zip code	−4,903.18 [732.222]	−4,676.34 [704.495]	367.812 [76.838]	376.07 [159.347]
Observations	827	827	811	794
R^2	0.05	0.05	0.03	0.01
Know someone in a gang	−10.636 [2.541]	−15.706 [2.411]	0.992 [0.271]	2.94 [0.552]
Observations	819	819	803	786
R^2	0.05	0.05	0.02	0.03
Witnessed shooting last year	−15.65 [4.302]	−18.144 [4.122]	1.359 [0.451]	3.365 [0.926]
Observations	827	827	811	794
R^2	0.02	0.02	0.01	0.02
Robbed last year	−10.556 [3.181]	−7.33 [3.068]	0.495 [0.330]	1.413 [0.676]
Observations	826	826	810	793
R^2	0.01	0.01	0	0.01
Neighborhood (zip code) controls				
Assault rate in zip code	−332.286 [1,105.978]	732.312 [1,057.376]	191.221 [120.283]	61.696 [250.346]
Observations	827	827	811	794
R^2	0.13	0.14	0.05	0.02
Know someone in a gang	−7.168 [2.430]	−12.124 [2.300]	0.772 [0.269]	2.727 [0.556]
Observations	819	819	803	786
R^2	0.14	0.17	0.06	0.05
Witnessed shooting last year	−10.361 [4.094]	−12.867 [3.905]	0.932 [0.448]	2.907 [0.933]
Observations	827	827	811	794
R^2	0.14	0.15	0.06	0.03
Robbed last year	−9.478 [3.000]	−6.075 [2.877]	0.45 [0.325]	1.366 [0.677]
Observations	826	826	810	793
R^2	0.14	0.14	0.05	0.03

Neighborhood (zip code) and family controls

Assault rate in zip code	131.784 [1,139.301]	1,023.61 [1,054.268]	266.94 [124.276]	171.19 [266.645]
Know someone in a gang	-3.406 [2.474]	-7.705 [2.280]	0.446 [0.274]	2.232 [0.584]
Witnessed shooting last year	-3.029 [4.136]	-6.247 [3.824]	0.757 [0.454]	2.066 [0.978]
Robbed last year	-10.715 [3.121]	-6.074 [2.905]	0.412 [0.340]	0.665 [0.732]
Observations	740	740	725	708
R^2	0.27	0.32	0.15	0.12
Observations	732	732	717	700
R^2	0.27	0.33	0.14	0.14
Observations	740	740	725	708
R^2	0.27	0.32	0.14	0.12
Observations	739	739	724	707
R^2	0.28	0.32	0.14	0.12

Neighborhood (zip code) fixed effects and family controls

Know someone in a gang	-2.473 [2.633]	-5.802 [2.365]	0.508 [0.274]	2.274 [0.581]
Witnessed shooting last year	-3.743 [4.354]	-5.938 [3.912]	0.862 [0.455]	2.22 [0.975]
Robbed last year	-10.233 [3.184]	-5.412 [2.879]	0.341 [0.340]	0.595 [0.727]
Observations	732	732	717	700
R^2	0.35	0.44	0.13	0.13
Observations	740	740	725	708
R^2	0.35	0.43	0.13	0.12
Observations	739	739	724	707
R^2	0.36	0.43	0.12	0.11

other types of disadvantage (racial, income, etc.). If these omitted variables are correlated with violence (i.e., if otherwise disadvantaged children are also exposed to more violence), then our estimate of β_1 will suffer from omitted variable bias—capturing not only the impact of violence on child outcomes, but also other types of disadvantage that can negatively affect child outcomes independent of violence. The bias in most cases will likely be upward if violence and disadvantage are positively correlated and child outcomes are negatively correlated with disadvantage. An upward bias means that our estimate of β_1 will be an overestimate of the true impact of violence on child well-being. It is possible, however, for our estimate of β_1 to be an underestimate of the impact of violence on child outcomes if either disadvantage is positively correlated with child outcomes and exposure to violence or disadvantage is negatively correlated with both child outcomes and exposure to violence. There is evidence, for example, that poor and minority families underreport their children's behavioral problems so that disadvantage and child outcomes are positively correlated for behavioral problems (Lambert et al. 1992; McMiller and Weisz 1996). It might also be the case that children in the most disadvantaged families are less likely to report exposure to violence if it might implicate them in criminal activity (such as knowing a gang member).

To correct for this bias, we include many detailed controls for locational, racial, income, and parental education disadvantage. As we control for these variables, the estimate of β_1 should decrease in magnitude. The second regression is:

(2) $Y = \beta_0 + \beta_1 \text{Violence} + \beta_2 \textbf{Child} + \beta_3 \textbf{Family} + \beta_4 \textbf{Neighborhood} + \varepsilon,$

where **Child** refers to a vector of child characteristics (sex, age, race, and number of siblings) and **Family** refers to a vector of family characteristics that include income and parental education disadvantage (maternal education, maternal age, marital status, family earnings, and welfare receipt). **Neighborhood** refers to a vector of neighborhood characteristics (share receiving welfare, share below poverty, share with less than a high school degree, the unemployment rate, and the share black) defined at the neighborhood level (either the zip code or the census tract, depending on the analysis) and based on data from the 2000 Census.

Estimates of equation (2) are presented in panel 2 of table 9.6. The following neighborhood (zip code level) controls are included: share on welfare, share below poverty, share with less than a high school degree, the unemployment rate, and the share black. When we include these controls for other neighborhood characteristics, many of the previous estimates of the impact of violence on child outcomes fall considerably. The impact of neighborhood violence falls by more than 80 percent for math and reading scores and is no longer significant. The impact of neighborhood violence on behavioral problems also falls and is no longer statistically significantly different from zero. The impact of peer violence and witnessing a shooting on cognitive test scores and behavioral problems both fall by approximately 30 percent. The impact of being robbed, however, falls the least once we control for neighborhood characteristics, falling only between 10 and 15 percent.

In the third panel, we include controls for neighborhood and family characteristics. When we do, the impact of peer violence on cognitive performance and behavioral problems falls further still and remains significant for externalizing behavioral problems and math scores only. The impact of witnessing a shooting on all but externalizing behavioral problems falls and is no longer statistically significantly different from zero. Interestingly, the impact of being robbed in the past year on child scores changes very little when we control for family characteristics and is still significantly negatively associated with child test scores in reading and math.

In table 9.7 we present estimated regression coefficients for the full set of family and neighborhood controls from the previous regression. Of the neighborhood characteristics included, only the share of adults with less than a high school degree appears to largely, significantly, and negatively affect child outcomes. However, it could be that we are simply not including the most important neighborhood characteristics because they are intangible or unobservable to the researcher, a point to which we return. As for personal or family characteristics, race (being black or Hispanic), maternal education, family earnings, and welfare receipt have the largest effects on child outcomes.

But these estimates are still subject to the criticism that many important forms of neighborhood disadvantage are not captured in the data. If true, then our estimates of β_1 may still be biased. To address this, we include neighborhood fixed effects. The inclusion of fixed effects defined at the neighborhood level essentially limits our analysis to a comparison of children who have been exposed to violence with children who have not been exposed and reside in the same neighborhood. In so doing, we implicitly control for all sources of neighborhood disadvantage, observed or unobserved, that might be correlated with exposure to violence and could bias our results.

Panel 4 includes family controls and neighborhood (zip code) fixed effects. By including zip code fixed effects we are able to isolate the impact of exposure to violence separate from other forms of neighborhood disadvantage. When we do, the impact of violent peers on reading scores falls further still, while the impact on math score also falls but is still significant (5.8 points), as does the impact on externalizing behavioral problems. Again, the inclusion of these controls does not affect the impact of being robbed on child test scores, which is still negative and significant (10.2 and 5.4 points on reading and math, respectively) and the null effect on behavioral problems remains.

We reestimate the regressions presented in table 9.6, redefining the neighborhood at the census tract and the measure of neighborhood violence as

Table 9.7 Impact of violence on child outcomes—Full set of neighborhood, family, and individual controls

	Reading	Math	BPI (int)	BPI (ext)	Reading	Math	BPI (int)	BPI (ext)	Reading	Math	BPI (int)	BPI (ext)	Reading	Math	BPI (int)	BPI (ext)
Assault rate in neighborhood	131.784 [1,139.301]	1,023.61 [1,054.268]	266.94 [124.276]	171.19 [266.645]												
Know someone in a gang					-3.406 [2.474]	-7.705 [2.280]	0.446 [0.274]	2.232 [0.584]								
Witnessed shooting last year									-3.029 [4.136]	-6.247 [3.824]	0.757 [0.454]	2.066 [0.978]				
Robbed last year													-10.715 [3.121]	-6.074 [2.905]	0.412 [0.340]	0.665 [0.732]
Community characteristics																
Share on welfare	29.569 [16.179]	-7.224 [14.972]	-2.393 [1.760]	-1.057 [3.786]	29.371 [16.334]	-4.783 [15.050]	-2.381 [1.781]	-1.496 [3.789]	29.706 [16.171]	-6.737 [14.952]	-2.353 [1.762]	-1.015 [3.774]	30.458 [16.059]	-6.589 [14.946]	-2.347 [1.766]	-1.031 [3.787]
Share below poverty	14.865 [24.787]	-9.062 [22.937]	3.965 [2.691]	9.208 [5.801]	16.792 [23.037]	4.549 [21.225]	5.866 [2.513]	9.446 [5.377]	17.397 [22.984]	2.408 [21.251]	5.792 [2.507]	9.692 [5.401]	11.222 [22.791]	-3.539 [21.211]	6.32 [2.509]	10.917 [5.417]
Share < high school	-36.401 [26.303]	-61.485 [24.340]	1.079 [2.884]	4.361 [6.206]	-33.688 [25.940]	-56.727 [23.899]	2.252 [2.853]	5.506 [6.068]	-36.183 [25.802]	-57.676 [23.856]	2.337 [2.834]	5.266 [6.069]	-34.957 [25.614]	-56.443 [23.839]	2.242 [2.839]	5.071 [6.089]
Unemployment rate	-1.061 [0.676]	0.583 [0.626]	-0.069 [0.072]	-0.286 [0.156]	-1.092 [0.676]	0.455 [0.622]	-0.079 [0.072]	-0.291 [0.155]	-1.093 [0.675]	0.481 [0.624]	-0.074 [0.072]	-0.279 [0.155]	-0.97 [0.670]	0.6 [0.624]	-0.084 [0.072]	-0.301 [0.156]
Share black	-0.207 [9.829]	-5.403 [9.096]	-0.478 [1.050]	1.205 [2.252]	1.091 [9.385]	-2.358 [8.647]	0.129 [1.009]	1.536 [2.139]	0.176 [9.353]	-2.625 [8.648]	0.194 [1.004]	1.625 [2.143]	3.06 [9.325]	-1.096 [8.679]	0.097 [1.009]	1.473 [2.159]
Family characteristics																
Maternal education	1.353 [0.316]	1.336 [0.293]	-0.028 [0.035]	-0.046 [0.075]	1.381 [0.318]	1.383 [0.293]	-0.032 [0.035]	-0.06 [0.075]	1.351 [0.316]	1.331 [0.292]	-0.027 [0.035]	-0.046 [0.075]	1.322 [0.314]	1.315 [0.292]	-0.026 [0.035]	-0.043 [0.075]
Black	1.198 [6.246]	2.034 [5.779]	-0.198 [0.676]	-0.674 [1.491]	0.905 [6.260]	1.722 [5.767]	-0.1 [0.679]	-0.584 [1.481]	1.23 [6.242]	2.18 [5.771]	-0.162 [0.676]	-0.661 [1.486]	0.237 [6.205]	1.565 [5.775]	-0.117 [0.678]	-0.574 [1.493]
Hispanic	-4.928 [5.793]	0.293 [5.361]	0.731 [0.626]	-0.191 [1.382]	-4.882 [5.762]	0.191 [5.309]	0.547 [0.624]	-0.522 [1.365]	-4.956 [5.750]	-0.22 [5.317]	0.556 [0.622]	-0.318 [1.369]	-6.401 [5.723]	-1.127 [5.327]	0.621 [0.625]	-0.197 [1.377]

	(1)	(2)	(3)	(4)	(5)	(6)	(7)	(8)	(9)	(10)	(11)	(12)	(13)	(14)	(15)	(16)
White	7.292	8.636	0.112	1.031	6.822	7.304	-0.032	1.001	7.21	7.947	-0.084	0.919	6.436	7.474	-0.054	0.967
	[6.025]	[5.575]	[0.652]	[1.441]	[5.983]	[5.513]	[0.649]	[1.419]	[5.971]	[5.520]	[0.646]	[1.425]	[5.933]	[5.521]	[0.648]	[1.431]
Asian	7.746	15.628	0.241	-1.248	7.645	14.532	0.103	-1.28	7.666	15.111	0.106	-1.31	5.82	14.083	0.172	-1.21
	[6.221]	[5.757]	[0.673]	[1.478]	[6.212]	[5.723]	[0.673]	[1.462]	[6.196]	[5.729]	[0.670]	[1.468]	[6.176]	[5.748]	[0.674]	[1.479]
Married	-1.976	1.084	-0.263	-0.747	-2.142	0.577	-0.253	-0.625	-1.92	1.177	-0.275	-0.792	-1.587	1.298	-0.279	-0.774
	[2.317]	[2.144]	[0.252]	[0.548]	[2.326]	[2.143]	[0.254]	[0.546]	[2.317]	[2.143]	[0.253]	[0.547]	[2.303]	[2.143]	[0.254]	[0.549]
Family earnings in 1,000s	0.061	0.098	-0.005	-0.009	0.061	0.099	-0.005	-0.009	0.059	0.094	-0.005	-0.008	0.056	0.094	-0.005	-0.009
	[0.027]	[0.025]	[0.003]	[0.006]	[0.027]	[0.025]	[0.003]	[0.006]	[0.027]	[0.025]	[0.003]	[0.006]	[0.027]	[0.025]	[0.003]	[0.006]
Welfare participation	-5.973	-5.92	0.929	3.753	-5.528	-5.222	0.827	3.421	-5.661	-5.441	0.799	3.472	-5.186	-5.724	0.861	3.684
	[3.333]	[3.084]	[0.370]	[0.796]	[3.343]	[3.080]	[0.373]	[0.794]	[3.354]	[3.102]	[0.374]	[0.803]	[3.308]	[3.079]	[0.372]	[0.798]
SSI receipt	-15.245	-15.36	-1.329	-4.084	-14.898	-14.693	-1.396	-4.323	-15.395	-15.772	-1.295	-4.011	-15.678	-15.473	-1.328	-4.099
	[4.781]	[4.424]	[0.544]	[1.243]	[4.793]	[4.416]	[0.548]	[1.236]	[4.780]	[4.420]	[0.544]	[1.240]	[4.775]	[4.444]	[0.549]	[1.255]
Maternal age	0.257	0.181	-0.006	-0.004	0.245	0.167	-0.003	-0.003	0.257	0.184	-0.004	-0.003	0.218	0.161	-0.003	0
	[0.140]	[0.130]	[0.016]	[0.035]	[0.141]	[0.130]	[0.016]	[0.035]	[0.140]	[0.129]	[0.016]	[0.035]	[0.139]	[0.130]	[0.016]	[0.035]
Child age 10–12	-10.356	24.198	-2.959	-3.509	-13.296	18.761	-2.858	-3.154	-10.064	25.621	-2.969	-3.549	-7.99	26.591	-3.049	-3.658
	[22.855]	[21.150]	[1.014]	[2.167]	[22.940]	[21.136]	[1.019]	[2.154]	[22.814]	[21.094]	[1.016]	[2.160]	[22.660]	[21.090]	[1.020]	[2.174]
Child age 13–15	-12.482	21.907	-2.852	-4.058	-14.797	17.417	-2.825	-3.961	-12.097	23.463	-2.905	-4.187	-10.88	23.814	-2.932	-4.177
	[22.768]	[21.069]	[0.985]	[2.104]	[22.835]	[21.039]	[0.989]	[2.090]	[22.733]	[21.019]	[0.987]	[2.099]	[22.573]	[21.009]	[0.990]	[2.109]
Child age 16–18	-13.022	19.273	-3.61	-5.212	-15.231	14.624	-3.623	-5.115	-12.694	20.691	-3.659	-5.3	-11.506	21.079	-3.698	-5.331
	[22.770]	[21.071]	[0.990]	[2.117]	[22.841]	[21.044]	[0.994]	[2.102]	[22.736]	[21.021]	[0.991]	[2.111]	[22.576]	[21.011]	[0.994]	[2.121]
Male	-1.745	5.991	-0.343	0.261	-1.895	5.803	-0.314	0.343	-1.655	6.207	-0.363	0.21	-0.456	6.785	-0.395	0.179
	[1.893]	[1.752]	[0.208]	[0.451]	[1.904]	[1.755]	[0.210]	[0.450]	[1.895]	[1.753]	[0.209]	[0.450]	[1.917]	[1.784]	[0.213]	[0.460]
Number of siblings	0.286	1.723	-0.036	0.165	0.219	1.656	-0.022	0.178	0.299	1.767	-0.03	0.157	0.259	1.735	-0.025	0.173
	[0.832]	[0.770]	[0.093]	[0.203]	[0.834]	[0.768]	[0.094]	[0.201]	[0.831]	[0.768]	[0.093]	[0.202]	[0.825]	[0.768]	[0.094]	[0.202]
Observations	740	740	725	708	732	732	717	700	740	740	725	708	739	739	724	707
R^2	0.27	0.32	0.15	0.12	0.27	0.33	0.14	0.14	0.27	0.32	0.14	0.12	0.28	0.32	0.14	0.12

Note: Standard errors in brackets.

the nature log of the violent crime rate. We do this because, as noted previously, the crime rate is available at a considerably smaller area (census tract) than the zip code that may better approximate a neighborhood. Note that since the violent crime data at the level for the census tract is available only for Los Angeles City (and not all of Los Angeles County), the sample size available for these analyses is smaller (approximately 500 versus 800). When we exclude all controls (top panel of table 9.8) we see that the violent crime rate has a negative and significant impact on all child outcomes, though the effect is not very large. For example, a 100 percent drop in violent crime would raise reading scores by 16 points (slightly more than a standard deviation). As we include neighborhood and family controls (second and third panels), the point estimates decrease considerably and lose significance, just as we observed for the zip code-level regressions. The remaining columns (columns [4] through [15]) present estimates of the impact of personal exposure to violence on child outcomes with controls for neighborhood characteristics defined at the smaller geographic level (census tract). In the last panel, we include neighborhood (census tract) fixed effects. In general, the results are very similar to those in which neighborhood is defined at the larger level of the zip code.

The results from the previous regressions suggest that once we control for other forms of disadvantage, violent neighborhoods, violent peers, and witnessing a shooting do not significantly negatively affect child cognitive achievement or internalizing behavioral problems—suggesting that underlying sources of disadvantage associated with both exposure to violence and child outcomes are likely responsible for the poor outcomes observed. They do seem to be correlated with externalizing behavior problems. The fact that the estimated impact of these types of violence on child outcomes falls as more child, family, and neighborhood controls are included underscores the importance of controlling for underlying disadvantage that may be correlated with both exposure to violence and child outcomes to produce unbiased estimates.

In contrast, the negative impact of one measure of violence (being robbed in the past year) on child test scores remains once we control for neighborhood and family characteristics, though there do not appear to be any significant effects on behavioral problems. It could be that we are not adequately controlling for differences across families within neighborhoods that are correlated with both exposure to violence and poor child outcomes. Recall from table 9.5 that the observed family characteristics of those who were robbed were very different from those who were not, even when limiting the comparison to families in violent neighborhoods. If families differ in observed ways, they may also differ in unobserved ways for which we cannot control and that may continue to bias our estimates. An important example may be domestic violence—as noted previously, children in disadvantaged families are more likely to witness domestic violence, which may also be correlated with exposure to street violence. Because the LA FANS does not

Table 9.8   Impact of violence on child outcomes—census tract level

	Reading	Math	BPI (int)	BPI (ext)
No controls				
ln (violent crime in census tract)	−16.333 [1.486]	−14.961 [1.543]	1.244 [0.196]	1.661 [0.345]
Know someone in a gang				
Witnessed shooting last year				
Robbed last year				
Observations	528	528	509	503
R²	0.19	0.2	0.08	0.05
Neighborhood (census tract) controls				
ln (violent crime in census tract)	−11.132 [2.501]	−11.924 [2.617]	0.478 [0.333]	0.745 [0.600]
Observations	528	528	509	503
R²	0.22	0.21	0.11	0.06
Know someone in a gang	−6.125 [2.417]	−11.17 [2.265]	0.671 [0.263]	2.732 [0.562]
Observations	819	819	788	771
R²	0.16	0.2	0.1	0.07
Witnessed shooting last year	−7.88 [4.102]	−11.967 [3.868]	0.84 [0.439]	2.746 [0.946]
Observations	827	827	796	779
R²	0.16	0.19	0.1	0.05
Robbed last year	−8.908 [3.013]	−8.048 [2.852]	0.44 [0.320]	1.11 [0.690]
Observations	826	826	795	778
R²	0.16	0.19	0.09	0.04

(continued)

Table 9.8 (continued)

	Reading	Math	BPI (int)	BPI (ext)	Reading	Math	BPI (int)	BPI (ext)	Reading	Math	BPI (int)	BPI (ext)
ln (violent crime in census tract)	-3.525 [2.871]	-4.532 [2.947]	0.07 [0.387]	1.151 [0.720]								
Neighborhood (census tract) and family controls												
Know someone in a gang	-3.603 [2.445]	-7.985 [2.248]	0.484 [0.273]	2.339 [0.586]								
Witnessed shooting last year					-3.058 [4.123]	-6.313 [3.806]	0.863 [0.452]	2.098 [0.981]				
Robbed last year									-10.197 [3.096]	-5.727 [2.875]	0.243 [0.337]	0.496 [0.729]
Observations	472	472	457	450	732	732	705	688	739	739	712	695
R^2	0.31	0.31	0.19	0.13	0.26	0.32	0.12	0.13	0.27	0.32	0.12	0.11
Neighborhood (census tract) fixed effects and family controls												
Know someone in a gang	-2.964 [2.657]	-6.049 [2.379]	0.458 [0.292]	2.047 [0.636]								
Witnessed shooting last year					-4.294 [4.423]	-6.242 [3.961]	0.503 [0.480]	2.067 [1.041]				
Robbed last year									-10.285 [3.217]	-5.4 [2.899]	0.327 [0.347]	0.458 [0.754]
Observations	732	732	705	688	740	740	713	696	739	739	712	695
R^2	0.33	0.42	0.23	0.23	0.33	0.42	0.22	0.22	0.34	0.42	0.22	0.22

Note: Standard errors in brackets.

contain credible measures of domestic violence, we are not able to control for this directly.

To address this concern, we present estimates of the impact of exposure to violence on child outcomes including family fixed effects in table 9.9. By including family fixed effects we limit our analysis to a comparison to children who have been exposed to violence with their siblings who have not been exposed, thereby implicitly controlling for all measures of family disadvantage, both observed and unobserved, that may be correlated with worse child outcomes and exposure to violence. This would include, for example, exposure to domestic violence. An analysis that includes family fixed effects must, by definition, include only those children in families with at least two children included in the LA FANS survey. This limits our sample to roughly 575 children in the case of violent peers, and 375 for the two other measures of exposure to violence (witness a shooting or being robbed last year). Because the sample has changed, for purposes of comparison in the top panel of table 9.9 we present OLS estimates of the impact of exposure to violence on child outcomes including family controls and neighborhood fixed effects (but not family fixed effects), and in the bottom panel we include family fixed effects. When we include family fixed effects in the last panel the large and significant effects of being robbed on reading and math scores are close to zero and no longer significant. However, those who know someone in a gang still have lower reading scores (8 points or 60 percent of a standard deviation). One concern over interpreting this latter estimate as causal, however, is that those of lower cognitive ability may choose to associate with violent appears. While the family fixed effect estimate does partially address this concern because cognitive ability within families is highly correlated (and much more so than across families), differences in cognitive ability across siblings still exist and may drive this relationship.

Interestingly, the impact of all three measures of violence on internalizing behavioral problems increases and becomes borderline significant when family fixed effects are included. The point estimates of 1.23, 1.99, and 1.50 suggest that exposure to violence increases the BPI by half a standard deviation. This is an interesting finding that may be explained by the fact that the BPI is based on parent reports and parents in disadvantaged families may be less likely to report behavior as problematic. For example, in the LA FANS, the average internalizing BPI of black children is 2.84 compared with 3.17 for nonblack children (the numbers are 6.1 and 7.7 for the externalizing BPI score). This is consistent with the findings of others (see Spencer et al. 2005; Ng 2006) based on other larger data sets. As such, when we limit our comparison to that between siblings within the same family, we eliminate the family-based reporting bias that can bias downwards our estimates of the impact of exposure to violence on children's internalizing behavioral problems.

Table 9.9 Impact of violence on child outcomes, family fixed effects

	Reading	Math	BPI (Int)	BPI (Ext)	Reading	Math	BPI (Int)	BPI (Ext)	Reading	Math	BPI (Int)	BPI (Ext)
	Family controls and neighborhood fixed effects											
Know someone in a gang	-2.397 [2.954]	-7.623 [2.996]	1.112 [0.382]	2.569 [0.712]								
Witnessed shooting last year					-6.681 [6.252]	-12.147 [5.426]	-0.679 [0.747]	1.741 [1.413]				
Robbed last year									-11.244 [4.606]	-6.157 [4.057]	0.226 [0.550]	-0.043 [1.044]
Observations	577	576	570	561	384	384	381	371	384	384	380	370
R^2	0.47	0.51	0.31	0.43	0.51	0.62	0.33	0.49	0.52	0.62	0.33	0.49
	Family fixed effects											
Know someone in a gang	-4.601 [3.666]	-8.259 [3.913]	1.23 [0.452]	0.723 [1.153]								
Witnessed shooting last year					7.23 [11.103]	-3.892 [9.428]	1.991 [1.192]	4.735 [2.486]				
Robbed last year									-1.776 [7.048]	1.436 [5.965]	1.497 [0.770]	-1.165 [1.556]
Observations	577	576	570	561	384	384	381	371	384	384	380	370
R^2	0.77	0.79	0.78	0.81	0.88	0.91	0.86	0.88	0.87	0.91	0.86	0.88

Note: Standard errors in brackets.

9.7   Conclusion

Together these results suggest that care should be taken in interpreting estimates of the impact of exposure to neighborhood violence on child outcomes. Previous work has found that exposure to violence is associated with many negative child outcomes (both cognitive and behavioral) but much of this work, while acknowledging that children exposed to violence are often more disadvantaged in other ways, rarely controls for such differences. Without controlling for such differences estimates of the impact of exposure to violence on child outcomes are likely biased—reflecting the impact of both exposure to violence and underlying neighborhood and family disadvantage on child outcomes. In the work presented here we employ econometric strategies to control for such differences by including multiple measures of neighborhood and family disadvantage as covariates. We also include neighborhood and family fixed effects, which control for both observed and unobserved characteristics of a child's neighborhood and family that might bias estimates of the impact of violence on child outcomes.

Once we control for underlying disadvantage, the impact of violence declines for some child outcomes, suggesting that underlying disadvantage does explain some of the negative outcomes observed, but not all. In fact, for internalizing behavior problems, controlling for underlying differences across families actually tends to increase the impact of all three measures violence. And it is still the case that even when we control for observed and unobserved underlying disadvantage, having violent peers (knowing a gang member) is negatively correlated with cognitive test scores.

These findings have implications for public policies regarding the reduction of violence as well as housing for the poor. In particular, the evidence presented here suggests that reducing neighborhood violence via enhanced law enforcement policies without reducing other sources of neighborhood disadvantage may have a limited impact on the youth outcomes examined here. Housing policies, and in particular, housing subsidies that enable low-income families to move to less disadvantaged neighborhoods, may be more effective in this regard, especially if they improve the personal circumstances (i.e., employment and income) of the target families. In this respect, policies aimed directly at lessening the income and educational disadvantages of families may prove the most effective.

References

Aizer, A. 2007. Wages, violence and health in the household. NBER Working Paper no. 13494. Cambridge, MA: National Bureau of Economic Research, October.
Bell, C. C., and E. J. Jenkins. 1993. Community violence and children on the southside of Chicago. *Psychiatry* 56:46–54.

Boney-McCoy, S., and D. Finkelhor. 1996. Is youth victimization related to trauma symptoms and depression after controlling for prior symptoms and family relationships? A longitudinal, prospective study. *Journal of Consulting and Clinical Psychology* 64:1406–16.

Cooley-Quille, M. R., S. M. Turner, and D.C. Beidel. 1995. Emotional impact of children's exposure to community violence: A preliminary study. *The American Academy of Child and Adolescent Psychiatry* 34 (10): 1362–68.

Currie, J., and E. Tekin. 2006. Does child abuse cause crime? NBER Working Paper no. 12171. Cambridge, MA: National Bureau of Economic Research, April.

Currie, J., and D. Thomas. 2001. Early test scores, school quality and SES: Long-run effects on wages and employment outcomes. *Research in Labour Economics* 20:103–32.

Fonagy, P., M. Target, M. Steele, and H. Steele. 1997. The development of violence and crime as it relates to security of attachment. In *Children in a violent society,* ed. J. D. Osofsky, 150–77. New York: Guilford Press.

Gorman-Smith, D., and P. Tolan. 1998. The role of exposure to community violence and developmental problems among inner-city youth. *Development and Psychopathology* 10:99–114.

Grogger, J. 1998. Local violence and educational attainment. *Journal of Human Resources* 32 (4): 659–82.

———. 2002. The effects of civil gang injunctions on reported violent crime: Evidence from Los Angeles county. *Journal of Law and Economics* 45 (1): 69–90.

Hill, H. M., and L. P. Jones. Children's and parents' perceptions of children's exposure to violence in urban neighborhoods. *Journal of the National Medical Association* 89 (4): 270–76.

Jenkins, E. J. 1995. Violence exposure, psychological distress and risk behaviors in a sample of inner-city youth. In *Trends, risks, and interventions: Proceedings of the Third Annual Spring Symposium of the Homicide Working Group,* ed. R. Block and C. Block, 287–98. Washington, D.C.: U.S. Department of Justice.

Kling, J., and J. Liebman. 2005. Experimental analysis of neighborhood effects on youth. Industrial Relations Section Princeton University Working Paper no. 483.

Kling, J., J. Liebman, and L. Katz. 2005. Bullets don't got no name: Consequences of fear in the ghetto. In *Discovering successful pathways in children's development: Mixed methods in the study of childhood and family life,* ed. T. S. Weisner, 243–82. Chicago: University of Chicago Press.

Lambert, M., J. Weisz, F. Knight, M. Desrosiers, K. Overly, and C. Thesiger. 1992. Jamaican and American adult perspectives on child psychopathology: Further exploration of the threshold model. *Journal of Consulting Clinical Psychology* 60 (1): 146–49.

Loeber, R., P. Wung, K. Keenan, B. Giroux, and M. Stouthamer. 1993. Developmental pathways in disruptive child behavior. *Development and Psychopathology* 5:101–33.

Ludwig, J., G. J. Duncan, and P. Hirschfield. 2001. Urban poverty and juvenile crime: Evidence from a randomized housing-mobility experiment. *Quarterly Journal of Economics* 116 (2): 655–80.

Ludwig, J., and J. Kling. 2007. Is crime contagious? *Journal of Law and Economics* 50 (3): 491–518.

McMiller, W., and J. Weisz. 1996. Help-seeking preceding mental health clinic intake among African-American, Latino, and Caucasian youths. *Journal of the American Academy of Child and Adolescent Psychiatry* 35 (8): 1086–94.

Murname, R., F. Levy, and J. Willett. 2005. The growing importance of cognitive skills in wage determination. *Review of Economics and Statistics* 77 (2): 251–66.

Ng, I. 2006. The effect of intergenerational and neighborhood factors on adolescent problem behavior. University of Michigan, Unpublished Manuscript.

Osofsky, J. 1999. The impact of violence on children. *The Future of Children: Domestic Violence and Children* 9 (3): 33–49.

Pynoos, R. S., C. Frederick, K. Nader, W. Arroyo, A. Steinberg, S. Eth, F. Nunez, and L. Fairbanks. 1987. Life threat and posttraumatic stress in school-age children. *Archives of General Psychiatry* 44 (12): 1057–63.

Schwab-Stone, M. E., T. S. Ayers, W. Kasprow, C. Voyce, C. Barone, T. Shriver, and R. P. Weissberg. 1995. No safe haven: A study of violence exposure in an urban community. *Journal of the American Academy of Child and Adolescent Psychiatry* 34 (10): 1343–52.

Spencer, M., D. Fitch, A. Grogan-Kaylor, and B. McBeath. 2005. The equivalence of the behavior problem index across U.S. ethnic groups. *Journal of Cross-Cultural Psychology* 36 (5): 573–89.

Straus, M. A. 1992. Children as witness to marital violence: A risk factor for life long problems among a nationally representative sample of American men and women. In *Children and violence. Report of the twenty-third Ross roundtable on critical approaches to common pediatric problems,* ed. D. F. Schwarz, 98–109. Columbus, OH: Ross Laboratories.

Zax, J. S., and D. I. Rees. 2002. IQ, academic performance, environment, and earnings. *Review of Economics and Statistics* 84 (4): 600–16.

Contributors

Anna Aizer
Brown University
Department of Economics
64 Waterman Street
Providence, RI 02912

Patricia M. Anderson
Department of Economics
Dartmouth College
6106 Rockefeller
Hanover, NH 03755-3514

Kristin F. Butcher
Department of Economics
Wellesley College
Wellesley, MA 02481

Julie Berry Cullen
Department of Economics-0508
University of California, San Diego
9500 Gilman Drive
La Jolla, CA 92093-0508

Janet Currie
International Affairs Building
Department of Economics
Columbia University-Mail code 3308
420 W. 118th Street
New York, NY 10027

Rajeev Dehejia
Department of Economics and The
 Fletcher School
Tufts University
114A Braker Hall
8 Upper Campus Road
Medford, MA 02155-6722

Thomas DeLeire
La Follette School of Public Affairs
209 Observatory Hill Office Building
University of Wisconsin, Madison
1225 Observatory Drive
Madison, WI 53706

David Figlio
Institute for Policy Research
Northwestern University
2040 Sheridan Road
Evanston, IL 60208

Jonathan Gruber
MIT, Department of Economics
E52-355
50 Memorial Drive
Cambridge, MA 02142-1347

Brian A. Jacob
Gerald R. Ford School of Public Policy
University of Michigan
735 South State Street
Ann Arbor, MI 48109

Melissa S. Kearney
Department of Economics
University of Maryland
3105 Tydings Hall
College Park, MD 20742

Phillip B. Levine
Department of Economics
Wellesley College
Wellesley, MA 02481

Jason Lindo
Department of Economics
University of California, Davis
One Shields Avenue
Davis, CA 95616

Erzo F. P. Luttmer
Kennedy School of Government
Harvard University
79 John F. Kennedy Street
Cambridge, MA 02138

Josh Mitchell
John F. Kennedy School of
    Government
Harvard University
79 John F. Kennedy Street
Cambridge, MA 02138

Philip Oreopoulos
Department of Economics
University of British Columbia
997-1873 East Mall
Vancouver, British Columbia V6T 1Z1
    Canada

Marianne Page
Department of Economics
University of California, Davis
Davis, CA 95616-8578

Jeffrey Roth
Maternal Child Health and Education
    Research and Data Center
Department of Pediatrics, University
    of Florida
1701 SW 16th Avenue
Building A, Room #3224
Gainesville, FL 32608

Diane Whitmore Schanzenbach
Harris School of Public Policy
University of Chicago
1155 E. 60th Street
Chicago, IL 60637

Mark Stabile
School of Public Policy and
    Governance
University of Toronto
Canadiana Building, 3rd Floor
14 Queen's Park Crescent West.
Toronto, Ontario M5S 3K9 Canada

Ann Huff Stevens
Department of Economics
University of California, Davis
One Shields Avenue
Davis, CA 95616

Author Index

Subject Index